THE ANCIENT MEDITERRANEAN SOCIAL WORLD

A Sourcebook

Edited by Zeba A. Crook

WILLIAM B. EERDMANS PUBLISHING COMPANY
GRAND RAPIDS, MICHIGAN

Wm. B. Eerdmans Publishing Co.
4035 Park East Court SE, Grand Rapids, Michigan 49546
www.eerdmans.com

26 25 24 23 22 21 20   1 2 3 4 5 6 7

ISBN 978-0-8028-7356-9

Library of Congress Cataloging-in-Publication Data

Names: Crook, Zeba A., editor.
Title: The ancient Mediterranean social world : a sourcebook / edited by Zeba A. Crook.
Description: Grand Rapids, Michigan : William B. Eerdmans Publishing Company, 2020.
   | Includes bibliographical references and index. | Summary: "Makes the rich social
   context of the ancient Mediterranean available to readers through the selection of
   translated primary sources and by emphasizing the interrelatedness of the topics"—
   Provided by publisher.
Identifiers: LCCN 2019054550 | ISBN 9780802873569 (hardcover)
Subjects: LCSH: Sociology, Biblical—Sources. | Mediterranean Region—Civilization—
   Sources. | Mediterranean Region—Social conditions—Sources. | Bible—Social scien-
   tific criticism.
Classification: LCC BS670 .A63 2020 | DDC 930/.5—dc23
LC record available at https://lccn.loc.gov/2019054550

Contents

Contents

PART II: SOCIAL INTERACTION

Contents

PART III: SOCIAL INTERACTION WITH GOD AND THE GODS

PART IV: SOCIAL COMMODITIES

PART V: SOCIAL SUBTERFUGE AND CONTROL

Contents

Foreword

One of the most fortunate points in my doctoral studies came when my submission of a conference paper abstract was redirected from an already-full seminar on Paul to a seminar on the social world of the New Testament, chaired by Philip Esler. He promptly set me to read Thomas Carney, *The Shape of the Past: Models and Antiquity*, and the work of Bruce Malina, John Pilch, and other members of the Context Group for Biblical Research. I discovered the great potential of triangulation between text, historical evidence, and conscious reflection on social-scientific theory.

In the book before you, scholars, who, between them, have an unparalleled wealth of experience in using various theoretical approaches, share with the reader lists of ancient texts that they have found particularly helpful in applying these theories to biblical studies. Some of the texts indicate the degree of prominence of concepts, such as honor, patronage, or envy, associated with specific theoretical areas. Others give a sense of the shape of that concept in the writer's culture. Others indicate links into biblical texts. Lists of Hebrew, Greek, or Latin terms also help the reader investigate relationships between non-biblical and biblical texts in each area.

The overall effect of this book is to give you a sense of what it is about the ancient evidence that has led these scholars into seeing each of the theoretical approaches as a worthwhile way into study of the biblical text. More importantly, it also offers you resources for assessing and pursuing each of those routes into the text.

Experience counts. The sad deaths of Dietmar Neufeld and, more recently, John Pilch and Bruce Malina bring home to me the importance of the transmitting of the fruits of extended experience working in specific areas. Each of the established writers in this book has, of course, published studies elsewhere. However, this book is a particular treasury of what each scholar has found to be key go-to texts in their area. The virtue of transmission is also shown in the volume in another sense, in the appearance of several younger scholars, who have received and are exploring this academic legacy for the coming generation. The resources developed through the concentrated and persistent work of the book's contributors are a valuable provision for biblical study, presented in a way readily accessible to every student and scholar. Whatever your approach to the biblical text, you will find that the use of this collection of texts will considerably enrich your study.

PETER OAKES
Manchester
August 31, 2017

Abbreviations

ABD	*Anchor Bible Dictionary*
ANRW	*Aufstieg und Niedergang der Römischen Welt*
BCH	*Bulletin de correspondence hellénique*
BGU	*Ägyptische Urkunden aus den Königlichen Museen zu Berlin, Griechische Urkunden*
BTB	*Biblical Theology Bulletin*
CBQ	*Catholic Biblical Quarterly*
CCCA	*Corpus cultus Cybelae Attidisque.* Edited by M. J. Vermaseren. Leiden, 1977–89
CIJ	*Corpus Inscriptionum Iudaicarum.* Edited by J. B. Frey. Rome, 1936–62
CIL	*Corpus Inscriptionum Latinarum.* Berlin, 1863–1974
CIRB	*Corpus Inscriptionum Regni Bosporani.* Edited by V. V. Struve. Moscow, 1965
CPJ	*Corpus Papyrorum Judaicarum.* Edited by V. Tcherikover. Cambridge, 1957–1964
FC	Fathers of the Church
HvTSt	*Hervormde teologiese studies*
IAM	*Inscriptions antiques du Maroc.* Edited by M. Euzennat and J. Marion. Paris, 1966–2003
IAsMinLyk	*Reisen in Lykien und Karien.* Edited by O. Benndor and G. Niemann. Vienna, 1884
IBM	*The Collection of Greek Inscriptions in the British Museum.* Edited by F. H. Marshall. London, 1874–1916
ICret	*Inscriptiones Cretae Insulae.* Edited by M. Guarducci. Rome, 1935–1950

IDelos	*Inscriptions de Délos.* Edited by P. Roussel and M. Launey. Paris, 1937
IDidyma	*Didyma. Zweiter Teil. Die Inschriften.* Edited by A. Reim. Berlin, 1958
IEph	*Die Inschriften von Ephesos.* Edited by Engelman, Wankel, and Merkelbach. Bonn, 1979–84
IEurJud	*Jewish Inscriptions of Western Europe.* Edited by David Noy. Cambridge, 1993–1995
IG	*Inscriptiones Graecae. Editio Minor.* Berlin: de Gruyter, 1924–
IGladiators	Les gladiateurs dans l'orient grec. Edited by L. Robert. Amsterdam, 1971
IGLSkythia	*Inscriptiones Scythiae Minoris Graecae et Latinae.* Edited by Pippidi and Stoian. Bucharest, 1983–2000
IGRR	*Inscriptions Graecae ad Res Romanas Pertinentes.* Edited by Cagnat, Toutain, Henry, and Lafaye. Rome, 1964
IGUR	*Inscriptiones Graecae Urbis Romae.* Edited by L. Moretti. Rome, 1968–1990
IHierapJ	Walther Judeich, "Inschriften." Pages 67–181 in *Altertümer von Heiropolis.* Edited by Carl Humann, Conrad Cichorius, Walther Judeich, and Franz Winter. Jahrbuch des kaiserlich deutschen archäologischen Instituts, Ergänzungsheft 4. Berlin: Georg Reimer, 1898
IJO	*Inscriptiones Judaicae Orientis.* Edited by D. Noy, A. Panayotov, and H. Bloedhorn. Tübingen, 2004
IKilikiaHW	*Reisen in Kilikien.* Edited by Heberdy and Wilhelm. Vienna, 1894
ILS	*Inscriptiones Latinae Selectae*
IMagnMai	*Die Inschriften von Magnesia am Maeander.* Edited by O. Kern. Berlin, 1900
IMylasa	*Mylasa Inscriptions. Texts and List.* The Princeton Project on the Inscriptions of Anatolia. Edited by D. F. McCabe. Princeton, 1991
IPergamon	*Die Inschriften von Pergamon.* Edited by M. Fränkel. Berlin, 1890–1895
IPrusaOlymp	*The Inschriften von Prusa ad Olympum.* Edited by T. Corsten. Bonn, 1991–1993
ISelge	*Städte Pamphyliens und Pisidiens*, II. Edited by E. Petersen. Vienna, 1892

ISmyrna	*Die Inschriften von Smyrna.* Edited by G. Petzl. Bonn, 1982– 1990
JAAR	*Journal of the American Academy of Religion*
JBL	*Journal of Biblical Literature*
JSHJ	*Journal for the Study of the Historical Jesus*
JSNT	*Journal for the Study of the New Testament*
JSOT	*Journal for the Study of the Old Testament*
LABS	*Letters from Assyrian and Babylonian Scholars*
LAS	*Letters from Assyrian Scholars to the Kings Esarhaddon and Assurbanipal*
LCL	Loeb Classical Library
LSCG	*Lois sacrées des cités grecques.* Edited by Franciszek Soko-lowski. Paris: E. de Boccard, 1969
LSS	*Lois sacrées des cités grecques, Supplément,* Paris, 1962
MAMA	*Monumenta Asiae Minoris Antiqua.* Manchester and London, 1928–1993
NewDocs	*New Documents Illustrating Early Christianity.* Edited by Greg H. R. Horsley and Stephen Llewelyn. North Ryde, NSW: The Ancient History Documentary Research Centre, Macquarie University, 1981–
OGIS	*Orientis Graeci Inscriptiones Selectae.* Edited by W. Ditten-berger. Leipzig, 1903–5
PGM	*Papyri Graecae Magicae: Die griechischen Zauberpapyri.* Edited by Karl Preisendanz. 2nd ed. Stuttgart: Teubner, 1973–1974
SEG	Supplementum epigraphicum graecum
SGDI	*Sammlung der griechischen Dialekt-Inschriften.* Edited by H. Collitz and F. Bechtel. Göttingen, 1884–1915
SIG	*Sylloge Inscriptionum Graecarum*
TAM	*Tituli Asiae Minoris*
TDP	*Traité akkadien de diagnostics et prognostics médicaux*
VAT	Vorderasiatische Abteilung Tontafel. Vorderasiatische Museum Berlin
WUNT	Wissenschaftliche Untersuchungen zum Neuen Testament

Cited Primary Sources

Biblical references in the text are either citations or adaptations of the New Revised Standard Version.

Other translations of primary sources are, unless otherwise noted, citations or adaptations of the translations in the following sources. References at the end of entries below are to chapter and selection numbers in this volume.

Achilles Tatius

Leucippe and Clitophon. Translated by S. Gaselee. LCL. Cambridge: Harvard University Press, 1969. | 7.8, 19.8

Aelius Aristides

P. Aelius Aristides. *The Complete Works Translated into English.* Translated by C. A. Behr. 2 vols. Leiden: Brill, 1981–1986. | 3.15, 13.3

Aeschylus

Translated by Alan H. Sommerstein. 3 vols. LCL. Cambridge: Harvard University Press, 2009. | 6.2, 11.10

Andocides

Minor Attic Orators, Volume I: *Antiphon. Andocides.* Translated by K. J. Maidment. LCL. Cambridge: Harvard University Press, 1941. | 7.11

Appian

Roman History. Translated by Horace White. 4 vols. LCL. Cambridge: Harvard University Press, 1912–1913. | 5.8

Aristophanes

Birds. Lysistrata. Women at the Thesmophoria. Translated by Jeffrey Henderson. LCL. Cambridge: Harvard University Press, 2000.　|　11.8, 11.15

Aristotle

The Athenian Constitution. Eudemian Ethics. Virtues and Vices. Translated by H. Rackham. LCL. Cambridge: Harvard University Press, 1935.　|　16.14

Economics. Translated by H. Tredennick and G. C. Armstrong. LCL. Cambridge: Harvard University Press, 1935.

Meteorology. Translated by H. D. P. Lee. LCL. Cambridge: Harvard University Press, 1952.

Nicomachean Ethics. Translated by H. Rackham. LCL. Cambridge: Harvard University Press, 1926.　|　4.1, 4.17, 5.13, 18.1

On Dreams. Translated by W. S. Hett. LCL. Cambridge: Harvard University Press, 1957.

On Prophecy in Sleep. Translated by W. S. Hett. LCL. Cambridge: Harvard University Press, 1957.　|　13.1

On the Generation of Animals. Translated by A. L. Peck. LCL. Cambridge: Harvard University Press, 1943.　|　9.7

Politics. Translated by H. Rackham. LCL. Cambridge: Harvard University Press, 1932.

Rhetoric. Translated by J. H. Freese. LCL. Cambridge: Harvard University Press, 1926.　|　4.5, 5.13, 17.9

[Pseudo-Aristotle] *Rhetoric to Alexander.* Translated by H. Rackham. LCL. Cambridge: Harvard University Press, 1957.　|　9.8, 15.13

Artemidorus

Daniel E. Harris-McCoy. *Artemidorus' Oneirocritica: Text, Translation, and Commentary.* Oxford: Oxford University Press, 2012.　|　10.2

Augustine

Confessions. Translated by Henry Chadwick. Oxford: Oxford University Press, 2008.　|　13.11

Rhetoric. Translated by Carolyn J.-B. Hammond. 2 vols. LCL. Cambridge: Harvard University Press, 2014–2016.

Aulus Gellius

Attic Nights. Translated by J. C. Rolfe. 3 vols. LCL. Cambridge: Harvard University Press, 1927.　|　4.14

Babylonian Talmud

Hebrew-English Edition of the Babylonian Talmud. Edited by Isidore Epstein. London: Soncino, 1989.　|　7.9, 20.20

Bacchylides

Greek Lyric, Vol. 4: *Bacchylides, Corinna, and Others.* Translated by David A. Campbell. LCL. Cambridge: Harvard University Press, 1992. | 11.2

2 Baruch

R. H. Charles and William John Ferrar. *The Apocalypse of Baruch and the Assumption of Moses.* Boston: Weiser, 2006. | 13.8

Basil

Letters. Translated by Roy J. Deferrari. 4 vols. LCL. Cambridge: Harvard University Press, 1926–1934. | 7.4, 17.18

M. M. Wagner. *St. Basil: Ascetical Works.* Fathers of the Church 9. Washington, DC: Catholic University of America Press, 1962. | 20.7

Callimachus

Hymns and Epigrams. Lycophron: Alexandra. Aratus: Phaenomena. Translated by A. W. Mair and G. R. Mair. LCL. Cambridge: Harvard University Press, 1921. | 17.17

Cato

Cato and Varro. *On Agriculture.* Edited by W. D. Hooper and Harrison Boyd Ash. LCL. Cambridge: Harvard University Press, 1934. | 14.20

Catullus

Catullus. Tibullus. Pervigilium Veneris. Translated by F. W. Cornish, J. P. Postgate, and J. W. Mackail. LCL. Cambridge: Harvard University Press, 1913. | 12.18, 16.6

Cicero

Translated by H. Rackham et al. 29 vols. LCL. Cambridge: Harvard University Press, 1913–2010. | 1.9, 2.4, 3.3, 6.15, 8.13, 11.6, 12.17, 15.2, 15.4, 15.7, 16.15, 17.13, 18.7, 19.3, 19.16

Clement of Alexandria

Christ the Educator. Translated by Simon P. Wood. Fathers of the Church 23. Washington, DC: Catholic University of America Press, 1954. | 9.5

Columella

On Agriculture. Translated by Harrison Boyd Ash et al. 3 vols. LCL. Cambridge: Harvard University Press, 1941–1955. | 8.17, 10.18

Cornelius Nepos

On Great Generals. On Historians. Translated by J. C. Rolfe. LCL. Cambridge: Harvard University Press, 1929. | 4.4

Dead Sea Scrolls

The Dead Sea Scrolls: Study Edition. Translated and edited by Florentino García Martínez and Eibert J. C. Tigchelaar. Leiden: Brill, 1997–1998. | 6.14, 13.19, 19.20

Mayer I. Gruber. "Purity and Impurity in Halakic Sources and Qumran Law." Pages 65–76 in *Wholly Woman, Holy Blood: A Feminist Critique of Purity and Impurity*. Edited by Kristin De Troyer, Judith A. Herbert, Judith Ann Johnson, and Anne-Marie Korte. Harrisburg, PA: Trinity Press International, 2003. | 12.3

Carol A. Newsom. "Religious Experience in the Dead Sea Scrolls: Two Case Studies." Pages 205–22 in *Linking Text and Experience*. Vol. 2 of *Experientia*. Edited by Colleen Shantz and Rodney Alan Werline. Early Judaism and Its Literature 35. Boston: Brill, 2012. | 13.19

Demosthenes

Translated by A. T. Murray. 7 vols. LCL. Cambridge: Harvard University Press, 1926–1949. | 10.9, 12.15, 15.1

Dio Cassius

Roman History. Translated by Earnest Cary. 9 vols. LCL. Cambridge: Harvard University Press, 1914–1927. | 19.15

Dio Chrysostom

Discourses. Translated by H. Lamar Crosby. 5 vols. LCL. Cambridge: Harvard University Press, 1932–1951. | 3.2, 3.8, 4.7, 7.10, 9.4, 15.14

Diodorus Siculus

Library of History. Translated by Francis R. Walton et al. 12 vols. LCL. Cambridge: Harvard University Press, 1932–1951. | 10.17, 14.16

Diogenes

Abraham J. Malherbe. *The Cynic Epistles: A Study Edition*. Missoula: Scholars Press, 1977. | 18.18

Diogenes Laertius

Lives of Eminent Philosophers. Translated by R. D. Hicks. 2 vols. LCL. Cambridge: Harvard University Press, 1932–1951. | 5.19, 16.8, 17.12

Dionysius of Halicarnassus

Roman Antiquities. Translated by Earnest Cary. 7 vols. LCL. Cambridge: Harvard University Press, 1937–1950. | 6.6

1 Enoch

George W. E. Nickelsburg and James C. VanderKam. *1 Enoch*. Hermeneia. Minneapolis: Fortress, 2012. | 13.14

Epictetus

Discourses. Translated by W. A. Oldfather. 2 vols. LCL. Cambridge: Harvard University Press, 1925–1928. | 3.17, 12.19

Euripides

Translated by David Kovacs et al. 8 vols. LCL. Cambridge: Harvard University Press, 1994–2009. | 10.6, 18.2

Eusebius

Ecclesiastical History. 2 vols. LCL. Cambridge: Harvard University Press, 1926–1932. | 7.5, 18.10

Fronto

Letters. Translated by C. R. Haines. 2 vols. LCL. Cambridge: Harvard University Press, 1919–1920. | 17.5

Gaius

O. F. Robinson and W. M. Gordon. *The Institutes*. London: Gerald Duckworth, 1988. | 10.8

Galen

Of Temperaments. Translated by P. N. Singer. *Galen: Selected Works*. Oxford: Oxford University Press, 1997. | 9.15

Galen on the Usefulness of the Parts of the Body. Translated by Margaret Tallmadge May. Ithaca: Cornell University Press, 1968. | 9.9

Gezer Calendar

http://www.kchanson.com/ | 1.1

Gospel of Thomas

Stephen Patterson and Marvin Meyer. "The Gospel of Thomas." Pages 305–22 in *The Complete Gospels: Annotated Scholars Version*. Edited by Robert J. Miller. Sonoma: Polebridge, 1994. | 1.6

The Greek Anthology

Discourses. Translated by R. Paton et al. 5 vols. LCL. Cambridge: Harvard University Press, 1918–2014. | 10.1, 10.5

The Greek Magical Papyri (*PGM*)

Hans Dieter Betz. *The Greek Magical Papyri in Translation, Including the Demotic Spells.* 2 vols. 2nd ed. Chicago: University of Chicago Press, 1996. | 19.18

Heliodorus

B. P. Reardon. *Collected Ancient Greek Novels.* Berkeley: University of California Press, 1989. | 10.7

Herodotus

The Persian Wars. Translated by A. D. Godley et al. 4 vols. LCL. Cambridge: Harvard University Press, 1920–1925. | 2.20, 4.10, 6.1, 8.2, 8.4, 12.9, 16.5, 17.3, 17.11, 18.3

Hesiod

Translated by Glenn Most. 2 vols. LCL. Cambridge: Harvard University Press, 2018. | 14.11, 16.1, 16.13

Hippocrates

Ann Ellis Hanson. "Hippocrates: Diseases of Women 1." *Signs* 1 (1975): 567–84. | 14.8

Translated by Paul Potter et al. 11 vols. LCL. Cambridge: Harvard University Press, 1923–2018. | 14.9, 14.15

Homer

Odyssey. Translated by A. T. Murray. 2 vols. LCL. Cambridge: Harvard University Press, 1919. | 6.3, 8.1, 11.16, 16.11

Homeric Hymns

Homeric Hymns. Homeric Apocrypha. Lives of Homer. Translated by Martin L. West. LCL. Cambridge: Harvard University Press, 2003. | 11.18

Horace

Satires. Translated by H. Rushton Fairclough. LCL. Cambridge: Harvard University Press, 1920–1926. | 3.9, 16.19, 19.1

Inscriptions

Inscriptions of Cilicia (IKilikiaBM)

Richard S. Ascough, Philip A. Harland, and John S. Kloppenborg. *Associations in the Greco-Roman World: A Sourcebook.* Waco: Baylor University Press, 2012. | 16.20

Inscriptions of Aphrodisias (IAph)

Richard S. Ascough, Philip A. Harland, and John S. Kloppenborg. *Associations in the Greco-Roman World: A Sourcebook.* Waco: Baylor University Press, 2012. | 17.19

Inscriptiones Graecae (IG)

H. F. J. Horstmanshoff. "The Ancient Physician: Craftsman or Scientist?" *Journal of the History of Medicine and Allied Sciences* 45 (1990): 191–92. | 12.7, 14.4

Barbara Levick. *The Government of the Roman Empire: A Sourcebook*. London: Routledge, 2000.

Keilschrift Texte aus Ugarit Keilalphabetische Texte aus Ugarit (KTU).

J. N. Ford. "'Ninety-Nine by the Evil Eye and One from Natural Causes.' KTU 1.96 in Its Near Eastern Context." *Ugarit-Forschungen* 30 (1998): 201–78. | 20.9

New Documents Illustrating Earliest Christianity. Edited by Greg H. R. Horsley and Stephen Llewelyn. North Ryde, NSW: The Ancient History Documentary Research Centre, Macquarie University, 1981–.

Inscriptiones Latinae Selectae (ILS)

Barbara Levick. *The Government of the Roman Empire: A Sourcebook*. London: Routledge, 2000. | 3.12

Die Inschriften von Kyme (IKyme)

F. C. Grant. *Hellenistic Religions: The Age of Syncretism*. New York: Liberal Arts Press, 1953. | 3.19

Phrygian Inscriptions (IPhrygR)

http://philipharland.com | 2.11

Supplementum epigraphicum graecum (SEG)

Richard S. Ascough, Philip A. Harland, and John S. Kloppenborg. *Associations in the Greco-Roman World: A Sourcebook*. Waco: Baylor University Press, 2012. | 3.13, 12.2, 12.4

P. J. Rhodes and Robin Osborne. *Greek Historical Inscriptions, 404–323 BC*. New York: Oxford University Press, 2003.

Irenaeus

The Apostolic Fathers with Justin Martyr and Irenaeus. Volume 1 of The Ante-Nicene Fathers. Edinburgh: T&T Clark, 1867. | 18.16

Isaeus

Translated by E. S. Forster. 3 vols. LCL. Cambridge: Harvard University Press, 1927. | 10.4, 11.11

Isocrates

Translated by George Norlin and La Rue Van Hook. 3 vols. LCL. Cambridge: Harvard University Press, 1928–1945. | 4.12, 4.19, 17.20

John Chrysostom

Discourses against Judaizing Christians. Translated by P. W. Harkins. Fathers of the
Church 68. Washington, DC: Catholic University of America Press, 1977. | 18.11

Joseph and Aseneth

James H. Charlesworth. *The Old Testament Pseudepigrapha*. 2 vols. Garden City, NY:
Doubleday, 1983–1985. | 7.17

Josephus

Translated by Henry St. J. Thackeray et al. 10 vols. LCL. Cambridge: Harvard Univer-
sity Press, 1926–1965. | 1.13, 2.5, 2.14, 3.18, 5.3, 5.14, 6.10, 8.19, 12.20, 13.6, 17.4,
18.5, 18.17, 18.19

Jubilees

James H. Charlesworth. *The Old Testament Pseudepigrapha*. 2 vols. Garden City, NY:
Doubleday, 1983–1985. | 2.6

Juvenal

Juvenal and Persius. Translated by Susanna Morton Braund. LCL. Cambridge: Harvard
University Press, 2004. | 12.11

Libanius

A. F. Norman. *Libanius' Autobiography (Oration I)*. London: Oxford University
Press, 1965. | 14.3

Livy

History of Rome. Translated by J. C. Yardley et al. 11 vols. LCL. Cambridge: Harvard
University Press, 1919–2018. | 8.10, 9.20, 10.16, 11.3, 11.7, 11.20

Lucian

Translated by A. M. Harmon et al. 8 vols. LCL. Cambridge: Harvard University Press,
1913–1967. | 7.1, 13.5, 18.13, 19.2

Lucretius

On the Nature of Things. Translated by W. H. D. Rouse. Cambridge: Harvard University
Press, 1924. | 5.5, 15.19

Martial

Epigrams. Translated by D. R. Shackleton Bailey. LCL. Cambridge: Harvard University
Press, 1993. | 3.10

Minucius Felix
Translated by Gerald H. Rendall. LCL. Cambridge: Harvard University Press, 1931. | 18.6, 19.17

Origen
Contra Celsum. Translated by Henry Chadwick. Cambridge: Cambridge University Press, 1980. | 18.15

Ovid
Art of Love. Cosmetics. Remedies for Love. Ibis. Walnut-Tree. Sea Fishing. Consolation. Translated by J. H. Mozley. LCL. Cambridge: Harvard University Press, 1929. | 9.19
Fasti. Translated by James G. Frazer. LCL. Cambridge: Harvard University Press, 1931. | 10.15
Metamorphoses. Translated by Frank Justus Miller. 2 vols. LCL. Cambridge: Harvard University Press, 1916. | 5.18, 11.4, 17.15
Tristia. Ex Ponto. Translated by A. L. Wheeler. LCL. Cambridge: Harvard University Press, 1924. | 6.16

Papyri

London Papyri (P.London)
Select Papyri. Translated by A. S. Hunt et al. 3 vols. LCL. Cambridge: Harvard University Press, 1932–1941. | 1.15

Michigan Papyri (P.Michigan)
http://papyri.info | 2.8

Yadin Papyri (P.Yadin)
Naphtali Lewis. *Documents from the Bar Kokhba Period.* Jerusalem: IES, 1989. | 1.7, 1.16

Passion of Perpetua and Felicity
Thomas J. Heffernan. *The Passion of Perpetua and Felicity.* Oxford: Oxford University Press, 2012. | 9.14

Pausanias
Translated by W. H. S. Jones. 5 vols. LCL. Cambridge: Harvard University Press, 1918–1935. | 8.20, 14.13

Persius
Juvenal and Persius. Translated by Susanna Morton Braund. LCL. Cambridge: Harvard University Press, 2004. | 20.19

Petronius

Satyricon. Translated by Michael Heseltine. Cambridge: Harvard University Press, 1913. | 3.7

Philo

Translated by F. H. Colson et al. 12 vols. LCL. Cambridge: Harvard University Press, 1926–1965. | 1.17, 4.2, 4.11, 6.7, 6.8, 6.9, 9.17, 15.8, 17.6

Philostratus

Life of Apollonius. Translated by Christopher P. Jones. 3 vols. LCL. Cambridge: Harvard University Press, 2005–2006. | 19.7

Phlegon of Tralles

William Hansen. *Phlegon of Tralles' Book of Marvels.* Exeter: University of Exeter Press, 1996. | 9.10

Pindar

Translated by William H. Race. 2 vols. LCL. Cambridge: Harvard University Press, 1997. | 15.6

Plato

Translated by R. G. Bury et al. 12 vols. LCL. Cambridge: Harvard University Press, 1921–2017. | 5.4, 7.3, 8.7, 10.20, 12.16, 13.12, 13.15, 14.1, 14.5, 14.10

Plautus

Translated by Wolfgang de Melo. 5 vols. LCL. Cambridge: Harvard University Press, 2011–2013. | 7.13

Pliny the Elder

Natural History. Translated by H. Rackham. 10 vols. LCL. Cambridge: Harvard University Press, 1914–1963. | 1.20, 8.5, 10.12, 18.12, 20.10, 20.18

Pliny the Younger

Letters. Translated by Betty Radice. 2 vols. LCL. Cambridge: Harvard University Press, 1969. | 3.4

Plotinus

Translated by A. H. Armstrong. 7 vols. LCL. Cambridge: Harvard University Press, 1966–1988. | 13.20

Plutarch

Lives. Translated by Bernadotte Perrin et al. 11 vols. LCL. Cambridge: Harvard University Press, 1914–1926. | 2.12, 2.14, 2.18, 3.5, 4.13, 14.18, 19.6

Moralia. Translated by Frank C. Babbitt et al. 16 vols. LCL. Cambridge: Harvard University Press, 1927–2004. | 3.5, 4.6, 4.13, 6.5, 7.2, 7.15, 7.16, 9.1, 10.11, 10.14, 10.19, 16.16, 16.17, 17.2, 17.16, 20.1, 20.2, 20.12, 20.16

The Poem of the Righteous Sufferer

W. G. Lambert. *Babylonian Wisdom Literature*. Oxford: Clarendon, 1959. | 14.12

Polemo of Laodicea

Translation of the Arabic version by Robert Hoyland. "A New Edition and Translation of the Leiden Polemon." Pages 329–464 in *Seeing the Face, Seeing the Soul: Polemon's Physiognomy from Classical Antiquity to Medieval Islam*. Edited by Simon Swain. Oxford: Oxford University Press, 2007. | 9.3

Polybius

The Histories. Translated by W. R. Paton. 6 vols. LCL. Cambridge: Harvard University Press, 2010–2011. | 15.15

Sallust

Translated by J. C. Rolfe et al. LCL. Cambridge: Harvard University Press, 2013. | 18.4

Seneca

Moral Essays. Translated by John W. Basore. 3 vols. LCL. Cambridge: Harvard University Press, 1928–1935. | 3.1, 3.14, 4.18, 15.3, 15.17, 15.20, 16.7, 16.18

Septuagint

A New English Translation of the Septuagint. Edited by Albert Pietersma and Benjamin G. Wright. Oxford: Oxford University Press, 2007. | 1.8, 1.12, 2.13, 4.8, 4.16, 5.7, 5.12, 5.17, 6.12, 8.12, 9.2, 11.9, 12.10, 14.19, 15.9, 20.5

Sextus Empiricus

Translated by R. G. Bury. 4 vols. LCL. Cambridge: Harvard University Press, 1933–1949. | 14.2

Shepherd of Hermas

B. D. Ehrman. *The Apostolic Fathers*. Cambridge: Harvard University Press, 2003. | 5.10

Sophocles

Translated by Hugh Lloyd-Jones. 3 vols. LCL. Cambridge: Harvard University Press, 1994. | 10.13, 15.5, 15.12

Statius

Thebaid. Translated by D. R. Shackleton Bailey. 2 vols. LCL. Cambridge: Harvard University Press, 2004. | 12.13

Strabo

Geography. Translated by Horace Leonard Jones. 8 vols. LCL. Cambridge: Harvard University Press, 1917–1932. | 6.17, 8.8, 8.11, 15.16

Suetonius

Lives of the Caesars. Translated by R. C. Rolfe. 2 vols. LCL. Cambridge: Harvard University Press, 1914. | 1.10, 5.15, 19.10

Tacitus

Translated by Clifford H. Moore et al. 5 vols. LCL. Cambridge: Harvard University Press, 1914–1937. | 1.14, 6.18, 11.19, 18.8, 19.12

Testaments of the Twelve Patriarchs

H. C. Kee. "Testaments of the Twelve Patriarchs." Pages 775–828 in *The Old Testament Pseudepigrapha*. Edited by James H. Charlesworth. Garden City, NY: Doubleday, 1983. | 20.6

Thucydides

History of the Peloponnesian War. 4 vols. LCL. Cambridge: Harvard University Press, 1919–1923. | 8.14, 17.10

Tibullus

Catullus. Tibullus. Pervigilium Veneris. Translated by F. W. Cornish, J. P. Postgate, and J. W. Mackail. LCL. Cambridge: Harvard University Press, 1913. | 7.6, 12.5

Tobit

Robert J. Littman. *Tobit: The Book of Tobit in Codex Sinaiticus*. Septuagint Commentary Series. Leiden: Brill, 2008. | 2.13

Ulpian

Digest. Jane F. Gardner and Thomas E. J. Wiedemann. *The Roman Household: A Sourcebook*. London: Routledge, 1991. | 2.1

Urkunden des aegyptischen Altertums

Edward Bleiberg. *The Official Gift in Ancient Egypt*. Norman: University of Oklahoma Press, 1996. | 16.4

Valerius Maximus

Memorable Doings and Sayings. 2 vols. LCL. Cambridge: Harvard University Press, 2000. | 2.3

Vergil

Translated H. Rushton Fairclough. 2 vols. LCL. Cambridge: Harvard University Press, 1999–2000. | 6.19, 7.12, 8.3, 10.10, 12.6

Wadi Murabba'at

Ada Yardeni. *Textbook of Aramaic, Hebrew and Nabatean Documentary Texts from the Judean Desert and Related Material.* 2 vols. Jerusalem: Hebrew University of Jerusalem, 2000. | 2.7

Xenophon

Translated by E. C. Marchant et al. 7 vols. LCL. Cambridge: Harvard University Press, 1914–2013. | 4.3, 8.16, 9.12

Introduction

Social-scientific criticism takes as its first principle that readers and writers are conditioned to create, read, and interpret by their social environment and that this applies as much to ancient writers as to modern readers. Traditional historical-criticism, as practiced by biblical scholars, has always sought to situate the reader in the ancient past and to provide the means for interpreters to interrogate texts, and to this end, social-scientific critics see their enterprise as an important extension of that approach.[1] But social-scientific criticism takes the position that it is not enough merely to understand the past; one needs simultaneously to enter the world of one's ancient subjects (like in historical criticism) and to filter out one's own (modern and anachronistic) enculturation. Put differently, readers from one culture must, to a certain extent, enter the culture of another in order to understand its discourses, rhetoric, arguments, and humor.

This is the benefit of models, though few critics understand this.[2] Models are not meant to be perfect or to reveal everything. Far from it; models are intended to filter out some data, some that might be interesting and enriching, in order to highlight the data pertinent to the model, like lenses constructed to filter certain kinds of light in order to show particular things and obscure others.[3] The use of models is also intended to produce results that are, in true scientific spirit, replicable. Since we all make assumptions when reading—that is, we all read from within models—it is better to be explicit about one's interpretive assumptions and models. The modeling enterprise allows for this;

---

1. J. H. Elliott, *What Is Social-Scientific Criticism?* (Minneapolis: Fortress, 1993), 11–15.

2. David Horrell, "Models and Methods in Social-Scientific Interpretation: A Response to Philip Esler," *JSNT* 78 (2000): 83–105.

3. Elliott, *What Is Social-Scientific Criticism?*, 42.

1

anything else pretends we are objective readers, which is impossible. We all use models when interpreting: the options available to us as readers are either to do so explicitly by presenting the model up front or to do so implicitly and risk projecting our modern assumptions onto ancient Mediterranean texts.[4]

Thus, over the history of social-scientific criticism, much effort has been placed on defining and defending the use of particular models and the modeling enterprise more broadly.[5] This history has been summarized many times, as has the variety of criticisms of the approach, and neither needs to be summarized again. Only one of these criticisms is pertinent here, namely, that the models used by social-scientific critics were developed in the modern world and imposed anachronistically on ancient texts and subjects, and by extension that this was done not only in the absence of data but in fact that the models themselves generate the data.[6] Far from generating the data, however, the models used by social-scientific critics are built on tremendous amounts of ancient data. Thus, this work seeks to depart from the practice of presenting and defending the models (as well the modeling enterprise) and focus on the data.

One of the strengths of models and indeed a measure of their appropriateness is their heuristic capacity: What do they succeed in explaining? This analytical component of the modeling enterprise might be foreign to the actors themselves; the very process of analysis is generally an outsider's prerogative. The anthropological language for this is *etic*: The analyst's explanation is etic by virtue of being foreign to the world being analyzed. As valuable and necessary as the etic perspective in the modeling enterprise is, the *emic* perspective—or language the subject would recognize—is, and always has been, valuable as well. This is not new; the models used in biblical studies were never

---

4. Philip Francis Esler, "Models in New Testament Interpretation: A Reply to David Horrell," *JSNT* 78 (2000): 107–13.

5. See Jerome H. Neyrey, "Social Science Modeling and the New Testament," *BTB* 16 (1986): 107–10; T. F. Carney, *The Shape of the Past: Models and Antiquity* (Lawrence, KS: Coronado, 1975); Richard L. Rohrbaugh, "Methodological Considerations in the Debate over the Social Class of Early Christians," *JAAR* 52 (1984): 519–46; Richard L. Rohrbaugh, "Models and Muddles: Discussions of the Social Facets Seminar," *Forum* 3.2 (1987): 23–33; Bruce J. Malina, *The New Testament World: Insights from Cultural Anthropology*, 3rd ed. (Atlanta: John Knox, 2001); Elliott, *What Is Social-Scientific Criticism?*, 42.

6. Louise Joy Lawrence, *An Ethnography of the Gospel of Matthew: A Critical Assessment of the Use of the Honour and Shame Model in New Testament Studies*, WUNT 2.165 (Tübingen: Mohr Siebeck, 2003); Cyril S. Rodd, "On Applying a Sociological Theory to Biblical Studies," *JSOT* 19 (1981): 95–106; Michael Herzfeld, "Honour and Shame: Some Problems in the Comparative Analysis of Moral Systems," *Man* NS 15 (1980): 339–51; Richard A. Horsley, *Sociology and the Jesus Movement* (New York: Crossroad, 1989).

constructed in the absence of data. They were sometimes developed in the absence of *biblical* data, but cross-cultural analysis has proven useful for explaining social transcripts that are easily accessible to insiders, but not always easily accessible to the scholars who study them. Most other social-scientific models have been constructed from ancient data, even as they sometimes help to illuminate in a passage the dynamics that might go unnoticed by a modern reader. Nonetheless, the nature of a sourcebook, and this one in particular, is that its focus is entirely emic, even while the nature of categories sometimes reflects the presence of a model. The passages and references in the chapters below, about which more will be said shortly, are ancient productions in their own words. The categories might be model based and our own, but the evidence is theirs.

If this book serves in any way to address the criticism that social-scientific models anachronistically generate data that cannot be found in antiquity, then that would be a beneficial contribution to the debate. Nonetheless, it would also be a secondary goal of this book. The primary goal of this work is to serve as a resource for teaching or research: to provide easy access to a vast and representative array of texts relating to many topics of social-scientific interest to scholars of antiquity. The sourcebook has a long and rich history in the field of biblical studies, and there is a good variety of fine ones still in circulation. None of them, however, prioritize exclusively social-scientific categories (though some of them touch briefly on some of these topics). Thus, we have deliberately avoided some topics that *are* socially interesting but that are covered well in these other sourcebook collections, such as education, marriage, or slavery. Instead, we have sought a balance of recently emerging areas of social-scientific scholarship (e.g., dress, alternate states of consciousness, space, gossip, and secrecy) and traditional social-scientific categories (e.g., honor, patronage, shame, evil eye, and friendship).

As the primary goal of this work is as a teaching and research resource, the structure of each chapter is largely uniform. The chapters each have five sections. They begin with a short introduction to the topic; then twenty passages are offered in translation, each with a brief introduction to the writer and the context of the passage. These translations were selected to highlight particular features of each topic, and thus the translations are grouped together into subunits. In addition, the passages were selected to show the prevalence of these data: These topics can be found in texts and material remains from the iron age to the period of the rabbis and church fathers, in Greek, Latin, Hebrew, Assyrian, and other languages, in historical writings, philosophical writings, poetry, satire, drama, oratory, inscriptions, letters, moral essays, and of course, biblical writings. In other words, the twenty passages are not exhaustive, but rather representative of the circum-Mediterranean and southwest Asia. Following the twenty translated passages, one finds a list of ancient vocabulary related to each topic (with the exception of a couple of topics that do not have a discrete vocabulary) followed by a very brief scholarly bibliography. Finally, each chapter ends by offering usually hundreds of additional citations where the topic can be found, and these citations are grouped together in the same subunits as used for the translations.

All of the topics in this book revolve around a shared theme: they all speak to the lived experience of people in the ancient Mediterranean. Honor (**chap. 4, Honor**: Richard Rohrbaugh) has been called the pivotal value of the ancient world. This can be expanded in two ways: Honor is that value around which everything else revolves; or honor is what explains the dynamic and the nature of so many other values. For instance, a concern for honor explains shame, deviance or labeling, the construction of gender, kinship, space, and so on. The concern for honor explains much of the lived experience of ancient people. Shame (**chap. 5, Shame**: Ron Roberts), which is *not* the opposite of honor, is the concern people have to show appropriate honor to others. Thus, men must have shame, too; shame is gendered, but it is not gendered in only one direction. The worst kind of person in this world is the shameless person, that is, the person who cannot be shamed into falling in line with the group.

Honor and shame are such powerful social values because the world was collectivistic (**chap. 6, Collectivism**: Dennis Duling and Richard Rohrbaugh). What others thought of you was extremely important to many people; their opinion not only mattered, but it also shaped and constrained people's options. Of course, there were some who rejected the peer pressure that inheres in collectivistic culture; in those cases, the charge that they were deviants (**chap. 18, Deviance**: Giovanni Bazzana) was a threat of expulsion, often intended to encourage them to correct their behavior and uphold group expectations. Talking behind the backs of others (**chap. 7, Gossip**: Dietmar Neufeld and John Daniels) was another way that charges of deviance could be disseminated. Gossip was a key means of maintaining group boundaries and enforcing group expectations. Publicly making fun of others and lying to or withholding information from them (**chap. 19, Mockery and Secrecy**: Dietmar Neufeld and Zeba A. Crook) were additional ways to exercise power over others. And one very common way of coming into possession of secrets was through revelatory dreams and visions (**chap. 13, Alternate States of Consciousness**: Colleen Shantz). In this world, information and experience derived from alternate states of consciousness were taken very seriously.

Another feature of ancient life that affected daily living was whether one was born male or female. This determined the rules (**chap. 9, Gender**: Alicia Batten) by which one was expected to live. Gender expectations also affected the ways in which one was expected to show shame and influenced the ways one could gain honor. It also affected the rules relating to where one could go (**chap. 8, Space**: Eric Stewart), for different spaces (home, temple, public square) were governed by different expectations. In public places, one needed to be aware of protecting and projecting honor. But one also needed to be wary of those who were envious of you, whether it was because you were wealthy, healthy, Roman, male, the mother of a baby boy, and so on. These things could provoke the evil eye (**chap. 20, Evil Eye**: John H. Elliott). Evil Eye beliefs and practices are explained not only by the ancient understanding of how vision worked, but by the belief that envy (**chap. 17, Limited Good and Envy**: John H. Elliott, Zeba A. Crook, and Jerome Neyrey) was natural, unavoidable, and utterly destructive.

Relationships and social interaction would also obviously affect one's lived experience in the world. One's first point of contact with the world was one's family, but family also shaped one's interaction with that world (**chap. 2, Kinship**: Erin Vearncombe), in terms of marriage practices, inheritance, and genealogy, which of course overlaps with honor. Kinship was such a basic social institution that it offered the foundational metaphor for other social relationships. Antiquity was a vertically structured world, in which power was expressed by controlling access. Whoever has access—to money, goods, gods, or other people—has power. People in need must approach those with access (**chap. 3, Patronage**: Zeba A. Crook). Kinship also provided the foundational metaphor for friendship, as the truest friends share as if they are family (**chap. 16, Friendship and Gifts**: Zeba A. Crook and Gary Stansell). Thus, both patronage and friendship were forms of what has been called fictive kinship. What connected clients to patrons, friends to friends, and manumitted slaves to their former masters was a bond of loyalty (**chap. 15, Loyalty**: Jason Lamoreaux).

Lived experience in the ancient world also involved ritual. Sometimes these rituals were located primarily in the home (**chap. 10, Ritual, Domestic**: Jason Lamoreaux), in which case they involved childbirth, marriage, death, festivals, and meals, and sometimes they were primarily public in nature (**chap. 11, Ritual, Public**: Amy Marie Fisher), in which they might be directed at the well-being of the emperor or the placation of the gods. Both types of ritual could be called politico-religious, as religion did not exist in a sphere all its own, separate from and independent of politics. Ritual was also sometimes governed by expectations of purity (**chap. 12, Purity**: Ritva Williams), so one had to be aware of the various ways in which one came into contact with impurity. Sacrifice was a common feature of ritual, including rituals one might undertake in the pursuit of healing (**chap. 14, Healing**: Agnes Choi). Illness and disease had social and cosmic, as well as personal, ramifications and implications. Being healthy was very important; being sick might be interpreted as disfavor with the gods or blamed on outsiders and deviants.

And last not because it is least, but because of how all-encompassing it too is, nothing affects one's lived daily experience more than economy (**chap. 1, Economy**: Douglas Oakman). Economy covers issues such as taxes, rents, tributes, agrarian life, labor, hunger, self-sufficiency or dependence, and livelihood.

It is also worth noting that not only do the topics of each chapter relate together, but also many of them relate to each other. Thus, while reading one entry, you will commonly be directed to a related entry. For instance, social expectations governing who can go where (**chap. 8, Space**) overlaps with gender, honor, purity, healing, deviance, and shame. The social construction of properly masculine or feminine behavior (**chap. 9, Gender**) overlaps with honor, deviance, mockery, patronage, kinship, purity, and space. The worry that being in possession of that which others lack can bring withering, damaging, or even fatal looks from people (**chap. 20, Evil Eye**) and overlaps with envy, honor, gender, space, economics, and patronage.

This book does not claim that these topics encompass the whole of lived experience in the ancient Mediterranean, but merely that an understanding of these topics (among others) deeply enriches our sense of their lived experience and of the ways in which our own lived experiences are to varying degrees different. It is not that we share nothing in common with these people, but that what we do not share in common is extremely important. In addition, this book does not claim that these topics were experienced in the same way by ancient Mediterranean people. While some generalization is possible, generalization is not necessary for understanding ancient experience.

Another feature of this book that I hope will contribute to current conversations relates to *religion*. Unlike most other sourcebooks, this one is not divided into categories, like politics, literature, philosophy, religion, economy, and culture. Such an approach imagines that religion exists in a sphere of its own, separated from other institutions by a set of concerns or by an intrinsic nature that is uniquely and essentially (in the philosophical sense of the term) its own. There is no category for religion in this book. Rather, "religion" (practices and ideas relating to superhuman beings) is a component of nearly every topic in this book, as it should be. Every chapter in some way demonstrates how ancient notions of any topic (e.g., honor, economy, loyalty, etc.) help explain how they interacted with their gods, and *vice versa*, their understanding of the gods informs each one of these topics. We have attempted, in other words, to reflect in our categories the now common notion that religion was embedded in antiquity, not a stand-alone institution. The one section that makes reference to the gods and God exists solely in the service of arranging the chapters, not for reflecting (or constructing) reality. Those happen to be topics that focus more explicitly on superhuman beings than do the other topics, but this does not lessen their social significance.

This project had more than its share, I think, of bumps along the way. With the exception of the chapter on collectivism, the essays were originally assigned to individual authors, but over the course of the project, Jerry Neyrey retired and changed careers, Gary Stansell fell ill, and most shocking of all, Dietmar Neufeld passed away. All four essays of these colleagues had to be completed in their absence, and it is my hope that justice was done to their contributions.

Professor Dietmar Neufeld was a longtime member of the Context Group, a devoted teacher and mentor, a rigorous interlocutor at meetings, and a dear friend to many. He was my MA thesis director at UBC, and it was a wonderful experience having him contribute two chapters to a book I was editing. He will be missed by all the contributors to this volume, by other members of the Context Group, and by many members of the international biblical studies guild. This book is dedicated to his memory. We miss you, Diet.

Select Bibliography

Carney, T. F. *The Shape of the Past: Models and Antiquity*. Lawrence, KS: Coronado, 1975.

Elliott, J. H. *What Is Social-Scientific Criticism?* Minneapolis: Fortress, 1993.

Esler, Philip Francis. "Models in New Testament Interpretation: A Reply to David Horrell." *JSNT* 78 (2000): 107–13.

Herzfeld, Michael. "Honour and Shame: Some Problems in the Comparative Analysis of Moral Systems." *Man* NS 15 (1980): 339–51.

Horrell, David. "Models and Methods in Social-Scientific Interpretation: A Response to Philip Esler." *JSNT* 78 (2000): 83–105.

Horsley, Richard A. *Sociology and the Jesus Movement*. New York: Crossroad, 1989.

Lawrence, Louise Joy. *An Ethnography of the Gospel of Matthew: A Critical Assessment of the Use of the Honour and Shame Model in New Testament Studies.* Tübingen: Mohr Siebeck, 2003.

Malina, Bruce J. *The New Testament World: Insights from Cultural Anthropology.* 3rd ed. Atlanta: John Knox, 2001.

Neyrey, Jerome H. "Social Science Modeling and the New Testament." *BTB* 16 (1986): 107–10.

Rodd, Cyril S. "On Applying a Sociological Theory to Biblical Studies." *JSOT* 19 (1981): 95–106.

Rohrbaugh, Richard L. "Methodological Considerations in the Debate over the Social Class of Early Christians." *JAAR* 52 (1984): 519–46.

———. "Models and Muddles: Discussions of the Social Facets Seminar." *Forum* 3.2 (1987): 23–33.

PART I

Institutions

1. Economy

Douglas E. Oakman

Introduction

It is difficult to read anywhere in the Bible without coming across social institutions and practices shaped by economics. The economies of the biblical periods were a mix of commercial and agrarian dimensions. But while elites might enjoy long-distance commerce in luxuries, and even some bulk goods, most biblical traditions were shaped under exploitative conditions characteristic of agrarian societies where the majority had limited material security. The details vary by locality and period, but the general economic picture is fairly static over the time the Bible was being compiled.

Advanced agrarian societies are characterized by manual and animal labor and the use of the iron plow. Approximately 90 percent of the population is engaged in direct agricultural work, the purpose of which is consumption and not sale for profit. Minimal *labor-saving devices* are at the disposal of village or small-town peasantry, and annual crops are always at the mercy of environmental (e.g., drought) and social (e.g., exploitation by land owners, taxes, rents) variables; the cumulative effect often results in tense social relations between those who own the land and those trying to survive on it. Elites, for the most part, live in cities and on estates. Elite-controlled commercial ventures, whether by land or sea, add further stresses on the subsistence "bottom line," because they send local agrarian wealth elsewhere without adding to food security. Elite building programs and corvées siphon labor away from peasant village agriculture. Because of the significant level of coercive relations and means, biblical economies were always political economies.

The agricultural year is very important in the biblical traditions. For instance, three major festivals were aligned with agricultural harvest times—Festival of Passover with the early grain harvest, Festival of Weeks with

11

the full grain harvest, and Festival of Booths with the vintage (Deut 16). Deuteronomy 8:8 envisions agrarian riches in seven kinds: wheat, barley, fig, pomegranate, grape, olive, and honey. Preindustrial agrarian production is more restricted by natural and sociopolitical factors, thus giving rise to distinctive cultural values, like disdain of manual labor among elites, mistrust of money (including those who handle it), reciprocity, generosity/ stinginess, **Patronage (chap. 3), Limited Good and Envy (chap. 17), Evil Eye** beliefs **(chap. 20)**, self-sufficiency, and peasant "wantlessness" (being content with very little).

Labor was organized by family units at the lowest level of agrarian societies. Villages were ordinarily comprised of extended families ("relatives"); towns and cities were expressions of state-level formations and nonagricultural labor organization. Large estates, for instance, could depend upon slave or free labor. Tenancy was often disadvantageous to the peasant, and estate stewards (*oikonomoi*) were carefully watched by landlords. Town and urban artisans might be made up of surplus village children or declassed elites, but landless laborers were also needed for estate harvest times. Tax or rent collectors were ordinarily bonded or indentured in some way, so as to remain under control of the major collectors and elites.

In addition to agricultural work, a limited number of the population, perhaps 5–10 percent, engaged in some specialized productive pursuits. These would include merchants, weavers, potters, stone masons, metal workers, and the like. Such specialization was again pursued by families (see **chap. 2, Kinship**), normally involving trade secrets, and possibly controlled by elite interests in organized workshops (see **chap. 19, Mockery and Secrecy**).

While Solomon (1 Kgs 9:26–28) and Herod the Great (building of Caesarea Maritima) respectively attempted to control transit trade and establish seaborne commerce, the major tribute takers of this region over the millennia were indigenous monarchies or the kingdoms or empires of Egypt and Mesopotamia, and later Rome. In other words, integration of the biblical lands into commercial networks (overland luxury caravans or seaborne products) primarily benefited the elites and put stresses upon traditional domestic production and the peasantry. It is possible to attribute unrest and revolt occasionally seen in the biblical traditions to such agrarian stresses and crises (1 Kgs 12:18–19). From time to time as well, pestilence (Joel 1:4) and famine (Acts 11:28) brought on crises. Honi the circle-maker was famous for his prayers for rain (m. Ta'anit 3:8). In straitened circumstances, familial solidarity and sharing ensured survival; ordinarily, then, family economy was characterized as sharing without expecting immediate return (generalized reciprocity), and such values came to symbolize healing and salvation in various places in biblical traditions.

The New Testament was written during the first century and a half of the Roman Empire, when Syro-Palestine again came to be firmly integrated into the mixed agrarian-Mediterranean commercial economy of the urban-based imperial elites. The canonical Gospels thus speak about money, economy, markets, large absentee landlords, and a host of exploited landless who are addressed as honored in Jesus's vision of the kingdom of God that will upend all imperial relations. This picture gives way in the later New Testament literature to the appearance of urban artisans, laborers, and commercial agents who move more naturally within the commercial economy of Rome (Acts 18:1–3; Jas 2:2–7). For some New Testament writers, who straddled the divide between city and country, the social tensions could evoke great anger (Jas 5:1–6; Rev 18:9–20).

The Bible is acutely aware of agrarian social institutions or conditions that endanger the primary producer. Paramount among dangers are the loss of land (or land access) and the crushing affliction of indebtedness. These two recurring problems are addressed in a number of places in the Bible, notably Deut 15; Lev 25; Neh 5; and in certain traditions associated with Jesus (Matt 18:23–35; Luke 7:41–42; 11:2–4). Indeed, debt forgiveness becomes a major biblical metaphor for salvific healing and release. Jesus speaks of the incompatibility of trusting mammon (wealth in the bank or storehouse) and loyalty to God (Luke 16:13). However, the later New Testament writers, stemming from the urban service strata, indicate that the problem is love of money (Acts 5:1–11; 1 Tim 6:9–10). The conventional ethos (consonant with household economy) among early Christ-followers came to value sharing among members of the household (Acts 4:32–37; 20:35).

Ancient Texts

MEDITERRANEAN/BIBLICAL AGRICULTURE

1. GEZER CALENDAR
The Gezer Calendar is an inscribed piece of limestone with seven lines of writing. It was found near Jerusalem and dates from approximately the tenth century BCE. It describes the annual agricultural cycle and presupposes a Mediterranean climate that allowed grains to be planted in fall and harvested in spring; grapes and olives were harvested in the early fall.

The two months of [olive] harvest; the two months of planting [grain]
The two months of late planting
The month of hoeing up of flax
The month of harvest of barley
The month of harvest and storage
The two months of vine-tending
The month of summer-fruit.[1]

2. JOHN 4:35–37

The Gospel of John shows that agriculture serves as an important reservoir of biblical metaphors, in this case harvest.

> Do you not say that the harvest is still four months away? I say to you, "Lift up your eyes and look at the fields—they are already white for harvest." Indeed, the harvester receives payment and gathers fruit for eternal life, in order that the sower and the reaper rejoice together. For in this matter, the saying is true, "One sows, and another reaps."

MEDITERRANEAN/AGRARIAN ECONOMIC VALUES

3. MATTHEW 20:15

The phenomenon of all resources being limited results in envy, which according to ancient science naturally leads to the "evil eye" (see **chap. 17, Limited Good and Envy**; **chap. 20, Evil Eye**). The evil eye was believed to do bodily harm.

> Is it not permitted me to do what I want with my wealth? Or is your eye evil because I am good?

4. LUKE 10:35

In an environment of subsistence, generosity was highly valued and stinginess despised. In the parable of the good Samaritan, the Samaritan character treats a foreign enemy like a family member, that is, generously and without the expectation of return.

> Drawing out two denarii, [the Samaritan] gave them to the innkeeper and said to him, "Take care of [the Israelite victim of robbery]. And whatever additional expense, I will repay you when I return."

1. http://www.kchanson.com/.

5. LUKE (Q) 16:13

Mistrust of money by the non-elite was common.

> You cannot serve God and mammon.

POLITICAL ECONOMY:
ELITE CONTROL OF PRODUCTION, ESTATES, AND LAND TENURE

6. GOSPEL OF THOMAS 65

Much economic life took place on large estates worked by tenant farmers. Elites and farmers conflicted constantly, as the former tried to control production and the latter tried to survive. This typically led to conflicted relations between landlord and producer, as is seen in Thomas's dark version of the parable of the tenants.

> A person owned a vineyard and rented it to some farmers, so they could work it and he could collect its crop from them. He sent his slave so the farmers would give him the vineyard's crop. They grabbed him, beat him, and almost killed him, and the slave returned and told his master. His master said, "Perhaps he didn't know them." He sent another slave, and the farmers beat that one as well. Then the master sent his son and said, "Perhaps they'll show my son some respect." Because the farmers knew that he was the heir to the vineyard, they grabbed him and killed him. Anyone here with two ears had better listen![2]

7. P.YADIN 16

Abundant documentary evidence for political control and taxation of agriculture is extant. In this papryus from the second century CE, land is being registered.

> At the time of the census of Arabia under Titus Aninius Sextius Florentinus, legate of Augustus pro praetore, I Babatha daughter of Simon of Maoza of the Zoarene region of Petra, dwelling on my own property in Maoza itself, have recorded the things that I own ... a date plantation within the boundaries of Maoza called Bethphaaraia, the area of sown barley seed of twenty sata, paying three kors of Syrian and Noaran [?] dates, two kors from those struck down, for the crown tax eight lepta forty-five adjacent to the property of Tamar daughter of Thamous and the road.[3]

2. Patterson and Meyer, "The Gospel of Thomas," in *The Complete Gospels*, 316.
3. Lewis, *Documents from the Bar Kokhba Period.*

POLITICAL ECONOMY: ORGANIZATION OF LABOR

8. SIRACH 38:24–30

This second-century BCE apocryphal work called Sirach (also called Ecclesiasticus, and the Wisdom of Jesus ben Sirach) illustrates the relationship between labor and leisure. Scribes in service of power elites played important roles in tax and rent accounting; they also inscribed the biblical traditions. The commoner lived life in service of the elites as well, but subject to the heavy labor demands of agriculture, trades, or elite-requisitioned labor (for instance, as a requirement of a patron).

> The wisdom of the scribe lies in the opportunity of leisure, and the one who decreases his business activity will become wise. How shall one who grasps the plow become wise? Or who drives cattle at the point of a goad? Or turns back and forth as they draw? Or whose conversation is about bulls' male calves? He will devote his heart to plowing straight furrows, and he is sleepless over heifer's feed. Likewise is every craftsman and master craftsman who labors night and day—those who engrave engravings on signets, and the carefulness of him who effects intricate designs—he will give his heart to craft a lifelike portrait, and he is sleepless to complete the work. So is the smith sitting near the anvil and carefully observing his work; a vapor of fire will melt his flesh; he will contend with sound of hammer in the heat of a furnace, and he will devote himself to perfection of product and concern himself to effect a beautiful ornamentation. Similarly, the potter sits with his vessel and turns the wheel with his feet. He reclines in worry every night over his work, and all his work aims to fulfill a number. He will mold clay with his arm, and he will shape its strength before his feet. He is devoted to a perfect glaze, and he is careful to clean the oven.

9. CICERO, *ON DUTIES* 1.69

Naturally, elites preferred leisure, and they associated busyness with the poor and non-elite. Leisure allows the cultivation of wisdom, naturally not the domain of the laboring masses. This passage comes from Cicero, a wealthy first-century BCE philosopher, politician, and lawyer. In this work, he discusses at length the best lifestyles and proper moral obligations.

> Moreover, there both are and were many who, seeking that tranquility that I spoke of, are the sort to have withdrawn themselves from public business and fled to leisure.[4]

4. Adapted from Miller, LCL.

10. SUETONIUS, *VESPASIAN* 18

Labor-saving devices were rarely accessible to non-elites and, in this passage, were avoided even by the elite. In this passage from Suetonius—a first-century CE Roman biographer—even the emperor recognizes the deleterious effects that a labor-saving device would have on the non-elite.

> To a mechanical engineer, who promised to transport some heavy columns to the capitol at small expense, [Vespasian] gave no mean reward for his invention, but refused to make use of it, having prefaced the deed by saying that it would not allow the commons to feed themselves.[5]

POLITICAL ECONOMY: TAXATION, RENTS, AND SO-CALLED SURPLUSES

11. 1 KINGS 4:7, 22–23

Solomon, the third king of Israel, is renowned in Israelite tradition for his wealth. This wealth was substantially derived from the agriculture of his kingdom, but he also benefited from some commercial dealings.

> Solomon had twelve revenue officers over all Israel, and they supplied the king and his house for one month out of the year, each in charge of one month's supply. . . .
>
> This was the provision of Solomon for one day: thirty kors of fine flour, and sixty kors of meal; ten fattened oxen and ten pasture-fed cattle; one hundred sheep, in addition to deer and gazelle; and fattened fowls.

12. 1 MACCABEES 10:29–31

Taxation, which in antiquity amounts to elite extraction of produce from the producers, could take the form of coin or produce. Either way, it was exorbitant, as reflected in this second-century BCE apocryphal work, which in part reflects the existence of multiple forms of taxation.

> I [Demetrius] now set you free and release all the Judeans from the tributes and the honor tax and the salt tax and from the crown taxes. I release the land of Judah and the three districts added to it from Samaria and Galilee, from this day and henceforth, from the collection of the third of the grain and the half of the fruit of the trees that I should receive. From this day and for all time, Jerusalem and its environs, its tithes and its revenues, shall be inviolable and free from tax.

5. Adapted from Rolfe, LCL.

13. JOSEPHUS, *JEWISH ANTIQUITIES* 17.306–9

The level of rents and taxes has been much debated, but combined they amounted to nearly 66 percent of all agrarian product. Josephus was a first-century CE Judean historian and military commander in the war against Rome. His writing was done as a client of the Roman emperors, Vespasian and Titus.

> [Herod the Great] was refusing to stop adorning neighboring cities and those inhabited by foreigners, despite the destruction to dwellers in his own kingdom. The nation by contrast was left full of desperate poverty, though it had been received in exceedingly good shape. Through baseless charges, he was killing those formerly of the nobility in order to expropriate their estates. And those whom he allowed the unpleasantness to live he stripped of their property. Even with the tributes due from each subject for the year, he was confiscating forfeited court money for himself and his household and the slaves who would go out to collect tributes. This was so that it not be returned to the lowly or to those who were making bribes.[6]

14. TACITUS, *ANNALS* 2.42

Tacitus was a first- and second-century (56–117 CE) Roman historian and senator. His work *Annals*—Tacitus's final work—is a history of Rome. He does not speak well of Tiberius, who in this passage is criticized for his manner of taxation.

> [Under Tiberius] the provinces of Syria and Judea, wearied by oppressive exactions, were petitioning for a diminution of the tribute.[7]

15. P.LONDON 306

This second-century CE papyrus manuscript illustrates a variety of tax agents serving provincial and imperial elites during the Greco-Roman period.

> In year eight of Emperor Caesar Titus Aelius Hadrianus Antoninus Augustus Pius, the fifth month of Caesareus, in Heraklea in the Themistes district of the Arsinoite nome. Stotoetis son of Stotoetis son of Horus, collector of taxes in silver of the before-mentioned village of Heraklea, twenty-six years old with a scarred shin, publicly acknowledges Saturnilus son of Apion son of Didymus, fifty years old with a scarred middle forehead, as collector for two years start-

---

6. Adapted from Marcus and Wikgren, LCL.
7. Adapted from Jackson, LCL.

ing with the coming ninth year of Lord Antoninus Caesar and to pay into the public treasury a third part for which Stotoetis is responsible, while Saturnilus should likewise fulfill in numbered payments the third part entrusted to him. In addition, Saturnilus will submit records of the collection at the usual appointed times; Saturnilus will provide papyrus, and other expenses will be his, and he will receive as salary from Stotoetis each year 252 silver drachmas, the payment of which will be made to him in four installments alike equally every three months. Stotoetis will help with collection whenever there is need, because the contract was made on these terms.[8]

POLITICAL ECONOMY:
CONTROL OF PEASANT LABOR THROUGH AGRARIAN DEBT

16. P.YADIN 11

Low-level scribes produced contracts such as this for those who invariably could not read or write; similar scribes were concerned with the earliest Jesus traditions. Default on debt brought serious consequences, as envisaged in this papyrus document.

When Manius Acilius Glabrio and Torquatus Tebanianus were governing, one day before the nones of May [May 6], in En-gedi village of Lord Caesar, Judah son of Elazar Khthousion, En-gedian, to Magonius Valens, centurion of Cohors I Miliaria Thracum, greeting. I acknowledge to have and owe to you in loan sixty denarii of Tyrian silver, which are fifteen staters, upon the security of the courtyard in En-gedi that belongs to my father Elazar Khthousion—which courtyard is on the east near the tents and the property of Jesus Mandronos, on the west tents and workshop of the same Elazar my father, on the south the agora and property of Simon Matthaios, on the north the road and presidio—silver that I will repay to you in the month of January of the interest of the same year, and the interest I will provide to you from the same silver each month to the amount of six denarii on one hundred denarii. And if I should not repay you at the appointed time as has been written beforehand, then you will have the right to seize, to possess, to sell, to dwell the same security without . . . and you can execute or another who might represent you or have your authority to do so.[9]

8. Adapted from Hunt and Edgar, LCL.
9. Lewis, *Documents from the Bar Kokhba Period.*

17. Philo, *Special Laws* 3.159–60

Philo of Alexandria was a first-century CE Judean philosopher and defender of Judean civic rights in Alexandria. In a work entitled *De specialibus legibus*, he writes at length about the special laws of Judaism, relating them to the Ten Commandments. In this section, he is considering laws relating to the seventh commandment, prohibiting murder. In the process, he presents evidence about how violence (and the threat of violence) was used against the whole family of a debtor in order to teach a lesson to others.

> Recently, a certain man was appointed a tax collector among us. When some who were in arrears on account of poverty fled for fear of cruel punishments, he violently led away their wives, children, parents, and other clan, striking them, hurling abuse at them, and tormenting them with all manner of outrages, in order that either they might betray the fugitive or they might settle on his behalf. Being able to do neither, and because they had even fewer resources than the fugitive, the tax collector did not give up before stretching their bodies on racks and torture implements in order to kill them with newly invented modes of death. Having tied baskets full of sand hanging down by nooses from the neck, a grievous weight, he stood them out in the open in the middle of the market. This was so that punished by a multitude of torments—wind and sun and the insults of those passing by and the hanging weights—they, broken by force, might perish wretchedly, while those witnessing the victims' torments might anticipate a similar fate.[10]

18. Nehemiah 5:1–5

The biblical traditions show familial/covenant concern for redemption from debt slavery.

> There was a great outcry of the people and their wives against their Judahite brothers. Some were saying, "We with our sons and our daughters are many, so let us take grain, eat, and live." Others were saying, "We are pledging our fields, vineyards, and houses, so let us take grain on account of famine." Others were saying, "We have borrowed silver for the king's tax on our fields and vineyards. Now, the flesh of our brothers is like our flesh, and we are like their brothers. We are subjecting our sons and daughters to slavery; some of our daughters are already enslaved. There is nothing we can do about it. Both our fields and vineyards belong to others."

10. Adapted from Colson, LCL.

POLITICAL ECONOMY:

ELITE CONTROL OF AND BENEFIT FROM COMMERCE

19. Ezekiel 27:12–17

In the sixth century BCE, the prophet from priestly lineage, Ezekiel, wrote a lamentation for the city of Tyre, a Phoenician (enemy) city. In the midst of the lament, which is in typical poetic form, there is a sudden prose section that is an economic accounting of Tyre's many trade relationships. This is approximately half of the section, which starts and ends with Tarshish, a key port city in southern Spain.

> Tarshish was your trade-partner because of all the wealth in silver, iron, tin, and lead given for your goods. Javan, Tubal, and Meschech were your traffickers in human life, and they gave bronze vessels for your wares. From Togarmah they exchanged horses, steeds, and mules for your goods. Sons of Dedan [Rhodes] were purveyors of your merchandise to many coastlands. Horns of ivory and ebony they brought back in return for your gifts. Aram was your merchant because of your abundant work. They traded your goods for precious stone, purple wool, decorated cloth, byssus, coral, and rubies. In exchange, Judah and the land of Israel gave wheat of Minnith, *pannag*, honey, oil, and balm.

20. Pliny the Elder, *Natural History* 12.32.63–65

Pliny the Elder (23–79 CE) was a Roman naval commander and naturalist. His work became the model for later natural science and geography. In this section of his encyclopedic *Natural History*, Pliny discusses land-borne commerce and the toll expenses that affected it. They add up and contribute significantly to the cost of goods once they reach a market.

> After frankincense is gathered, it is conveyed to Sabota by means of camels. A single gate is left open for the caravan. The kings have made it a capital offense to depart from the road. There priests take a tithe by volume, not by weight, for the god they call Sabis. Nor is it allowed to be sold at market beforehand. From this the public expenses are sustained. For indeed the god liberally supplies food to guests for a certain number of days. It is not allowed to be exported except through the Gebbanites, and for this reason a tax is weighed out for their king. Their chief city Thomna is distant from Gaza (a town on our shores in Judea) 1370 miles, a journey that is divided into sixty-five stopping places for camels. There are select portions of frankincense that are given to priests and to royal scribes. Besides these, guards and attendants and gatekeepers and servants grab their portions.

Now in some places, portions are weighed out for water, in some places for fodder, in some places for lodging, and in some places for various duties. All together up to the coast, 688 denarii are collected for a single camel, and even then, tolls are exacted by our imperial tax farmers.[11]

Vocabulary of Economy

Economy, as a topic of study, of course has certain vocabulary words associated with it: market, coin, tax, tribute, and so on. But words like this do not tell us anything about the features of the economic world of antiquity. For that, we must simply read texts to see the economy that stands behind them. Thus, no vocabulary is offered for this chapter.

Select Bibliography

Borowski, Oded. *Agricultural Life in Iron Age Israel.* Winona Lake, IN: Eisenbrauns, 1987.

Finley, Moses I. *The Ancient Economy.* 2nd ed. London: Hogarth, 1985.

Hamel, Gildas. *Poverty and Charity in Roman Palestine, First Three Centuries C.E.* Berkeley: University of California Press, 1990.

Oakman, Douglas E. *Jesus and the Economic Questions of His Day.* Lewiston: Edwin Mellen, 1986.

Rohrbaugh, Richard. "Peasant Reading of the Parable of the Talents/Pounds: A Text of Terror?" *BTB* 23 (1989): 32–39.

Scheidel, Walter, Ian Morris, and Richard Saller, eds. *The Cambridge Economic History of the Greco-Roman World.* Cambridge: Cambridge University Press, 2007.

Additional Texts

MEDITERRANEAN/BIBLICAL AGRICULTURE

Acts 11:28	Babylonian Talmud
Ambrose, *On Duties* 3.45–47	Avodah Zarah 30a

11. Adapted from Rackham, LCL.

Menahot 85a–b
Mo'ed Qatan 17b
Josephus, *Jewish Antiquities* 15.299–316;
 Jewish War 3.271, 277
Luke 6:43
Mark 11:13
Mishnah

Kil'ayim 4:4–7
Menahot 8:1, 3, 6
Pe'ah 7:1
Pliny the Elder, *Natural History* 8, 14–15,
 17, 19–20
Sifre 135b
Varro, *On Agriculture* 1.54–55

MEDITERRANEAN/AGRARIAN ECONOMIC VALUES AND ATTITUDES

Aristotle, *Nicomachean Ethics*
 1119b–1123a, 1163b5–19, 1177a–1178a;
 Politics 1291a; *Rhetoric* 1390b–1391a
Cicero, *On Duties* 1.150; 3.1
Dio Chrysostom, *Kingship 1* (*Or.* 1) 33;
 The Hunter (*Or.* 7) 108; *Slavery and
 Freedom* (*Or.* 14) 14
Gospel of the Nazarenes 18
Gospel of Thomas 45, 63, 76
Jerome, *Commentary on Jeremiah* 2.5.2
John 3:30

Lucian, *The Dream* 9
Luke 6:32–38; 7:5; 11:2–4; 12:16–20;
 16:1–13; 16:19–31; 19:12–24; 22:25
Mark 6:21
Matthew 6:2; 19:24; 20:1–16
Philippians 4:11–12
Plotinus, *Enneads* 2.9.9
Proverbs 10:15; 18:11
Psalms of Solomon 5:19
Sirach 5:8; 10:31; 31:13; 38:24

POLITICAL ECONOMY:
ELITE CONTROL OF PRODUCTION, ESTATES, AND LAND TENURE

Babylonian Talmud
 Gittin 56a
 Hagigah 2:13
CIL 8.10570, 14464, 25902, 25943
Columella, *On Agriculture* 1.6–9
Gospel of Thomas 45, 63, 76
Josephus, *Against Apion* 1.51; *Jewish
 Antiquities* 17.175; 18.138, 273; 19.353,
 355; 20.140, 147; *Jewish War* 1.660;
 Life 71, 73, 119
Luke 2:8; 9:58; 12:16–20; 15:25; 16:1–8
Mark 12:1–12
Matthew 20:1–16

Mishnah
 Bava Batra 3
 Bava Metzi'a 5:8
P.Amherst 91, 105
P.Milan 6
P.Rylands 171
Pliny the Elder, *Natural History* 18.7.35
Pliny the Younger, *Letters* 3.19; 9.37; 10.8
Plutarch, *Life of Tiberius Gracchus* 9.4
Varro, *On Agriculture* 1.16–17; 11.10
Xenophon, *Oeconomicus* 13

POLITICAL ECONOMY: ORGANIZATION OF LABOR

CIL 6.2305; 8.11824

Columella, *On Agriculture* 1.7–8;
  2.12.1–4; 11.2, 11, 20

Deuteronomy 24:19

Josephus, *Jewish Antiquities* 13.52; 18.37

1 Kings 5:13–16

Leviticus 19:9

Luke 10:2; 16:1–7

Mark 4:3–8, 29; 15:21

Matthew 5:41

Pliny the Elder, *Natural History* 18.117–19

Revelation 14:15–20

Varro, *On Agriculture* 1.50–51

POLITICAL ECONOMY: TAXATION, RENTS, AND SO-CALLED SURPLUSES

Acts 5:37

Babylonian Talmud
  Sanhedrin 25b

Cicero, *On Duties* 1.150; *Against Verres*
  2.3

Deuteronomy 26:1–11

Dio Chrysostom, *Slavery and Freedom 1*
  (*Or.* 14) 14

Exodus 13:11–13

Josephus, *Jewish Antiquities* 12.154–55,
  169; 12.175–77; 14.203, 274–75; 16.153–
  54; 17.308–9; 18.1–2, 312; 19.299;
  20.181, 206; *Jewish War* 1.170, 221, 524;
  2.118, 433; 6.422–24; 7.253; *Life* 80

Judith 11:13

Julian, *Against the Galileans* 238e

1 Kings 4:1–19

Leviticus 27:30–32

Lucian, *The Mistaken Critic* 30

Luke 2:1–2; (Q) 7:34; 15:1; 18:10–13

1 Maccabees 3:49

Mark 2:14–16

Matthew 17:24–27

Mishnah
  Bava Qamma 10:2
  Ma'aserot 1:1
  Nedarim 3:4
  Sheqalim 8:8
  Teharot 7:6

Numbers 18:15–18

Origen, *Against Celsus* 1.63

P.Oxyrhynchus 251, 288

Philostratus, *Life of Apollonius* 8.7

Tacitus, *Annals* 13.50–51

Tobit 1:6–7

POLITICAL ECONOMY:
CONTROL OF PEASANT LABOR THROUGH AGRARIAN DEBT

Aristotle, *Constitution of Athens* 6.1

Cicero, *Against Catiline* 2.8

CIL 6.967

Deuteronomy 23:19–20

Dio Cassius, *Roman History* 71.32.2

Josephus, *Jewish Antiquities* 14.200–02;
  15.365; 17.204; *Jewish War* 2.426–27;
  6.354

Leviticus 25:10, 13, 25, 35–55

Luke 6:34–35; 7:36–50; (Q) 12:58–59;
  19:12–26
1 Maccabees 11:32–36
Matthew 18:23–35
P.Kronion 1–29

Pliny the Younger, *Letters* 9.37.2–3
Plutarch, *Solon* 15.3, 5
Proverbs 22:7
Tacitus, *Annals* 2.42

POLITICAL ECONOMY: COMMERCE

Aristotle, *Politics* 1258a35–b8; *Nico-
  machean Ethics* 1096a5–10, 1122a,
  1127b10–14, 1163b5–19
Cicero, *On Duties* 1.150
Gregory of Nazianzus, *Epistles* 2
Gospel of Thomas 45, 63, 64, 76, 109
Horace, *Epodes* 2
Julian, *Against the Galileans* 238e

1 Kings 10:14–15, 22
Luke 12:18–20
Philostratus, *Life of Apollonius* 4.32
Revelation 18:11–13
Sirach 26:29; 27:2
Suetonius, *Augustus* 2.3; 3.1; 4.2
1 Timothy 6:10

2. Kinship

Erin K. Vearncombe

Introduction

To the modern reader, the detailed genealogical accounts found throughout both the Hebrew Bible and the books of the New Testament may not excite the mind or stimulate reflection in the same way that the more dramatic events enclosed in these narratives might; the meticulous list of the descendants of Adam to Noah in Gen 5 does not generate the same sort of enthusiasm in the modern audience as the story of the flood that it precedes, and the tracing of Jesus's lineage back to Abraham at the beginning of Matthew's Gospel does not pull the reader's focus in the same way as the recounting of Jesus's birth and Matthew's famous story of the wise men. However, the importance of these genealogies must not be underestimated; in the ancient contexts in which these lists of descent and ancestry were compiled, genealogy served a variety of important social functions, particularly in terms of the establishment of claims to social status (see **chap. 4, Honor**), privilege, and authority. In Matthew's text, for example, the tracing of Jesus's genealogy back to Abraham through David links Jesus both to Israel's greatest patriarch, Abraham—establishing Jesus's social position as an Israelite—and to Israel's greatest king, David—linking Jesus to Israel's royal history and, according to Matthew, to its future as the fulfillment of this royal line.

Indeed, genealogy is so important that the author of the Gospel of Matthew chooses to categorize the entirety of the text as "an account of the genealogy of Jesus the Messiah" (Matt 1:1). Genealogy draws its significance from the matrix of kinship in the ancient Mediterranean, a matrix that influences almost every social relationship or context. "Kinship" refers to relationships we might think we are familiar with—parents and children, brothers and sisters, spouses and in-laws, as well as births and deaths—but these relationships cannot be conceptualized through simple biology, blood, marital linking, or reproduction. All people have mothers and fathers, and most have siblings and cousins, but *kinship* is a system of value and culture that is much bigger than biological relationships. For example, in terms of lineage, children were related to parents but could also be related to gods, ancestors, and other persons outside the biological line.[1]

In the social world of the ancient Mediterranean, the structuring of descent and descent groups not only established the connections between kin through common ancestry, but also set up a variety of social relationships. Kinship should therefore be thought of as a social construction, heavily dependent upon sociohistorical context. "Family" has no comprehensive, collective meaning. Kinship matters because of the different social frameworks its structures support, including families and households (see **chap. 8, Space**), but also including ritual observance, political practice, and economic distribution (see **chap. 10, Ritual, Domestic**). In the ancient Mediterranean, these frameworks were very different from our own.

The basic kinship unit in the ancient Mediterranean world was the household. The ancient Greek and Latin terms for "household" (see below) refer to physical space (dwelling, architectural structure), property (material goods and slaves, ancient slavery being a very complicated kinship category), and to social relationships, including both direct kin structures ("direct" meaning connected through blood, or carnally through reproduction: father, mother, child, etc.) and relationships with dependents, which could also be configured through the language of fictive kinship (see **chap. 3, Patronage; chap. 16, Friendship and Gifts**). The imperial household (*domus Caesaris*) is an extreme example of a household unit, including blood relatives, various clients and officials (see **chap. 3, Patronage**), slaves, and a huge network of freedpersons. Similarly, the ancient terms for "family" are not limited to the "nuclear family" of modern understanding, but to this diverse and extended network of family relationships, dependents, slaves, and property. The household was the center of social identity and location; indeed, ancient Mediterranean societies were collectivistic, meaning that orientation was toward social relationship, one's place in a group or as part of a group, rather than toward the individual. A person "was" in relation to another (see **chap. 6, Collectivism**).

The head of the household was the *paterfamilias*, the ultimate (male) authority figure (see **chap. 9, Gender**). The *paterfamilias*, generally the eldest

1. Robert Parkin, *Kinship: An Introduction to the Basic Concepts* (Oxford: Blackwell, 1997), 14.

surviving male of the kin group, was responsible for the efficient social and economic operation of the household until his death. He held a considerable degree of power (*potestas*) over property and persons in the household, from his wife (especially if the marriage involved the transfer of authority over the bride, from the bride's father to her new husband, so that she was now incorporated into her husband's kin group; a woman could also remain under the power of her father, through a "free marriage") and children to slaves and other dependents. The decisions of the *paterfamilias* therefore impacted the entire household.

Pater is the Latin word generally translated as "father," so one might consider a reasonable translation of *paterfamilias* to be "father of the family." However, an understanding of ancient kinship structures changes the translation significantly. *Pater* can mean "father," but also "older" or "aged man," "forefathers" in the plural, or "parent" more generally; it can be used as an honorific title for senators, statesmen, patrons, and benefactors (see **chap. 3, Patronage**); it refers to the generative or creative capacity of gods and is also applied to gods themselves, especially "high" or supreme gods like Jupiter. *Vir*, the Latin word usually translated as "man," has a similar range of meanings: man (as opposed to woman or boy, very important distinctions), husband, soldier, someone who is courageous, and someone who is worthy of honor. The range of meanings implicit in apparently simple terms like "man" and "father" is a good demonstration of the profoundly social character of kinship structures. Far beyond biology, the kinship matrix located the person in social space, influencing and influenced by constructions of gender and the body, economics, politics, and religion. The social group is the constant frame of reference.

Ancient Texts

THE FAMILY UNIT, OR HOUSEHOLD

1. ULPIAN, *DIGEST* 50, 16.195

Ulpian (died ca. 230 CE) was a Roman jurist originally from Phoenicia who served under several Roman emperors, rising to the rank of chief advisor to Alexander Severus (Roman emperor 222–235 CE). While we have only extracts from his writings, his legal work survives in the emperor Justinian's codification of Roman law, the *Corpus Iuris Civilis*, in the section called the *Digest*. In this lengthy excerpt, Ulpian breaks down the referents of the term *familia*, which begins with property, including freedmen, and moves to people.

As for people, *familia* can refer to something as broad as a tribe. This passage from the longer section delineates how different the ancient *familia* was from the modern nuclear family.

> The term *familia* is also used to mean a certain body of persons, defined either by a strict legal bond between the persons themselves or in a general sense of people joined by a looser relationship of kinship. In the strict legal sense, we call a *familia* a number of people who are by birth or by law subjected to the *potestas* [power] of one man, for example, *paterfamilias, mater* [mother], son or daughter of a *familia*, and so on in succession, for example, grandsons, granddaughters, etc. *Paterfamilias* is the title given to the person who holds sway in the house, and he is correctly so called even if he has no children, for we are designating not only him as a person, but his legal right: indeed, we call even a minor *paterfamilias*. When a *paterfamilias* dies, all the persons subject to him begin each to have a separate *familia*; for each individual takes on the title *paterfamilias*. The same will happen when someone is emancipated, for he becomes legally independent and begins to have his own *familia*.[2]

2. ACTS 16:25–34

The excerpt above from the *Digest* mentions the most authoritative figure in the household unit, the *paterfamilias*, or male head of the household. The decisions of the *paterfamilias* had an impact on all members of the household, from blood relations to slaves. In Acts, the second-century CE sequel to the Gospel of Luke, when a *paterfamilias* becomes a follower of Jesus, the whole household also converts.

> And around midnight, Paul and Silas were singing hymns to God, and the prisoners were listening to them. But suddenly there was a great earthquake, so that the foundations of the prison were shaken; and immediately all the doors were opened, and everyone's chains were unfastened. And the jailor, having been awoken and having seen that the doors of the prison were open, having drawn his sword, was about to kill himself, supposing the prisoners to have escaped. But Paul called out with a loud voice, saying, "Do no harm to yourself; indeed, we are all here." Having called for lights, [the jailer] rushed in, and he fell down trembling before Paul and Silas, and after he brought them outside, he said, "Lords, what is necessary for me to do, that I might be saved?" And they replied, "Believe on the Lord Jesus, and you will be saved, you and your household." And they spoke

2. Adapted from Gardner and Wiedemann, *Roman Household*, 3–4.

the word of the Lord to him, and to all those in his household. And having taken them at the same hour of the night, he washed their wounds, and he was baptized at once, he and all who were of him [his household]. And having brought them up into his house, he set a table for them, and he rejoiced, with all his household, having believed in God.

3. VALERIUS MAXIMUS, *MEMORABLE DEEDS AND SAYINGS* 6.3.9

Valerius Maximus (first century CE) authored a collection of historical "doings and sayings," rather like a book of anecdotes, under the patronage of the emperor Tiberius. This particular anecdote emphasizes the potentially extreme nature of the power exercised by the *paterfamilias*.

> Egnatius Mecennius . . . beat his wife to death with a stick because she had drunk wine. And his act went without any formal accuser or even someone who reproved it. Everyone judged the penalty she paid to Injured Sobriety an excellent precedent. And it is correct that any female seeking immoderate use of wine closes the door to every virtue and opens [it] to every fault.[3]

4. CICERO, *ON DUTIES* 1.54

The separation of "household" (kinship), economics, religion, and politics into discrete social domains is artificial in the ancient context; each overlaps with and is embedded in the others. It is fruitful to attempt to untangle them here, however, in order to demonstrate the deep roots of kinship structures in diverse social structures. Marcus Tullius Cicero (106–43 BCE), a well-known orator and statesman writing alongside the fall of the Roman Republic, makes a connection between the household and the political domain; again, the household acts as ultimate sociopolitical constituent.

> For since, by nature, the common feature of all living creatures is that they have the desire to reproduce, the first social bond is that of marriage itself, the next, that with one's children, then the household unit, with everything in common; and this is the foundation of the city, the nursery, as it were, of the state. And following are the bonds between brothers, and next those of first and second cousins, and when they can no longer be contained within one household, they go out into other households, as into colonies. And following these come marriages and connections [arising from marriage], and from these again even more relations; and from this propagation and progeny, states have their origin. For shared blood

3. Adapted from Shackleton Bailey, LCL.

binds men together in goodwill and affection; for it means a great deal to have the same [family] memorials, the same forms of domestic worship, and the same ancestral tombs.[4]

MARRIAGE AND DIVORCE

5. JOSEPHUS, *JEWISH WAR* 1.241

As the ancient vocabulary referring to "family" and "household" extends to include a more complex group of relationships than "husband-wife," "parent-child," etc., so the institution of marriage in the ancient context must be interpreted as a "group" endeavor, rather than the linking of two individuals. The signing of a marriage contract represented the linking of two households, two kinship groups for the purpose of creating a new household (in terms of economic production, the transfer of wealth and property, and sexual reproduction) and for the fortification, transmission, or augmentation of honor. One did not simply marry an individual, therefore, but married into a family, as demonstrated in this text from Josephus (37–100 CE), who fought in the Judean war against Rome and is best remembered for his defense of Judean religious life in terms appealing to Romans.

> Herod, having held his ground against them at the entry points into the land of the Judeans, prevailed in the combat. Once Antigonus was driven out and Herod returned to Jerusalem, he was beloved by all for his virtuous action; and even those who in the past had not paid court to him claimed him as kin now, because of his intermarriage into the line of Hyrcanus. For formerly he had a wife from his own land of some significant social status, called Doris, from whom he conceived Antipater, but now he married Mariamne, the daughter of Alexander, son of Aristobolus, and granddaughter of Hyrcanus, and so became kin of the king.[5]

6. JUBILEES 30:7–12

King Herod is described as formerly marrying a wife "out of his own country"; this marriage strategy may be interpreted as *endogamy*, marriage within the kin group (contrasted with *exogamy*, the exclusion of marriage between close kin, the most prevalent approach to marriage among Greeks and Romans).

4. Adapted from Miller, LCL.
5. Adapted from Thackeray, LCL.

Endogamous marriage is stressed in a wide variety of Israelite texts as a way of maintaining identity boundaries. The book of Jubilees is a Hebrew text composed around 135–105 BCE, potentially during the reign of the Maccabees. It shows particular concern for Judean group boundary maintenance, particularly through marriage.

> And if there is any man in Israel who wishes to give his daughter or his sister to any man who is from the seed of the gentiles, let him surely die, and let him be stoned because he has caused shame in Israel. And also the woman will be burned with fire because she has defiled the name of her father's house and so she will be uprooted from Israel. And do not let an adulteress or defilement be found in Israel all the days of the generations of the earth, because Israel is holy to the Lord. . . . And there is no limit of days for this law. And there is no remission or forgiveness except that the man who caused defilement of his daughter will be rooted out from the midst of all Israel, because he has given some of his seed to Moloch and sinned so as to defile it. And you, Moses, command the children of Israel, and exhort them not to give any of their daughters to the gentiles and not to take for their sons any of the daughters of the gentiles, because that is contemptible before the Lord. Therefore, I have written for you in the words of the law all of the deeds of the Shechemites that they did against Dinah and how the sons of Jacob spoke, saying, "We will not give our daughter to a man who is uncircumcised, because that is a reproach to us."

7. Wadi Murabba'at 19

The dissolution of the relationship of marriage through divorce was possible for both men and women in the ancient Mediterranean. As marriage involved more than the bride and groom, divorce also meant the severing of ties between kinship groups or households in terms of the renegotiation of property (e.g., dowry and living arrangements) and honor status. Divorce could be initiated by either party for a variety of reasons, including adultery, refusal to fulfill conjugal duties, or for issues relating to religious purity. Divorced parties were often presented with a bill of divorce to officially confirm the dissolution of the relationship, as we see in Murabba'at 19, an Aramaic text from a cave in the Wadi Murabba'at, not far from the discovery site of the Dead Sea Scrolls, dating to the period of the Bar Kokhba Revolt in Roman Palestine (132–135 CE).

> On the first of Marheshvan, year six, in Masada, of [my] own free will, this day, I, Yehosef son of >N Yehosef son of < Nqsn, from . . . , residing in Masada, dismiss and divorce you, my wife, Miriam daughter of Yehonathan [from] *hn/rb/klt'*, residing in Masada, who has been my wife before this, (so) that you are allowed to

go by yourself and be the wife of any Judean man whom you desire. And this shall be for you from me a document of divorce and a bill of dismissal according to the law of [Mos]es and the people of Judea. All . . . and damages and . . . [. . .] . . . to/for you according to the law will be established and paid in quarterly rates [?]. And at (any) t[ime] that you will tell me, I shall exchange for you the deed as it is fitting.[6]

INHERITANCE

8. P.Michigan 5.322a

Inheritance was generally the passing down of property from the male head of the household to his kinship group upon his death, though there are cases in which fathers or parents presented one or more of their children with a "deed of gift," a distribution of inheritance while the parents were still living (often containing directives for the children concerning the continued support of the parents). P.Michigan 5.322, a lengthy papyrus document from Tebtynis (Egypt) dated November 1, 46 CE is such a "deed" from a man to his various children. It explains in great clarity how property is to be divided and governed, and at the end has been signed by all parties named in the document. Here is a short portion of that deed (from lines 1–5).

> Psyphis who is also called Harpochration son of Serapion also called Marepke-mis, about sixty-nine years old with a scar on the shin, acknowledges that he has divided from the present time among the children born to him from Tetosiris also called Dionysia daughter of Maron also called Marepsemis, with whom he lives without written contract, among his sons Onnophris and Psyphis and the one of his other son Psenkebkis, who has died, his son Psenkebkis and the daughters born to him by the same Tetosiris, Tamarres and Thaubastis, on the one hand, to Onnophris the land that belongs to him, Psyphis who is also called Harpochration, around the above-mentioned village of Tebtynis, namely, three arourai of the land sacred to the god Seknebtynis counted as unirrigated land, of which the neighboring places are south of the canal, called that of Taketon, on the north of the public land and on part of the uncultivated land, on the west of the public land, east of the allotment formerly counted to Konnas, but now is of the estate of Herakles the younger, son of Orsenouphis.[7]

---

6. Adapted from Yardeni, *Textbook of Aramaic, Hebrew and Nabatean Documentary Texts from the Judean Desert and Related Material*, 2:57.

7. Adapted from "Division of Property and Account of a Beer Shop" (http://papyri .info/ddbdp/p.mich;5;322a). Last accessed May 30, 2019.

FICTIVE KINSHIP

9. 1 PETER 4:17

The vocabulary of kinship could be applied not only to biological relationships or close kin relationships within a household or within extended families, but also to "fictive kin" groups, groups modeled on the household or family as a way of constructing or understanding social identity. These "surrogate family" structures could provide group members with the same kinds of social patterns and functions as kin groups. Fictive kinship language provides the primary framework for the early Jesus groups; Paul, for example, frequently addresses group members as "brothers." Similarly, members of the Jesus movement were identified as belonging to the "household of God," as we see in 1 Peter, a pseudepigraphical letter written in the name of the disciple Simon Peter. The letter assumes that the recipients have faced persecution or alienation from their home communities and thus works to create a "fictive" family or insider group for these rejected outsiders.

> For the time of judgment is come and has begun with those from the household of God; and if the first are from us, then what will be the end for those disobeying the good news of God?

10. MARK 3:31–35

The author of the Gospel of Mark, the earliest surviving gospel we have, presents a very clear statement about the radical move away from biological family as articulated in the proclamation of Jesus. Giving up one's kin group for a fictive kin group or surrogate family was not without cost; it could mean breaking with one's entire social network.

> And his mother and his brothers arrive, and standing outside, they sent to him, calling him. And a crowd was sitting around him, and they say to him, "See, your mother and your brothers [and your sisters] are outside, asking for you." And answering them, he says, "Who are my mother and [my] brothers?" And having looked at those who were sitting around him, he says, "See, here are my mother and my brothers! Whoever should do the will of God is my brother and sister and mother."

11. *IPHRYGR* 30

The terminology of fictive kinship, though "fictive," was not "fictional," in that someone referred to as a "mother" or "father" could have a functional role or position as a community or group leader. Calling someone "father" was an honorific title, but in the case of ancient voluntary associations and diaspora synagogues as well, a "father" could be a prominent benefactor, a leader of important ritual practices, or a well-liked or well-respected insider of the group. Many voluntary associations in the Greco-Roman world, groups that met for a variety of purposes (meals, funerals, rituals) under a variety of auspices (groups based on ritual observance, ethnicity, occupation, etc., rather like modern "clubs" or "guilds") used fictive-kinship language to honor members, designate various roles, and to show affection for special insiders. This particular association from second-century CE Phrygia, in Asia Minor, honored some of its members (named following this excerpt) with a special monument decorated with reliefs of gods, like Hermes and Zeus.

> The people of the district of Thiounta honored with a stele and a crown the broth-
> erhood [*phratra*: in a political sense, "association"] that is gathered around The-
> odotos Diogeneianos and Glykon son of Diodoros, the president of the contests.[8]

LINEAGE, ANCESTRY, AND DESCENT

12. PLUTARCH, *ALEXANDER* 2.1–3

Lineage was used to place persons in their proper social location and to iden-
tify positive or negative potential. A person of humble origins could not be expected to accomplish great deeds, while those who do accomplish great things must have high social associations. A person did not develop over time in terms of qualities or attributes; one's potential and abilities were inherent in the person at and through birth. The Greek historian and biographer Plutarch (46–120 CE), for example, suggests that the impressive accomplishments of Alexander the Great are a product of his divine origins.

> Alexander's lineage is as follows: on the side of his father, on the one hand, he was
> from Herakles from Caranus, and on the side of his mother, on the other hand,
> from Aeacus from Neoptolemus; this is altogether believed, without doubt. But
> it is said that Philip [his father], after being initiated into the mysteries of Sa-
> mothrace at the same time with Olympias, when he was still a youth and she an

8. Adapted from Philip Harland, "Honours by Thiounta Village for a Brotherhood [A and B] (II CE)," http://philipharland.com/greco-roman-associations/honours-by -thiounta-village-for-a-brotherhood-a-ii-ce/. Last accessed May 24, 2019.

orphan child, he desired her passionately and betrothed himself in marriage to her, having persuaded her brother, Arymbas. So then, the bride, the night before she was enclosed in the bride-chamber, dreamt that there was thunder, and that a thunderbolt fell upon her womb, from which a great fire was kindled, which burst into flames that burned on every side, then was dissolved. And Philip, at a time after the marriage, knew in a dream that he was affixing a seal on his wife's womb; and the emblem on the seal, he thought, was the image of a lion. But while the other seers suspected, because of the vision, that Philip needed to put a stricter watch on his marriage, Aristander of Telmessus affirmed that she was pregnant, as nothing empty could be sealed, and that she bore in her womb a child whose nature would be high-spirited and lion-like.[9]

13. TOBIT 5:11–14

An excellent example of ancestry motivating social behavior is seen in the apocryphal book of Tobit (ca. 225–175 BCE). The focus of the main character is on the continuation and safeguarding of kinship ties through lineage, and relationships are avoided or created based on ancestral connections. This focus is important in Tobit's eastern diaspora context, in which a heightened threat to identity or communal boundaries and an increased concern with what loyalty to God means and involves prevail. In this passage, after Tobit's son discovers a fellow Israelite, Tobit interrogates him.

> And [Tobit] said to him, "Kinsman, of what lineage are you and from what tribe [or descent]? Teach me, kinsman." And he replied, "What need do you have of my tribe?" And [Tobit] said to him, "I wish to know truthfully, kinsman, whose [son] you are and what your name is." And he said to him, "I am Azariah, the son of the great Hananiah, of your kin." And [Tobit] said to him, "Hearty welcome, and God save you, kinsman! Do not be bitter toward me, kinsman, because I wished to know truthfully about your lineage; as it happens, you are kin, and you are from honorable and good descent. For I knew Hananiah and Nathan, the two sons of the great Shemeliah, and they used to go with me into Jerusalem and prostrate themselves with me to the Lord there, and they were not led astray. Your kin are good men; you come from good roots. Hearty welcome!"[10]

9. Adapted from Perrin, LCL.

10. Adapted from Robert J. Littman, *Tobit: The Book of Tobit in Codex Sinaiticus*, Septuagint Commentary Series (Leiden: Brill, 2008), 17.

GENEALOGY

14. JOSEPHUS, *JEWISH ANTIQUITIES* 18.134–41

Genealogy as an approach to "knowledge" refers to knowledge in a constructed form, as it calculates kinship links in order to present a specific perspective on these relationships or to achieve a specific social purpose; genealogies are not historically or socially disinterested. Rather, the articulation of family relationships through genealogical lists can be used to encode or represent a wide variety of social contexts and claims. Genealogies can be constructed to defend or refute claims to honor, establish political or economic rights (the right to rule or to inherit), identify appropriate marriage partners, and determine religious purity. In this passage, Josephus provides us with a genealogy used as an honor claim in the context of his detailed discussion of Herodian kinship relations. This description is particularly interesting because it combines relationships from both patrilineal and matrilineal lines of descent.

> But this Herod, who was the brother of Agrippa, married Mariamne, the daughter of Olympias, [herself] the daughter of Herod the king, and of Joseph, the son of Joseph, brother to this Herod the king, when they were brought up into adolescence; and he conceived by her a son, Aristobolus. And the third brother of Agrippa, Aristobolus, married Jotape, the daughter of Sampsigeramus, the king of Emesa, and a daughter was born to them who was deaf; her name was also Jotape. And these were the children of the male line. And Herodias their sister was married to Herod, the son of Herod the Great, the child born of Mariamne, who was [the daughter] of Simon the high priest, and from them was born Salome, after whose birth Herodias, minded toward the ruin of the lineage, married Herod, her husband's brother by the same father, separating from a living husband. This [Herod] was the tetrarch of Galilee. . . . And Alexander, the child of Herod the king, the one who was killed by his father, conceived two sons, Alexander and Tigranes, through the daughter of Archelaus, the king of Cappadocia. . . . And immediately, right from birth, Alexander's kin [descendants] left off the divine honors of the Judeans, allying themselves with the Greek lineage.[11]

---

11. Adapted from Feldman, LCL.

15. MATTHEW 13:53–58

Genealogy could be invoked to discredit an individual or to shame them by drawing attention to unsuitable ancestors. In the Gospel of Matthew, the people of Nazareth, hearing Jesus teach in the synagogue, take offense at this action, based upon their understanding of Jesus's genealogy. According to his hearers, Jesus's genealogy does not give him the authority to teach in the synagogue.

> And Jesus, when he had finished these parables, went away from that place. And coming into this own country, he taught them in their synagogue, so that they were astonished and were saying, "From where do the wisdom and deeds of power of this man come? Isn't this the carpenter's son? Isn't his mother named Mary, and are his brothers not James and Joseph and Simon and Judas? And his sisters, aren't they all with us? From where, then, do these things come to this man?" And they took offense at him. But Jesus said to them, "A prophet is not without honor except in his own country and in his own household." And he did not do many deeds of power there due to their unbelief.

16. 2 SAMUEL 5:9–16

Genealogy could be used in a political context to justify an individual's right to rule or bolster a claim to leadership. David's success in conquering Jerusalem and his right to that success, as well as his authority as newly anointed king over all Israel, is reinforced in 2 Samuel, a chronicle of Israelite royal history, through the use of a genealogy to conclude the narrative of his conquest.

> So David occupied the fortress and called it the city of David. David built the city around from the Millo inward. And David became greater and greater, because the LORD, the God of hosts, was with him. King Hiram of Tyre sent messengers to David, along with carpenters and cedar logs, and masons and stones, and they built David a house. David then perceived that the LORD had established him king over Israel, and that he had exalted his kingdom for the sake of his people Israel. And David took more concubines and wives to himself from Jerusalem after he came from Hebron, and more sons and daughters were born to David. These are the names of those who were born to him in Jerusalem: Shammua, Shobab, Nathan, Solomon, Ibhar, Elishua, Nepheg, Japhia, Elishama, Eliada, and Eliphelet.

17. EXODUS 28:1

Claims to membership or authoritative positions, particularly positions that rely on heredity, in a religious group or context often rely on genealogical reckoning. Ezra 2, for instance, not only includes a list of returned exiles in terms of the leaders of specific kin groups and their descendants, but also identifies some of these returned exiles as "unclean," and therefore as unfit for ritual office. The book of Exodus presents genealogy as essential in the determination of priestly eligibility.

> And you, take to yourself from among the children of Israel your brother Aaron, and with him his sons, to serve as priests—Aaron and Aaron's sons, Nadab and Abihu, Eleazar and Ithamar.

18. PLUTARCH, *NUMA* 1.1

Lists of descent may not always be literal, as we saw above in the case of Alexander the Great and shall see below in Luke's genealogy of Jesus; they may skip generations or add fictive descendants. Because lineage is so important in encoding social relationship, including fictive links in the chain of one's descent can also be used as social strategy. For example, in his *Life of Numa Pompilius*, Plutarch describes a complaint against a group of compilers, alleging that they had forged ancient genealogical records in order to "gratify the pride" of certain families. By including the names of these families in lists of descent from Numa Pompilius, a legendary king of Rome with direct ties to the gods, these families secured greater honor for themselves, and therefore also for the compilers, through their association with the families. The word *stemma* here is usually translated as "genealogy" but has a more primary meaning of pedigree; the honor involved in the term is more explicit when translated as "pedigree."

> But concerning the time in which King Numa lived, there is also active disagreement, although from the beginning leading down to this time the pedigrees [genealogies] seem accurate. But a certain Clodius, in a book inscribed as "In Refutation of Historical Time," maintains strenuously that the original records went missing when the city was taken by the Celts [or Gauls], and that those that we currently have are forgeries, those who composed them courting favor with certain men by inserting their names among the first families and most distinguished households, forcing their way in where they do not belong.[12]

19. LUKE 3:23-38

Luke includes a genealogy in his Gospel, though it is not right at the very beginning of the narrative, as is Matthew's. Luke's genealogy excludes the

---

12. Adapted from Perrin, LCL.

39

possibility that anyone could have a greater honor claim than Jesus. With his apical ancestor as God, who could challenge his authority? This presentation of authority *is* challenged, however, in Luke's next chapter, and verified in Jesus's triumph in various honor tests.

> And Jesus was himself, when he began his work, about thirty years of age, being the son, it was believed, of Joseph, son of Heli, son of Matthat, son of Levi, son of Melchi, son of Jannai, son of Joseph, son of Mattathias, son of Amos, son of Nahum, son of Esli, son of Naggai, son of Maath, son of Mattathias, son of Semein, son of Josech, son of Joda, son of Joanan, son of Rhesa, son of Zerubbabel, son of Shealtiel, son of Neri, son of Melchi, son of Addi, son of Cosam, son of Elmadam, son of Er, son of Joshua, son of Eliezer, son of Jorim, son of Matthat, son of Levi, son of Simeon, son of Judah, son of Joseph, son of Jonam, son of Eliakim, son of Melea, son of Menna, son of Mattatha, son of Nathan, son of David, son of Jesse, son of Obed, son of Boaz, son of Sala, son of Nahshon, son of Amminadab, son of Admin, son of Arni, son of Hezron, son of Perez, son of Judah, son of Jacob, son of Isaac, son of Abraham, son of Terah, son of Nahor, son of Serug, son of Reu, son of Peleg, son of Eber, son of Shelah, son of Cainan, son of Arphaxad, son of Shem, son of Noah, son of Lamech, son of Methuselah, son of Enoch, son of Jared, son of Mahalaleel, son of Cainan, son of Enos, son of Seth, son of Adam, son of God.

20. HERODOTUS, *HISTORIES* 1.134

Genealogy as expressive of actual biological links between familial generations, the way a modern reader might approach such a listing, misses the complex social functioning of genealogical reckoning in the ancient Mediterranean context. Genealogy was used to construct sociocultural reality in very specific ways, ranging from honor claims to the definition of religious "insider" status. Like the broader concept of kinship, understandings of genealogy link to a myriad of social and anthropological relationships. As the general patrilineal slant of ancient genealogy, the tracing of lineage through the male line references ancient understandings of gender, sex, bodies, and reproduction, which emphasize generation through the male (Jesus is born "of" Mary in Matt 1:16; he is "conceived in her," Matt 1:20, and she "bears" him, Matt 1:21, but she does not actively "generate" him; see also 2 Macc 7:22). Genealogical knowledge was essential for determining an individual's location on the social (honor) scale, impacting the most basic human interactions. The importance of "ranking" is referenced in the Greek historian Herodotus's (fifth century BCE) description of the habits of the Persians. Genealogy served a variety of social functions and was essential for the "mapping" of basic social relationships.

> When men come across one another along their way, one may readily discern whether those meeting are social equals: If they are, instead of greeting one another [verbally], they kiss each other on the mouth; if there is a small difference in social status, the cheek is kissed; if the difference is great, the inferior prostrates himself before the other.[13]

Vocabulary of Kinship

HEBREW

אָב (ab) .... father
אִישׁ (ish) .... man, husband
אִשָּׁה (ishshah) .... woman, wife
בָּעַל (baal) .... to marry, rule over
יָלַד (yalad) .... to beget, bear, bring forth
כְּרִיתוּת (keritut) .... divorce
מֹהַר (mohar) .... dowry

GREEK

ἀδελφός, ἀδελφή
  (adelphos, adelphē) .... brother, sister
ἀνήρ (anēr) .... man, male, husband
γαμίζω (gamizō) .... to give in marriage
γενεά (genea) .... family in relation to national or ethnic
                         identity
γένος (genos) .... offspring, family
γεννάω (gennaō) .... to bear, beget
γυνή (gynē) .... woman, wife
θυγάτηρ (thygatēr) .... daughter
κληρονομία (klēronomia) .... inheritance
μήτηρ (mētēr) .... mother

13. Adapted from Godley, LCL.

μονογενής (*monogenēs*) . . . . only child, sole offspring

νύμφη (*nymphē*) . . . . bride, daughter-in-law, young woman

οἰκοδεσπότης (*oikodespotēs*) . . . . master of a household, head of the household

οἶκος, οἰκία (*oikos, oikia*) . . . . household, property, estate, inheritance,
                                                                         dwelling, home

παρθένος (*parthenos*) . . . . virgin, maiden

πατήρ (*patēr*) . . . . father

πατριά (*patria*) . . . . family, lineage

πενθερά (*penthera*) . . . . mother-in-law

πενθερός (*pentheros*) . . . . father-in-law

στέμμα (*stemma*) . . . . pedigree, family tree, genealogy

συγγένεια (*syngeneia*) . . . . kinship, kindred, relative

υἱός (*huios*) . . . . son

χωρίζω (*chōrizō*) . . . . to separate, divorce, divide

LATIN

dos . . . . dowry

familia . . . . domestic collective of spouses, children,
                                                                        slaves, or property

mater . . . . mother

pater . . . . father

paterfamilias . . . . head of the household

vir . . . . man, male, husband, soldier

Select Bibliography

Hanson, K. C. "All in the Family: Kinship in Agrarian Roman Palestine." Pages 27–46 in
   The Social World of the New Testament: Insights and Models. Edited by Jerome H.
   Neyrey and Eric C. Stewart. Peabody, MA: Hendrickson, 2008.

Harland, Philip A. "Familial Dimensions of Group Identity (II): 'Mothers' and 'Fathers'
   in Associations and Synagogues of the Greek World." *Journal for the Study of Judaism in the Persian, Hellenistic and Roman Period* 38 (2007): 57–79.

Moxnes, Halvor, ed. *Constructing Early Christian Families: Family as Social Reality and
   Metaphor*. London: Routledge, 1997.

Oden, Robert A., Jr. "Jacob as Father, Husband, and Nephew: Kinship Studies and the
   Patriarchal Narratives." *JBL* 102 (1983): 189–205.

Parkin, Robert. *Kinship: An Introduction to the Basic Concepts*. Oxford: Blackwell, 1997.

Zerubavel, Eviatar. *Ancestors and Relatives: Genealogy, Identity, and Community*. Oxford: Oxford University Press, 2012.

Additional Texts

THE FAMILY UNIT, OR HOUSEHOLD

Acts 16:13–15
Acts of Paul and Thecla 9–10
Apuleius, *Apology* 47
Aristotle, *Politics* 1253b, 1254b–1255a,
   1260a
CIL 1.1007; 6.11602
Colossians 3:18–4:1
Columella, *On Agriculture* 1 (preface)
   7–8
1 Corinthians 11:4–16
Dionysius of Halicarnassus, *Roman
   Antiquities* 2.26
Ephesians 5:21–6:9
Gaius, *Institutes* 1.48–165
Genesis 2:7–25
John 2:12; 7:2–10; 19:25–27
Josephus, *Against Apion* 2.181, 190–203
Judith 9

Luke 20:28–33
Mark 3:31–35; 10:29–31; 12:19–23
Matthew 20:1–15; 22:24–28
1 Peter 2:18–3:7
Petronius, *Satyricon* 57
Philo, *Hypothetica* 11.14–17; *Questions in
   Genesis* 1.33; *Special Laws* 2.226–27;
   3.169–78
Pliny the Younger, *Letters* 9.15
Proverbs 31:10–31
Sirach 7:18–28; 42:9–14
Suetonius, *Augustus* 64
1 Timothy 2:9–15
Titus 2:1–10
Varro, *On Agriculture* 1.17
Wisdom of Solomon 7:1–6
Xenophon, *Oeconomicus*

MARRIAGE AND DIVORCE

Acts 18:1–3
Aulus Gellius, *Attic Nights* 10.23
Dio Cassius, *Roman History* 54.16
1 Corinthians 7:27–40
Damascus Document 7
Deuteronomy 7:3–4; 22:13–30; 24:1–5
Exodus 34:16
Genesis 27:46
John 4:1–26
Joseph and Aseneth 8, 19–21
Josephus, *Life* 75–76

Judges 3:5–6
Judith 8:1–8
Luke 16:18
Mark 10:2–12; 12:18–27
Matthew 5:31–32; 19:3–12
Mishnah
   Gittin 9.10a
   Ketubot 7
   Nedarim 11:12
Nehemiah 13:23–27
1 Peter 3:1–7

Pliny the Younger, *Letters* 6.31.4–6

Plutarch, *Advice to Bride and Groom*;
   Consolation to His Wife

P.Michigan 1.87; 5.350

P.Oxyrhynchus 903

P.Rylands 2.154

P.Tebtunis 2.334

P.Yadin 18

Tacitus, *Annals* 2.85; 11.26–27; 12.53

Testament of Job 6

1 Timothy 3:2–5

Tobit 1:9; 4:12–13; 6:11–18; 7:9–16

INHERITANCE

Code of Hammurabi 137–84

Deuteronomy 21:17

Genesis 30:20; 31:14–16

Job 42:15

Joshua 15:18–19

1 Kings 9:16

Luke 12:13–21; 15:11–32

Mishnah

Bava Batra 8:3–5

Ketubot 6.6

Numbers 27:3–4

P.Fiorentini 99.6–7

P.Michigan 18.789

Sirach 33:20–24

Ulpian, *Digest* 22–23

FICTIVE KINSHIP

CIJ 694, 720

CIL 3.633, 882, 1207, 4045, 7505, 8837

2 Corinthians 8:1–24

CPJ 3.473

Galatians 5:11–26

IEurJud 1.5, 18, 115, 116; 2.209, 251, 288,
   406, 540, 542, 544, 560, 576, 577, 578,
   584

Luke 9:57–62; 12:51–53; 14:26; 18:28–30

Matthew 8:18–22; 10:34–39; 19:23–30

Philippians 4:1, 20–23

Philemon

Romans 16:1–2

1 Thessalonians 1:4–5; 5:25–27

ANCESTRY, LINEAGE, DESCENT, GENEALOGY

1 Chronicles 2:5–8:40; 9:1

1 Esdras 5

Ezra 2:1–68; 10:18–44

John 1:46; 4:9

Josephus, *Jewish Antiquities* 17.12–22

Luke 3:7–9

1 Maccabees 2:1–5

2 Maccabees 7:22

Mark 8:27–30; 14:70

Matthew 3:7–10; 13:54–58

Nehemiah 7

Philippians 3:4–6

Ruth 4:13–22

1 Samuel 9:1–3

2 Samuel 3:2–5; 9:6

Titus 1:12

3. Patronage

ZEBA A. CROOK

Introduction

Patronage and benefaction are two forms of asymmetrical reciprocity: That is, they relate to exchanges of asymmetrical value between parties of asymmetrical social status. Anything that a person or group needs that he, she, or they cannot get on their own becomes something that can be exchanged. The key, when it comes to asymmetrical reciprocity, is that what is returned cannot be similar to what is given. Thus, if a person gives money or grain, money or grain cannot be paid back. That would symmetrical and would be called a loan. When something is exchanged between people who are relatively close in social status, we call that a gift (see **chap. 16, Friendship and Gifts**). What is exchanged and the social status of those undertaking the exchange are both fundamentally different with patronage and benefaction: one reciprocates the bestowal of grain, money, dinner, a political post, legal protection, tax exemption, a villa, a games, a new building roof, and so on, with loyalty, praise, honor, deference, and glory.

Patronage differs from benefaction, however. Following Richard Saller's definition, patronage pertains where the relationship is personal, face-to-face. Benefaction pertains when the relationship is anonymous: when an emperor grants a city exemption from taxes or hosts a games or festival. Or when a wealthy man pays for the city liturgies, they are benefactions, for the recipients of their generosity never meet them personally. Conversely, when a person represents someone in court, gives money for his family, or appoints him to a civic position of some prestige, there is a personal relationship. Because of this, patronage is also long lasting: it is not at all the case that a person would receive an act of patronage, thank the giver, and be done with it. The assumption is that the bond of clientage is long-lasting and even crosses generational lines. This is not expected with benefaction.

Where patronage and benefaction are indistinguishable, however, is in reciprocity. Both forms of exchange require the recipient (whether a person or a group, like an association, a city, or a nation) to honor and praise the patron or benefactor: Individuals speak well of their patron, avoid criticizing them, follow them around town, laugh at their jokes, clap for their poetry, and generally do their bidding. When the public sees these things, they ascribe honor to the patron (see **chap. 4, Honor; chap. 6, Collectivism**). Groups respond to benefactions similarly: a city or an association sets up a stele with an inscription thanking the emperor, a governor, or a wealthy individual for the good things that person has bestowed upon the group.

Because patronage is personal (as opposed to benefaction), it admits of two additional features. First, the language of friendship is commonly used to mask what is distasteful to most: the relationship of dependence. There are many more words for patron than there are for client. In fact, "friend" is the word used most for patron. Yet we know that clientage is what is meant when the "friend" in question and the patron are not status equals exchanging goods of equal value (that is, friends exchanging gifts). Second, patronage is more susceptible to extortion and abuse. It is not uncommon for clients to complain that their patron demands much yet gives as little as possible (see **chap. 16, Friendship and Gifts**).

Sometimes a client requires a benefit from someone very much higher in status. In this case, the client requires a broker, or a chain of brokers, to mediate that relationship. Thus, a broker is both patron to a client (for he gives the favor of representation) and client to a patron (for he has a lower status than the patron who is the ultimate goal). Brokers thus play a very important and somewhat liminal role in this system.

The relationships of patronage, benefaction, brokerage, and clientage that existed among humans also existed in perfect parallel between humans and the gods. A god could be seen as a benefactor, benefiting all humanity with the gift of language or civilization; a god could also be seen as a patron, helping individuals by healing them or leading them safely in travel. Just as a person might abandon a human patron for failing to help, one could also abandon a patron deity who had failed to heal or protect. Some interactions with a patron god required a broker (e.g., a priest, an angel, a prophet, etc.), while others allowed direct access, but in all instances, the receiving client was obligated to express gratitude: by testifying concerning the god, making sacrifices, singing hymns of praise, converting others, and so on.

It can be argued whether the ancient Israelites thought of their God in a patron-client rubric, since the language and the analogy do not line up perfectly. But there can be no dispute that thoroughly Hellenized writers such as Second Temple Judeans and Christ followers did precisely this. The language they use of their God is distinguishable from Greek and Roman usage by mere degrees.

Ancient Texts

SOCIAL IMPORTANCE OF PATRONAGE AND BROKERAGE

1. SENECA, *ON BENEFITS* 1.4.2–3

Seneca (ca. 4 BCE–65 CE) was a Roman philosopher, statesman, and eminent citizen. Among the many works he wrote on topics he considered of moral importance, one concerned patronage and benefaction. It is a very idealized treatment, in many ways not a practical one. Because of this, two texts from Seneca appear in this chapter (see also no. 14). Many writers considered the challenges and the "rules" of patronage and clientage, but few did so as thoroughly as Seneca. The ability to give and receive benefactions properly was for Seneca the core of human society, and one linked to the gods.

> We are to speak of benefits and to define a matter that constitutes the most important bond of human society; standards are what we need, so that thoughtless indulgence may not be confused for generosity, and yet that our concern, while it moderates may not quench our generosity. For when it comes to giving, we should be neither excessive nor cheap. People must be taught to give willingly, receive willingly, and reciprocate willingly, and to place above all not merely to equal but to surpass those to whom they are indebted, both in good offices and in good feeling. The one who feels the duty to repay can never do so unless he outdoes his benefactor; some must be taught to look for no return, others to feel deeper gratitude for what they have received.[1]

2. DIO CHRYSOSTOM, *REPUTATION (OR. 66)* 1–2

Dio Chrysostom (40–115 CE) was a Greek historian, orator, and philosopher of the Roman Empire. Dio has harsh words for those who spend everything they own in pursuit of the honor that accrues to generous benefactors: while their names live on, they destroy their lives and families in the process.

1. Adapted from Basore, LCL.

On the one hand, there are some people who denigrate as irredeemable and unlucky those who love money, or delicacies, or getting drunk, or lusting after women or boys, considering each of these the greatest matter of reproach, when, on the other hand, they praise those who love honor and love glory, as if those are splendid things. . . . Of the many people, each one praises a disease of this sort, considering it due to him. Furthermore, by popular decree, nearly every single city has concocted all sorts of traps to incite the ignorant fools—crowns and front-row seats and proclamations. Because of this, some of those who were eager for these things have been rendered miserable and poor.[2]

TYPES OF PATRONAGE

3. CICERO, *FOR ARCHIAS* 5

Cicero (106–43 BCE) was a Roman philosopher, statesman, lawyer, and orator of highest reputation. The present work is an act of patronage in and of itself: it is an oration he delivered on behalf of a poet named Aulus Licinius Archias, whom Cicero defended from political persecution. In this passage, Cicero refers to the act of literary patronage that Archias received from a leading family of Rome, the Luculli. We do not, unfortunately, know the outcome of the trial.

Though Archias was underage, the Luculli admitted him into their home in short order. It is not only due to his natural virtue and his literary genius, but also his natural constitution and manly virtue that the house that was the first to extend its patronage to him in his adolescence is still the one with which he is most familiar at the end of his life.[3]

4. PLINY THE YOUNGER, *LETTERS* 10.104

Pliny the Younger (61–113 CE) was a politician, serving in many elected and appointed positions in the Roman Empire. He was also a noted orator and letter writer. Book 10 of his collection of letters is a series of missives exchanged between himself and the Emperor Trajan, his patron. In this letter, he contributes to our understanding of what sorts of things constituted acts of patronage: not only physical objects, but also, in this case, citizenship. This passage also illustrates the role of a broker (Pliny) who stands above his own clients yet

2. Adapted from Crosby, LCL.
3. Adapted from Watts, LCL.

below his patron (the emperor). Also evident in this text is the relationship between manumission and clientage.[4]

> My Lord, Valerius Paulinus has left me the right of patronage over all his Latin freedmen, except one. I ask you to grant the freedom of Rome to three of them. To wish you to extend this kindness to all of them would, I fear, be an unreasonable draw upon your indulgence, which I have amply experienced.

5. Plutarch, *The E at Delphi* 384E

Plutarch (46–120 CE) was a Greek historian, essayist, moralist, and a citizen of the Roman Empire. He was also a priest at Delphi, which clearly informs his pontificating on the letter E that is inscribed there: this letter was called EI, which was also the Greek word for "you are," for "if," and for "five." This passage comes from the opening of this work and articulates the view that even a learned discourse and wisdom are considered not only benefactions, but also superior benefactions to material gifts.

> It is necessary to look at the ways in which gifts of money, when it comes to freedom and honor, are eclipsed by learned speech or wisdom. Both to give is good and, having given, to ask in return similar gifts from those who receive them.[5]

6. 2 Samuel 9:1, 7

Saul, whom David defeated in war, had once been patron over an area called the Machir in the northern Transjordan. After defeating Saul, David must attempt to convert the loyalty of those clients into loyalty to himself, which he does by treating Saul's former servant (Ziba) with dignity and by extending a benefaction to a son of a house in that area (Machir). David also uses his friendship with one of Saul's sons, Jonathan, to justify taking over Saul's clients, but he cannot do so by fiat. He does so by offering patronage to them.

> And David asked whether there was anyone still from the house of Saul whom he could benefit on account of Jonathan. . . . And David said to him [Mephibosheth, a son of the house of Machir], "Do not be afraid, because I promise to do you a favor on account of your forefather Jonathan: I will return to you all the land of Saul your forefather, and no matter what, you will eat bread at my table."

4. Adapted from Radice, LCL.
5. Adapted from Babbitt, LCL.

7. PETRONIUS, *SATYRICON* 57

The *Satyricon* is a Latin satirical novel, possibly composed late in the first century CE. It narrates the adventures of two men, including an extravagant dinner at the home of a wealthy freedman named Trimalchio. This passage depicts the loyalty that a manumitted slave was expected to show to a former master, for manumission turned one from a slave to a client.

> I spent forty years as a slave; nobody, however, knew whether I was servile or free. The portico was not yet built when I came to this colony, and I was a long-haired lad. Nevertheless, I surrendered in service in order to satisfy my master, an honorable and most dignified gentleman, whose little fingernail was worth more than the whole of you.[6]

RELATIONSHIP TO FRIENDSHIP

8. DIO CHRYSOSTOM, *KINGSHIP* 3 (*OR.* 3) 94–96

In this work, Dio Chrysostom discusses the nature of true kingship, and given that he is likely addressing Trajan, the friendship referred to here is really clientage. Kings (i.e., patrons) must have "friends" (i.e., clients) in order for everything to run smoothly.

> Our greatest needs—armaments, fortifications, soldiers, and cities—without friends to manage them are of no use, nor effective. . . . Without friendship, neither is it possible to live safely even in times of peace.[7]

9. HORACE, *SATIRES* 1.6.45–62

Horace (65–8 BCE) was a leading and highly respected poet and an essayist on the poetic art. He was equally capable of highly literary work, as well as poetry that shamed and humiliated people whose lifestyles he disliked. Horace had a famous literary patron, Maecenas. As was typical, Horace uses the language of friendship, not clientage, to refer to the relationship. Horace originally wrote this as poetry, but it reads more easily in English as prose. It is very telling of ancient Mediterranean friendship that this very same passage appears in chapter 16 on **Friendships and Gifts**.

---

6. Adapted from Heseltine, LCL.
7. Adapted from Cohoon, LCL.

Now, let's get back to me: the son of a freedman, disparaged by everyone as "the son of a freedman," because now, Maecenas, I share a table with you, while of old because as tribune I led a Roman legion. This situation and that one differ, for the same person who envies me for the honor of the office should not envy me your friendship, particularly since you adopt only those who are worthy, those who are far from prone to self-seeking. . . . Standing before you the first time, I spoke only a few stuttering words; I was prevented by quiet shame from going on. . . . You were quiet, as is your way. I went away, and nine months later you recalled me, inviting me to number among your friends.[8]

OPPOSING, CRITIQUING, AND AVOIDING PATRONAGE

10. MARTIAL, *EPIGRAMS* 9.88

Martial (40–104 CE) was a Roman poet from what is now Spain. He is most known as a writer of epigrams, which are short, memorable, witty, and satirical poems. Martial's epigrams frequently lampoon society. In this one, he implies that patronage is about winning control over people, but not in reciprocity.

When you courted me, you used to send me gifts;
Once you laid hold of me, Rufus, you give me nothing.
To maintain what you have caught, send gifts also to the captured,
So that the wild boar, though poorly fed, may not flee its pen.[9]

BENEFACTION/EUERGETISM

11. *BGU* 1.19

This papyrus contains two columns of twenty-one lines each. It was found in Fayum, Egypt, and was written in the early second century CE. It is a lengthy list of benefactions received from the "Lord" Emperor Hadrian. These are not acts of personal patronage, but of universal benefaction. Note also the divinizing language related to benefaction.

The means of distinguishing might exceed what is displayed, which has now been sent up from me to them, he thought worthy to flee for refuge into the benefactions of the manifest god emperor.

8. Adapted from Fairclough, LCL.
9. Adapted from Shackleton Bailey, LCL.

CLIENT OBLIGATION

12. *ILS* 6109

This eleven-line Latin bronze inscription from 222 CE shows the council of Clunia (now in Spain) publicly proclaiming their patron not only for themselves, but for future generations as well. This inscription, like so many others, was made in order to discharge the duty of clients to publicly honor their patron.

> In the consulship of Imperator Caesar Marcus Aurelius Severus Alexander, April 14: The council of the religious assembly of Clunia elected by itself Gaius Marius Pudens Cornelianus, legionary legate, he of the highest merit, as its patron for itself, for its children, and forever, owing to his many and distinguished benefactions to them individually and collectively.[10]

13. SEG 36.1207

This Greek inscription (5–4 BCE) from Roman-occupied Pisidia comes from two groups of foreigners and Roman businessmen in gratitude and loyalty to Caesar Augustus. The inscription illustrates not only the client's required reciprocity, but also the need to do so publicly (hence, the publicly displayed inscription for all to read).

> Dedicated to Rome and the emperor Caesar Augustus son of God, high priest with the authority of tribune . . . and consul . . . and emperor . . . , to their own savior, from the Milyadians, and the Romans who do business around them, and the Thracians living near them.[11]

14. SENECA, *ON BENEFITS* 4.18.1

As a Stoic philosopher, Seneca philosophizes on gratitude in book 4 of *On Benefits*: is gratitude a desirable object in and of itself? Here he goes beyond the mere practical importance of client gratitude.

> The proof that gratitude is to be sought after and that ingratitude is to be fled from, purely and simply, is this: no vice more thoroughly disintegrates and destroys human concord.[12]

---

10. Barbara Levick, *The Government of the Roman Empire: A Sourcebook* (London: Routledge, 2000), no. 147.

11. Richard S. Ascough, Philip A. Harland, and John S. Kloppenborg, *Associations in the Greco-Roman World: A Sourcebook* (Waco: Baylor University Press, 2012), no. 208.

12. Adapted from Basore, LCL.

DIVINE PATRONAGE AND BROKERS

15. AELIUS ARISTIDES, *SPEECH FOR ASCLEPIUS* 40.1–2

Aelius Aristides (117–181 CE) was a young scholar and part of a movement that championed higher learning and imitation of the ancient Greek writers. He fell seriously ill at the age of twenty-six, and his activities were curtailed at that point. He spent his remaining years writing and lecturing in Smyrna. In some of his writings, he details his illness and his frustrating attempts to find a divine patron who could ease his suffering, which he finally did in Asclepius. In this passage, Aristides alludes to all he has received from the god, but most of all to his oratorical skills, which allow him all the more to praise Asclepius as he does in this speech as a whole.

> As for me, O Lord Asclepius, just as I said, I have received many and manifold things from you and on account of your philanthropy, but the greatest and most worthy of gratitude and quite nearly the dearest of all to me is the ability to deliver speeches.

16. 1 CORINTHIANS 15:10

Paul, the apostle to the gentiles, uses the term *charis* many times as a technical term to refer to what he feels was the most important thing he ever received from God: the vision of the resurrected Christ. In this passage, he refers to how that benefaction changed him.

> By the benefaction of God, I am what I am, and his benefaction toward me was not in vain, but rather I labored more excessively than any of them, not I but rather the benefaction of God that was with me.

17. EPICTETUS, *DISCOURSES* 4.1.97–98

Epictetus (55–135 CE) began life as a slave and became a well-known Stoic philosopher. He wrote extensively within his Stoic worldview, which includes a passage on the divine benefactions of Zeus. He writes earlier in this passage that a traveler, hearing that there are robbers on the road, takes precautions such as traveling in groups and, if that does not work, becomes a "friend" (or client) of Caesar. But even that cannot protect the traveler from the wilderness. He concludes by recommending God for the divine benefaction of protection.

> [The wise traveler asks himself,] "What, therefore, will happen? Is safe association with one who is loyal, strong, and treachery-free not to be found?" Thus, he

pauses on it and considers that if ever he might bind himself to a god, he will pass through everything safely.[13]

18. Josephus, *Jewish Antiquities* 4.315–18

Josephus (37–100 CE) was a Judean commander in the war against Rome. He surrendered and eventually became a writer under the patronage of the Flavian emperor Titus. While sometimes an apologist for Rome, he was also a strong defender of the religion of the Judeans. In this passage, he remembers Moses's last words to Joshua—a speech in which Moses remembers God as a divine patron to whom he owes gratitude.

> Therefore, when Moses urged Joshua to lead out an army against the Canaanites, assuring him that God would work with him in all things, and having loudly praised the multitude, he said, "Since I am going away to our forefathers, and God has decided that this should be the day of my departure, I proclaim gratitude to him, while I still live and am among you, for the foresight he has exercised over you. This relates not merely to releasing you from bad things, but also to bestowing the best gifts upon us. In addition, he has assisted me in the pains I took, and in all the contrivances I had in my intentions to improve your condition, and he favors us all in everything. But really, it was he who conducted our business, imparting favors to the end by making use of me as a general and servant in those matters in which he wished to be a benefactor to our whole people. Therefore, I think it proper, before departing, to praise in advance the ability of God, which will take care of you for the time to come, and this in order to give back that debt of reciprocity.[14]

19. *IKyme* 41.3–29

This fifty-seven-line inscribed hymn of praise was written in the voice of Isis (making it an aretalogy), perhaps dating from the second century CE, and reveals the belief that she was the benefactor of all humanity; the ways that humanity has benefited from her are considerable and wide ranging, and this inscription lists thirty-six ways she benefited humanity. It was found at Kyme in Asia Minor and is partially preserved in a number of other ancient locations as well.

> I am Isis, the mistress of every land, and I was taught by Hermes, and with Hermes I discovered letters, both the holy and the demotic letters, so that not all things

13. Adapted from Oldfather, LCL.
14. Adapted from Thackeray and Marcus, LCL.

would be written with the same letters. . . . I have founded laws for humanity, which no one is able to have altered. . . . I am the one who discovered fruit for people. . . . I divided land and sky. I showed the paths of the stars. . . . I destroyed the rule of tyrants. . . . I legislated that truth should be considered good.

20. JOHN 10:7–9

On the patron-client model, Jesus is more often than not depicted as the broker, the one who mediates between a distant patron (God) and the needy client. The writer of the Gospel of John expresses this clearly in the text below.

And then Jesus said again, "Truly truly I say to you that I am the door for the sheep. All those who came before me are thieves and highway bandits, but the sheep did not hear them. I am the door; if ever a person comes through me, he will be saved and will enter and exit and will find pasture.

Vocabulary of Patronage

HEBREW

חֵן (*khen*). . . . . favor, act of benefaction
חֶסֶד (*khesed*) . . . . favor, loving-kindness

GREEK

ἄγγελος (*angelos*). . . . . messenger, angel
ἀπόστολος (*apostolos*). . . . . apostle, envoy, ambassador
ἐπίτροπος (*epitropos*) . . . . agent, representative
εὐεργέτης (*euergetēs*) . . . . benefactor
ἱερεύς (*hiereus*). priest
λειτουργός (*leitourgos*) . . . . minister
μεσίτης (*mesitēs*) . . . . mediator
παράκλητος (*paraklētos*). . . . . broker, mediator, paraclete
προφήτης (*prophētēs*) . . . . prophet
φίλος (*philos*). . . . . friend
χαρίζομαι (*charizomai*). . . . . to benefit
χάρις (*charis*) . . . . benefaction, favor

LATIN

amicus	friend
cliens	client
gratia	benefaction, favor
meritum	benefaction, merit, service

Select Bibliography

Crook, Zeba A. *Reconceptualising Conversion: Patronage, Loyalty, and Conversion in the Religions of the Ancient Mediterranean.* Berlin: de Gruyter, 2004.

Danker, Frederick W. *Benefactor: Epigraphic Study of a Graeco-Roman and New Testament Semantic Field.* St. Louis: Clayton, 1982.

Gellner, E., and J. Waterbury, eds. *Patrons and Clients in Mediterranean Society.* London: Gerald Duckworth, 1977.

Neyrey, Jerome H. "'I Am the Door' (John 10:7, 9): Jesus the Broker in the Fourth Gospel." *CBQ* 69 (2007): 271–91.

Saller, Richard P. *Personal Patronage under the Early Empire.* New York: Cambridge University Press, 1982.

Wallace-Hadrill, Andrew, ed. *Patronage in Ancient Society.* London: Routledge, 1989.

Additional Texts

SOCIAL IMPORTANCE OF PATRONAGE AND BROKERAGE

Dio Chrysostom, *Law (Or. 75)* 7

Exodus 20:19; 32:32

Genesis 18:22–33; 20:17

Herodotus, *Histories* 1.21, 96

Isocrates, *Demonicus* 26

Josephus, *Jewish Antiquities* 4.194–95

Philo, *Who Is the Heir?* 19

Pliny the Younger, *Letters* 10.2, 4–6, 12, 26, 51

Plutarch, *Precepts of Statecraft* 814c; *Solon* 14.2

Seneca, *On Benefits* 1.1.1; 2.11.5; 2.23.1; 6.24.1–2

TYPES OF PATRONAGE

Acts 1:1

Athenaeus, *The Dinner Sophists* 6.253

Cicero, *For Archias* 26; *On Duties* 2.15; *Tusculan Disputations* 5.5

Diodorus Siculus, *Library of History* 3.21.5

Dionysius of Halicarnassus, *Roman Antiquities* 5.21.3

Josephus, *Jewish Antiquities* 1.8

Luke 1:1; 7:4–5

Martial, *Epigrams* 1.59; 3.7

Polybius, *Histories* 20.11.10; 30.31.7

Propertius, *Elegies* 3.9.43–44

Seneca, *On Benefits* 1.2.4; 2.35.3; 3.8.3; *Epistles* 90.1

Sidonius, *Epistles* 1.1

Sophocles, *Oedipus the King* 771–74

Theocritus, *Idylls* 16

Vergil, *Georgics* 3.41

Xenophon, *Memorabilia* 1.2.61; 1.3.1; 4.8.11

RELATIONSHIP TO FRIENDSHIP

Aristotle, *Nicomachean Ethics* 1163b

IG II² 457

Isocrates, *Demonicus* 2

James 2:23

John 19:12

Plutarch, *How to Tell a Flatterer from a Friend* 52b; *On Having Many Friends* 94b

Seneca, *Epistles* 3.2–3

Sidonius, *Epistles* 1.1

Sirach 30:6

Wisdom of Solomon 7:27

Xenophon, *Memorabilia* 2.9

OPPOSING, CRITIQUING, AND AVOIDING PATRONAGE

Aristotle, *Nicomachean Ethics* 1124a–b

Horace, *Epistles* 1.18

Juvenal, *Satires* 5.19, 161

Lucian, *Nigrinus* 22–24

Martial, *Epigrams* 5.22

Polybius, *Histories* 1.31.6; 30.18

Seneca, *On the Shortness of Life* 19.3

Theophrastus, *Characters* 2.2–3; 23.5–6

Xenophon, *Memorabilia* 2.9

BENEFACTION/EUERGETISM

1 Corinthians 16:3

2 Corinthians 8:6–7

Dio Chrysostom, *Law (Or. 75)* 6

Epictetus, *Discourses* 1.4.29

Josephus, *Jewish Antiquities* 16.98, 146–47, 212; *Jewish War* 1.215, 388; 2.607; 3.459; 4.113; 7.71; *Life* 244, 259

2 Maccabees 4.2; 9.26

Seneca, *On Benefits* 6.19.2–5

Wisdom of Solomon 3:5; 7:23; 11:5; 16:2, 11

CLIENT OBLIGATION

Aristotle, *Nicomachean Ethics* 1163b

Cicero, *For Archias* 27; *On Duties* 1.45–48; 2.63, 70; *Against Verres* 2.2

Demosthenes, *On the Crown* (*Or.* 18) 131

Dio Chrysostom, *His Past Record* (*Or.* 50) 9; *Law* (*Or.* 75) 6; *To the People of Rhodes* (*Or. 31*) 7, 20, 37, 38

Horace, *Epistles* 1.7.9; 2.1.103–7; *Satires* 1.1.9–10; 2.6.16; 11.2.4

IDelos IV 1521

IG XII⁹ 899

Isocrates, *Demonicus* 24

Luke 16:4–9

Martial, *Epigrams* 2.18, 57; 6.48

OGIS 248

Philo, *On the Decalogue* 167

Pliny the Younger, *Letters* 10.51

Pseudo-Phocylides, *Sentences* 80

Pseudo-Plato, *Greater Alcibiades* 135d

SEG 24.1100

Seneca, *On Benefits* 1.1.2; 1.10.4; 2.22.1; 2.24.4; 2.25.3; 3.1.1; 3.1.3; 3.2.1; 3.6.2; 3.7.2; 3.11.1; 3.14.1; 3.17.1–12; 4.8.2; 4.16.3; 4.34.2–4; 5.11.5; *Epistles* 81.21

SIG 721, 587

Sirach 12.1

Tobit 12:6–7

DIVINE PATRONAGE AND BROKERS

Acts 2:33–34; 3:26; 4:21; 10:38; 11:15–18; 14:3, 17; 17:24–28; 24:2–4

Aelius Aristides, *Sacred Tales* 2.292.14; 2.294.8; 4.322.1–2; 4.323.14; 4.330.13–16; 4.337.11; *Speech for Asclepius* 4.329.16; 44.2

Apuleius, *The Golden Ass* 11.25; 13; 15

Aristotle, *Nicomachean Ethics* 1162a

BGU 4.1085

Colossians 1:3; 4:12

1 Corinthians 3:10; 8:6

2 Corinthians 1:10–11, 22; 5:5

Dio Chrysostom, *Kingship 2* (*Or.* 2) 75; *Kingship 4* (*Or.* 4) 22; *Borysthenic Discourse* (*Or.* 36) 35–36, 60; *Man's First Conception of God* (*Or.* 12) 21, 27–28, 32, 39

Diodorus Siculus, *Library of History* 1.70.6; 3.73.6

Ephesians 1:13–14; 6:11

Epictetus, *Discourses* 1.4.32; 1.10.3; 2.23.5; 4.4.7; 4.7

Exodus 20:19; 32:31–32

Galatians 3:1–5; 4:8–9

Genesis 6:8; 18:22–33; 20:17; 32:11

Hebrews 7:24–25; 8:6; 9:15; 12:24

Hesiod, *Theogony* 501–6

IBM 4.1034

IG II² 4636; *IG* XI⁴ 1299.29–36; *IG* XIV 966

James 4:10; 5:15–16

John 4:34; 5:23, 30, 37; 6:38–39; 7:16; 8:18; 9:4; 12:44; 14:6

1 John 5:14–16

Jonah 4:2

Josephus, *Jewish Antiquities* 1.229; 2.196; 4.212; 5.115; 6.60; 8.111

Luke 1:54, 68–75; 4:25–30; 7:16; 11:2–4; 17:15–18; 18:43; 19:37

2 Maccabees 6:13; 10:38

4 Maccabees 8:5–7; 13:13; 16:18–22

Matthew 6:9–13

Numbers 14:19

P.Fayum 124.16

P.Giessen 1.17.6

P.Hibeh 1.79.6

P.Oxyrhynchus 963.6

P.Petrie 1.29.2

Philippians 1:19; 4:6–7

Philo, *On Dreams* 1.140–43; *On the Change of Names* 24; *On the Cherubim* 122–23; *On the Creation of the World* 23, 77; *On Drunkenness* 32; *On the Embassy to Gaius* 76–78, 215; *On the Migration of Abraham* 73; *On the Life of Moses* 2.166; *On the Posterity of Cain* 143; *On the Sacrifices of Cain and Abel* 57–58, 127; *On Rewards and Punishments* 126; *On Sobriety* 55; *That God Is Unchangeable* 107; *Who Is the Heir?* 32

Pindar, *Nemean Odes* 9.45

Plato, *Republic* 613b–d

Plutarch, *Isis and Osiris* 351c–d, 356a–b, 361c, 377a

Psalms 116:12

Revelation 4:9–11

Romans 1:5, 8; 5:1–2, 15–17; 11:35–36; 12:3; 15:8, 15; 16:27

Seneca, *On Benefits* 1.10.5; 2.1.1–4; 3.15.4; 4.3.2–3; 4.5; 4.26.1; 4.28.1; 7.31.2–4; 7.32

Sirach 3:18

SIG 365; 708.25, 30; 709.47; 731.17; 1172.9–10

Theocritus, *Idylls* 16

1 Thessalonians 5:17, 25

2 Thessalonians 3:1–2

1 Timothy 2:1–5

2 Timothy 1:9; 2:25

Wisdom of Solomon 11:5, 13

PART II

Social Interaction

4. Honor

Richard L. Rohrbaugh

Introduction

In ancient Mediterranean societies, especially among the socially elite, honor was the passion of all who aspired to excel. One's honor status determined nearly everything in life: how one behaved, interacted with others, dressed, ate, married, and even what happened at the time of death. Public rights and responsibilities, public speech, approved gestures, friends, associates and even the guests one could invite to a meal were all determined by one's place on the scale of honor. It even determined which seat a guest should occupy at a dinner table. Critics complain that it was a craving nearly impossible to control.

Put very simply, honor was the status one claimed in the community, together with the all-important public recognition of that claim. Lacking public recognition, honor claims were the boast of fools (see **chap. 5, Shame**). Honor acknowledged by one's peers, however, was a treasure of great value. Thus, Philo could talk about noble birth, honor, reputation, and an all-pervasive lust for glory. Josephus has long lists of those on whom honor is bestowed, including kings, generals, consuls, governors, priests, village leaders, and even cities. Plutarch thought it empowered a person to speak in public.

To some ancient writers, the love of honor distinguished the superior from the inferior and even humans from animals. Others identified happiness with honor and even thought being loved and being honored were indistinguishable. Since honor meant access to power and privilege that could be gained no other way, it is not surprising that comments on honor, shame, and related matters are everywhere in the literature of antiquity.

While the love of honor and a code of honorific behavior were universal in Mediterranean antiquity, the *content* of the behavioral code could vary a great deal from one area to another, even among the cities and villages of a single region. That is because community standards could be distinctly local; hence, Aristotle might define honor one way for Greeks in fourth-century BCE Athens, while Seneca would define it quite another way for those of Stoic outlook in first-century CE Rome. What unites them all, however, is the universal concern for and love of personal honor.

Honor typically came in two forms: ascribed and acquired. Ascribed honor came first of all from family, because an honorable birth was the foundation on which a good reputation rested. To be "lowborn" was to bear an indelible, lifelong disgrace that closed the doors to power and privilege. Acquired honor, however, came as the result of good behavior. It accrued to those who lived in accord with community values and was considered a public reward for virtuous behavior. It was especially important because in the collectivist societies of the ancient Mediterranean world (see **chap. 6, Collectivism**), observance of community standards was considered the ultimate display of group loyalty.

People who used their resources for the good of others were also thought to deserve special honors (see **chap. 3, Patronage**). Thus, patrons who helped subordinate clients and benefactors who funded buildings, events, or services for the whole community were often accorded the highest praise. Augustus was widely honored for just that kind of behavior. Philo thought Egyptians took special care in honoring their benefactors and patrons. Nonetheless, cynical writers often criticized those who publicly paraded their praise of patrons as seekers after unending and undeserved favors.

It is especially important to recognize that honor could be accorded to both men and women (see **chap. 9, Gender**). Ascribed honor, the honor that came from family of birth, was naturally ascribed to both male and female members. Acquired honor could likewise be attributed to both genders, even though the content of the honor code was different for each and written comment about male honor was far more prevalent.

For many, shame, as the lack or loss of honor, was a deeply painful experience. Like honor, shame could be either ascribed, as to those of lowly birth, or acquired, as happened to those who violated community standards (see **chap. 18, Deviance**). Position or occupation mattered as well. For occupations like barber, porter, prostitute, tax collector, tanner, or sailor, shame came with the territory. Greeks thought being non-Greek inevitably reduced one's honor rank, though Herodotus notes how often ascribed honor was considered higher for those near the homeland and diminished in direct proportion to geographical distance.

In contrasting honor and shame, however, it is important to understand the difference between *being* shamed and *having* shame (see **chap. 5, Shame**). Being shamed meant a public loss of honor, a loss of reputation. Aristotle likens it to the fear of death—both make one go pale. It is described in the New Testament as being "thrown into outer darkness, where there will be weeping and gnashing of teeth." By contrast, having shame was positive and necessary for both men and women. It meant knowing right from wrong and was considered an essential form of everyday wisdom. The "shameless," those who lack sensitivity to community standards, make fools of themselves in public.

Finally, honor was a relative matter in which one claimed superiority over others. Moreover, because honor was a limited good, the result was the intense competition and the pervasive envy that characterized these agonistic societies (see **chap. 17, Limited Good and Envy**). Both positive (compliments or gifts) and negative (insults, dares, or public questions) honor challenges were possible, and either had to be answered to avoid a loss of honor. Failure to respond was attributed to cowardice or bad character. Success often provoked envy.

Ancient Texts

THE LOVE OF HONOR

1. ARISTOTLE, *NICOMACHEAN ETHICS* 1123B18–20

Aristotle (384–322 BCE) was one of the truly eminent philosophers and scientists of ancient Greece. He was also the tutor of Alexander the Great. In his long discussion of virtues and vices, Aristotle comments on those virtues associated with honor. In so doing, he acknowledges the value placed on honor by the noblest persons.

> Now the most valuable of external goods, it is said, is the thing we offer to the gods and that is most prized by those of high reputation, and that is honor. It is clearly the greatest of external goods. It is the thing worthy people most desire and the reward for the noble deeds. Such is honor, the greatest of all external goods.[1]

2. PHILO, *ON GOD* 150

Philo of Alexandria (25 BCE–50 CE) was a Hellenistic Jewish thinker who attempted to harmonize what he saw as the truth of the Hebrew Bible with Stoic

---

1. Adapted from Rackham, LCL.

philosophy. In describing what had been learned by all Israel in the "school of Moses," Philo illustrates by recounting how the envoys to the king of Edom, who were asking the king's permission to pass through his land, showed their wisdom and self-control. They asserted that they would "pass by" all the treasures of Edom and take nothing without returning equal value. The king in turn asked whether they would not be swayed by what they saw, including the honors of the Edomite nobility.

> Will you ignore the ancestors thought worthy of honor, from either father or mother, and the noble birth that so many celebrate? And the glory, for which people will exchange everything, will you leave that behind as something not worthy of honor?[2]

3. Xenophon, *Hiero* 7.3

Xenophon (ca. 430–354 BCE) was a Greek historian, soldier, mercenary, and student of Socrates. This work is a dialogue between Hiero, tyrant of Syracuse, and the poet Simonides (ca. 474 BCE), comparing the lives of rulers and ordinary citizens. Xenophon argues that a ruler does not have any more access to happiness than a private person, because both can share a love of honor.

> For in this, Hiero, it seems to me that man differs from all other living things: in the craving for honor. For all living things take similar delight in eating, drinking, sleeping, and sexual pleasures. But the love of honor is implanted neither in the brute beasts nor in all human beings. But in anyone in whom are implanted both honor and the love of praise, these are already the ones differing the most from the beasts, being considered men and not merely human beings.[3]

THE HONOR CODE

4. Cornelius Nepos, *On Eminent Foreign Leaders*, preface

Cornelius Nepos (ca. 110–25 BCE) was a Roman biographer. Before writing his biographical accounts of the great generals of the nations, he indicates that each nation has a different index of what constitutes honor and shame; here he compares Greece and Rome.

2. Adapted from Colson, LCL.
3. Adapted from Bowersock, LCL.

If these men can understand that not all peoples look upon the same acts as honorable or shameful, but rather judge by the standards of their ancestors, they won't be surprised that, when evaluating the worthiness of the Greeks, I take account of the customs of that nation. An example: Cimon, a respected citizen of Athens, felt no shame in having his sister as a wife, because others in that region do the same thing. Of course, we consider that kind of union to be wrong. Cretans think the highest possible number of love affairs is an honorable thing for young men. No matter how highly respected, a single woman in Lacedaemon would not refrain from being a hired entertainer at a dinner party. Everywhere in Greece, it is thought to be a high honor to be proclaimed a winner at Olympia. They do not consider appearing on stage and exhibiting oneself to invite shame. To us, all those things are considered dishonorable and shameful behavior.

By the same token, behavior that is deemed honorable by our standards is considered shameful by the Greeks. For instance, what Roman would be embarrassed to take his wife to a dinner party? Or what married woman is not regularly in the front rooms of her house or shows herself in public? In Greece, it is very different. There a woman is not allowed into a dinner party unless only her relatives are present. Instead, she stays in the private parts of the house called "the women's quarters," which cannot be entered by males who are not blood relatives.[4]

ASCRIBED AND ACQUIRED HONOR

5. Aristotle, *Rhetoric* 1390b20–25

In this section of his work on rhetoric, Aristotle comments on the impact good fortune has on human character. Here he begins with noble birth and the way it ascribes honor to the descendants of honorific ancestors. In a later section, however, he hastens to add that the value of noble birth often degenerates among later generations, who grow less mindful of its benefits.

> Thus, it is characteristic of those of noble birth to hold a greater love of honor, because whenever they start anything, they are accustomed to heap it up. Nobility is the honor-rank that comes from one's ancestors.[5]

4. Adapted from Rolfe, LCL.
5. Adapted from Freese, LCL.

6. Plutarch, *On the Education of Children* 1a–c

Plutarch (46–120 CE) was a Greek historian, essayist, and moral philosopher. He was born into a family of considerable means and enjoyed an education that included mathematics, music, and later the study of philosophy. He was also a priest at the great shrine center of Delphi. Though it is uncertain whether this text is actually from Plutarch, it nonetheless reflects both the common view of his time and his own personal experience of ascribed honor.

> For those not wellborn, on either the mother's or the father's side, bear an indelible disgrace that dogs the steps of the lowborn throughout life and offers anyone wishing to use it a ready subject for insult and abuse. Wise was the poet who declares, "A family foundation incorrectly laid, inevitably the offspring are unfortunate." A good treasure, therefore, is freedom of action for those of honorable birth, which should be held in the highest regard by those striving for legitimate offspring. And in fact, the spirits of those having been born a mixture and low down are always being demeaned and humiliated. Correct was the poet who declares: "Though bold-hearted a man might be, he becomes a slave whenever he learns of his mother's or his father's shame."[6]

7. Dio Chrysostom, *Friendship for His Native Land* (Or. 44) 1–5

Dio Chrysostom (40–115 CE) was a Greek orator, philosopher, and historian of the Roman Empire. The following address was probably given in the winter of 96–97 CE, not long after Dio returned to Prusa from fourteen years in exile. It was occasioned by a meeting at which city honors were proposed for him as a result of his virtuous behavior: advocacy on behalf of Prusa with the emperor Nerva. The honorific funeral orations he cites that were given for his family members doubtless followed the *epitaphios* tradition begun in fifth-century BCE Athens. On the close connections here between friendship and patronage, see **chapter 3, Patronage.**

> To me, O citizens, nothing is sweeter than the sight of you all, no voice more agreeable, no honors greater than the ones here [at Prusa], no praise more splendid than what comes from you. And even if all Greeks together and the Roman people themselves were to admire and praise me, that would never so gladden my thoughts. For of all the wise and inspired things Homer said, none is wiser or more truthful than this: "Nothing is sweeter than one's native land." Indeed, you may well fix in your mind that because of all the honors [*timas*]

6. Adapted from Babbitt, LCL.

I have, both the many you now propose and any others there might be, coming from your goodwill and friendship, I need nothing else. For this is sufficient for any person: to be loved by his own compatriots. And having this, why is there any need for things like statues or proclamations or seats of honor [*proedriōn*]—of anything of beaten gold set up in distinguished shrines? For one word spoken in goodwill and friendship is worth more than all the gold and crowns and all the other things people think magnificent. So, being persuaded, act this way with me.[7]

8. SIRACH 10:19

Sirach is a work of ethical teachings from approximately 200 to 175 BCE, written by the scribe Shimon ben Yeshua ben Eliezer ben Sira of Jerusalem. It was translated into Greek by the author's grandson, who added a prologue. It is the longest wisdom book to have been preserved from antiquity. This passage relates loyalty to the God of Israel as a source of both ascribed and acquired honor.

Whose progeny are to be held in honor? Human progeny. Whose progeny are to be held in honor? The ones fearing the Lord. Whose progeny are dishonorable? Human progeny. Whose progeny are dishonorable? The ones flouting the commandments.

9. AUGUSTINE, *CITY OF GOD* 5.12

Augustine of Hippo (354–430 CE) was the Bishop of Hippo Regius in the Roman province of Africa and one of the most important early theologians of Western Christianity. Here he describes the Roman sense that honor and virtue are closely connected.

Both the hero and the coward want these things, but the hero gets there by an honest path: virtue. By that means, he ascends to the prize he is eager to obtain: glory, honor, and power. That this ideal was deeply rooted among the Romans is demonstrated by the close proximity in which they arranged the temples of two of their gods, Honos and Virtus—gifts of God that they took as gods. Moreover, this makes clear their chosen goal of virtue and the standard of judgment used by the good among them: honor.[8]

---

7. Adapted from Crosby, LCL.
8. Adapted from Green, LCL.

GIVING, RECEIVING, AND RECOGNIZING HONOR

10. HERODOTUS, *HISTORIES* 1.134

Herodotus (ca. 484–425 BCE) was a Greek whose history of the Greco-Persian wars includes a wealth of cultural and geographical information. While his "history" was mocked by many of his later Greek readers, he claims to have reported the stories, anecdotes, and information just as they were told by those he interrogated. In describing the customs of the Persians, Herodotus indicates the gestures they employ when persons of varying honor rank meet on the streets.

> By this, anyone may know whether the persons meeting each other on the street are of the same rank. If they are, instead of greeting each other, they kiss on the mouth. But if one is a little inferior, the kiss is offered on the cheeks. And if one is much inferior, being lowborn, he falls down and prostrates himself before the other.[9]

11. PHILO, *ON THE LIFE OF JOSEPH* 203–4

Joseph is said by Philo to have retained a strong commitment to the ancestral custom of honoring age in arranging the seating of dinner guests, even though neither Hebrews nor Egyptians had yet the Roman custom of reclining at a meal.

> The guests being seated in the order of age, according to his commands (at that time, it was not yet the custom to recline at gatherings), they marveled that the Egyptians sought to emulate the arrangements of the Hebrews, being careful to distinguish between the older and the younger in the honors paid to them.[10]

12. ISOCRATES, *TO DEMONICUS* 1.16

Isocrates (436–338 BCE), an ancient Greek rhetorician, was one of the ten great Attic orators honored by Aristophanes of Byzantium, the librarian of the great Alexandrian library. He was a friend of Socrates and a strong defender of the timeless honor of Athens.

> Do not think you can hide something shameful you have done, for even if you conceal it from others, you yourself will know. Fear the gods, honor your parents

---

9. Adapted from Godley, LCL.
10. Adapted from Colson, LCL.

and friends, obey the laws. Seek out the pleasures bringing honor, for pleasures characterized by virtue are the best. Those without it are the worst.[11]

13. PLUTARCH, *DINNER OF THE SEVEN WISEMEN* 147D

A tradition passed down by Plato and others tells how seven wise men, living at the beginning of the historic period in Greece, met at Delphi for the dedication of two inscriptions on the temple of Apollo. Using that tradition and the sayings of these wise men then current, Plutarch constructs an imaginary dinner conversation among the seven. They are discussing the position of tyrant. Thales is the speaker.

> Alongside all the evils that come from the love of power, there stands one good thing: honor and the glory that comes from ruling over good men—especially if they themselves are thought to be even greater. As for those who love safety more than honor, they should rule over sheep, horses, and cattle, but not over men.[12]

14. AULUS GELLIUS, *ATTIC NIGHTS* 2.2.1–10

Aulus Gellius (ca. 125–after 180 CE) was a Latin author and grammarian who was probably born and raised in Rome but educated in Athens. In this text, he recounts how a governor of Crete brought his father along on a visit to an Athenian philosopher. Only one chair was available, and the philosopher invited the older man to sit. But the father deferred to his son, saying his son's honor as a Roman magistrate outranked his own honor as the older man. A discussion of honor protocols then ensued.

> The essence of the discussion came down to this: in public places, functions, or affairs, the rights of a father diminish and are eclipsed by those of sons who are magistrates. But when they are at home, or walking around, or reclining with close friends at a dinner, then the official distinction between a father who is a private citizen and a son who is a magistrate disappears and the natural or inherent distinctions reemerge. Thus, he said, "Your visit here, our present conversation, and this discussion of duties are all private actions. Consequently, as an older man, you must enjoy the same honor-priority here that you properly receive in your own home."[13]

11. Adapted from Norlin, LCL.
12. Adapted from Babbitt, LCL.
13. Adapted from Rolfe, LCL.

15. PROVERBS 31:25–31

An acrostic poem on the ideal wife details her wisdom, her industrious way of providing for her household, and her compassion for the poor. It ends with this acknowledgment of the honor and praise that is her due.

> She is clothed with strength and honor; she laughs at the days to come. She opens her mouth with wisdom, and instruction in kindness is on her tongue. She carefully watches the doings of her home and does not eat the bread of idleness. Her children stand up and give her honor; her husband praises her as well: "Many women have done things well, but you outdo them all." Charm is a deception, beauty is transitory, but a woman who fears God is to be honored. Give her the fruit of her own hands, and let her deeds praise her at the city gates.

16. JUDITH 13:18–20

Probably written in the latter part of the second century BCE, this fictional story tells of the gruesome decapitation of Holofernes, a Babylonian general, by the pious Israelite widow Judith. Though honor accorded for military heroism is more typical of males, here it is given to a woman.

> And Uzziah said to her, "You, daughter, are praised by the Most High God above all other women on earth. Honored be the Lord God who created the heavens and the earth, the one who guided you to wound the ruler of our enemies. Your hope will never leave the hearts of people remembering the power of God into the age. God grant that you be held in high honor forever and bring good things to you because you risked your own life on account of the humiliation of the nation, preventing our ruin, and walking a straight path before our God. And all the people said, "So let it be, so let it be."

CHALLENGE AND RESPONSE

17. ARISTOTLE, *NICOMACHEAN ETHICS* 1163B13–19

In considering relations between friends, Aristotle acknowledges that friendship is possible between those who are not social equals. The question then becomes how the inferior can repay benefits received from the superior.

> This, actually, is the way to deal with unequals. To the one benefiting us in money or virtue, we must repay with honor, making what return we can. But friendship seeks a return of what is possible, not what corresponds to worth, for that is

impossible in some cases, as with the honors due the gods or parents. For no one could ever make a return matching their honor, but the one doing what service to them that is in his power seems to be a proper person.[14]

18. SENECA, *ON ANGER* 2.34.1

Seneca (ca. 4 BCE–65 CE) was an influential Roman Stoic philosopher, statesman, dramatist, and occasional humorist. Ever the Stoic, he believes that there is much to be gained from a reputation for forbearance. It is only the "petty and sorry person" who strikes back.

> We must, therefore, refrain from anger, whether a challenge [*lacessendus*] comes from an equal or a superior or an inferior. A contest with one's equal is hazardous, with a superior full of madness, with an inferior degrading.[15]

HONORING GOD

19. ISOCRATES, *TO DEMONICUS* 1.13–14

This discourse is addressed to Demonicus, son of the late Hipponicus, who had been one of Isocrates's good friends. Knowing the son was eager for education, Isocrates offers to instruct him in the moral values and behaviors befitting those of noble aspirations, contrasting these with those of persons of base and common outlook.

> First, act reverently toward the gods, not only by making burnt offerings, but also by remaining faithful to your oaths. The one is a sign of abundance in the things one needs, the other is a sure sign of noble character. Always honor divinity, especially in the midst of the community. For in this way, you will be respected for both sacrificing to the gods and abiding by the laws.[16]

20. REVELATION 4:8–11

Though there is considerable scholarly debate about the origins of this New Testament book, it was probably written around 96 CE during the reign of the Roman emperor Domitian. It is an apocalyptic work that imagines a terrible

---

14. Adapted from Rackham, LCL.
15. Adapted from Basore, LCL.
16. Adapted from Norlin, LCL.

end for the Roman Empire, and thus this passage (and similar ones in the book) is likely intended to honor God far above the Roman emperor.

> And the four living creatures, each one of them having six wings, are full of eyes all around as well as within. Day and night, without rest, they are saying, "Holy, holy, holy is God, the ruler of all, the one who was, and is, and is to come. And whenever the living creatures give glory and honor and gratitude to the one sitting upon the throne, the one living into the age of ages, the twenty-four elders fall down before the one sitting on the throne and worship the one living into the age of ages. They lay their crowns before the throne, saying, "Worthy are you, the Lord and our God, to receive glory and honor and power, because you created all things and by your will they existed and were created."

Vocabulary of Honor

HEBREW

הָדַר (*hadar*) . . . . to honor
שֵׁם (*shem*) . . . . name, renown, reputation
תְּהִלָּה (*tehillah*) . . . . praise
תִּפְאֶרֶת (*tipheret*) . . . . glory

GREEK

δόκιμος, -ον (*dokimos, -on*) . . . . honored, respected
δόξα (*doxa*) . . . . glory, honor, reputation
δοξάζω (*doxazō*) . . . . to give glory
ἔντιμος, -ον (*entimos, -on*) . . . . esteemed, honored
ἐντρέπω (*entrepō*) . . . . to show respect for those of high status
εὐγενής, -ές (*eugenēs, -es*) . . . . wellborn
εὐσχήμων, -ον (*euschēmōn, -on*) . . . . . . esteemed
κλέος (*kleos*) . . . . reputation
μεγαλύνω (*megalynō*) . . . . to hold in high honor
μεγιστάν (*megistan*) . . . . person of high status
πρωτοκλισία (*prōtoklisia*) . . . . place of honor
σεμνός, -ή, -όν
    (*semnos, -ē, -on*) . . . . honorable

τιμάω (*timaō*) . . . . to honor, bestow honor
τιμή (*timē*) . . . . honor
ὑπερυψόω (*hyperypsoō*) . . . . to regard as exceptionally honored
φιλοτιμία (*philotimia*) . . . . love of honor

LATIN

dignitas . . . . rank, esteem, importance
honor . . . . honor
veneror . . . . to give honor

Select Bibliography

Barton, Carlin A. *Roman Honor: The Fire in the Bones*. Berkeley: University of California Press, 2001.
Fisher, N. R. E. *Hybris: A Study in the Values of Honour and Shame in Ancient Greece*. Warminster: Aris & Phillips, 1992.
Gilmore, David G., ed. *Honor and Shame and the Unity of the Mediterranean*. Washington, DC: American Anthropological Association, 1987.
Neyrey, Jerome H. *Honor and Shame in the Gospel of Matthew*. Louisville: Westminster John Knox, 1998.
Peristiany, J. G., and Julian Pitt-Rivers, eds. *Honor and Grace in Anthropology*. Cambridge: Cambridge University Press, 1992.
Rohrbaugh, Richard L. "Legitimating Sonship—A Test of Honour: A Social-Scientific Study of Luke 4:1–30." Pages 183–97 in *Modelling Early Christianity: Social-Scientific Studies of the New Testament in Its Context*. Edited by P. F. Esler. London: Routledge, 1995.

Additional Texts

LOVE OF HONOR

Aristotle, *Nicomachean Ethics* 1095b1–8, 1123b1–1125a33, 1159a13–35
Augustine, *City of God* 5.12
Demosthenes, *On the Crown* (*Or.* 18) 66; *Olynthiac* 2.15

Dio Chrysostom, *Kingship 4* (*Or.* 4) 83–96
Philo, *On the Life of Abraham* 185, 263, 264; *That the Worse Attacks the Better*

33, 122; *Allegorical Interpretation* 3.87;
  On the Migration of Abraham 172
Plutarch, *A Pleasant Life Impossible*
  1100; *Lycurgus* 19.3

Seneca, *On Benefits* 4.16.2; 4.17.3
Xenophon, *Memorabilia* 3.3.13

THE HONOR CODE

Acts 5:13
1 Chronicles 16:27; 29:12, 28
2 Chronicles 1:11; 12:1–16; 17:5; 26:18;
  32:27; 33:1–25
1 Corinthians 12:23, 26
2 Corinthians 6:8
Daniel 2:6; 4:37; 11:38–39
Deuteronomy 5:16; 26:19
Ecclesiastes 6:2; 10:1
Esther 1:20; 6:3, 6–7, 9, 11; 8:16
Eunapius, *Lives of the Philosophers* 496
Exodus 20:12
Ezekiel 39:13
Genesis 30:20
Hebrews 2:7; 3:3
Isaiah 9:15; 22:23; 29:13; 43:20; 58:13
Job 14:21; 30:15
John 4:44; 5:23, 41; 8:54
Judges 13:17
1 Kings 3:13
2 Kings 5:1
Lamentations 4:16
Leviticus 19:32
Livy, *History of Rome* 6.34.7–9
Luke 14:7–11; 20:13
Malachi 1:6

Mark 15:43
Matthew 15:8; 23:6
Numbers 22:17, 37; 24:11
1 Peter 1:7; 2:20
2 Peter 1:17
Philippians 2:9
Philo, *On the Virtues* 195; *On Sobriety* 16
Plutarch, *On Affection for Offspring*
  479c; *Table Talk* 617d; *Sertorius* 23.5
Proverbs 3:9, 16, 35; 4:8; 5:9; 8:18; 15:33;
  18:12; 20:3; 21:21; 22:4; 25:7; 26:1, 8;
  29:23
Psalms 4:2; 8:5; 45:9; 62:7; 84:11; 91:15;
  96:6; 104:1; 111:3; 112:9
Revelation 4:9, 11; 5:12; 19:1, 7; 21:26
Romans 2:7, 10; 12:10; 14:18
1 Samuel 2:8, 29, 30; 9:6; 15:30
2 Samuel 6:22
Seneca, *On Benefits* 4.19.4; 5.12.3–7;
  5.3.3–4; *On Anger* 3.37.4
1 Thessalonians 4:4
1 Timothy 1:17; 5:17; 6:1
2 Timothy 2:20
Xenophon, *Hiero* 1.27
Zechariah 6:13

ASCRIBED AND ACQUIRED HONOR

Aristotle, *Nicomachean Ethics*
  1123b1–1125a33, 1125b1–1126; *Rhetoric*
  1361a28–b3, 1366a23–1368a38
1 Chronicles 16:27

Cicero, *On Duties* 2.43
Diogenes Laertius, *Lives of Eminent*
  Philosophers 5.19
Euripides, *Hercules Furens* 1261

Josephus, *Jewish War* 4.149

Plutarch, *On the Education of Children* 4b–c; *On Moral Virtue* 446c; *On Brotherly Love* 478b, 486b

Proverbs 3:16; 8:18; 22:4; 25:27; 26:1, 8; 29:23

Seneca, *On Benefits* 2.19.2; 2.29.5; 3.28.1–2; 4.30.4; 4.12.4; *Moral Letters* 8.2–3; 19.3; 66.16–18; 76.18

Sirach 5:13

Stobaeus, *Anthology* 4.2.51

Theon of Alexandria, *Lexicon to the Greek Comedians* 9.35–38

Thucydides, *History* 6.2

Xenophon, *Memorabilia* 3.3.13; 4.1.5

GIVING, RECEIVING, AND RECOGNIZING HONOR

Acts 5:13, 34

Aristotle, *Nicomachean Ethics* 1128b22–30, 1165a22–33; *Rhetoric* 1365a10–22, 1378b47–1379a12, 1383b12–1385a18, 1408a33–b2

Aulus Gellius, *Attic Nights* 7.14.2–4

1 Chronicles 29:12, 28

2 Chronicles 16:14; 17:5; 18:1; 21:19; 26:18; 32:27, 33

[Cicero] *Rhetoric for Herennius* 3.9–12

Cicero, *On Duties* 2.69

1 Corinthians 4:10; 12:23–24

2 Corinthians 6:8

Daniel 2:6; 4:37; 11:38–39

Deuteronomy 5:16; 26:19

Ecclesiastes 6:2; 10:1

Ephesians 6:2

1 Esdras 8:4; 9:45

Esther 1:20; 6:3, 6–7, 9, 11; 8:16; 10:2

Exodus 20:12

Ezekiel 39:13

Genesis 30:20

Hebrews 2:7, 9; 3:3; 5:4; 13:4

Herodotus, *Histories* 1.134

Isaiah 22:23; 23:9; 58:13

James 2:1–13

Job 14:21; 30:15

John 4:44; 12:26

Josephus, *Jewish Antiquities* 6.168, 251; 7.117; 10.92; 13.102; 14.152–54; 19.292; *Jewish War* 1.194, 199, 358, 396, 607; *Life* 5.80, 429

Judges 9:16, 19; 13:17

Judith 13:20; 15:12

1 Kings 3:13

Lamentations 4:16

Luke 14:7–8; 18:20; 20:46

1 Maccabees 1:39; 2:8, 51, 64; 3:14; 9:10; 10:3, 24, 64; 11:42, 60; 12:8, 43; 14:4, 21, 23, 40; 15:9

2 Maccabees 5:16; 6:7, 19; 14:21

3 Maccabees 1:12; 3:16–17; 4:16; 7:21

4 Maccabees 1:10, 26; 17:5, 20

Mark 6:4; 7:10; 10:19; 12:39

Martial, *Epigrams* 1.5.13

Matthew 13:57; 15:4–5; 19:19; 23:6

Numbers 22:17, 37; 24:11

1 Peter 1:7; 2:17; 3:7

2 Peter 1:17

Philippians 2:29

Philo, *On the Confusion of Tongues* 18; *That God Is Unchangeable* 17; *On the Special Laws* 2.226–27; 4.6

Philostratus, *Lives of the Sophists* 1.19

Plutarch, *Cicero* 13.2; 22.5–7; 39.4; 45.1; *Demosthenes* 16.2; *Fabius Maximus*

23.3; *How a Man May Become Aware of His Progress in Virtue* 84e; *On Moral Virtue* 446c; *On Tranquility of Mind* 470e; *On Brotherly Love* 478b, 486b; *Table Talk* 615d, 617d

Proverbs 3:9, 35; 4:8; 5:9; 11:16; 15:33; 18:12; 20:3; 21:21; 26:8; 29:23

Psalms 4:2; 8:5; 45:9; 62:7; 71:21; 84:11; 91:15; 112:9

Quintilian, *Institutes of Oratory* 3.7.10–18

Romans 2:10; 12:10; 13:7

Seneca, *Moral Essays* 3.37.4; 4.30.1–4; 5.1.3–4; 5.28.6

1 Samuel 2:8, 29–30; 9:6; 15:30

2 Samuel 6:22

Sirach 3:8; 5:13; 7:4, 27, 29, 31; 10:5, 19–20, 23, 28–29; 12:12; 38:1, 16; 47:20

1 Thessalonians 4:4

1 Timothy 5:3, 17; 6:1

Tobit 4:3; 10:12; 14:13

Wisdom of Solomon 3:17; 5:4; 6:21; 8:10; 10:14; 14:17

Zechariah 6:13

CHALLENGE AND RESPONSE

Aristotle, *Rhetoric* 1378b34–50, 1383b31–1385a18, 1388a1–7; *Nicomachean Ethics* 1158b13–28, 1163b15–29

Lucian, *Nigrinus* 3–5

Luke 4:1–13, 22, 25–27; 6:9; 20:40

Mark 11:29

Martial, *Epigrams* 1.5.36

Matthew 19:17; 21:24; 22:46

Philo, *On the Cherubim* 122

Plato, *Laws* 625e, 626d

Plutarch, *How a Man May Become Aware of His Progress in Virtue* 84e

Seneca, *Moral Essays* 1.19.3; 2.11.1; 2.12; 2.19.2; 3.5.8; 4.2.34; 4.32.1; 5.5.8; 10.1–4

Stobaeus, *Anthology* 3.14.17

HONORING GOD

Aristotle, *Nicomachean Ethics* 1163b5–29

Isaiah 29:13; 43:20

John 5:23; 8:49

Leviticus 19:32

2 Maccabees 6:19

3 Maccabees 4:16

Malachi 1:6

Philo, *On the Decalogue* 6–9; *That the Worse Attacks the Better* 54; *On Drunkenness* 110

Plutarch, *Roman Questions* 266a–e

Proverbs 3:16

Psalms 96:6; 104:1; 111:3

Revelation 4:9, 11; 5:12–13; 7:12; 21:26

Romans 1:21; 2:7; 14:6

Sirach 3:20

1 Timothy 1:17; 6:16

5. Shame

Ronald D. Roberts

Introduction

As a Mediterranean cultural value, *shame* is closely related to *honor*, but shame and honor are not binary opposites. According to anthropologists like Julian Pitt-Rivers, shame is "a concern for repute, both as a sentiment and also as the public recognition of that sentiment"; thus, shame "is what makes a person sensitive to the pressure exerted by public opinion." Shame can therefore be both positive and negative. A profusion of shame is extremely undesirable; however, the complete lack of shame is equally undesirable. The possession of a sense of shame allows a person to understand his or her role in society and to live appropriately within that role (see **chap. 4, Honor**). Therefore, *having shame* is a positive value, demonstrated through sensitivity to the court of public opinion, appropriate deference to social superiors, and demonstrating a sense of propriety. Shame can even function as a form of honor, such as when a person expresses deference toward a social superior or when a woman's modesty (often referred to as her shame) gains her the reputation in these cultures of being a good, moral, or honorable woman. However, a shameless person possesses no honor, since he or she has no sense of decorum or morality. For example, moral and criminal deviants are often considered shameless because they disregard social norms and laws (see **chap. 18, Deviance**).

Being shamed or *being put to shame* is the negative experience of shame that results in dishonor. When a person is shamed, public opinion determines that the person or someone intimately connected with that person, especially a family member, has acted dishonorably or has been acted upon dishonorably. Thus, the same activities and arenas that present opportunities for gaining honor also present opportunities for being shamed. A favorable outcome in public engagements provides honor, and an unfavorable outcome results in dishonor (see **chap. 4, Honor**). Reciprocally, the shaming of someone increases the honor of the person doing the shaming (see **chap. 19, Mockery and Secrecy; chap. 18, Deviance**). Therefore, a paradox exists in which a person engaging in the public arena demonstrates a willingness to be shamed. Not only must a person in the public arena expose himself or herself to situations that hold the potential for honor or shame, but also that person must be willing to demonstrate public deference (positive shame) to social superiors (see **chap. 3, Patronage; chap. 8, Space**). In turn, positive shame may lead to an increase in honor for the one who defers to social superiors.

When someone's honor is challenged, he or she is expected to offer a riposte defending his or her honor or even challenging the honor of the challenger. However, the best defense sometimes is no defense. By offering no response, the challenged person treats the challenger as unworthy of a response, such as when the challenged person considers the challenger to have a much lower social status. At other times, a person may decide to defer to the challenger and gain honor through a demonstration of humility. In addition, when a person's actions threaten the honor of his or her social group, such as his or her family, the group may take punitive actions against the offender.

The relationship between shame and honor has numerous subtle variations from one local sociocultural context to another. For example, in the Mediterranean sociocultural context, representations of shame are intimately linked to conceptions of gender; however, the exact construction of gender roles varies among localized contexts (see **chap. 9, Gender**). Within a broad Greco-Roman context, honor for men was expressed in the culturally constructed value of manliness, and it was shameful for a man to act unmanly. Greco-Roman conceptions of masculinity were not entirely universal, since Greek expressions of manliness were sometimes at odds with Roman expressions of manliness. For instance, in the second century CE, the rhetor Polemo drew upon the traditional Roman concept of manliness in order to criticize his rival Favorinus. While this concept of manliness considered high concern over physical appearance as feminine behavior, Favorinus followed a more Greek concept of manliness that enabled rhetors to be highly concerned with physical appearance (Polemo, *Physiognomy* 1:160–64).

Nearly universal in Mediterranean cultures is the concern over the potential for shame represented by the women of a family. A Mediterranean man is typically very concerned about the potential shame that a female relative's sexual impropriety could bring upon the family. Thus, a man is expected not only to protect his female relatives from shameful sexual attacks and sexual overtures from other men but also to control his female relatives in order to reduce the risk of sexual promiscuity. The Mediterranean concern over female promiscuity should not be taken as an indication that Greco-Roman women were always veiled and strictly cloistered; instead, the cloistering of women was more an ancient elite ideal than a reality (cf. Philo, *On the Special Laws* 3.169). Nevertheless, female sexual promiscuity was a major concern for Greco-Roman men to the extent that it was shameful for a man to be perceived as unable to control his wife or daughters.

Although positive shame can function as a virtue for men, shame is most often associated with the feminine in Mediterranean cultures. Behaviors typically considered feminine are also considered to be expressions of shame. In particular, modesty, bashfulness, and blushing were ideal feminine behaviors; however, these behaviors could function as expressions of positive shame for men. Similarly, the conceptual association between women and shame implies neither that women had no honor nor that they could never act in "masculine" ways. Ethnographical work among contemporary Mediterranean cultures suggests that women in these cultures have their own systems of honor and shame that, although not completely disconnected from the men's systems of honor and shame, are quite distinct from male honor and shame. For example, anthropologist Unni Wikan found that the women in the Omani town of Sohar were not as preoccupied with the shame of sexual promiscuity as men in the town were and that the women determined the relative honor of other women more upon the values of loyalty and hospitality.

Ancient Texts

SHAME AS THE LOSS OF HONOR

1. 1 SAMUEL 20:30

As Jonathan's father, King Saul claims that Jonathan's protection of David has shamed their family before the court of public opinion, presumably other elite Israelites. Furthermore, the connection between Jonathan's shameful deed and his mother's nakedness not only illustrates the link between shame and female sexuality but also serves as a euphemistic reference to the shame that Saul may experience from Jonathan's actions.

> Saul was angry with Jonathan and said to him, "Son of a perverse, rebellious woman, do I not know that you chose the son of Jesse, resulting in your own shame and the shame of your mother's nakedness?"

2. 3 MACCABEES 7:14

After King Ptolemy of Egypt unsuccessfully attempts to force Alexandrian Judeans to worship Dionysus (third century BCE), he ends the persecution and even allows the Judeans to punish those Judeans who *polluted* themselves by participating in the Dionysian cult (see **chap. 12, Purity** and **chap. 18, Deviance**). Killing the apostates functions as an honor killing that simultaneously shames the "apostate" Judeans and removes the dishonor from the Judean community.

> Thus, any of their polluted compatriots that they came across along the way they punished and killed as shameful examples.

3. JOSEPHUS, *JEWISH WAR* 3.137

The captive Judean general Josephus (first century CE) explains that he complied with the Romans not because he wanted to betray his people, but because he saw this as the only way of saving the Judeans from utter destruction.

> For indeed Josephus saw what sort of endings would prevail upon the Judeans and knew that their only salvation was surrender. For although he expected to be pardoned by the Romans, he similarly hoped more that he would die many times than completely betray his homeland and the military command entrusted to him in order to prosper shamefully with the one whom he was sent to fight.[1]

4. PLATO, *LAWS* 646E–647A

The philosopher Plato (fifth to the fourth century BCE) discusses two basic human fears. One fear is worry over bad things occurring or being done to one's own self. The second fear, shame, is concern over personally behaving or speaking inappropriately.

> Athenian: Tell me, are we able to perceive two fears that are indeed nearly opposites?
>
> Clinias: Which ones then?
>
> Athenian: These here: we fear some sort of harm that we expect to happen.
>
> Clinias: Yes.

---

1. Adapted from Thackeray, LCL.

Athenian: Also, we frequently fear reputation, when considering how we might be accredited with bad things, specifically practicing and saying things that are not good; this that we ourselves already call fear we all also know as shame.[2]

5. LUCRETIUS, *ON THE NATURE OF THINGS* 3.41–42

The Roman poet and Epicurean philosopher Lucretius (ca. 99–55 BCE) provides a concise demonstration of the importance of shame in Roman culture, where suicide could be an honorable form of death when a person is faced with severe ignominy.

> For people frequently claim that more than the underworld of death,
> Diseases and the life of dishonor are feared.[3]

6. 2 CORINTHIANS 4:2

Paul explains how avoidance of shameful activities enables a person to be honorable and demonstrate a proper sense of shame. Paul's avoidance of shameful deception gives him the confidence to place himself openly before the court of public opinion, which here consists of the Corinthian Christ-followers.

> However, we renounced the secret things of shame, by neither conducting ourselves in trickery nor distorting God's word but in the full disclosure of the truth, commending ourselves to every person's conscience before God.

POSITIVE SHAME

7. SIRACH 4:20–21

In a section of proverbs clustered around the concepts of shame and truthfulness (Sir 4:20–28), the Judean sage Ben Sirach (second century BCE) discusses the balance between courageous honesty and regard for shame. In addition, Ben Sirach demonstrates a close connection between wisdom and positive shame.

> Watch carefully for the right time, and watch out for evil,
> And do not be shamed concerning yourself.
> For there is a shame that results in sin
> And a shame that is good reputation and favor.

2. Adapted from Bury, LCL.
3. Adapted from Rouse, LCL.

8. Appian, *Illyrian Wars* 3.4.20

During the first-century-BCE siege of the city of Metulus, the Roman army constructed four bridges between their siege mounds and the top of the city walls. After three bridges were destroyed, Caesar Augustus (63 BCE–14 CE) went out onto the fourth bridge to keep the opponent from destroying the bridge after he failed verbally to rouse the Roman army. In this selection, shame spurs the army into not letting Augustus do their job for them.

> But since the Romans were not provoked by Augustus's speech, he took a shield and ran onto the bridge. Two of his generals, Agrippa and Hiero, the bodyguard Lucius, and Volas (I know of only these four), along with some armor-bearers, ran with him. He had already crossed the bridge, when the army, feeling shame, started up in numbers.[4]

9. Mark 12:6–12

In the Markan account of the parable of the wicked tenants, the landlord eventually sends his son to collect rent from the murderous farmers leasing the vineyard. The landlord expects the farmers to defer to his son, but the farmers demonstrate shamelessness when they murder the son. Jesus's opponents recognize that the farmers represent them, and their fear of the crowd suggests that the crowd deems Jesus the winner of this agonistic honor competition. The crowd, thus, considers Jesus's opponents as the losers that are shamed.

> The landlord still had one beloved son. At last, he sent him to the farmers, while saying, "They will show deference to my son." Those farmers said to themselves, "This is the heir. Come, let's kill him, and the inheritance will belong to us." They grabbed him and killed him, and they threw him outside the vineyard. Therefore, what will the master of the vineyard do? He will come and destroy the farmers, and he will give the vineyard to some others. Did you not read this scripture?
>
> > The stone that the builders rejected,
> >> This one became the cornerstone.
> > This occurred through the Lord,
> >> And it is amazing in our eyes.
>
> Jesus's opponents were seeking to seize him, and they feared the crowd, since they knew that he spoke the parable about them. Letting him be, they departed.

---

4. Adapted from White, LCL.

10. Shepherd of Hermas, *Similitudes* 9.11.1–3 (88.1–3)

While waiting for the Shepherd, Hermas finds himself in a potentially morally compromising situation. Hermas's reluctance to stay the night with the virgins demonstrates a positive sense of shame.

> The virgins say to me, "Wait here for the shepherd until evening. If he does not come, stay here with us until he comes." I say to them, "I will wait for him until evening, and if he does not come, I will depart for home and will return early in the morning." In response, they say to me, "You were entrusted to us. You cannot leave us." I say, "Then, where will I stay?" They say, "You will sleep with us as a brother and not as a husband. For you are our brother, and we are about to live with you from here on, since we love you very much." I was shamed to stay with them.[5]

SHAMELESSNESS

11. Jeremiah 6:15

The absence of regard for shame is a state worse than being shamed. The shameless person is not only treated as one who has no awareness of propriety and morality, but also he or she is considered to be without honor. Through the prophet Jeremiah, God states that the Judahite prophets' and priests' proclamation of the false message of peace is shameful and reflects the shamelessness of the prophets and priests, who lack the appropriate sense of deference toward God. In response, God will publicly shame them.

> They caused shame because they made an abomination,
>> they have no shame,
>> but they did not know shame.
> Therefore, they shall fall with those who fall.
>> At the time of punishments, they will stumble,
>> says the Lord.

12. Tobit 14:9 (14:10 ET)

In Tobit's deathbed instructions, the dying Judean hero provides his sons and grandsons an unflattering description of Nineveh, where they live as foreign residents.

5. Adapted from Ehrman, LCL.

On the day that you bury your mother with me, on that day do not stay within the borders of Nineveh, since I see that there is much unrighteousness in it and much deceit is accomplished in it, and they are not shamed.

13. ARISTOTLE, *RHETORIC* 1383B13–22

The philosopher Aristotle (fourth century BCE) initially defines shame in terms of positive shame. He continues on, however, to explain that inappropriate behavior results in negative shame. The motivation for someone to act according to his or her sense of shame is to avoid dishonoring not only himself or herself but also family and friends.

> Now let shame be some pain or disturbance concerning the kinds of bad actions that appear to bring someone into dishonor, whether occurring in the present, having already occurred, or being about to occur, and let shamelessness be some contempt and apathy concerning these same things. Now, if this defines shame, it is necessary to be shamed by these sorts of bad actions that seem to be as disgrace either to a person or to those for whom that person cares. Such things are the commission of bad deeds, such as throwing away a shield or fleeing, since these deeds come from cowardice or the defrauding of or damaging of a deposit, since this is injustice.[6]

14. JOSEPHUS, *JEWISH ANTIQUITIES* 4.267–68

Josephus (first century CE) attempts to show the civility and liberality of the Mosaic law's lending regulations. He describes those who do not repay their loans as *shameless*, that is, lacking regard for the divine mandate requiring honorable people to repay their loans (see **chap. 1, Economy**).

> Those who receive either gold or some wet or dry commodity, if things should go by God the way they thought they would, let them repay what was loaned by bringing happily the repayment to those who gave it to them just as if the lendees were storing it up for themselves and if they were to have need, they would have it again. In regard to whoever is shameless concerning repayment, do not go around that house in order to take a pledge before the judgment concerning this matter is rendered.[7]

15. SUETONIUS, *NERO* 39.3

The Roman biographer Suetonius (ca. 69–140 CE) describes a period of intense public criticism against the Roman emperor Nero. Suetonius explains

---

6. Adapted from Freese, LCL.
7. Adapted from Thackeray and Marcus, LCL.

that Nero's failure to deal appropriately with his brash critics was possibly the result of Nero's shamelessness.

> Nero did nothing more than exile the actor [Datus] and the philosopher [Isidorus] from the city and from Italy; either he despised all dishonor or he did not acknowledge pain that would upset his inherent qualities.[8]

WOMEN AND SHAME

The following selections illustrate not only the close association between shame and the feminine in ancient Mediterranean societies but also how women in these same societies could experience both positive and negative shame.

16. HOSEA 2:7–9 (2:5–7 ET)

Hosea 2:3–25 (2:1–23 ET) metaphorically portrays Israel as Hosea's promiscuous wife, Gomer. The Lord labels Gomer's/Israel's infidelity as shameful and proposes a new solution. It is interesting that God does not make the customary public response to a promiscuous wife in the Mediterranean region, specifically, divorce her and have no further concern for her.

> Since their mother has been prostituting herself,
>> the one who conceived them acted shamefully,
> Because she said, "I will chase after my lovers,
>> they provide my bread and my water,
>> my wool and my flax,
>> my oil and my drink."
> Therefore, I will block
> her ways with thorns.
> I will build walls,
>> and she will not find her pathways.
> She will pursue her lovers,
>> and she will not catch them.
> She will look for them and not find them,
>> and she will say, "I will go
> And return to my first husband,
>> because it was better then than now."

8. Adapted from Rolfe, LCL.

17. SIRACH 26:13–15

In these instructions to his young male students, the Judean sage Ben Sirach (second century BCE) emphasizes the honor of a modest woman, that is, a woman with a proper sense of shame.

> The favor of a woman delights her husband,
> And her skill fleshes out his bones.
> A gift from the Lord is a silent woman,
> And there is reward for her disciplined life.
> An exceedingly generous benefit is a modest woman,
> And there is not any scale worthy of her self-controlled life.

18. OVID, *METAMORPHOSES* 1.596–99

In Ovid's account of the rape of Io, the virgin Io flees Jupiter after she refuses his invitation to have sexual relations, but Jupiter catches and rapes her. The Latin term *pudorem* (shame), which occurs in this passage, is lexically related to *pudenda* (female genitals). Ovid seems to refer to Io's stolen virginity as her shame; thus, Jupiter also steals away her modesty, that is, her reputation as a chaste virgin.

> Jupiter said, "Don't run away from me!" But she was already fleeing.
> She had already run past the pastures of Lerna and the cultivated trees of
>   Lyrcea.
> And the god introduced mist into the wide land,
> Concealed her route of escape, and snatched hold of her shame.[9]

19. DIOGENES LAERTIUS, *LIVES OF EMINENT PHILOSOPHERS* 8.43

The biographer Diogenes Laertius (third century CE) reports an incident from the philosophical career of Theano, the mother of the philosopher Telauges. The brief dialogue demonstrates not only the link between feminine sexuality and feminine shame as honor but also the central position that modesty played in the construction of gender for Greco-Roman women.

> It is reported that Telauges wrote nothing, but his mother Theano wrote a few
> things. However, according to a report, when she was questioned concerning on
> which day a woman is clean from sexual relations with a man, she explained, "If
> it was with your own husband, immediately; if with some other man, never." She

9. Adapted from Miller, LCL.

advised her, "When you are about to be with your own husband, take off your shame at the same time you remove your clothing, and when you stand up, pick it up again with your clothes." The questioner said, "How?" She answered, "On account of these things, I am called a woman."[10]

20. 1 Corinthians 11:3–15

Paul explicates a symbolic moral universe in which socially constructed gender roles are not only legitimized as the natural order but also symbolized through the veiling of women.

I want you to realize that the head of every man is Christ, the man is the head of woman, and God is the head of Christ. Every man who prays or prophesies with his head veiled shames his head. Every woman who prays and prophesies with an unveiled head shames her head, since it is the same as having her head shaved. For if a woman does not veil herself, let her hair be cut off. If it is shameful for a woman to have her hair cut off or shaved off, let her veil herself. Since indeed a man ought not to veil his head because he is the image and reputation of God, but the woman is the reputation of man. For man is not from woman, but woman from man. For also a man was not created for the sake of woman, but woman for the sake of man. On account of this, the woman ought to have authority over her head because of the angels. However, neither is woman separate from man nor man separate from woman in the Lord. Just as the woman came from the man, thus also the man comes through the woman, and all come from God. Determine among yourselves whether it is proper for a woman to pray while veiled. Does nature itself not teach us that it is dishonorable if a man has long hair, but if a woman has long hair, it is reputable because hair was given to her as a covering?

Vocabulary of Shame

HEBREW

בּוֹשׁ (*bosh*) . . . . to shame
בֹּשֶׁת (*boshet*) . . . . shame
חָפֵר (*khafer*) . . . . be shamed, be put to shame
כְּלִמּוּת (*kelimut*) . . . . ignominy, shame, humiliation
קִיקָלוֹן (*qiqalon*) . . . . dishonor

10. Adapted from Hicks, LCL.

קָלַל (*qalal*) .... to be cursed

שִׂמְצָה (*shimtsah*) .... derisive whisper

GREEK

αἰσχύνω (*aischynō*) .... to shame
ἀσχημοσύνη (*aschēmosynē*) .... shame, shameful act
ἀτιμάζω (*atimazō*) .... to dishonor
ἐντρέπω (*entrepō*) .... to shame, show deference
ἐπαισχύνω (*epaischynō*) .... to shame
καταισχύνω (*kataischynō*) .... to shame
ὕβρις (*hybris*) .... arrogance, insult, mistreatment

LATIN

dedecoro .... to dishonor
impudentia and related words .... shamelessness
infamis .... disreputable
opprobrium .... dishonor, abuse, reproach
probrum .... shameful act
pudeo .... to shame
rubor .... blushing
verecundia .... shame, modesty

Select Bibliography

Crook, Zeba. "Honor, Shame, and Social Status Revisited." *JBL* 128 (2009): 591–611.

Gleason, Maud C. *Making Men: Sophists and Self-Presentation in Ancient Rome.* Princeton: Princeton University Press, 1995.

Kressel, Gideon M. "Shame and Gender." *Anthropological Quarterly* 65 (1992): 34–46.

Malina, Bruce J. *The New Testament World: Insights from Cultural Anthropology.* 3rd ed. Louisville: Westminster John Knox, 2001.

Pitt-Rivers, Julian. "Honour and Social Status." Pages 19–77 in *Honour and Shame: The Values of Mediterranean Society.* Edited by J. G. Peristiany. The Nature of Human Society Series. Chicago: University of Chicago Press, 1966.

Wikan, Unni. "Shame and Honour: A Contestable Pair." *Man* NS 19 (1984): 635–52.

Additional Texts

SHAME AS THE LOSS OF HONOR

Aeschines, *Against Timarchus* 1.29

Appian, *Civil Wars* 2.9.60; 2.13.93–94; 4.15.113; 18.134; *Mithridatic Wars* 2.14; *Samnite History* 1.2–5, 7

Apuleius, *The Golden Ass* 6.22

Aristotle, *Economics* 1348a1–36; *Politics* 1302a30–35, 1315a15–20; *Rhetoric* 1383b15

Cicero, *On the Republic* 4.10

1 Corinthians 6:5; 11:14

2 Corinthians 12:10

Deuteronomy 21:23

Diodorus Siculus, *Library of History* 12.16.1–2

Ephesians 5:4

Epictetus, *Discourses* 1.6.20; 3.7.27

Euripides, *Helen* 687–88

Exodus 10:3; 32:25

Ezekiel 22:5

Ezra 9:7

Genesis 38:23

Habakkuk 2:16

Hebrews 6:6

Hosea 10:6

Isaiah 66:24

Isocrates, *Plataicus* 14.50

Jeremiah 3:25; 23:40; 50:2, 11–12; 51:17–19, 51

Job 19:3

Josephus, *Jewish Antiquities* 4.262; 9.154; 12.175–79; 16.195; 18.147, 243; 19.39; *Jewish War* 3.542; 6.362; 7.376–77

Julius Caesar, *Gallic War* 4.25.5

Livy, *History of Rome* 2.45.5–6; 9.7.1–7; 23.3.11; 25.6.18–23; 28.15.6–9

Luke 13:17; 14:9

Lycurgus, *Against Leocrates* 1.51, 107

2 Maccabees 5:7; 9:2; 11:12

3 Maccabees 4:11

4 Maccabees 16:17

Mark 6:4

Nehemiah 3:36 (Ezra 4:4 ET)

Ovid, *Metamorphoses* 1.754–55; 6.614–18

1 Peter 4:16

Plato, *Laws* 727c–d, 878b–c; *Republic* 604a; *Statesman* 309e; *Symposium* 194c

Pliny the Younger, *Letters* 7.31.1

Plutarch, *Alexander* 50.4

Proverbs 10:5; 13:5; 14:35; 18:3; 19:26; 28:7; 30:17

Psalms 35:4; 44:14–17; 69:7–13, 20–22; 89:46 [Psalm 89:45 ET]

Revelation 16:15

Romans 2:23; 6:21

2 Samuel 6:20–23; 10:5; 16:5–13

Seneca the Elder, *Controversies* 8.1.11

Sirach 13:7

Suetonius, *Claudius* 16; *Julius* 59

Tacitus, *Annals* 2.38; *Histories* 3.24; 4.11; 4.72

2 Thessalonians 3:14

Titus 1:11

Wisdom of Solomon 2:20; 3:17; 13:17

POSITIVE SHAME

Appian, *Mithridatic Wars* 7.49; *Wars in Spain* 5.27

Aristotle, *Eudemian Ethics* 1233b25–30

Cicero, *Against Verres* 1.5.14; *Letters to Friends* 248

Demosthenes, *1 Philippic* (*Or.* 4) 10; *4 Philippic* (*Or.* 10) 27; *On the Chersonese* (*Or.* 8) 51

Diogenes Laertius, *Lives of Eminent Philosophers* 6.2.36

Epictetus, *Discourses* 1.25.4; 3.7.27

Horace, *Odes* 1.24.1

Josephus, *Jewish War* 4.283–86; 6.362

Julius Caesar, *Civil War* 1.67.4; 2.31.7; *Gallic Wars* 1.39.3

Livy, *History of Rome* 2.10.7; 10.9.7

Hebrews 12:9

Petronius, *Poems* 28

Plato, *Laws* 671c–d

2 Samuel 6:22

Seneca, *Moral Letters* 11.1–5

Strabo, *Geography* 13.3.6

Terence, *Brothers* 1.1.32–33

SHAMELESSNESS

Catullus, *Poems* 16, 57

Cicero, *Against Piso* 17.39; *For Caelius* 47; *For Scaurus* 2.8

Demosthenes, *1 Against Aphobus* (*Or.* 27) 62; *Against Spudias* (*Or.* 41) 24

Epictetus, *Discourses* 1.5.3; 3.17.1–3; 4.5.21

Galen, *Natural Faculties* 1.16

Genesis 2:25

Jeremiah 3:3; 8:8–12

Josephus, *Jewish Antiquities* 15.287–88

Livy, *History of Rome* 30.12.19

Lycurgus, *Against Leocrates* 1.90

Ovid, *Metamorphoses* 10.238–46

Pausanias, *Description of Greece* 4.9.7

Plato, *Laws* 732b, 871d; *Republic* 388d, 571d, 573a–b

Sirach 10:8; 30:13

Tacitus, *Annals* 6.51; 12.52; 14.14; 16.26; *History* 4.36

WOMEN AND SHAME

Diodorus Siculus, *Library of History* 10.21.4; 16.64.2

Euripides, *Hippolytus* 420–30

Ezekiel 16:23–29, 61

Josephus, *Jewish Antiquities* 5.146–48; 7.170–71; 17.46–47

Judith 14:18

Ovid, *Metamorphoses* 1.481–87; 6.533–48; 7.741–46; 9.23–26; 10.238–42

Pausanias, *Description of Greece* 2.20.9–10; 4.4.2; 7.21.5; 8.47.6; 9.13.5

Plautus, *Amphitryon* 3.2.1–17

Plutarch, *Alexander* 12.1

Proverbs 6:32–33; 12:4

Sirach 22:4; 26:8, 15

Tacitus, *Annals* 2.85; 12.65

Vergil, *Aeneid* 4.320–24

Vitruvius, *Architecture* 1.1.5

6. Collectivism

Dennis Duling and Richard Rohrbaugh

Introduction

In individualistic cultures, people are taught to think of themselves as having unique and distinctive personalities, thus to aspire to be independent and self-reliant. In addition, they are taught self-directed learning, admiration for self-sufficiency, and the value of self-fulfillment. Young people typically want to leave their families to live independent lives and choose their own mates. In marriage, they desire to care for their own immediate families, especially children, but not for their more distant relatives. They value privacy, freedoms, and rights. They generally believe that developing their own special talents will lead to success. Although teamwork is valued, they tend to think that individual competition and heroic victory will usually receive the greatest fame and fortune. Slogans representative of individualism are "standing on your own two feet," becoming a "self-made man (sic)," and "different strokes for different folks."

Collectivist cultures, however, are different. People are taught to think that it is more important to be accepted by the group. They usually expect their groups to protect them through their lifetimes in exchange for their unquestioning loyalty. They are socialized in interdependence, not independence. Their private, individual lives are subordinated to their communal lives. They are *allocentric* (other-directed) or *dyadic* (they honor a "significant other" [dyad = two] or others, thus *dyadism*), because they are socialized to live in harmony with others. Custom, conformity, and correct manners are encouraged; "standing out" from others is discouraged. Although there are public challenges to an individual's honor by other individuals, reputation in the eyes of others is inseparable from, and subordinate to, honor among family members and closest friends. Tradition, order, and duty are very deeply held values.

With respect to mates, marriages are usually arranged—they are marriages between families, not individuals—and families often live in family clusters. Where they are not arranged, family approval of a mate would be extremely important.

Generalizations such as these represent extremes on a continuum. A table illustrates them as cultural contrasts:

Individualistic Cultures	Collectivistic Cultures
Independent; idiocentric; "I-consciousness"	Interdependent; allocentric; "we-consciousness"
Adults care most for self, nuclear family	Adults care for adult parents, extended family
Individual rights	Obligations to others
Self-reliance; self-sufficiency	Reliance on group
Innovation, new ideas	Maintaining culture, tradition
Pursuing individual goals/interests	Fulfilling accepted roles within group
Individual competition and rewards	Group competition and group rewards
Self-determination and individual choices	Group or hierarchical decision-making
Innocence/guilt based on individual behavior	Honor/shame based on judgment by group
Independent living	Living with kin
Individual property rights	Property shared communally
Individuals seek knowledge (usually texts)	Elders transmit knowledge (usually oral)
"Low-context" communication (meanings are direct, explicit)	"High-context" communication (meanings are indirect, implicit)

Specialists who compare cultures with one another have discovered that the most important contrast between them is the contrast between *individualism* and *collectivism*. Sociologist Geert Hofstede, for example, surveyed over a hundred thousand people in some ninety-three countries around the world and, based on their answers to certain questions, placed their countries on a 0–100 collectivism/individualism continuum. The most individualistic countries (the high end of the scale) are in northwestern continental Europe, the United Kingdom, and UK-influenced English language countries in northern North America and southeast Asia. The most collectivistic countries (the lower end of the scale) are in the Latin cultures of North America (e.g., Mexico 30; Guatemala 6) and South America (e.g., Honduras 20; Columbia 13), Asia (e.g., China 20; Indonesia 14), and Africa (e.g., Ethiopia 20; Ghana 15). The key point for this chapter is that *countries surrounding the Mediterranean Sea (and Portugal as part of the Iberian Peninsula) are also predominantly collectivistic,* as a second chart demonstrates. (Note that based on the scale 0–100, Italy, Israel, and Spain are above 50, the midpoint, and might justifiably be considered individualistic; however, *southern* Italy and *southern* Spain are much more collectivistic, and Israel is distinctive in having many immigrants and "Western" influences.)

Most Individualistic Countries: Northwestern Europe, the UK, and UK-Influenced Countries	Collectivistic Countries of the Mediterranean
100. United States	76. Italy
99. Australia	54. Israel
98. United Kingdom	51. Spain
87. Canada	40. Lebanon
87. The Netherlands	38. Libya
81. Belgium	37. Turkey
79. New Zealand	35. Greece
76. Sweden	33. Croatia
74. Norway	32. Morocco
74. Denmark	27. Portugal
73. Switzerland	25. Egypt
72. Germany	25. Serbia
71. France	20. Albania

That modern countries of the Mediterranean are predominantly collectivistic is a significant finding. Many contemporary anthropologists and social historians of the Mediterranean think that, despite a rich ethnological diversity, one can discern "family resemblances" that are not simply modern, but are ancient and have persisted over time into the present. This point suggests that ancient Mediterraneans, like their modern counterparts, were also predominantly collectivistic and dyadic, not individualistic. Both conclusions, modern and ancient, are important since interpreters from more "Western," that is, more individualistic, cultures have often misunderstood ancient Mediterranean texts by reading them too individualistically. A further conclusion, then, is that interpreters from "the West"—the most individualistic countries—

should always be very careful not to interpret ancient Mediterranean collectivistic texts from the perspective of their own individualism. This chapter collects ancient texts that illustrate ancient Mediterranean collectivism and dyadism.

Collectivism and dyadism are related to another theme, *stereotyping*. Stereotypes can be found in all cultures but are especially common in collectivistic cultures because of their group centeredness. Groups form subjective opinions about themselves and other groups. These opinions are typically "ethnocentric" (Greek *ethnos* = "group"; see vocabulary list). Rumor, report, and especially direct contact with peoples who are different all lead to subjective judgments about their physical features, odors, dialects, languages, trades, origins, ancestors, habitats, beliefs, values, foods, clothing, women, sexuality, habits, rituals, character, military prowess, intelligence, and the like. Such judgments are usually prejudicial. They contribute to the formation of sharp social boundaries and can lead to social conflict, often with catastrophic consequences for indigenous minorities, migrants, and those defeated in war. Some of the text selections below illustrate stereotyping.

Finally, collectivism, dyadism, and stereotyping can be correlated with other themes in this sourcebook, especially honor/challenge-riposte, shame, deviance, gossip, kinship/fictive kinship/lineage/ancestry, friendship/gifts, and unclean/purity/pollution.

Ancient Texts

ETHNIC COLLECTIVISM

1. HERODOTUS, *HISTORIES* 8.144.2

The Greek historian Herodotus (ca. 485–425 BCE) relates a story about the Greco-Persian Wars in which Persia warned Athens to make peace or face the consequences (ca. 480 BCE; see text no. 2). This proposal greatly concerned the nearby Lacedaemonians, who, like Athenians, were also Greeks. They pleaded with the Athenians to reject the Persian offer, which the Athenians did. The rationale of the Athenians was that past Persian aggression had to be avenged and that the Greeks could not break their strong ethnic ties.

> For many and excellent are the reasons that prevent us [Athenians] from doing these things [making peace with Persians], supposing that we actually wanted to; in the first place—and most important—their setting ablaze and destroying the

images and temples of our gods, for which we must exact the most extreme retribution rather than make a treaty with those who have carried out such atrocities; in the second place, there is a bond of kinship among the Greeks who are of the same stock, speak the same language, [have] the same temples of the gods and sacrifices, and [share the same] customs; it would not be right for Athenians to betray such values.[1]

2. Aeschylus, *Persians* 402–5

In the same Greco-Persian Wars, the greatly outnumbered Greek alliance of city-states tricked the Persian navy to sail into the straits of the Saronic Gulf between the Greek mainland (not far from Athens) and the island of Salamis. There the Greeks defeated the Persians (the battle of Salamis, 480 BCE). The Greek poet Aeschylus, who fought at Salamis, wrote that before the battle, the Greeks lifted up a battle cry that, like the previous text (no. 1), appealed to Greek ethnic identity.

> "Charge, O sons of Hellas! Set free your fatherland! Liberate your children, your wives, the dwelling places of the gods of your fathers and the graves of your fore-fathers! Today you are fighting for everything that is yours!"[2]

3. Homer, *Odyssey* 10.325

The *Iliad* and the *Odyssey* are culturally influential epic poems of the ancient Greeks, to which they attached the name Homer. They are probably from the ninth or eighth century BCE. The assumption behind the questions in the sentence from the *Odyssey* is that in order to understand strangers, one needs only to know something about their significant origins (nation, city, family, etc.).

> [The goddess-witch Circe to the much-traveled Odysseus:] "Who are you, and where are you from? What is your city? And who are your parents?"[3]

4. Jonah 1:8

The Book of Jonah, usually dated to the fifth or fourth century BCE, caricatures a prophet who attempts to understand why God has exiled his people. At the beginning of the story, Jonah resists Yahweh's command to prophesy against the Assyrians by fleeing in the opposite direction on a ship. When the

1. Adapted from Godley, LCL.
2. Adapted from Smyth, LCL.
3. Adapted from Murray, LCL.

ship encounters a violent storm, the sailors draw lots and, when they fall on Jonah, demand that Jonah explain their fate. They try to identify him by asking questions about his significant groups, in this case his geographical and ethnic origins and occupation.

> So they [the sailors] said to him [Jonah], "Tell us who brought this disaster on us? What is your occupation? Where do you come from? What is your country and who are your kin?"

CITY-STATE COLLECTIVISM

5. PLUTARCH, *ON THE DELAYS OF DIVINE VENGEANCE* 559D

Plutarch, the Greek historian, moral philosopher, essayist, and biographer (ca. 45–120 CE) compared the character of a city to a family unit whose likenesses are inherited from a common ancestor.

> And if a city is a single, continuous, concrete reality, that is doubtless also true of a family. With a single origin, a certain power and inseparable commonality take hold, making it unlike some artistic creation he wishes to get rid of as if it were not his. . . . For what is begotten originated from him and has not been disconnected from him. Thus, it carries within itself a share of what is his, whether that is properly punished or honored.[4]

6. DIONYSIUS OF HALICARNASSUS, *ROMAN ANTIQUITIES* 6.86.2–4

The body, with its many inseparable parts, was commonly cited as an analogy for the unity of the city, as illustrated by the following quotation from the Greek historian and rhetorician Dionysius of Halicarnassus (a city in Asia Minor, now western Turkey), whose *Roman Antiquities* was written about 7 CE (cf. 1 Cor 12:12–27).

> In some ways, the human body is similar to a city: a composite of many parts in which no part has the same function as the others, or can, on its own, produce what is needed. So then, if the parts of the human body should each gain a perception and voice of their own, and factions appear among them, the whole joining against the stomach alone, and if the feet might say that they carry the entire body, and the hands that they do the skilled labor and provide the necessary things,

4. Adapted from De Lacy, LCL.

and fight the wars, and supply many other good things to the group, and the shoulders that they carry everything themselves, and the mouth that it speaks up, and the head that it sees, hears, and has a comprehension of all the other senses through which it preserves the thing, then these might say to the stomach: You, O soothsayer, which of these things do you do? Or what is your benefit or favor to us? . . . So then, think about the same situation in a city. It too is made up of many kinds of people who are not all alike. Each one contributes a particular thing to the common good in the same way the parts do for a body. Some farm the fields, some fight the wars concerning them, others do much useful trading via the sea, and some work at the necessary skilled labor.[5]

KINSHIP AND HOUSEHOLD COLLECTIVISM

7. PHILO, *ON THE UNCHANGEABLENESS OF GOD* 17

According to levirate law in ancient Israel (Deut 25:5–10), it was a brother's duty to marry the widow of his deceased brother to ensure that there would be children in the family and clan and the property would remain as an inheritance within the family (an economic motive). According to Genesis, Onan did not live up to his levirate duty regarding his brother Er's widow, instead "spilling his semen on the ground" (*coitus interruptus*). For some unknown deed, Yahweh had punished Er by death and now so punished Onan (Gen 38:1–11). Centuries later, the Judean philosopher Philo of Alexandria (20 BCE–50 CE) interpreted the story allegorically as an example of individualistic self-seeking that did not benefit the laws, customs, and religion of family and country.

> For if any are altogether self-seeking in everything they do, not honoring parents, not requiring decent behavior of their children, disregarding the security of their country, not maintaining the laws or safekeeping proper customs, not setting right private or public matters, not celebrating the sacred rites, not turning toward proper reverence of God, demonic evil shall come to them.[6]

8. PHILO, *ON THE UNCHANGEABLENESS OF GOD* 19

Philo of Alexandria criticized anyone who placed the individual self above family and country—and even the world, the creation, and the heavenly Father.

5. Adapted from Cary, LCL.
6. Adapted from Colson, LCL.

For we must indeed reject all the ones producing offspring for themselves, the ones chasing only their own profit and looking down on others, as if born only for themselves and not for countless others: for father, mother, wife, children, country, and all humankind. And if it is necessary to add or explain anything further, also for heaven, for earth, for the whole world, for knowledge, for virtues, for the Father and leader of all, being obligated to all for what is their just due, not assuming all things an appendage of himself, but considering himself an appendage of all.[7]

9. PHILO, *ON THE SPECIAL LAWS* 1.68

Philo of Alexandria believed that belonging to one's groups—kin, friend, and compatriot—is more important than even religion itself.

For the one intending to offer an unpolluted sacrifice would never leave fatherland, friends, or kin group to live abroad, but being held by a stronger attraction than piety would clearly remain with his accustomed group and closest friends who are essentially parts of himself.[8]

RELIGIOUS COLLECTIVISM

10. JOSEPHUS, *AGAINST APION* 2.195–96

In defending the antiquity of the Judeans against the anti-Judean philosopher and rhetorician Apion of Alexandria, the Judean historian Josephus (ca. 37–100 CE) argued that prayers for the people as a whole take precedence over prayers for oneself and are rewarded because there is one God common to all.

Our sacrifices are not occasions for drunken self-indulgence—such practices are abhorrent to God—but for sobriety. At these sacrifices, prayers for the welfare of the community must take precedence of those for ourselves; for we are born for fellowship, and he who sets its claims above his private interests is especially acceptable to God.[9]

11. TOBIT 4:12–13

The book of Tobit, an originally Aramaic work of fiction from the fourth to the third century BCE and now in translation in the Greek version of the Hebrew

---

7. Adapted from Colson, LCL.
8. Adapted from Colson, LCL.
9. Adapted from Thackeray, LCL.

Bible called the Septuagint, contains Judean customs about family, marriage, burial, meals, patriarchs, and concern for the poor. The following selection comes from the scene portraying Tobit's deathbed words to his son and heir, Tobias (a "testament"). Having told Tobias to care for his aging mother, bury her beside him, act justly, and give alms to the poor, he continues with fatherly advice about not engaging in illicit sex and especially not taking a wife from outside one's kinship group.

> Son, avoid every kind of sexual immorality, and above all take a wife from the seed of your ancestors; and do not take for your wife a foreigner, who is not from the tribe of your fathers, because we are descended from the prophets. Remember, son, that Noah, Abraham, Isaac, and Jacob, our ancient forefathers, all took wives from among their kin and were blessed in their descendants, and their offspring will inherit the land. So now, son, love your own people and do not have contempt in your heart for your kin, the sons and daughters of your people, declining to take wives for yourself from among them, because in arrogant superiority there is destruction and much instability, and failure to act leads to despair and great poverty, for "sloth is the mother of famine."

12. 1 MACCABEES 1:10–15, 41–43, 62 (LXX 1:11–15, 41–43, 62)

A generation after the death of Alexander ("the Great") of Macedonia (356–323 BCE), Palestine was controlled first by the Ptolemies of Egypt (301–198 BCE) and then by the Seleucids (198–167 BCE). Some Judeans were initially attracted to Hellenistic Greek culture, but when the Seleucid king Antiochus IV Epiphanes ("[God] Manifest") imposed on his client kingdoms the tribute demanded from him by Rome and forced on the Judeans Greek religion and customs, many Judeans revolted under Maccabean leadership in 167 BCE. In recounting these events, the ancient Judean historian of 1 Maccabees wrote that some Judeans assimilated to Hellenistic ways, but others, like the Maccabees, held firmly to their ancestral beliefs, even if it led to martyrdom.

> In those days [of Antiochus IV Epiphanes], Israelite men who did not keep the law appeared and deceived many people, saying, "Let us go and make a covenant with the gentiles who surround us, because many bad things have happened to us since we separated ourselves from them." This plan was considered to be a good one, and some of the people, determined to carry it out, went to the king, and he gave them authority to implement the customs of the gentiles. So they constructed a gymnastic school in Jerusalem according to the design of the gentiles, made foreskins for themselves to reverse their circumcisions, withdrew from the

holy covenant, joined themselves together with the gentiles, and sold themselves to do evil. . . .

And the king [Antiochus IV Epiphanes] issued a proclamation throughout his whole kingdom that all should become one people and that each should abandon his customs. All the gentiles accepted the king's command and many from Israel preferred his form of worship, sacrificed to idols, and profaned the Sabbath. . . .

However, many in Israel were strengthened and were fortified within themselves not to eat unclean food. Indeed, they accepted death rather than be defiled by food or profane the holy covenant—and they died.

VOLUNTARY COLLECTIVISM

13. *CIL* 6.26032

Scribonia (68 BCE–16 CE) was the second wife of Caesar Augustus (who reigned 27 BCE–14 CE), the mother-in-law of the emperor Tiberius, the great-grandmother of the emperor Gaius Caligula, grandmother-in-law of the emperor Claudius, and great-great-grandmother of the emperor Nero. The following funerary inscription illustrates a domestic voluntary association in which the members of Scribonia's household, or extended family, including freed slaves, are buried together with her.

The household of Scribonia Caesar together with her freedmen and freedwomen have gathered together [are buried] in this monument.

14. RULE OF THE COMMUNITY (1QS) V, 1–7A

The Rule of the Community (*yachad*) from the Dead Sea Scrolls contains the requirements of a male "voluntary association" that, led by rebel priests who claimed descent from the ancient high priest Zadok, considered itself to be the truly pure and obedient Israel in contrast to disobedient Israelites and gentiles. The following selection illustrates the group's hierarchical order and community norms; most importantly, it gives a dire warning against individual human desires that threaten to pollute the whole community—thus, the necessity "to circumcise the foreskin of [evil] inclination and [to relax] the stiffness of the neck," a common image in the Bible (Deut 10:16; cf. Acts 7:51).

And this is the rule for the men of the community who freely volunteer to turn away from all evil and to strengthen all that he according to his pleasure has commanded. They are to separate themselves from the congregation of the men of perversion and become a community of law and possessions. They are to sit under the authority of the sons of Zadok, the priests, the keepers of the covenant, and under the authority of the men of the community who strictly observe the covenant. Under their authority, every decision shall be determined by lot about everything pertaining to the law, riches, and judgment. They are to practice truth combined with humility, righteousness, and justice, and they are to perform loving-kindness and walk humbly in all their ways; and no man shall walk in the stubbornness of his heart and fall prey to his heart, his eyes, and the thoughts of his [evil] inclination. It follows that in the community, they are to circumcise the foreskin of inclination and [relax] the stiffness of the neck in order to lay a foundation of truth for Israel, for the community of the eternal covenant. They are to atone for all those who freely volunteer for the holy in Aaron, the house of truth in Israel, and for the joiners in community with them, and to bring a lawsuit and judgment against anyone who is guilty of transgressing a statute.[10]

FRIENDSHIP AND DYADISM

15. CICERO, *ON FRIENDSHIP* 23

An excellent example of ancient Mediterranean dyadism was true friendship (1 Sam 18:1–5; Plato, *Symposium*). It was important to distinguish a true friend from a mere flatterer (see **chap. 16, Friendship and Gifts**). The following excerpt comes from an essay/dialogue titled (*Laelius*) *On Friendship* (44/45 BCE) by the Roman orator, lawyer, politician, and philosopher Marcus Tullius Cicero (ca. 106–43 BCE). Dedicated to his friend Atticus, Cicero emphasized that true friendship among humans is rare and can exist only among two, or at most a few, compatriots; indeed, its absence threatens the stability of households and cities, thus society itself. Cicero also observed that friendship has many benefits and that a life without the mutual love of friends is not worth living.

> Furthermore, if you remove the ties of friendship from the natural order of things, not one house or city will be able to stand, in fact no cultivation of fields will endure. If this [statement] sounds silly, think about how great are friendship and harmony by considering the possibility of being overcome by dissension and discord. For example, what household is so stable, what city is so strong, that it cannot be turned upside down at its very foundation by animosities and disagreements? From this it can be determined what great good there is in friendship.[11]

10. Martínez, *The Dead Sea Scrolls Translated*.
11. Adapted from Falconer, LCL.

STEREOTYPING

16. OVID, *SORROWS* 5.10.29–38

The Roman rhetorician and poet Ovid (Publius Ovidius Naso, 43 BCE–17/18 CE) was for some unknown reason banished by the emperor Augustus in 8 CE to the remote Greek colony of Tomis on the western shore of the Black Sea (in modern Romania). Far from his beloved Rome and his friends, he wrote with sadness of his harsh, trying exile. In the following passage, Ovid complains of having to live side by side with the Getae, one of the Thracian tribes whose rugged appearance, dress, and language offended his cultural sensitivities. The passage illustrates Greek and Roman stereotypes about other peoples, whom they labeled "barbarians" (see vocabulary list).

> We are scarcely protected by the defenses of the fortress, and yet inside it, there is a hubbub in a barbarian tongue mixed with Greek speech [that] produces apprehension. We live right next to the barbarians with no space between [us], and they are in possession of a greater number of dwellings. You might not be afraid of them, but you would despise looking at their chests covered with animal hides and their long hair. Those who are believed to have been born in a city of the Greeks hide it by wearing Persian pants in place of the clothing common to their native land. They carry on their daily affairs in their common language; I have to communicate using gestures. Here I am the one who is a barbarian, understood by nobody; the Getae laugh idiotically at Latin words.[12]

17. STRABO, *GEOGRAPHY* 1.2.34

Strabo (64/63 BCE–24 CE), a Greek geographer, philosopher, and historian, was favorably impressed with Posidonius's theory that peoples who are geographically contiguous and have similar languages, customs, and physical features can also have similar-sounding names: Armenians, Arammaeans [Syrians], Arabians, and Erembians. From this perspective, ethnic identity, physical proximity, and group names are interrelated (see **chap. 8, Space; chap. 18, Deviance**).

> In this case, Posidonius seems to be right in relating the etymologies [of the similar-sounding names] of peoples to their kinship and common features since the people of the Armenians and that of the Syrians and Arabians appear to be very much the same tribe with respect to their language, their ways of living, and their physical features, and mostly because they are neighboring regions, [although their different climates in the north, the south, and in between contribute to some variations]. . . . Also, both

---

12. Adapted from Wheeler, LCL.

the Assyrians and the Arians have in some ways a great similarity to them and to each other. Indeed, Posidonius supposes that the names of these peoples also bear a resemblance to each other. For those whom we call "Syrians" are called "Arammaeans" by the Syrians themselves; and similar to this [are the names of] the "Armenians" and the "Arabians" and "Erembians," [a name] the Greeks of long ago possibly called the Arabians, and therefore the etymology reinforces his theory.[13]

18. TACITUS, HISTORIES 5.4–5

Tacitus, a Roman historian who wrote about 110 CE, echoed a commonly held opinion about the origin of the Judeans, that they were lepers who had been expelled from Egypt. In his description of them, he offered several negative stereotypes: their laziness, greed, sexuality, and strange and repulsive religious customs.

Moses, wanting to establish himself over his people forever, introduced a new religious cult that is totally different from any found in the rest of humanity. All things that are sacred among us are profane to them and, contrariwise, things that are pure to them are polluted among us.... They avoid pigs because of their memory of a most awful plague, a certain itching that had polluted them, for which they hold the animal to be responsible. By frequent fasts, they still bear witness to a protracted famine [that happened] long ago, and the produce they hurriedly carried off they remember by a sign, Judean bread without yeast. On the seventh day, they love to rest, because this day will have brought an end of their toils; thereafter, allured by the pleasure of laziness, the seventh year also has been set aside for idleness.... This cult, having been introduced, is justified by its antiquity; other customs, perverse and detestable, have gained strength because of their depravity. For some of the worst of them, despising the religion of their homeland, collect tributes and monetary gifts, whence the wealth of the Judeans increases; and because there is a stubborn trust and open compassion among themselves, but a hostile animosity toward all others, they separate themselves at banquets, and do not sleep in the same bed, although as a people they are especially inclined to lust. They abstain from having sexual relations with foreign women, but among themselves nothing is prohibited. They have adopted circumcision of their genitalia in order to be perceived as different. Those who convert to their way of life adopt the same practices and are soon indoctrinated in how to despise the gods, renounce their country, and hold [their] parents, children, and brothers [to be] of little value.... The religion of the Judeans is irrational and disgusting.[14]

13. Adapted from Jones, LCL.
14. Adapted from Moore, LCL.

19. VERGIL, *AENEID* 2.65

Mediterranean stereotypes are well illustrated by a number of examples of ancient insults and humor.

> If you know one [Greek], you know them all.[15]

20. TITUS 1:12

The New Testament letter to Titus, likely written by an anonymous "Pauline" follower late in the first century, purports to be addressed to Paul's coworker Titus who has been left on the island of Crete to assist the congregation there with issues of theology and leadership. The letter repeats this saying attributed to the (perhaps mythical?) Cretan sage and poet Epimenides, who is said to have lived in Knossos during the sixth century BCE. It typifies the ancient/collectivist habit of stereotyping people based on place of origin.

> Cretans always lie, are evil beasts and idle gluttons.

Vocabulary of Collectivism

HEBREW

בַּיִת (*bayit*) . . . . house
גּוֹי (*goy*) . . . . people, nation
חֲבוּרָה (*khavurah*) . . . . fellowship
מִשְׁפָּחָה (*mishpakhah*) . . . . family
קָהָל (*qahal*) . . . . assembly, congregation
שֵׁבֶט (*shevet*) . . . . tribe

GREEK

βάρβαρος, -ov (*barbaros, -on*) . . . . foreign, barbarian
ἔθνος (*ethnos*) . . . . kind, people
ἐκκλησία (*ekklēsia*) . . . . assembly, group
γένος (*genos*) . . . . people, nation
κοινωνία (*koinōnia*) . . . . participation, sharing, agreement

15. Adapted from Fairclough, LCL.

οἶκος (*oikos*) . . . . house, tribe
φυλή (*phylē*) . . . . tribe
συναγωγή (*synagōgē*) . . . . gathering, synagogue

LATIN

collegium . . . . guild, society, group
domus . . . . building, home, house
gens . . . . people, nation
familia . . . . family, school, estate

Select Bibliography

Albera, Dionigi, and Anton Blok. "Introduction: The Mediterranean as a Field of Ethnological Study; A Retrospective." Pages 15–37 in *L'anthropologie de la Méditerranée: Anthropology of the Mediterranean*. Edited by Dionigi Albera, Anton Blok, and Christian Bromberger. Paris: Maisonneuve & Larose, 2001.

Hofstede, Geert, Gert Jan Hofstede, and Michael Minkov. *Cultures and Organizations: Software of the Mind*. 3rd ed. New York: McGraw-Hill, 2010.

Malina, Bruce J. "Collectivism in Mediterranean Culture." Pages 17–28 in *Understanding the Social World of the New Testament*. Edited by Dietmar Neufeld and Richard E. DeMaris. London: Routledge, 2009–2010.

———. "Is There a Circum-Mediterranean Person? Looking for Stereotypes." *BTB* 22 (1992): 66–87.

Triandis, Harry C., and Eunkook M. Suh. "Cultural Influences on Personality." *Annual Review of Psychology* 53 (2002): 133–60.

Additional Texts

ETHNIC COLLECTIVISM

Acts 2:9–11; 13:21; 16:14
Caesar, *Gallic Wars* 1.40.9; 3.14.4; 4.16.7; 4.17.10
Genesis 49

Hebrews 7:13–14
Herodotus, *Histories* 9.122.3
Hippocrates, *Airs, Waters, and Places* 16, 24

Isaiah 9:1–2
Josephus, *Jewish Antiquities* 18.23–25
Luke 2:36
Mark 3:8
Matthew 4:15–16
Philippians 3:5

Pliny the Elder, *Natural History* 4.29
Revelation 7:4–9; 13:7; 14:6
Romans 11:1
Tacitus, *Annals* 2.21; 3.21; 4.47; 6.31–32;
    12.35; *Germany* 1–4, 15–18

CITY-STATE COLLECTIVISM

Acts 21:37
Aristotle, *Politics* 1252a1–22

Plato, *Republic* 368c–369c, 433–435d,
    441c–442d
Stobaeus, *Anthology* 2.7

KINSHIP AND HOUSEHOLD COLLECTIVISM

Acts 10:6; 16:14; 21:39
Aristotle, *Politics* 1252a1–22; *Rhetoric*
    1390b1–1391b32
1 Chronicles 2:1–55
CIL 6.21096, 21715
Colossians 3:18–4:1
1 Corinthians 5:1–2
Deuteronomy 5:16; 21:18–21; 25:5–10
Dio Cassius, *Roman History* 16
Ephesians 5:21–6:9
2 Esdras 3:21
Exodus 20:12
Genesis 5:1–32; 10:1–32; 22:1–19; 25:5–6,
    19–26; 49:29–33; 50:4–14
Herodotus, *Histories* 8.139
Homer, *Odyssey* 6.175–85
John 8:19
Josephus, *Life* 1; *Jewish Antiquities*
    17.12–16; 18.130–41

Leviticus 18
Luke 3:23–38; 9:57–60; 15:11–32
1 Maccabees 4:30
2 Maccabees 7:22–23, 27b–29
Mark 3:17; 6:3; 7:10; 15:21
Matthew 1:1–16; 16:17
Ovid, *Metamorphoses* 7
1 Peter 2:18–3:7
Philo, *On the Special Laws* 3.12–13, 22–25
Plutarch, *Advice to Bride and Groom*;
    Consolation to His Wife
Proverbs 4:1; 7:2
Ruth 3–4
Stobaeus, *Anthology* 2.7
Suetonius, *Galba* 2–3; *Nero* 1
Tacitus, *Annals* 3.25; 6.19
1 Timothy 2:9–15
Tobit 4:3–4

RELIGIOUS COLLECTIVISM

Acts 2:44–47; 4:32–37; 5:1–16
CIL 6.467, 2233

Ephesians 5:1–20
Galatians 3:23–29

IJO 2.26, 44, 206
John 7:15
Josephus, *Jewish Antiquities* 13.171–72,
    297–98; 14.259–61; 18.11–22; *Jewish
    War* 2.119–61, 284–88; 7.44
1 Maccabees 2:42; 7:8–18
Matthew 9:11; 23:23–26
Philo, *On the Contemplative Life* 2.10–
    3.33; *On the Embassy to Gaius* 132–34,
    137–38, 155–58, 164–65, 191; *That*

Every Good Person Is Free 12.75–91;
    Against Flaccus 41–50
Pliny the Elder, *Natural History*
    5.15.73–81
Romans 8:28–30
Rule of the Community (1QS);
    4QRule of the Community
    (4QS^{a-j}=4Q255–264); 5Q11; 5Q13
Theodotus Inscription (Rockefeller
    Museum, Jerusalem)

VOLUNTARY COLLECTIVISM

Acts 9:43; 10:6, 32; 19:23–41
IEph 22, 215, 425, 454, 457, 719, 800,
    1161–67, 2213, 2402, 3079
IG II.5 1335b; *IG* XII¹ 867
IGladiators 200, 201
IGLSkythia 2.2.153
IGRR 4.548, 788–89, 1114, 1128
IHierapJ 36, 41, 50

IKilikiaHW 2.193–201
ISaitt 26, 28
ISmyrna 715
ITralles 79
Josephus, *Jewish Antiquities* 15.370;
    Jewish War 2.567
P.Rylands 4.604

FRIENDSHIP AND DYADISM

Cicero, *On Friendship* 26–27, 44–46
2 Esdras 7:102–5
Horace, *Satires* 1.5.44
James 2:23; 4:4
John 19:12
1 Maccabees 10:20; 15:32
Patronius, *Satyricon* 80

Philemon 1
Philo, *Against Flaccus* 40
Plutarch, *How to Tell a Flatterer from a
    Friend*; *Love* 754d
Seneca, *Moral Letters* 3
Sirach 18; 22:20–22; 27:16–17; 37:1–2

STEREOTYPING

Cicero, *For Flaccus* 9–10, 12, 17, 19, 65;
    Tusculan Disputations 1.1
Diodorus Siculus, *Library of History*
    5.26; 28

Herodotus, *Histories*, 1.1; 1.94.1; 3.38.1–4;
    4.2.1–2; 4.17.1; 5.78.1
John 1:46; 4:9
Josephus, *Against Apion* 2.121–24

Justin, *First Apology* 26; *Second Apology* 12

Juvenal, *Satires* 14

Lucian, *The Passing of Perigrinus* 11–13

Marcellinus, *History* 22.16.23

Martial, *Epigrams* 7.30.4

Origen, *Against Celsus* 3.44, 55–57

Petronius, *Fragments* 37; *Satyricon* 102.14

Philostratus, *Life of Apollonius* 5.33

Pliny the Younger, *Letters* 10.96–97

Plutarch, *Cicero* 7.3–8.2

Porphyry, *On Abstinence* 2.26

Strabo, *Geography* 4.4.5

Tacitus, *Annals* 15.44; *Histories* 5.5.2; *Agricola* 11.30

Tertullian, *Against Marcion* 3.6, 8

7. Gossip

DIETMAR NEUFELD AND JOHN W. DANIELS JR.

Introduction

Speech (talking) was the principal vehicle for the fabrication and dissemination of information in ancient Mediterranean societies. Whether news about the comings and goings of an emperor or the son of a peasant artisan, or a public discussion about the character of a certain individual, or even the execution of an infamous outlaw, word of mouth was the primary and preferred mode by which one came to knowledge about significant or strange events and made sense of civic and religious officials, neighbors (near and far), or kin. Thus, the content and character of information conveyed orally, especially about another group of people or an individual, often resulted in the formation of stereotypes and social identity (see **chap. 6, Collectivism**). Indeed, the distribution of the pivotal value of honor was initiated by conversation if the information that was transacted carried any valence (see **chap. 4, Honor; chap. 5, Shame**).

As it is, and has been across centuries and cultures, the peculiar kind of speech called *gossip* was part and parcel of the ancient Mediterranean world. As a genre of speech, gossip is discussed by ancient Greco-Roman authors and in ancient Israelite religious literature, including the Hebrew Bible and the New Testament. By and large, gossip was viewed in antiquity much like it is today—as divisive, dangerous, and flippant talk, often portrayed in the literature primarily as feminine discourse, even though it was practiced as much, or perhaps even more, by men (see **chap. 9, Gender**). Gossip is also depicted "in action" in ancient narratives. Sometimes, descriptions of a healthy gossip network are on offer, while elsewhere, characters are portrayed engaging vigorously in gossip. In fact, gossip is often implied in narratives to such an extent that it functions as a crucial motivator of a plot or storyline.

What we know about gossip in ancient Mediterranean societies is not only informed by the literature, but also by modern ethnographic research of "traditional" cultures/societies within the Mediterranean culture continent. In other words, by studying the sociocultural matrices of a "traditional Greek mountain village," one can learn a lot about the role and function of speech, including gossip, within such societies. Considering both sources of information—ancient literature and modern ethnographies—it becomes quite clear that the ancient Mediterranean world was a very gossipy world indeed.

According to psychologists and sociologists, and as it is often observed by ethnographers, gossip comprises evaluative, face-to-face speech between persons (or among groups) about an absent subject (individual or group). Such speech may evaluate its subject either negatively or, contrary to a typical view of gossip, positively. It is *face-to-face* discourse insofar as discussants are familiar, or "intimate," with one another somehow—connected perhaps by kinship or even social status—and engaging one another on a regular basis at social functions, in commerce, or occupation, or even in daily conversation in the village square. The subject of gossip (typically an individual) is usually absent and so out of "earshot." However, in peculiar and particularly agonistic situations, the subject may be rendered absent by several means, including physical gestures, body positioning, tone, and inflection, all the while remaining within earshot. Such instances are signaled in narratives by descriptions of groups "turning toward one another," "murmuring among themselves," or talking (gossiping) about the subject in the third person while he or she is standing right there.

Gossip has four social functions: friendship (intimacy), entertainment, information control, and influence. Gossip is also understood as a collective effort to make sense of an individual subject's words or deeds that animate the evaluative discourse. Gossip may arise among bored social familiars to entertain and so may not be intended to generate any significant social repercussions for the subject.

Alternatively, when gossip emerges during times of uncertainty and in agonistic interactions, it may have significant consequences, as it functions to evaluate a subject either positively or negatively. Gossip can thus be utilized by an individual to control information and so influence how a subject is perceived. Hence, the talk can either smear someone's reputation, if negative (see **chap. 19, Mockery and Secrecy; chap. 18, Deviance**), or bolster one's reputation (honor), if positive, and so play a pivotal role in constructing social identity. As information control, gossip may be initiated by someone to generate information about a subject in an attempt to influence the collective construction of a person's social identity, again either positively or negatively. Consequently, gossip often influences people (potential subjects) by "policing behavior" and so enforcing social conformity among groups.

Gossip has numerous trigger points, especially things people say and do, that challenge or affirm a society's sociocultural script. Gossip thus functions either to (re)affirm or reimagine the established social map and the subject's place (status) in it. This underscores gossip's role in remembering and making sense of significant events (words or deeds), while assessing the character of both the subject and the subject's words or deeds.

Trading in evaluative information often in the absence of the subject, gossip is closely related to the two concepts of self-regard (honor and shame) and can result in the distribution of either honor or shame onto an individual. Gossip operates frequently as a form of envy-aggression (see **chap. 17, Limited Good and Envy**), generated by a subject's good fortune or public grasp at reputation, or honor. In such cases, after saying or doing something unexpected, a subject may be rendered absent somehow, while the negative gossip is intended by the gossipers to be overheard by both the subject and everyone else around. In this way, the talk functions as a challenge (or counterchallenge) to a subject's unusual activity—words or deeds—that destabilizes the social status quo. So when Jesus is remembered in John's Gospel publicly claiming to be of heavenly origin (honor claim), those who overhear him *challenge* his claim, gossiping openly about his lineage (an insult in the Mediterranean world), using third-person speech (John 6:41–42). Jesus, of course, responds immediately to this challenging gossip here and elsewhere in John, as well as in the Synoptic Gospels.

Ancient Texts

EVALUATING GOSSIP, GOSSIPING, AND GOSSIPERS

1. LUCIAN, *SLANDER* 1

Lucian (ca. 125–180 CE) was a Greek rhetorician who, although well versed in persuasive oratory, is most well-known for his satire, which often comes out in his early rhetorical writing. In his rhetorical essay *Slander*, Lucian reflects on the ignorance displayed by characters of Greek tragedy. Here he focuses specifically on negatively evaluative speech, translated below as "slander," that clearly carries all the necessary earmarks of negative gossip that can have disastrous social outcomes.

I refer primarily to slanderous talk about familiars and friends, by which households have been upset, and cities completely destroyed, fathers driven mad against their children, and children against parents, and lover against beloved. Both many friendships have been severed and many oaths thwarted by the persuasion of slander.[1]

2. Plutarch, *On Being a Busybody* 519b

Plutarch (46–120 CE) was a Greek historian and essayist who excelled at composing, among other things, many splendid biographies. Some of his most important writings, written in the last decades of his life, were moral reflections on living. The following text underscores the appetites of inveterate gossips constantly seeking unsavory (negative) information to pass on.

As cooks pray for a crop of animals, and fishermen for fish, in this way busybodies pray for a crop of wickedness and a multitude of troubles, novelties, and changes, so that they might always have something to catch or butcher.[2]

3. Plato, *Crito* 44d

Plato (428–348 BCE) was a Greek philosopher, born in Athens into an aristocratic family. Some of his most influential work emerged during his early philosophical period (ca. 399–388 BCE) when, in nurturing the memory of Socrates (d. 399 BCE), he wrote many dialogues, including the *Crito*. In it, Plato underscores the social function of gossip as censuring behavior—in this case, the content of Socrates's teaching to the youth of Athens—when appealing to Socrates to escape from prison (see **chap. 18, Deviance**).

But you see it a necessity, O Socrates, to care about the opinion of the many, as is clear in this situation we now are in; they are able to bring about, by no small means, the greatest of evils, if one is slandered by them.[3]

4. Basil, *Letters* 22

One of the great Cappadocian fathers, Basil of Caesarea (330–379 CE) was bishop of Caesarea in the Roman province of Cappadocia. In his twenty-second letter, Basil encourages what he understands to be good Christian behavior. This portion of the letter warns against slanderous gossip but interestingly conveys that gossip can, in fact, convey the truth.

---

1. Adapted from Harmon, LCL.
2. Adapted from Helmbold, LCL.
3. Adapted from Fowler, LCL.

One [a Christian] ought not speak against a brother to slander him, since even if what is spoken is true, it is slander nevertheless. One ought to turn from the one who slanders a brother. One ought not talk frivolously. One ought not laugh or put up with jokesters. One ought not talk idly, chatting of things that are not useful—neither to listeners nor to things necessary and allowed to us by God.[4]

5. Eusebius, *Ecclesiastical History* 5.18
Eusebius of Caesarea (ca. 260–340 CE), a native of Caesarea Maritima, became bishop of Caesarea in 314 CE. Eusebius's *Ecclesiastical History* accounts for the history of early Christianity from its beginnings to the fourth century CE. The text below relates how a prominent Montanist named Themiso, who boasted of being a martyr even though he was never even a confessor, dared to write an epistle—in imitation of Paul—apparently instructing those loyal to dishonor the Lord with their words.

[I]mitating the apostle, [Themiso] composed a catholic epistle, intending to instruct those with faith better than his, to argue with vain talk and profane speech against the Lord, the apostles, and the holy church.[5]

6. Tibullus, *Incerti Auctoris* 19
Tibullus (ca. 48–19 BCE) has been described as a Roman elegiac poet, perhaps of the equestrian rank, famous for his love of poetry. The text below is from a poem that was part of a collection of miscellaneous poetry from the household of Marcus Messalla Corvinus, a patron of Tibullus—but not actually written by Tibullus himself. Here the poet seems to feign regret for the passionate bondage his gossipy speech has gotten him into.

Now will you be strong! Now will you boldly consume me [with passion]! This pitiable torment brought on by my prating tongue.[6]

7. Proverbs 16:27–28
The book of Proverbs is one of several texts comprising the Israelite wisdom tradition of the Hebrew Bible. Traditionally understood to have been written by King Solomon, the book is constituted by, among other things, dramatic personification of the "Wisdom Woman" and the "Strange Woman," and by a

4. Adapted from Defarrari, LCL.
5. Adapted from Lake, LCL.
6. Adapted from Postgate, LCL.

large collection of proverbial sayings imagined as advice from a father to his son. The text below advises against gossip and accentuates the social divisiveness of such talk (see **chap. 16, Friendship and Gifts**).

> A corrupt man digs for evil, and his lips are a fire. A wayward man spawns division, and a gossiper breaks friendships apart.

8. Achilles Tatius, *Leucippe and Clitophon* 6.10

Achilles Tatius was a Greek novelist of the second century CE. His writing *Leucippe and Clitophon* is a first-person adventure (told by Clitophon) describing how two lovers fall into the hands of pirates. In the excerpt below, the character Melite begins a lengthy rant on gossip in light of the talk about her caring for a shipwrecked fellow.

> Gossip and slander are two wicked siblings: Gossip is the daughter of slander. Slander is sharper than a blade, more violent than fire, more persuasive than sirens; Gossip is more fluid than water, faster than the wind, flies quicker than birds.[7]

9. b. Arakhin 15b

The Babylonian Talmud is the authoritative collection of Rabbinic traditions, laws, and teachings spanning seven centuries (ca. 200 BCE–500 CE). It incorporates rabbinic discussions (Gemara) on the text of the Mishnah. The text below, from Tractate Bavli Arachin ("vows"), illustrates the social dynamic involved in gossiping, as it identifies some of the necessary elements of such talk—the gossiper, the listener(s), and the subject.

> Gossip kills three persons: the person who tells it, the person who receives it, and the person whom it is about.[8]

10. Dio Chrysostom, *Reputation* (*Or.* 66) 23

Dio Chrysostom (ca. 40–115 CE) was a philosopher and rhetorician born in the Roman province of Bithynia in Asia Minor. His name "Chrysostom," which means "golden mouthed," was given to him because of the eloquence of his discourse. In his sixty-sixth speech (discourse), after lamenting the human desire to be the topic of "empty-headed" public discourse, Dio praises the strength of those who ignore such speech, despite its power to construe social identity.

---

7. Adapted from Gaselee, LCL.

8. Adapted from Isidore Epstein, ed., *Hebrew-English Edition of the Babylonian Talmud: 'Arakin* (London: Soncino, 1989).

[H]e who is uninhibited pays no attention to the foolish talk of the many; rather he laughs at their chattering, having long ago proclaimed to them all: "I care not; it's like a woman threw [something at] me, or a senseless child; for dull is the arrow of a feeble, impotent man."[9]

GOSSIP AND GENDER

11. ANDOCIDES, *ON THE MYSTERIES* 130

Andocides (ca. 440–390 BCE) was an Athenian orator and politician. He is remembered for holding a peculiarly liberal, anti-religious stance that eventually led to his participation in the defacing of the busts of Hermes throughout Athens to curse the Athenian expedition to Sicily during the Peloponnesian war. In his speech *On the Mysteries*, gossip is described as the frivolous, entertaining, and meaningless talk of children and women (see **chap. 9, Gender**).

> [T]hen, indeed, a tale familiar to you all, uttered by insignificant little boys and women ranging over the entire city: That Hipponikos has a wicked being [wicked spirit] in his house that overturns his table.[10]

12. VERGIL, *AENEID* 4.173–75

Vergil (70–19 BCE) was one of the greatest poets of Roman antiquity, whose works are remembered by some for reaching a nearly sacred status in Rome. Born in Gaul, Vergil would eventually study rhetoric and philosophy in Rome. His epic poem *Aeneid* tells the story of the founding of Rome by Aeneas. The text below describes the tenacity and voraciousness of gossip, gendered as female speech, growing over time and much talk.

> Straightaway, talk flies through Libya's great cities. Talk! An evil of which nothing is swifter, thriving by speed, she acquires strength as she goes.[11]

13. PLAUTUS, *A FUNNY THING HAPPENED ON THE WAY TO THE WEDDING* 2.8

Titus Plautus (254–184 BCE) was a remarkably successful Roman writer of comedy, who started as a stagehand in Rome before commencing his writing career, supposedly after finding work at a mill. In his play *Casina*, or *The Strata-*

---

9. Adapted from Crosby, LCL.
10. Adapted from Maidment, LCL.
11. Adapted from Fairclough, LCL.

gem Defeated, the character Stalino asks Olympio to go to the market for some fish. Olympio then asks Stalino if he would like for him to get *lingulacas*—a word that translates either as a kind of fish (sole) or as "a gossiper." Stalino's reply to the inquiry amounts to a pun reflecting the then common gendering of gossip as feminine speech (see **chap. 9, Gender**).

> Why bother, when my wife is home? She is tongue-fish [*lingulacas*] to us, and she is never silent.[12]

14. JOHN 4:39–42
The Gospel of John is the latest of the four New Testament Gospels, composed sometime between 90 and 120 CE. In the story of Jesus's encounter with a Samaritan woman, the woman gossips to the daytime inhabitants of Sychar (presumably men in the public square), conveying that Jesus was, at least, a prophet, and this leads to their believing in Jesus because of her "word" (*logos*). But after hearing Jesus's "word" (*logos*), the Samaritans seemingly go out of their way to disparage the woman's talk.

> Many Samaritans from the town believed in him because of the woman's word, "He told me all that I have ever done." Thus, as the Samaritans came to him, they asked him to stay with them, and he stayed there two days. Many more began to believe because of his word, so they said to the woman, "We no longer believe because of your chatter (*lalia*), for we have heard for ourselves and know that this truly is the Savior of the world."

15. PLUTARCH, *TABLE TALK* 716A
Although gossip was typically associated with women in antiquity, men enjoyed gossiping as much, or even more. In his essay *Table Talk*, Plutarch recalls the words of a well-known Greek philosopher describing the common discourse in barbershops—traditionally male spaces. This would, of course, be consistent with the public life people led in antiquity (see **chap. 4, Honor; chap. 6, Collectivism; chap. 19, Mockery and Secrecy**).

> But just as Theophrastus called barbershops "wineless symposia" on account of the chitchat, so a wineless drunkenness lingers in the lives of the uneducated.[13]

12. Adapted from Nixon, LCL.
13. Adapted from Minar, LCL.

16. PLUTARCH, *ON TALKATIVENESS* 509A

After describing how it was the gossip of old men in a barber shop (505b) who leaked information to the Romans before an attack on Athens, Plutarch later offers sweeping comment about the gossipy world of barbershops and the men who frequented them.

> It is fitting that barbers are a loquacious bunch, with babblers spilling in [to their shops] and sitting, so that they themselves are filled with the habit.[14]

NARRATIVE DESCRIPTIONS OF GOSSIPING

17. JOSEPH AND ASENETH 4.12–14A

Joseph and Aseneth is a pseudepigraphic, narrative romance written sometime between the first and second centuries CE, about the Israelite patriarch Joseph's marriage to the Egyptian daughter of Potiphera, priest of On. Upon hearing her father explain his intention to hand her over to Joseph in marriage, Aseneth interrogates her father's decision with questioning gossip amounting to a vain attempt to invite her father to construe Joseph negatively, as she does.

> Why are you speaking these words, my lord and father, considering to hand me over like a prisoner to a foreigner and fugitive who was himself sold? Is this not the shepherd's son from the land of Canaan, who was abandoned [by his father]? Is this not the one who had intercourse with his mistress so his lord threw him into the prison of darkness?[15]

18. MARK 1:25–28

The Gospel of Mark is the oldest of the four canonical Gospels, written sometime around the destruction of Jerusalem and the temple (70 CE). The text below bears a vivid testimony to the prevalence and power of gossip as a social process spreading information and constructing social identity in the ancient Mediterranean world—after Jesus exorcises a demon from a man.

---

14. Adapted from Helmbold, LCL.

15. Adapted from C. Burchard, "Joseph and Aseneth," in vol. 2 of *The Old Testament Pseudepigrapha*, ed. James H. Charlesworth (Garden City, NY: Doubleday, 1985), 207.

And Jesus rebuked him, saying, "Be silent and come out of him." And the unclean spirit shook him violently and cried out in a loud voice and came out of him. And everyone was amazed and began to talk among themselves saying, "What is this? A new teaching with authority? He even orders the unclean spirits, and they obey him." And the news about him immediately went out everywhere in the whole surrounding region of Galilee.

GOSSIP AND HONOR/CHALLENGE-RIPOSTE

19. MATTHEW 23:1–7

The Gospel of Matthew was written around the mid-80s CE. While Matthew's portrait of Jesus is noted by some scholars as being the most "Jewish" of the Gospels, ironically the vitriol shared between Jesus and the Pharisees is peculiarly acute in this Gospel. Here Jesus invites both the Jerusalem crowd and his disciples to construe the Pharisees along with him (gossip!) in a rather disparaging way—and apparently with the Pharisees standing right there! Thus, Jesus's words constitute challenging gossip that was intended to be overheard and responded to by the Pharisees.

> Then Jesus spoke to the crowds and his disciples, saying, "The scribes and the Pharisees sit on Moses's seat. Then observe and do whatever they tell you, but do not do the things they do, for they talk, but they do nothing. They chain heavy burdens on the shoulders of men, but they are unwilling to lift a finger to move them. They do all their works for men to behold; they widen their phylacteries and make their fringes long. And they love the first places at banquets and the first seats in the synagogues, and greetings in the market places, and being called rabbi by men.

20. JOHN 7:25–27

As in the three Synoptic Gospels, John's Jesus is typically at odds with his opponents and sometimes with the crowds. The text below has the Jerusalem crowd first gossiping about both Jesus and the authorities who are after him, and then questioning Jesus's origins and identity in what amounts to a public challenge.

> Thus, some from Jerusalem were saying, "Is this not the man they seek to kill? But look! He is speaking openly, and yet they say nothing to him. Perhaps the rulers actually know that this man is the Christ. We know where he is from. But whenever the Christ comes, no one will know from where."

Vocabulary of Gossip

HEBREW

אָמַר (*amar*) . . . . to say, spread news
דִּבָּה (*dibbah*) . . . . slander, slanderer
רָכִיל (*rakil*) . . . . slander, gossip

GREEK

ἀπαγγέλλω (*apangellō*) . . . . to spread news, report
ἀκριτόμυθος (*akritomythos*) . . . . babbling confusedly, confused babbler
βλασφημέω (*blasphēmeō*) . . . . to insult, defame, slander
γογγύζω (*gongyzō*) . . . . to grumble, complain, gossip
διαβολή (*diabolē*) . . . . slander, calumny
θρυλέω (*thryleō*) . . . . to babble
κατάλαλος (*katalalos*) . . . . slanderer, slander, gossiper
κενοφωνία (*kenophōnia*) . . . . empty talk, foolish chatter
κληδών (*klēdōn*) . . . . tale, rumor, report
λαλιά (*lalia*) . . . . talk, chatter
λῆρος (*lēros*) . . . . nonsense
μαρτυρέω (*martyreō*) . . . . to speak well of, witness
ματαιολογία (*mataiologia*) . . . . idle or meaningless talk
μωρολογία (*mōrologia*) . . . . stupid talk
φλύαρος (*phlyaros*) . . . . slander, gossip
ψιθυρισμός (*psithyrismos*) . . . . gossiper, whisperer

LATIN

calumnia . . . . slander
crimen . . . . blame, reproach, slander
fama . . . . talk, rumor
garrulus . . . . babbling, chattering, talkative
lingulaca . . . . gossip, chatterbox

Select Bibliography

Daniels, John W. *Gossiping Jesus: The Oral Processing of Jesus in John's Gospel*. Eugene, OR: Pickwick, 2013.

Du Boulay, Juliet. *Portrait of the Greek Mountain Village*. Oxford Monographs on Social Anthropology. Oxford: Clarendon, 1974.

Gluckman, Max. "Gossip and Scandal." *Current Anthropology* 4 (1963): 307–16.

Kartzow, Marianne. *Gossip and Gender: The Othering of Speech in the Pastoral Epistles*. Berlin: de Gruyter, 2009.

Rohrbaugh, Richard L. "Gossip in the New Testament." Pages 239–59 in *Social Scientific Models for Interpreting the Bible: Essays by the Context Group in Honor of Bruce J. Malina*. Edited by John J. Pilch. Leiden: Brill, 2001.

Van Eck, Ernest. "Invitations and Excuses That Are Not Invitations and Excuses: Gossip in Luke 14:18–20." *HvTSt* 68 (2012).

Additional Texts

EVALUATING GOSSIP, GOSSIPING, AND GOSSIPERS

Babylonian Talmud
  Arachin 15b, 16a
  Sanhedrin 103a
  Sotah 5a, 35a, 42a
Cicero, *For Caelius* 18
2 Corinthians 12:20
Ephesians 5:4
James 3:5–12
Job 27:4
Leviticus 19:16a
Lucian, *Slander* 1

Matthew 15:11
Pindar, *Olympian* 1.51
Plutarch, *On Being a Busybody* 516a–d, 518c–e, 519c–f
Proverbs 10:18; 11:13; 16:28; 20:19; 30:10
Psalms 15:3; 39:1; 101:5; 140:11
Romans 1:29–30
Sirach 19:6–16; 28:13
Tacitus, *Histories* 1.1
Wisdom of Solomon 1:10–11

GOSSIP AND GENDER

Aristotle, *Economics* 3.1
Augustine, *Confessions* 5.9; 9.9
Cicero, *For Caelius* 49
John 4:39
Juvenal, *Satires* 6.273, 398–412

Plutarch, *On Talkativeness* 507b–d, 508a–b; *On Being a Busybody* 519f
Polybius, *Histories* 3.20
1 Timothy 5:13; 6:20
2 Timothy 2:16

DESCRIPTIONS OF GOSSIP AND GOSSIPING

Acts 6:11; 9:21; 13:49–50; 16:2; 17:21; 21:31

Aeschines, *Speeches* 2.4; 3.216, 226, 254

Appian, *Civil Wars* 2.16.107–8

Aristophanes, *Knights* 810

Aristotle, *Politics* 1303b3, 1308a3

2 Chronicles 26:8, 15

Colossians 3:8

2 Corinthians 12:20b

Demosthenes, *Speeches* 1.7; 19.273

Deuteronomy 1:27

Epictetus, *Discourses* 3.25; 4.13

Esther 9:4

Euripides, *Iphigenia at Aulis* 1000

Exodus 15:24; 16:2–3, 7–9, 12; 17:3

Ezekiel 16:14; 22:9; 36:3

Herodotus, *Histories* 6.61

Homer, *Iliad* 22.280

Isocrates, *Orations* 3.52; 17.5

Juvenal, *Satires* 6.398–412

Jeremiah 6:28; 9:4

John 1:35–36, 40–41, 45–46; 3:26; 4:29; 5:15; 6:14, 41, 52, 60; 7:11–12, 31, 35–36, 40–43, 46–52; 9:2–3, 8–12,
16–17, 24–34; 10:19–21; 11:36–37, 46–47; 12:29; 16:17

3 John 10

Joseph and Aseneth 4.12–14; 24.4, 6

Josephus, *Jewish Antiquities* 6.196; 6.224; 14.14

Joshua 9:18; 10:21

Luke 1:65–66; 4:37; 6:11; 7:16–17; 8:34, 36, 39; 11:15; 15:2; 19:7

Lysias, *Speeches* 16.1; 18.9; 19.50; 20.30

1 Maccabees 11:39

3 Maccabees 3:7

Mark 1:27, 28, 44–45; 3:6; 4:41; 8:27–30; 15:31

Matthew 2:22; 4:12, 24; 8:27; 9:31; 22:34

Numbers 14:2, 27, 29, 36; 16:11

Plutarch, *On Talkativeness* 507c–d

Polybius, *Histories* 1.32; 4.87; 29.1

Romans 3:8

1 Samuel 16:18

Sirach 46:7

Sophocles, *Women of Trachis* 365–70

Strabo, *Geography* 13.4.9

Tacitus, *Histories* 1.13, 22; 4.11

Xenophon, *Anabasis* 2.5.1–2

GOSSIP AND HONOR/CHALLENGE-RIPOSTE

John 6:41–42, 52; 8:22

Luke 4:22; 5:21, 30, 33

Mark 2:16, 18, 24

Matthew 6:2–3; 9:3, 11; 12:2; 13:54–55

8. Space

Eric Stewart, with Mischa Hooker and Emil Kramer

Introduction

All societies, ancient and modern, passively and actively assign meanings to spaces. One need only consider a variety of associations with places in the contemporary United States, like "downtown," "the suburbs," a "back alley," a "vacant lot," or a "schoolyard," to appreciate how space can be perceived. People divide and attempt to control spaces by designating them for certain uses. Expressions such as "that's not the way we do things here" indicate attempts to designate certain spaces as appropriate for certain types of people, animals, things, and activities. Once defined, people attempt to control spaces, appropriating them for only those designated tasks, often by seeking to restrict access to them, by defending them from "invaders" or "trespassers." It is significant to note that the meanings associated with or assigned to places, and the ideologies attached to them, do not always reflect the lived experience of the people who use those spaces.

Control of space is a key feature of ancient Mediterranean societies in the same way that it is a key feature of all other societies. The ways in which ancient Mediterranean cultures arranged their mental maps show some consistency from one place/civilization to the next. Some common distinctions of spaces into binary pairs (e.g., public and private, cultivated and wild, city and village, city and countryside, ours and theirs, civilized and uncivilized/barbarous, central and peripheral) have been remarkably consistent for centuries across Mediterranean cultures (see **chap. 18, Deviance**). While the meaning attributed to the pairs might shift, the common practice of designating one member of the pair as "primary" or "favored" remains consistent through many centuries in the cultures that surround the Mediterranean Sea (see **chap. 6, Collectivism**).

Greek geographers debated the shape and extent of the *oikoumenē* (an abbreviation of *oikoumenē gē*, literally the "inhabited world"). Homer and Hesiod both considered the earth to be a circular disc encircled by *Ōkeanos*, a word often translated as "Ocean," but for both Homer and Hesiod, *Ōkeanos* was a stream that flows around the landmass. The ancient Greeks, and the Romans after them, knew only three continents: Africa (commonly called Libya then), Europe, and Asia. Ancient authors believed that at the edges of the *oikoumenē*, strange, marvelous, or grotesque peoples, things, and animals were to be found.

Not surprisingly, the binary pairs into which the world was divided favored elite males (see **chap. 9, Gender**). These types of pairs dealt with ideas like center and periphery, in which the writer's location defined both center and "normal" or "ideal." The Greek concept of latitudinal zones, or *klimata*, favors the position of those who live in proximity to the Mediterranean Sea, arguing that areas north were too cold for proper civilization, while those south were too hot to allow civilized life. Another way in which Greek and Roman authors conceived of centrality is through the use of the concept of a navel, or *omphalos*, of the world. The *omphalos* represented either the exact center of the landmass of the earth, as ancient thinkers understood it, or it represented the foundational point upon which the world was created or ordered. Sometimes the *omphalos* represented both of these ideas together. The "central" member of the pair is almost always valued positively, though sometimes the "peripheral" member represented a kind of innocence that Greeks and Romans thought had disappeared in the building of their city lives.

By the Roman period, a certain level of "urbanization" was developed. Even so, the vast majority of the population lived not in cities, but in villages that supported those cities. The elites resided in the cities at least part of the time, and those who attended to them lived with them there. The majority of the population, however, lived in villages outside the cities, and the elites who built and inhabited the cities exploited those in the villages for the food and wares they produced. For elites, however, in some ways, the "countryside" (*chōra*) was considered a preferable place to live. The countryside represented the idyllic, rustic past before the corruption of city life caused moral degeneration among its inhabitants. The elites withdrew to countryside estates, especially during the warmer summer months when city life was less pleasant. During times of war or important public business, however, elites would return to the cities for protection and the opportunity for gaining honor that came with public life there (see **chap. 4, Honor**).

The binary mode of thinking about space significantly impacts the description of male and female space through the notion of public and private space. Public spaces were considered "male," the space in which men saw to the matters of governance, enacted business, pursued their own families' interests, and proved their masculinity in any number of ways. Private spaces, largely contained within the household, were considered women's space. The distinction between public and private spaces, not necessarily representative of lived experience, is found throughout several millennia in a variety of southwest Asian and Mediterranean cultures.

Another classification of space in the ancient Mediterranean world is what I term here "restricted" space. Restricted spaces are those not accessible to everyone, sometimes on the basis of their being "sacred" and other times for ethnic or other reasons. Such spaces might include temples, sacred groves, and certain cities (or city spaces). Another space that is considered restricted and rather widely at risk is the heavenly realm of the gods. Humans tried, at various times, to force their way into the gods' abode (see **chap. 3, Patronage**).

What remains constant about descriptions of space/place during the periods investigated here is the conceptualization of space in binary categories, privileging one member of the category above the other. Certain conceptualizations of space could be used to critique others, such as the appeal to the bygone ideals of the "self-sufficient" person (most commonly "man") in the countryside in contrast to the morally degenerate person in the city, but the pairing of certain spaces is constant.

Ancient Texts

THE EDGES, RANGE, AND EXTENT OF THE OIKOUMENĒ

1. HOMER, *ODYSSEY* 9.275–80, 284

Homer (ca. 750 BCE), an epic poet responsible for the preserved form of the *Iliad* and the *Odyssey*, understood the earth to have "boundaries" or "edges," by which it was surrounded. For Homer, these ultimate edges were part of *Ōkeanos*, but even within the landmass encircled by *Ōkeanos*, there were edges to which one might sail. A famous episode involves Odysseus's meeting the cyclops, who describes why his kind has no respect for the gods. The land of the cyclops is a place of unlawfulness (see **chap. 18, Deviance**), where even the gods are not honored. Odysseus makes references to the edges in the second quotation in answer to the cyclops's question of how he came to the land of the cyclops.

> For the cyclopes have no respect for aegis-bearing Zeus or any of the blessed gods, since we are much better than they, nor shall I spare, avoiding the enmity

of Zeus, you or any of the others, except if my own spirit orders me. But say to me where, coming in, you have put your well-constructed ship, in order that I should know, whether any place far off or nearby.... My ship was shattered by earth-breaking Poseidon against the rocks, throwing it against the edges of your land.[1]

2. HERODOTUS, *HISTORIES* 4.36

Herodotus (ca. 484–425 BCE), among the earliest Greek historians, was more an ethnographer than a historian in the modern sense, and he provides numerous tales and descriptions about the peoples who populated the fifth-century BCE and earlier Mediterranean region. In this passage, he questions the received wisdom of his day regarding *Ōkeanos*, the earth-encircling stream around the *oikoumenē*, objecting to the notion that the landmass is a perfect circle, since he knows that Asia is much larger than Europe.

> I chuckle to see that before this time, many have drawn the circumference of the earth, but none of them carrying it out sensibly. For mentioning these matters, they draw Oceanus surrounding the earth, they make it circular, as with a compass, making Asia and Europe the same size.[2]

3. VERGIL, *AENEID* 1.255–79

Vergil (70–19 BCE) was a Roman epic poet who penned the *Aeneid, Eclogues,* and *Georgics.* He is perhaps best characterized as an apologist for the Octavian dynasty. In this section of the *Aeneid,* Vergil holds that the extent of the *oikoumenē* is essentially coterminous with the territory controlled by Octavian, now Caesar Augustus. The section is quite long, but significantly Vergil notes here what Jupiter has promised to the descendants of Aeneas.

> To them, I have laid down no limits to their time; I have given empire without end. . . . Return to better counsel, nurture the Romans, lords of everything, and people of the togas. . . . From this beautiful people, the Trojan Caesar will be born, his empire bound by Oceanus, and his fame by the stars, Julius, a moniker descended from mighty Julus.

4. HERODOTUS, *HISTORIES* 4.106

Herodotus notes that, among the most northerly tribes of the Scythians, one particular tribe feasts on human flesh. This charge that the tribes farthest from

1. Adapted from Murry and Dimock, LCL.
2. Adapted from Godley, LCL.

the Greeks were the wildest and least "civilized" is widespread both in Greek and Latin literature, and it says something about how the Greeks constructed the space of their world.

> The *anthrōpophagoi* ["human-eaters"] have the wildest customs of all people, neither recognizing righteousness nor holding a single law. But they are nomads, wearing clothing similar to the Scythians, but they have their own language, and they alone of these people eat humans.[3]

CENTRALITY AND KLIMATA

5. Pliny the Elder, *Natural History* 2.80.189–90

Pliny the Elder (23–79 CE), a soldier, lawyer, and writer whose description of the natural world set the course for much of the scientific activity in the West well into the Middle Ages, describes two permanently frozen zones (around the north and south poles) and two temperate zones separated by an excessively hot zone. People in the two temperate zones are permanently cut off from one another due to this hot zone in the middle.

> We must also discuss what follows from these celestial causes. For indeed, there is no doubt that the Ethiopians are scorched by the warmth of the neighboring star [i.e., the sun], and are born burnt-seeming, and have frizzled beards and hair. In the opposite region of the world are peoples with skin icy white, their locks blond and drooping down. These latter peoples are rough, on account of the harshness of the sky; the former are wise, on account of its volubility. And—by the very evidence of their legs—the bodily fluids in the former are drawn up to their upper parts by the nature of the heat, whereas in the latter they are pushed down into the lower parts by the descending moisture. In the one area [i.e., the cold], there are troublesome wild animals; in the other, diverse types of animals, especially birds, are produced. In both, bodies are tall—there, under pressure from the fires; here, nourished by the moisture. In the *middle* regions, however, by virtue of the healthful mixture of both, there are territories fertile for all things, moderate conditions of bodies with great temperateness even in complexion, mild practices, perspicuous senses, minds that are fruitful and can take in all of nature [read: *capacia* rather than *capacis*]; likewise, they have empires, which have never existed among the farthest peoples, just as those [peoples] have never served these

3. Adapted from Godley, LCL.

either, being separated and solitary in accord with the harshness of the nature that weighs them down.

6. Claudius Ptolemy, *Tetrabiblos* 2.2.55–57

Claudius Ptolemy (100–170 CE) was a natural scientist and astronomer who proposed a geocentric conception of the universe that stood as received wisdom until the time of Copernicus. Ptolemy understood the *klimata* as sure guides to understanding the social, political, and cultural habits of the peoples located within them. Perhaps naturally, he locates those peoples ringed around the Mediterranean as inhabiting the "perfect" position, in that it is a mix of heat and cold. This position gave the peoples of the temperate zone the ability to develop both agriculture and political philosophy in order to rule over the peoples of the other zones.

> The particularities of individual ethnic groups are determined in part by the parallels and angles. . . . And so our *oikoumenē* is in the northern quarters; the peoples who live under the southern parallels, I say from the equator to the summer tropic, are burned by the sun since it is over their heads, they have black skins and thick, curly hair, they are small of form and have a shrunken stature, are optimistic by nature, though mostly savage due to the oppressive heat. . . . Those who lived more to the north than us . . . , since they are distant from the zodiac and sun's heat, are thereby cold; but because they have more moisture . . . they are of white skin, have straight hair, are large and well fed, and naturally cold. . . . Those who live between the summer tropic and Ursa Major, the sun neither directly overhead nor distant along its noontime passing, share in the mildness of the air. . . . They are in the middle by color, of medium build, temperate naturally, they live close together and civilized by custom.[4]

CENTRALITY AND OMPHALOS

7. Plato, *Republic* 427c

The works of Plato (429–347 BCE) have been enormously influential in Western thought. He was a philosopher in ancient Athens, a student of Socrates, a onetime teacher of Aristotle, and the founder of the academy in Athens. In this segment of the *Republic*, Socrates answers a question from Adeimantus concerning what is left to discuss about legislation, once enculturating values into children through their education has been covered.

4. Adapted from Robbins, LCL.

[We ought to discuss] both the founding of temples and sacrifices, and also other services to gods, *daimones*, and heroes. And again, the burial of the ones who have died and whatsoever things are necessary to provide service to the ones there [the realm of the dead], to have them be gracious. Neither do we who are founding the city understand such things, nor do we trust any other person, if we have any sense, nor shall we make use of another interpreter except [the god] of our fathers. For this god doubtless is the one who interprets to all people the things of the fathers, seated in the middle of the earth upon the navel [*omphalos*], he interprets.[5]

8. STRABO, *GEOGRAPHY* 9.3.6

Strabo (ca. 64 BCE–21 CE), whose surviving first-century *Geography* is the most complete text of its kind, also understood the earth to be encircled by *Ōkeanos*. Like Herodotus, Strabo believed the earth not to have been exactly round, however, and was aware that Asia was considerably larger than Europe. In this passage, he repeats the tradition that Delphi was the navel of the earth and relates that there was a "navel" within the temple, apparently some kind of statue marking the status of the temple as the center point of the whole *oikoumenē*.

And so, the largest share of honor given to this temple was because of the oracle; being esteemed of all [the oracles] the least untrustworthy, the setting of the place increased it. For of the whole of Greece, it is in the middle, of the land inside and outside the isthmus, and it was considered the center of the *oikoumenē* and called the navel. . . . Some navel is displayed in the temple.[6]

9. TANHUMA, KEDOSHIM 10

Midrash is a collection of (largely) narrative material, though it also incorporates material that should be designated "legal." It is difficult to say with any precision when the collection was ultimately compiled, but rabbis of the Middle Ages made use of it. The collection has several elements attributed to a rabbi named Tanhuma, though the ascription of the entire collection to any individual rabbi is problematic. Here the text represents a development of the *omphalos* tradition, applying it to the temple of Jerusalem and associating it with the creation of the world.

So says the Scripture: "I made myself gardens and paradises, and I planted therein a tree of every fruit" [Eccl 2:5]). . . . Another interpretation [for] "I planted therein

5. Adapted from Shorey, LCL.
6. Adapted from Jones, LCL.

trees of every fruit" [Eccl 2:5]: Just as the navel is set at the center of a man, so the land of Israel is set at the center of the world—as is said: "They who sit at the navel of the earth" [Ezek 38:12]. And therefrom the foundations of the world go forth—as is said: "A psalm of Asaph. God, eternal God spoke and called the world from east to west" [Ps 50:1]—whence?—"from Zion, utterly beauteous, God appears" [Ps 50:2]. The land of Israel sits at the center of the world; Jerusalem, at the center of the land of Israel; the temple, in the middle of Jerusalem; the sanctum, in the middle of the temple; the ark, in the middle of the sanctum; and the foundation stone is before the ark, wherefrom the world was founded. Solomon, being wise, stood upon the roots that went out from it to all the world and planted in them every sort of tree and produced fruit. Therefore, he said, "I made myself gardens and paradises" [Eccl 2:5]. (translation by Brandon Bruning and Christopher Jones)

10. Livy, *History of Rome* 5.52.5
Livy (59 BCE–17 CE), a Roman historian whose overall perspective of the history of Rome is that morality was in decline during his lifetime, was from Patavium, a region battered during the civil wars of the 40s BCE. Unlike many other Roman historians, Livy was not a member of the senatorial class, nor was he especially influential in Rome during his lifetime. In the speech he composed for Camullus, he expresses the notion of Roman centrality, which was common among Roman authors. Aware that Rome was not centrally located, since it was too far west of the *oikoumenē* to make such a claim, Livy suggests that the gods had established in Rome certain rites and that these could not be transferred.

> Perhaps someone might suggest that we conduct our religious rites at Veii or that we should send our priests from Veii to Rome to carry out the rites there. Neither thing can be done without the risk of committing sacrilege.[7]

CITY AND VILLAGE

11. Strabo, *Geography* 3.4.13
Greek and Roman authors commonly distinguished between cities and villages. The distinction had to do not only with the buildings, goods and services, and honor of a place, but also, according to Strabo, the laws and civilized customs of its inhabitants. Regarding the Iberian Peninsula, Strabo dismisses what he considered to be wildly inflated numbers of cities for the region, due

7. Adapted from Foster, LCL.

to the lack of social customs among them and their inability to prevent "savages" from wooded areas having influence over their populations.

> When the ones affirming that there are more than a thousand cities of Iberia, they appear to me to be carried away in this matter, naming great villages cities. For the region by nature is not able to support so many cities, due to the poverty of its land or through the remoteness and savageness, nor do their lives and deeds (outside of those living alongside us on the seacoast) suggest such things. For the ones living in the villages are wild, and such are most of the Iberians. And the ones in cities cannot civilize them, when the ones living in the woods to work evil upon their neighbors outnumber them.[8]

12. 1 MACCABEES 5:65

First Maccabees is a second-century BCE source describing how the Maccabees (or the Hasmoneans, as they were also known) overthrew the Seleucid forces and established a Judean high priesthood to rule over Judea, telling the story of the Maccabean family from the priest Mattathias to the installation of his grandson John. This section describes the military victory of Judas, one of Mattathias's sons, over the descendants of Esau.

> And Judas and his brothers came out and waged war against the sons of Esau in the land that is in the south, and they struck down Hebron and its villages [lit. "daughters"], and they destroyed her strongholds, and they set fire all around their towers.

CITY AND COUNTRYSIDE

13. CICERO, *FOR ROSCIUS AMERINUS* 39

Cicero (106–43 BCE) was a Roman senator, philosopher, jurist, and orator who wrote copiously during his lifetime. The speech *For Roscius Amerinus*—a defense speech in which Cicero defended Roscius against the charge of parricide—appeals to the "naturalness" of life in the countryside and suggests that Roscius, interested only in his simple life working his land, is not the kind of person who is corrupted by city life to the point where he would murder his father. Those who work in the countryside do not even have passions, according to Cicero.

8. Adapted from Jones, LCL.

Sextus Roscius murdered his father. What sort of person are we talking about? A young man corrupted and led on by useless men? He is forty years old. Naturally, he is an old hand at murder, an outrageous sort of person for whom murder is a daily routine. But this you have heard not even his accusers claim. Luxury, then, no doubt, the enormity of his debts, and the desires of his uncontrollable lusts drove the man to this crime. As for luxury, Erucius cleared him of that when he said that he had hardly ever even taken part in a dinner party. In addition, he has never owed anyone anything. Furthermore, his desires? What sort of passions can there be in the sort of person who—as his accuser himself sarcastically noted—has always lived in the country and made his living by farming—the sort of life least associated with desire and most associated with duty?[9]

14. THUCYDIDES, *HISTORY* 2.41

Thucydides (ca. 460–400 BCE) served the Athenian army as a fleet commander during the Peloponnesian War and wrote its history. While little is known about Thucydides's life, it is quite likely that he wrote much of the *History* during a period of exile for failing to prevent Sparta from taking Amphipolis (424 BCE). The section of the text excerpted below is from Pericles's speech honoring those Athenians who died fighting for Athens in the first year of the war. In this section of the speech, Pericles praises those dead by extolling the virtues of Athens, demonstrating how the inhabitants of the city control and remake the spaces outside the city by "compelling" them to provide access to the Athenians and by marking them with memorials.

> Briefly, I say the whole city is a place of learning for Hellas, and each man among us seems to me, according to his own self, in the widest set of circumstances, also with the greatest elegance and dexterity, to supply a self-sufficient body. And this is not a boastful word in this moment, but it is more the truth of the deeds, it being a sign of the power of the city, which we procured for ourselves from these things. When it comes into trial, Athens alone compared to others is better than her reputation, and only of her the approaching enemy has neither vexation by what sorts of poor fates he suffers, nor does the subject find fault that he is ruled by unworthy ones. Furnishing many great signs of our power and not without a witness to it, we will cause amazement to the ones living now and to those in the future, needing neither Homer to make a paean to us, nor whoever's words delight at this moment, but whose conjecture about the deeds perverts the truth, but we compel the whole sea and earth to become accessible to us, by our boldness,

9. Adapted from Reese, LCL.

planting in every place eternal memorials of evil and good. And so, for this city these men, having fought nobly, rightly thinking that she should not be taken from them, died, and of those remaining, all should in like manner be willing to toil to the end for her sake.[10]

15. MARK 6:53–56

Mark was written around 70 CE, during the period of the Jewish-Roman War. Various locations have been suggested for its composition, ranging from Rome to Syria. In this section of the text, people bring to Jesus others suffering from illness. The places from which they come illustrate nicely the distinctions between city and village and city and fields.

> And having crossed over, they came into the land of Gennesaret and brought the boat to harbor. And when they came out of the boat, immediately recognizing him, that whole region rushed about, and they began to carry those who were ill on beds to whatever place they heard he went. And whatever place he entered, whether villages or cities or fields, they put the weak in the marketplaces and appealed to him that they might touch the edge of his garment. And however many as touched it were restored to health.

PRIVATE AND PUBLIC/GENDERED SPACES

16. XENOPHON, *OECONOMICUS* 9.2–5

Xenophon (ca. 430–350 BCE), a philosopher and historian, wrote works chronicling the history of Greece and the life of Cyrus II. In this section of the *Oeconomicus*, a treatise on household management, Isomachus relates to Socrates how he introduces his new wife into the household, showing her the various parts of the house. Key among the distinctions he makes is that between the women's areas of the house and the men's. This is a common distinction in discussions of Greek houses but is not a distinction in Roman architecture (see the reference to Vitruvius in the additional texts).

> And what else would I do, I thought first to show her the strength of the house. For it has not been adorned with many embroideries, Socrates, but the rooms are built having been prepared for the purpose to be most useful vessels for these things about to be contained in them, so that each room called these things to be in it. For

10. Adapted from Smith, LCL.

the inner room in its security called out for the most worthy bedding and utensils, and the dryness of the covered rooms for seed, the cool rooms for wine, and the lighted rooms for as many works and vessels as need light. And then I showed her the adorned dwelling places for the people in the household, which are cool in the summer and warmed by the sun in the winter. And I showed her that the whole house lies open to the south, with the result that it is in a nice sunny position in winter, and well shaded in the summer. And I showed her the women's areas, divided from the men's areas by a fastened door, in order that nothing be carried out from within which it should not be, nor can those living there bear children without our knowledge. For the most useful of them are kinder, even more having children, for the most part, while the evil ones, being married, become ever more resourceful in their evil doing.[11]

17. COLUMELLA, *ON AGRICULTURE* 12; PREFACE 2, 7

Columella (ca. 4–70 CE) was a Roman author who wrote about his farming life. Little is known about his life before he started farming. After serving in the military in Syria, he took up farming and wrote a twelve-volume work about it. Here he reproduces the notion that the outdoor, public world is the world of the males, while the indoor, private world is suitable to females.

In addition, since humans' nourishment and adornment had to be cared for in a house, indoors, not, as with wild beasts, in the open air and in woodland places, it was necessary for one or the other [of a couple] to be outdoors under the sky, to procure by labor and industry things to be stored indoors—because it was necessary to engage in farming, sailing, or some other kind of business, in order to secure some store of goods. But once the things acquired had been collected indoors, it was fitting for there to be another person to guard the things that had been brought in, and to accomplish those tasks that needed to be conducted at home. . . . For both among the Greeks and afterward among the Romans, even into the memory of our fathers, domestic work generally belonged to the matron, with the father of the household returning to hearth and home just in order to rest from his activities in the forum, all cares having been laid aside. For there was the highest respect, mingled with harmony and diligence; the most beautiful woman would burn with eager zeal to advance and improve her husband's business by means of her own carefulness.[12]

11. Adapted from Marchant and Todd, LCL.
12. Adapted from Forster and Heffner, LCL.

RESTRICTED SPACES

18. PSALM 24:3–4

Psalm 24 describes the earth, seas, and rivers, together with all the things living in them, as belonging to the Lord. The psalmist goes on to describe the "place" of the Lord and who is qualified to enter into it.

> Who will go up to the mountain of the Lord? And who will stand up in his holy place? They who have innocent hands and pure hearts, who do not raise their beings to deceit and do not swear fraudulently.

19. JOSEPHUS, *JEWISH WAR* 5.194–95, 198–99, 219

Titus Flavius Josephus (ca. 37–100 CE) was a Galilean writer and soldier who fought against Rome in the Jewish-Roman War (66–73 CE). He was commander of the Galilean forces until his capture by Vespasian, after which he was granted Roman citizenship and became an advisor to Vespasian's son, the emperor Titus. Here Josephus describes several different spaces within the temple and the restrictions that applied to them, covering ethnicity, sex, and title.

> In this place [the second court] itself, stelae were set up at equal intervals, announcing the law of purity, some of which are in Greek script, and others in Roman, saying that no one foreign is permitted within the holy place, for the second court is called *the holy place*. . . . For within this area a special, secluded place, having been walled off for women to worship, made necessary a second gate opposite the first. And of the other areas, one gate was on the south side, while the other one was on the north, through which they entered the women's place. For it is not permitted for a woman to enter by other gates, nor to go beyond, by way of her own gate, the walled-off area. . . . And the innermost part, measuring twenty cubits, was separated similarly by curtains from the outside, and nothing was laid in it. It was inaccessible, undefiled, and unseen by all, called the holy of holy.[13]

20. PAUSANIAS, *DESCRIPTION OF GREECE* 7.5.7–8

Pausanias, about whom little is known beyond his writings, is famous for his *Periēgēsis*, or *Description of Greece*. The text was written during the middle third of the second century CE. In this section of the work, Pausanias describes a certain temple of Herakles in Erythrae.

13. Adapted from Thackeray, LCL.

Finally, a certain Erythraean man, whose name was Phormio, whose life was made from the sea and fishing, and whose eyes were destroyed due to sickness, this seafaring man saw a vision in a dream that the Erythraean women were bound to cut off their hair, and thus the men, twisting a cord from the hair, would pull the raft to their territory. But among the women who were citizens, not one wished to heed the dream. But as many of the Thracian women who were enslaved, and the ones who lived there in freedom, offered to cut off their hair. Thus, the Erythraean men drew in the raft. So it is permitted only to the Thracian women to enter the Herakleion, and they tell me that the residents still guard the cord made from the hairs.[14]

Vocabulary of Space

HEBREW

מִדְבָּר (*midbar*) . . . . desert, wasteland, wilderness
טַבּוּר (*tabbur*) . . . . navel, center of the world

GREEK

ἀγορά (*agora*) . . . . marketplace, town square
ἀγρός (*agros*) . . . . field, sown areas outside the city
ἀνδρωνῖτις (*andrōnitis*) . . . . men's quarters or areas of the house
ἄστυ (*asty*) . . . . city, town
ἔσχατος (*eschatos*) . . . . edge of a territory
γυναικωνῖτις (*gynaikōnitis*) . . . . women's quarters or areas of the house
κλίμα (*klima*) . . . . climatic zone, latitudinal zone
κώμη (*kōmē*) . . . . village
οἰκουμένη (*oikoumenē*) . . . . inhabited world
οἶκος (*oikos*) . . . . house, household
ὀμφαλός (*omphalos*) . . . . navel, middle, center of a territory or the earth
πεῖραρ (*peirar*) . . . . edge/boundary of territories or the earth
πόλις (*polis*) . . . . city

---

14. Adapted from Jones, LCL.

LATIN

orbis terrarum . . . . inhabited world
pomerium . . . . dividing line between a city and its surrounding countryside
rus . . . . countryside
templum . . . . temple, area set aside for worship of the gods
urbs . . . . city

Select Bibliography

Clarke, Katherine. *Between Geography and History: Hellenistic Constructions of the Roman World*. Oxford Classical Monographs. Oxford: Clarendon, 1999.

Neyrey, Jerome H., S. J. *The Gospel of John in Cultural and Rhetorical Perspective*. Grand Rapids: Eerdmans, 2009.

Nicolet, Claude. *Space, Geography, and Politics in the Early Roman Empire*. Translated by Hélène Leclerc. Ann Arbor: University of Michigan Press, 1991.

Romm, James S. *The Edges of the Earth in Ancient Thought: Geography, Exploration, and Fiction*. Princeton: Princeton University Press, 1992.

Shepardson, Christine. *Controlling Contested Places: Late Antique Antioch and the Spatial Politics of Religious Controversy*. Berkeley: University of California Press, 2014.

Stewart, Eric C. *Gathered around Jesus: An Alternative Spatial Practice in the Gospel of Mark*. Matrix 6. Eugene, OR: Cascade, 2009.

Additional Texts

THE EDGES, RANGE, AND EXTENT OF THE OIKOUMENĒ

Agathemerus, *Sketch of Geography* 1.1–5
Aristotle, *Meteorology* 362b
Caesar, *Gallic War* 1.1
Cicero, *On the Republic* 6.21
Daniel 2:36–45
Diodorus Siculus, *Library of History* 1.9.1–10
Herodotus, *Histories* 1.131–39; 3.98, 102–6; 4.17, 97, 106, 185, 191; 5.9

Hesiod, *Theogony* 517–19, 620–25
Homer, *Odyssey* 1.22–25; 11.13–22
Isaiah 13:5–22
Josephus, *Against Apion* 1.33; 2.41; *Jewish Antiquities* 1.109–12; 1.38–39; 3.185; 4.115, 138, 190; *Jewish War* 2.360–64; 4.262
Pliny the Elder, *Natural History* 2.67; 3.1.3–4; 6.35.195

Strabo, *Geography* 1.1.8–10; 1.2.1; 2.5.26; 3.5.5

Tacitus, *Germany* 46

Testament of Naphtali 6.7

Thucydides, *History* 1.69.5

CENTRALITY AND KLIMATA

Aristotle, *Politics* 1327a13–28

Cicero, *On the Republic* 6.20–21; *Tusculan Disputations* 1.68–69

Hippocrates, *Airs, Waters, and Places* 24.43–67

Jubilees 8–9

Plato, *Laws* 747d–e; *Republic* 435e–436a

Pliny the Elder, *Natural History* 2.68.170

Vitruvius, *Architecture* 6.1.1–12

CENTRALITY AND OMPHALOS

Agathemerus, *Sketch of Geography* 1.2

Ezekiel 5:5; 38:10–13

Isaiah 19:24–25

Josephus, *Jewish War* 3.51–52

Jubilees 22:11–14

Pausanias, *Description of Greece* 10.16.3

Philostratus, *Life of Apollonius* 3.14.3

Pindar, *Pythian Ode* 6.3–4; *Nemean* 7.34

Plutarch, *The Disappearance of Oracles* 409e–410a

Strabo, *Geography* 9.3.6

CITY AND VILLAGE

Josephus, *Against Apion* 1.197; *Jewish War* 2.460

Joshua 15:20–63

Judges 1:27

Leviticus 25:29–34

Matthew 9:35–38

Numbers 21:21–32

Pausanias, *Description of Greece* 10.4.1

Philo, *On the Embassy to Gaius* 1.225; *On the Life of Moses* 1.143; *On the Confusion of Tongues* 12.46

Strabo, *Geography* 3.4.13

Tacitus, *Agricola* 21; *Histories* 4.64–65

CITY AND COUNTRYSIDE

Aristophanes, *Clouds* 43–55

Arrian, *Anabasis* 7.9.2

1 Kings 14:11; 16:4

Martyrdom of Polycarp 5.1

Menander, *Dyskolos* 169–78

Philo, *On the Contemplative Life* 19–20;

On the Decalogue 2–4

Plato, *Theaetetus* 173c–e

Pliny the Elder, *Natural History* 36.24.101

Strabo, *Geography* 3.3.5

PRIVATE AND PUBLIC/GENDERED SPACES

Acts 20:18–35
Aulus Gellius, *Attic Nights* 10.22.6–24
Cornelius Nepos, *On Eminent Foreign Leaders*, preface
John Chrysostom, *The Kinds of Women Who Ought to Be Taken as Wives* 4

Philo, *On the Virtues* 19; *Special Laws* 3.169–70
Plutarch, *Advice to Bride and Groom* 142c–d; *Greek Questions* 300a–e; *Old Men in Public Affairs* 785c–d
Vitruvius, *Architecture* 6.7.2, 4
Xenophon, *Oeconomicus* 7.19–22

RESTRICTED SPACES

Apuleius, *The Golden Ass* 11.17, 23–25
Deuteronomy 23:2–9
Exodus 19:9b–25
Genesis 11:1–9
Herodotus, *Histories* 6.134–35
Homer, *Odyssey* 11.305–20

Josephus, *Jewish Antiquities* 15.417–20
3 Maccabees 1:6–2:33
Pausanias, *Description of Greece* 7.5.8
Plutarch, *Isis and Osiris* 357d–e
Revelation 21:9–27

9. Gender

ALICIA J. BATTEN

Introduction

Ancient Mediterranean societies generally had a "one-sex" model, whereby the female was an ill-conceived and unfinished male with genitals inverted, while the male was properly made with appropriately unturned genitalia. Indeed, it has been argued that this paradigm exerted itself up until the early nineteenth century in Europe. Many think that these understandings of sexual difference are reflected in other ways that male and female are distinguished, such as with respect to space (public = male; private = female), and honor (= male) and shame (= female). Contemporary notions of "heterosexual," "homosexual," or "sexual orientation" did not exist in antiquity, and as Foucault has shown, even the concept of "sexuality" is a historically conditioned idea that is less related to nature than it is to forms of power.

In the ancient world, the categories of "masculine" and "feminine" are types that did not always correspond to a person's anatomy, although men were by and large expected to conform to certain ideals of masculinity (e.g., power, aggression, and courage) and women to those of femininity (e.g., chastity, deference, and obedience). If a person's "gender" was blurry, he or she was suspected of deviancy (see **chap. 18, Deviance**), and one of the chief means of insulting and humiliating a man was to accuse him of effeminacy. Women, likewise, had to tread delicately lest they be accused of mannish tendencies. A "manlike" woman could sometimes receive worse invective than a dandy or fop, reminding us of how notions of sex and gender are connected to power. Some argue, as well, that the primary way of understanding sexual and gender difference in the ancient world was not with regard to male and female, but "active" and "passive" categories. At the very least, these dimensions of sex and gender difference must be taken into account when examining the topic in antiquity.

Many Mediterranean peoples were preoccupied with physiognomy, or the idea that outward appearance and manner revealed inward disposition and character. The size and shape of the body, what one wore, as well as gestures, facial expressions, walk, and voice were all deeply significant, for they were felt to communicate aspects of a person's identity, status, and gender and were subject to relentless public scrutiny, also known as "the gaze." A mistake, such as a man being overly fastidious with his hair, or a woman dressing inappropriately for a given occasion, could incite stinging censure from onlookers and cost the person and his or her family and associates dearly in the court of public opinion (see **chap. 5, Shame**).

Individual body parts were perceived hierarchically. For example, the head was the most honorable component; one could swear by it (Matt 5:36) and anoint it (Matt 26:7). It was important to cover up body parts that were used to serve the needs of nature, and these aspects of the physique, such as sexual organs, were often referred to euphemistically with other terms, such as "feet" (Isa 7:20). The right hand was associated with power and with eating and drinking, while the left one was used for lavatory activities. A person who was disfigured, lame, blind, or in any way lacking a "whole" body was banned from cultic activity among the ancient Israelites and often, in Greco-Roman contexts, viewed as a type of barbarian (see **chap. 12, Purity**). Such people might be associated with the evil eye, as it was often assumed that these persons would be envious of those with whole bodies (see **chap. 20, Evil Eye**).

Although nudity was acceptable in certain contexts, ancient Mediterranean peoples were sensitive to nakedness in some situations. The Israelite had to be careful not to expose himself to the deity, for such an act would effectively shame God, as revealing the buttocks or genitals to another person or deity was a power grab and offended the onlooker. The priest is therefore commanded to wear a type of underwear beneath his robes in order to prevent accidental exposure (Exod 28:42). If a man or woman was forcibly stripped naked, he or she was shamed (Nah 3:5; Matt 27:28), and defeat by another nation could be represented by images of naked women. If a Roman woman wore transparent clothing, she could be accused of prostitution, and therefore fabrics such as Coan silks were associated with slave girls and low-level prostitutes. Involuntary nakedness indicated that one was at the bottom of the social scale, that one was uncivilized and barbaric.

The category of "dress" can include clothing, shoes, adornment (e.g., jewelry, hair, and cosmetics), tattoos, scarification, and various accoutrements or accessories, such as carrying a mirror or a basket of flowers. Clothing styles could vary across cultural groups, but social level, identity, culture, and moral stature were also recognizable and prescribed through dress. For example, the wives of Roman citizens, *matronae,* wore the stola, a long garment worn overtop the tunic with over-the-shoulder straps. It had a deep V neckline and was belted under the breast with a cord. A range of authors correlate the stola with a chaste matron; Martial refers to matronly propriety as "stolate modesty" (1.35.8–9). Probably the best-known Roman male item of dress was the toga, which could vary depending upon the life stage of the man. For example, when Roman boys came of age, they switched from bordered childhood togas to the plain white "masculine" togas of adulthood. The fabulous hairstyles that some elite Roman women sported reveal the degree of leisure and means (slaves to dress the hair, elaborate needles, clips, and combs) required to be well prepared for public display (see **chap. 4, Honor; chap 6, Collectivism**).

Ancient Texts

GENDER

1. Plutarch, *Advice to Bride and Groom* 139c

Plutarch (46–120 CE) was a Greek writer, priest at Delphi, and Roman citizen. He produced a wide variety of essays, including this guide for newly married couples. The passage reflects the widespread attitude that wives could be in public when they were in the company of their husbands, but otherwise, their primary realm was that of the domestic.

> When the moon is far from the sun, we see her bright and conspicuous, but she becomes invisible and hides when she is near. In contrast, the virtuous woman should be seen the most when she is with her husband, and remain in the house and be hidden when he is away.[1]

2. Sirach 25:16–26 (LXX)

The notion that a woman brought sin into the world is not prominent in the LXX but is stated squarely here in the second-century BCE writer, Jesus ben Sirach. The passage also reflects some of the common negative stereotypes about women.

> I would rather dwell with a lion and a dragon than dwell with an evil woman. The evil of a woman changes her appearance and darkens her face like that of

1. Adapted from Babbitt, LCL.

a bear. Her husband shall lose heart among the neighbors, and listening, he groans bitterly. Any vice is small compared to a woman's vice; may the lot of a sinner fall upon her! A sandy climb for the feet of the elderly man—so is the talkative wife to a quiet husband. Do not fall down on a woman's beauty, and do not long for a woman. Anger and shamelessness and great disgrace is a wife when she maintains her husband. A lowly heart, sad countenance, and injury of the heart come from an evil wife. Drooping hands and weak knees come from the wife who does not make her husband happy. From a woman is the beginning of sin, and because of her, we all die. Allow no opening to water, and no frank speech to an evil wife. If she does not walk as your hands direct, separate her from your flesh.[2]

3. POLEMO OF LAODICEA, *PHYSIOGNOMY* 2

Expert physiognomists, such as Polemo of Laodicea (90–144 CE), were able to detect gender deviants, sometimes referred to as *androgynos* in Greek and *cínaedus* in Latin, based upon subtle signs. Here Polemo talks about how "masculinity" and "femininity" can be classifications applied to both male and female creatures.

Nor should you ignore all that I have commanded you regarding the physiognomical scrutiny of the signs of masculinity and femininity. You should learn this from the gaze, the movement, and the voice and then measure up one part with the other until you come to know where resides precedence [of one over the other]. For in masculinity there is femininity, and in femininity there is masculinity, and the name [of male or female] falls to whichever has precedence.[3]

4. DIO CHRYSOSTOM, *TO THE PEOPLE OF RHODES* (*OR.* 31) 162–63

The Greek philosopher and orator Dio Chrysostom (40–115 CE) was from Bithynia, lived in Rome, but was exiled because of his criticism of the emperor Domitian. His writings provide a clear sense of how an ideal Greek male should behave, including how he should walk. Self-control and equanimity were widely associated with male virtue and were believed, by Dio, to set the Greeks apart.

---

2. Adapted from Albert Pietersma and Benjamin G. Wright, eds., *New English Translation of the Septuagint*, trans. Benjamin G. Wright (Oxford: Oxford University Press, 2007).

3. Robert Hoyland, "A New Edition and Translation of the Leiden Polemon," in *Seeing the Face, Seeing the Soul: Polemon's Physiognomy from Classical Anitiquity to Medieval Islam*, ed. Simon Swain (Oxford: Oxford University Press, 2007), 393.

On this account, you are praiseworthy for such characteristics—and they are known by all as no small matters—the walk, the haircut, that no one swaggers through the city, but that even foreigners staying here are forced by your customs to walk in a dignified manner . . . because of all these things you are marveled at; you are loved, more than for your harbors, your fortresses, or your shipyards.[4]

5. CLEMENT OF ALEXANDRIA, *CHRIST THE EDUCATOR* 3.21

Clement of Alexandria (150–215 CE) reflects keen awareness of physiognomics in this treatise, which offers harsh criticism of women who adorn themselves, and men who act like women by shaving and plucking out their hair or overly grooming themselves. In this passage, he reveals to what extent gender roles were connected to questions of power.

But to seek adornment in smoothness . . . is effeminacy if done by men and adultery if done by women. . . . He who denies his manhood by light of day will clearly prove himself a woman at night. . . . Wantonness has turned everything upside down. Luxurious living has put humanity to shame. It seeks everything, attempts everything, forces everything, and coerces nature. Men act like women and women act as men; confounding nature, women are both wives and husbands. No opening is protected from licentiousness.[5]

GENDER AND SEX

6. GENESIS 1:26–27; 5:1–2 (LXX)

The first creation story in Genesis was interpreted by some ancient writers, such as Philo, to be entirely different from the second story, in which male and female were created. Gen 1:26–27 evokes the myth of the androgyne, whereby the first human was not male or female, but rather made in the image of God, not corporeal. This is the ideal and essential human subject that existed prior to sexual difference. In Gen 5:1–2, "Adam" designates humanity as a whole, and thus some translate it as "humankind."

Then God said, "Let us make humanity according to our image and according to our likeness; and let humanity rule over the fish of the sea, and over the birds of the

---

4. Adapted from Cohoon, LCL.

5. Adapted from Clement of Alexandria, *Christ the Educator*, trans. Simon P. Wood, FC 23 (Washington, DC: Catholic University of America Press, 1954), 215–17.

sky, and over the livestock, and over all the earth, and over every creeping thing that creeps upon the earth. And God made humanity, according to the image of God he made humanity; male and female he made them. . . . This is the book of the beginning of humans. On the day that God made Adam, he made him according to the image of God. Male and female he made them, and he blessed them and named them "Adam" on the day that he made them.[6]

7. Aristotle, *On the Generation of Animals* 728A18

The fourth-century BCE philosopher here discusses conception, arguing that male sperm is generative, while female sperm, which is in fact menstrual fluid, provides nutrition for the embryo.

> In addition, a boy is actually like a woman in form, and a woman is as a barren male; for the female is female on account of a type of lack of power. The female does not have the power to make sperm out of the last state of the food (this is either blood or its equivalent in bloodless animals). . . . Therefore, clearly, it is logical to maintain that conception takes place from this. For the menses is sperm, not pure, but needs to be worked on. It is the same with fruit when it develops. There is food present, even before it has been filtered, and it needs to be worked on in order to cleanse it. That is why when the former is brought together with the seed, and when the latter is brought together with pure food, the one causes conception and the other causes growth.[7]

8. Pseudo-Aristotle, *Physiognomics* 809A26–B14

Although Aristotle examined the connections between physical appearance and character, this text is not by him and is generally dated to approximately 300 BCE. It is the oldest extant study of physiognomy and can be divided into two parts (it was probably two different treatises originally): the first deals with arguments about human behavior drawn from nature, while the second focuses upon animal behavior, especially that of males versus females and their correlations to the human species.

> The genus of animals is divided into two forms, male and female, attaching to each form what is appropriate. Of all the animals that we try to rear, the females are milder and gentler in spirit than the males, less robust, and more predisposed to

6. Adapted from Albert Pietersma and Benjamin G. Wright, eds., *New English Translation of the Septuagint*, trans. Robert J. V. Hiebert (Oxford: Oxford University Press, 2007).

7. Adapted from Peck, LCL.

rearing and managing. Because of these things, they are more fainthearted than males. . . . But in my view, it seems that the female has a more evil disposition than the male, is reckless and less courageous. Women and the female animals reared by us are quite manifestly so. . . . In addition, it is also clear that in each genus, each female has a smaller head, a narrower face, and a thinner neck than the male . . . and above all, the whole form of the body is made for pleasure rather than for high mindedness, with weaker nerves and with softer, moister flesh. The males are completely opposite to this; their nature is braver and more just, that of the female being more cowardly and less just.[8]

9. GALEN, *ON THE USEFULNESS OF THE PARTS OF THE BODY* 14.6

The philosopher and physician Galen of Pergamum (129–200 or 216 CE) served the emperor Marcus Aurelius. He based many of his ideas about the human body on dissections he completed upon animals (he did not dissect humans). The following excerpt reflects the widespread view that women were inverted and incomplete males.

All the constituent parts, then, that men have, women also have, the difference between them being a single thing only, which must be remembered throughout the discussion: in women the parts are inside, but in men they are outside, in the area named the perineum. First, think about whichever ones you want, turn outward those of the woman, turn inward and fold double those of the man, and you will find them to be the same in every way.[9]

10. PHLEGON OF TRALLES, *ON MARVELS* 6.2–3

The second-century CE Greek writer leaves a fragment testifying to pseudoher-maphroditism, or the appearance of a male organ in a child who had up to that point seemed to be female. These cases of mistaken sex could create philo-sophical and legal challenges for people, when a young wife turned out to be a young husband, for example.

A thirteen-year-old young woman of distinguished parents, who was very attractive, had received many offers of marriage. She was engaged to the one whom her parents wanted. The wedding day was near, and she was going to go out from her house when she had great pain and cried out. Those related to her were treating her for

---

8. Adapted from Hett, LCL.

9. Adapted from Margaret Tallmadge May, *Galen: On the Usefulness of the Parts of the Body* (Ithaca: Cornell University Press, 1968), 2:628.

stomach pains and twisted bowel. The pains continued for three days in a row, and everyone was confused as to the nature of her malady. There was no alleviation in her discomfort either during the night or in the day, despite the fact that every doctor in the city offered her every kind of treatment, but nobody was able to find a reason for her suffering. Then on the fourth day, at dawn, the pain intensified and she cried out with a great wail. Suddenly male parts appeared on her, and the girl became a man.[10]

GENDER AND THE BODY

11. LEVITICUS 21:16–21 (LXX)

For ancient Israelites, a body that was blemished, incomplete, or not capable of producing offspring meant that one was ostracized from various forms of cultic and social activity. Likewise, interaction with dead bodies, open lesions, bald spots, or marrying a woman who was not a virgin would render a priest impure (Lev 21:1–15).

> And the Lord spoke to Moses, saying: "Say to Aaron: 'If a person from your family among your relatives has a blemish, he may not approach to offer the gifts of his God. Any person who has a blemish shall not approach, a person who is lame or blind, or a person who has something cut or mutilated, or one who has a broken foot or a broken hand, or a hunchback, or one with white spots on the eye, or an inflammation in his eyes, or a man with an itching disease or scabs, like lichen, or with a single testicle. Anyone of the seed of Aaron the priest who has a blemish shall not come near to offer the sacrifices to your God; because he has a blemish, he shall not approach to offer the gifts of God.'"[11]

12. XENOPHON, *MEMORABILIA* 1.5.6

The historian Xenophon of Athens (430–354 BCE) had studied with Socrates, whom he describes here. Xenophon identifies a chief virtue associated with Greek masculinity: self-control. The notion that men had to control their bodies, including all their appetites as well as their finances, was key to what it meant to be a man and continued to exercise its centrality through the centuries.

10. Adapted from William Hansen, *Phlegon of Tralles' Book of Marvels* (Exeter: University of Exeter Press, 1996), 38–39.
11. Adapted from Albert Pietersma and Benjamin G. Wright, eds., *New English Translation of the Septuagint*, trans. Dirk L. Büchner (Oxford: Oxford University Press, 2007).

Speaking in this way, he displayed his own self-control more by his deeds than by his words. For he controlled not only the pleasures of his body, but also those of money, esteeming that the one taking money from a random person places himself under a master and is subject to a slavery of which nothing is more shameful.[12]

13. James 5:1–3, 5

In his characterization of the rich as wailing, with rotting clothes, rusting gold and silver that cuts into their pudgy flesh, and living luxuriously, the author of James evokes the image of the effeminate male who has lost control of all his appetites. Such an association with effeminacy would be deeply dishonorable to a male in Mediterranean antiquity.

> Come on now, you greedy ones, cry and howl for the hardships that are coming upon you. Your riches have rotted, and your clothes are moth-eaten. Your gold and silver have rusted, and their rust will be a witness against you, and it will eat your fleshy parts like fire. . . . You have lived on the earth in luxury and in pleasure; you have fattened your hearts in a day of slaughter.

14. *Passion of Perpetua and Felicity* 10.7

Perpetua was an aristocratic woman, martyred for her Christian loyalty in Carthage in 203 CE. This remarkable account narrates part of one of her visions, in which she turns into a man and fights like a gladiator, conquering her male opponent (including stepping on his head). Like other martyr accounts, her "masculinization" was a means by which some Christian writers asserted the masculinization of early Christianity.

> I was stripped naked, and I became a man. And my helpers began to rub me with oil as is the custom in a contest; and right opposite, I saw the Egyptian rolling about in the dirt.[13]

15. Galen, *Of Temperaments* 2.4

Galen, referred to in the previous section, was one of the most prolific writers in antiquity. Here he reflects the view that women and men are different with regard to heat. Galen does not indicate that he actually touched women to

---

12. Adapted from Marchant and Todd, LCL.

13. Adapted from Thomas J. Heffernan, *The Passion of Perpetua and Felicity* (Oxford: Oxford University Press, 2012), 130.

confirm that they were colder, but argues that their coldness is related to his observation that they are fatter than men (see **chap. 8, Space**).

> Therefore, hibernating animals are often found to be fatter, and women more than men; by temperament, the female is colder than the male and stays at the house most of the time.[14]

GENDER AND DRESS

16. 1 Corinthians 11:2–16

This text is much debated, and some of its references unclear, but it reflects to what extent gender, dress, and honor and shame were intimately connected. Women should dress and wear their hair like women, and men like men, reminiscent of a whole range of Greco-Roman texts.

> I praise you because you remember me in everything and keep the traditions just as I have given them to you. But I want you to know that Christ is the head of every man, and the man is the head of the woman, and God is the head of Christ. Every praying or prophesying man with something on his head shames his head, but any praying or prophesying woman with her head uncovered shames her head, for it is one and the same thing as having her head shaved. For if a woman will not be covered, then she should cut off her hair; but if it is shameful for a woman to have her hair cut off or to be shaved, she should be covered. For a man ought not to cover his head, since he is the image and glory of God; but woman is the glory of man. For man was not made from woman, but woman from man. Neither was man created for woman, but woman for man. For this reason, a woman ought to have power on her head because of the angels. Nevertheless, in the Lord, woman is not separate from man or man separate from woman. For just as woman is of man, so man is by woman; but all things come from God. Judge for yourselves; is it appropriate for a woman to pray to God with her head uncovered? Does not even nature itself teach you that if a man wears long hair, it is dishonorable to him, but if a woman has long hair, it is her glory? For her hair is given to her for a covering. But if anyone seems to be contentious—we have no such practice, nor do the churches of God.

14. Adapted from P. N. Singer, *Galen: Selected Works* (Oxford: Oxford University Press, 1997), 247.

17. PHILO OF ALEXANDRIA, *ON THE VIRTUES* 18–21

The Hellenistic Judean philosopher Philo (25 BCE–50 CE) explains the legal prescriptions concerning why men should look and dress like men, and women should look and dress like women.

> But such earnestness and love for honor is displayed by the law in attaining the object of disciplining and exercising the soul to manly courage, so that regulates the type of garment that men ought to wear, strictly forbidding a man from wearing the garments of a woman, in order that no trace of shadow of the female may be attached to the male to destroy his masculinity. . . . For as it perceived that the bodies of men and women, looking at them as if they had been sculptured or painted forms, were very dissimilar, and that each of the two has a different life assigned to it, for to the woman is assigned a household life, while a political one is more suited to the man, so in respect of other matters that were not actually the works of nature, but still were in strict accordance with nature, it judged it expedient to deliver prohibitions that were the result of sense and wisdom. And these related to the habits of living, and to dress, and to other things of that kind. It is thought desirable that he who is truly a man should show himself a man, particularly in the matter of dress, since, as he wears that both day and night, he ought to take care that there is no indication in it of any lack of manly courage. In the same way, having also trained the woman in the ornaments suited to her, the law forbids her from wearing the dress of a man, keeping at a distance men-women just as much as it does women-men. For the lawgiver knew that just as in buildings, if something is taken away, the rest does not remain the same.[15]

18. EZEKIEL 16:8–13A (LXX)

Ezekiel 16 famously personifies Jerusalem as a woman who is born, matures, and is bathed, anointed, and dressed (the dressing of her is a euphemism for engaging in sex with her) by God. However, Jerusalem becomes adulterous, using her adornment to "play the whore." She is then stripped by her lovers and eventually destroyed. The text illustrates how women's adornment is acceptable provided it is under male control.

> I passed by you and saw you, and behold, your season was a season of lodgers. I spread my wings over you and concealed your unseemliness: I swore to you and entered into a covenant with you, says the Lord, and you became mine. Then I bathed you with water and washed off your blood from you and anointed you with

15. Adapted from Colson, LCL.

oil. And I clothed you with embroidered clothes and put shoes on you of hyacinth color; I bound you in fine linen and covered you with a rich hair veil. I adorned you with an ornament: I put bracelets on your arms, a chain on your neck, a ring on your nose, earrings in your ears, and a crown of boasting on your head. And you were adorned with gold and silver, while your clothing was of fine linen, woven hair, and embroidered cloth.[16]

19. Ovid, *Cure for Love* 347–56

The Roman poet Ovid (43 BCE–17/18 CE) was known for describing how women should don their dress (*cultus*), yet in this excerpt, he levels nothing short of disgust at the filth that women put on their faces. Here he tells a lover to arrive at his girlfriend's home early before she has finished putting on her makeup.

Arrive unannounced: You are safe, you will catch her defenseless; the poor one will fall by her own faults. . . . Go see her face (do not let shame stop you) when she is painting her cheeks with concoctions of dyes. You will find boxes, and a thousand colors, and ointments dripping down into her tepid bosom. These drugs smell like your table, Phineus, and more than once have made me sick.[17]

20. Livy, *History of Rome* 34.7

The Roman historian Livy (64 or 59 BCE–17 CE) reconstructs a debate about whether the Oppian law of 215 BCE should be repealed. This law restricted how much gold a woman could carry, whether she could wear purple-trimmed clothes, or ride in carriages near Rome. Lucius Valerius wants to revoke the law and states the following. The debate is really about women's economic power, but it illustrates how closely women were associated with adornment.

[E]legance of appearance, adornment, clothes—these are the woman's *insignia*; in these they rejoice and glory; these our ancestors called the ornament [or "universe"] of women.[18]

16. Adapted from Albert Pietersma and Benjamin G. Wright, eds., *New English Translation of the Septuagint*, trans. Noel Hubler (Oxford: Oxford University Press, 2007).
17. Adapted from Mozley, LCL.
18. Adapted from Sage, LCL.

Vocabulary of Gender

HEBREW

אָדָם (*adam*) .... human being
אִישׁ (*ish*) .... man
אִשָּׁה (*ishshah*) .... woman
זָכָר (*zakar*) .... male
נְקֵבָה (*neqevah*) .... female

GREEK

ἀνδρεία (*andreia*) .... manliness, manhood
ἀνδρόγυνος (*androgynos*) .... "man-woman," "woman-man"
ἄρσην (*arsēn*) .... male, masculine
γυνή (*gynē*) .... woman, wife
Ἑρμαφρόδιτος
 (*Hermaphroditos*) .... person of both sexes
θῆλυς (*thēlys*) .... female, delicate, gentle
κίναιδος (*kinaidos*) .... deviant male
μαλακός, -ή, -όν
 (*malakos, -ē, -on*)............... soft one (often to designate an effeminate male)

LATIN

cultus .... clothing, personal care, adornment
femina............................ woman
femininus, -a, -um................ feminine
genus............................. grammatical gender
masculinus, -a, -um .... masculine
mulier............................ woman
ornatus........................... adornment
sexus .... biological division of male and female
vir .... man

Select Bibliography

Edwards, Douglas R. "Dress and Ornamentation." *ABD* 2:232–38.

Gleason, Maud W. "The Semiotics of Gender: Physiognomy and Self-Fashioning in the Second Century C.E." Pages 389–415 in *Before Sexuality: The Construction of Erotic Experience in the Ancient Greek World*. Edited by David M. Halperin, John J. Winkler, and Froma Zeitlin. Princeton: Princeton University Press, 1990.

Martin, Dale B. *Sex and the Single Savior: Gender and Sexuality in Biblical Interpretation*. Louisville: Westminster John Knox, 2006.

Moxnes, Halvor. "Conventional Values in the Hellenistic World: Masculinity." Pages 263–84 in *Conventional Values of the Ancient Greeks*. Edited by Per Bilde et al. Aarhus: Aarhus University Press, 1997.

Olson, Kelly. *Dress and the Roman Woman: Self-Presentation and Society*. New York: Routledge, 2008.

Osiek, Carolyn, and Jennifer Pouya. "Constructions of Gender in the Roman Imperial World." Pages 44–56 in *Understanding the Social World of the New Testament*. Edited by Dietmar Neufeld and Richard E. DeMaris. London: Routledge, 2010.

Additional Texts

GENDER

Aeschylus, *Seven against Thebes* 181–202

Augustine, *City of God* 6.9

Catullus, *Poems* 6

Chariton, *Chaereas and Callirhoe* 1.4.9

Cicero, *Letters to Friends* 352

Clement of Alexandria, *Christ the Educator* 3.2–5

Dio Cassius, *Roman History* 43.43.1–4

Euripides, *Medea* 569–75

Hesiod, *Theogony* 590–612

Horace, *Satires* 1.2

Hosea 1–3

Jerome, *Letters* 75, 84

Judges 11:34–40

Juvenal, *Satires* 6

Leviticus 12:1–8

Livy, *History of Rome* 1.47.1–6

Lucian, *Nigrinus* 13

Martial, *Epigrams* 8.12

Philo, *On the Creation of the World* 151–52; *Questions and Answers on Genesis* 1.33

Plutarch, *How to Profit by One's Enemies* 89b–f; *Life of Gaius Gracchus* 4.2–3

Quintus Curtius, *Histories of Alexander* 8.9.20–30

1 Samuel 16:17–18

Semonides, *On Women*

Sirach 9:1–9; 26:1–18

1 Timothy 5:3–16

GENDER AND SEX

Augustine, *City of God* 16.8
1 Corinthians 5:1–2; 6:9; 7:1–7
Dio Chrysostom, *The Hunger* (*Or. 7*) 149–52
Diodorus Siculus, *Library of History* 32.12
Galatians 3:28
Hippocrates, *Nature of the Child* 7, 9, 20
James 1:12–15
2 Kings 9:30–37
Leviticus 18:19–23
Livy, *History of Rome* 27.11.4–5; 27.37.5–7

Martial, *Epigrams* 1:9
Ovid, *Metamorphoses* 6.424–721
Gospel of Philip 70, 82
Philo, *Special Laws* 3.7–26
Plato, *Symposium* 189d7–192a1
Pliny the Elder, *Natural History* 7.38–43
Protoevangelium of James
Revelation 2:19–25; 17:1–2
Romans 1:26–28
Sappho, *Poems*, fragment 31
Song of Songs 5:7
Soranus, *Gynaecology* 1.13
Gospel of Thomas 22, 114

GENDER AND THE BODY

Augustine, *City of God* 16.8
Cicero, *On Duties* 1.126–27
1 Corinthians 15:35–58
Colossians 1:18; 2:10
Ephesians 1:22–23; 4:15; 5:23
Leviticus 18:6–18
Longinus, *On the Sublime* 32.5
1 Peter 3:12
Philo, *On the Life of Abraham* 151–53;

Questions and Answers on Genesis 4.99
Pliny the Elder, *Natural History* 7.63–77; 28.70–82
Plutarch, *Cato the Elder* 1.3–6
Quintilian, *Institutes of Oratory* 11.3.75–76
Sirach 26:17–18
Song of Songs 4:1–8

GENDER AND DRESS

Acts of Paul and Thecla
Augustine, *Epistles* 262.9–10
Babylonian Talmud Ketubbot 72a
Cicero, *Against Catiline* 2.22
LSCG 65
Colossians 3:9–12
Cyprian, *On the Dress of Virgins*; *On the Lapsed* 30

1 Enoch 8:1; 62:16
Ephesians 6:10–17
Epic of Gilgamesh 3.20–30
Esther 4:4
Exodus 28:6–12
Ezekiel 5:1–4
Genesis 3:1–21
Isaiah 3:16–4:1
James 2:2

Josephus, *Jewish Antiquities* 3.151–78

Judith 10

Juvenal, *Satires* 2.82–116; 6.457–507

Leviticus 13:45–59

Luke 10:4; 15:11–32

1 Maccabees 8:14

Mark 5:28–30; 14:51–52; 15:17

Martial, *Epigrams* 9.37

Gospel of Mary 15.13

Matthew 6:25–33

Ovid, *Loves* 1.5.9–22

P.Michigan 6551

P.Tebtunis 2.405

1 Peter 3:1–6

Philo, *On the Life of Moses* 2.133

Pliny the Elder, *Natural History* 9.105, 114

Psalm 30:11

4Q184

Revelation 3:18; 17:4–5; 19:8

Ruth 3:3

Seneca, *Questions of Nature* 7.31.2

Sirach 50:11

Tertullian, *On the Apparel of Women*; *The Veiling of Virgins*

Theodosian Code 15.7.11

1 Thessalonians 5:8

1 Timothy 2:8–15

PART III

Social Interaction
with God and the Gods

10. Ritual, Domestic

JASON T. LAMOREAUX

Introduction

Given the public nature of life in an honor and shame society, finding a way to divide domestic and public rituals is no easy task (see **chap. 6, Collectivism; chap. 8, Space**). The following is a selection of texts from the domain of ritual that concentrates on the everyday lives of Mediterraneans, as opposed to the ceremonies of a grander political nature (see **chap. 11, Ritual, Public**). Included are texts concerning childbirth, marriage, burial, festivals, and meals. This selection by no means covers all ritual and falls far short of anything that would be considered comprehensive. Furthermore, the selections were chosen because they contain instances of ritual actions. In other words, simple statements suggesting that a birth happened or that a certain group ate meals were not enough. Further, a comment about the inclusion of festivals is in order. Festivals can be a grand, public spectacle or a smaller, more intimate affair. Because this is the case, festivals are difficult to place either in a domestic or a political sphere. Therefore, festivals were included in this chapter as a compromise between the two chapters on ritual.

While there are some scholars who would argue that ritual should not be defined because definitions are too limiting or reductive, others see merit in defining "ritual" for particular projects. Yet the plethora of definitions of ritual in scholarship is overwhelming. For the purposes of our brief introduction, ritual will be defined not using a universal definition, but simply as a guide to the chapter. Ritual is verbal, nonverbal, and bodily expression—scripted and authorized—that establishes and maintains (situates/locates/orients) individuals and groups in socially defining (identity-giving) relationships. Rituals create possibilities for change in social arrangements and conditions, for the reinforcement of norms, for coping with outside change, and for engaging with transpersonal/ultimate values/realities. While modern ritual theorists discuss ritual in terms of the secular and the sacred, it is important to note that, in an ancient Mediterranean context, this dichotomy is anachronistic. Even mundane rituals, such as meals, were loaded with a religious symbolic nature. For example, meals were not just a time for consuming food, but they were also a highly ritualized form of status demonstration where one's station was put on display in a public forum. This station was viewed by ancient Mediterraneans as fated or ordained by the gods and therefore proper. Of course, there were rules about lavishness and excessive show, but the status of a wealthy individual was nonetheless contrasted with those of lesser status at banquets and dinner parties with various ritual actions and dedications to various gods in the pantheon (see **chap. 4, Honor; chap. 3, Patronage; chap. 5, Shame**).

As is evident below, there is a rich vocabulary relating to ritual in ancient languages: Several words in Greek refer to offerings and initiations; the English word *ritual* derives from the Latin *rite*, with other words referring to *celebration* and *sacrifice*. In Hebrew, however, terminology for ritual is more difficult to detect, where terms relate to carrying out the law. Regardless, it must be pointed out that illustrations of ritual in ancient texts are far more common than the presence of specific vocabulary pertaining to ritual. Further, we are often at a disadvantage in the ancient textual evidence. Texts often contain only echoes or small portions of a more complex ritual. Therefore, scholars must piece together whole rituals from disparate texts. In some cases, we may never know all the elements of a ritual and its enactment. The texts below often contain small mentions of ritual actions in different contexts, spanning a great deal of time. This means that the interpreter must be aware of cultural context (i.e., Greek, Roman, Judean) as well as aware of when the textual evidence was produced (i.e., Homer during the eighth century BCE, compared to Plutarch in the first century CE).

Ancient Texts

RITUAL OF CHILDBIRTH

1. *THE GREEK ANTHOLOGY* 6.200

Childbirth contains rituals not unlike those seen in marriage and death. In birthing rituals, the woman is prepared to enter into the community as a new mother, along with the child who enters the community as a new member. Following childbirth, other rituals are often performed to gods and goddesses in thanks for the safety and health of both the mother and child. In the following inscription, Ambrosia has already given birth and gives clothing to Artemis (here called Ilithyia) in gratitude for helping with a successful delivery of her twins.

LEONIDAS

Ilithyia! Ambrosia, saved from the bitter throes of childbirth, laid her headbands and her robe at your glorious feet, because in the tenth month she delivered twins from her womb.[1]

2. ARTEMIDORUS, *INTERPRETATION OF DREAMS* 1.13

Artemidorus was a second-century CE Greek author from Ephesus who traveled collecting accounts of dreams and their outcomes. In a section on childbirth, he notes the similarities between both death and birthing rituals and how the imagery is reflected in the actions of each.

The dead are wrapped in torn strips of cloth and placed on the ground like a newborn. The end has the same relation to the beginning as the beginning does to the end.[2]

3. LEVITICUS 12:1–8

In Leviticus, an entire chapter is devoted to Israelite rituals of childbirth. The impurity of the woman is explained, as are the ceremonies necessary for the new mother and child (in particular, a male child) to negotiate entrance into the community under new statuses.

The LORD spoke to Moses, saying, "Speak to the people of Israel: 'If a woman conceives and bears a male child, she will be unclean for seven days; she will be unclean like the time of her menstruation. On the eighth day his foreskin will be circumcised. Her period of blood purification will last thirty-three days; she will not touch any holy thing, or enter the sanctuary, until her days of purification are completed. If she bears a daughter, she will be impure for two weeks, like the time of her menstruation; her blood purification will be for sixty-six days. When she has completed her days of purification, whether for a son or for a daughter, she will bring a lamb in its first year for a burnt offering to the priest at the entrance of the

1. Adapted from Paton, LCL.
2. Daniel E. Harris-McCoy, *Artemidorus' Oneirocritica: Text, Translation, and Commentary* (Oxford: Oxford University Press, 2012).

tent of meeting and a pigeon or a turtledove for a sin offering. The priest will bring it before the face of the LORD and conduct the rite of atonement on her behalf; then she will be purified from her blood flow. This is the law for one who bears a son or daughter. If she cannot provide a lamb, she will take two turtledoves or two pigeons, one for a burnt offering and the other for a sin offering; and on her behalf the priest will perform the rite of atonement, and she will be declared pure.'"

RITUAL OF MARRIAGE

4. ISAEUS, *CIRON* 8.18

Isaeus (420–340 BCE) was an Athenian speechwriter and rhetorician. Meals were often a large part of wedding celebrations. In this passage, a grandson makes the case that his mother was the legitimate heir to his grandfather's estate by noting the many witnesses present at the wedding feast he threw in her honor.

> When her father received her [in marriage], he held a wedding feast and invited three of his friends along with his relatives; and for the tribe, he threw a wedding banquet according to their customs.[3]

5. *THE GREEK ANTHOLOGY* 6.280

The following anonymous inscription shows a young woman who dedicates her childhood toys to Artemis before her wedding. This act symbolized a break with her former status as a virgin, as she transitioned into married life.

> Timareta, before her wedding, dedicated her tambourine, lovely ball, her hair net that kept up her hair, her dolls and her dolls' clothing, as was suitable, to Artemis of the lake, pure things, for a pure goddess. Daughter of Leto, holding your hands over the daughter of Timaretus, rightly preserve her purity.[4]

6. EURIPIDES, *IPHIGENEIA AT AULIS* 905–8

Euripides was an Athenian tragic playwright during the fifth century BCE. In Euripides's play *Iphigeneia at Aulis*, Iphigeneia is going to be sacrificed in order to give passage for the Greeks to sail to Troy. Clytemnestra mourns for the coming sacrifice of her daughter and appeals to Achilles to protect her, since, initially, Agamemnon was going to give his daughter in marriage to him. In the descrip-

3. Adapted from Forster, LCL.
4. Adapted from Paton, LCL.

tion of her daughter's coming death, Clytemnestra mingles images of death and marriage while mentioning ritual elements of the marriage ceremony.

> For you, I crowned her head with garland and led her as if to marriage, but now I am carrying her off to slaughter. Shame will come upon you because you did not defend her; for even though you were not joined in marriage, you were a loving husband of my poor girl in name at least.[5]

7. HELIODORUS, *ETHIOPIAN STORY* 6.8

Heliodorus was a third-century CE novelist. In this scene from the *Ethiopian Story*, Nausikles is found out to have been part of a plot that befell the main characters at the beginning of the novel. As recompense for his wrongdoing, he promises to testify concerning his role in the plot and, as a gesture of trust, offers his daughter in marriage to Knemon, who loves her. The scene depicts a few ritual actions that one might find in a typical wedding celebration in the Greco-Roman world.

> When he presented his right hand, Nausikles placed his daughter's hand in his and announced the betrothal. Then, calling upon his servants to sing the wedding hymn, he initiated the dance himself, declaring the symposium to be an impromptu wedding feast. They were all dancing; without notice, they went to make merry at the bridal chamber, and the light of the wedding vigil illuminated the house.[6]

8. GAIUS, *INSTITUTES* 1.112

Gaius was a second-century CE Roman teacher of law. In a discussion of legal marital subordination, he discusses three ways in which a woman finds herself legally subordinated to her husband. In this second case, he notes a ritual in which bread is shared by the bride and groom in the presence of witnesses. *Manus*, which appears in the passage below, refers to the placing of a woman under the authority of a man through marriage.

> Women are joined in the rite of *manus*, in which a woman is wed to a man and placed under his authority, through a certain kind of sacrifice made to Jupiter of the Spelt Bread, in which spelt bread is employed, for which reason it is also called the sharing of bread. Furthermore, many other things have to be done and occur to complete this rite, along with the saying of specific and solemn words before ten

---

5. Adapted from Kovacs, LCL.

6. B. P. Reardon, *Collected Ancient Greek Novels* (Berkeley: University of California Press, 1989).

witnesses. This legal state is still found in our own times; for the higher priests, that is the priests of Jupiter, of Mars, and of Quirinus, as well as the Sacred Kings, are chosen only if they have been born in marriage made by the sharing of bread, and they cannot occupy priestly office without being married by the sharing of bread.[7]

RITUAL OF BURIAL

9. DEMOSTHENES, *AGAINST MACARTATUS (OR. 43)* 62

Demosthenes (384–322 BCE) was an Athenian orator. In a rather convoluted disagreement over the succession of property rights after the death of one Hagnias of Oeon, Demosthenes cites the laws of Solon, noting that certain types of relatives are obligated to bury kin (i.e., cousins and those closer in degree). In this regard, the cousins for whom the defendant is arguing in terms of property rights were in fact proven to be cousins, given their role in the burial of Hagnias.

> The deceased will lie in state in the house as one appoints, and they will carry out the deceased the day after they laid him out, before the sun rises. And the men will walk in front and the women behind, when they carry the deceased out. And no woman under sixty years of age is allowed to be in the chamber of the dead, or to follow the deceased when he is carried to the tomb, except those who are among the children of cousins or closer relation; nor is any woman allowed to enter the chamber of the dead when the body is carried out, except those who are children of cousins or closer relatives.[8]

10. VERGIL, *AENEID* 9.687–92

Vergil (70–19 BCE) was a Latin epic poet. In his epic poem the *Aeneid*, a night raid occurs on the Latin camps, during which a man named Euryalus, along with Nisus, moves through the camp but is cornered on the other side by horsemen and is killed. Euryalus's mother reacts to his death even though she is far off and recounts some elements of ritual burial.

> Nor did I, your mother, participate in your funeral, or close your eyes, or wash your wounds, shrouding you with the robe that, in haste, night and day, I toiled at for your sake, comforting with the loom the sorrows of an old woman.[9]

---

7. O. F. Robinson and W. M. Gordon, *The Institutes* (London: Gerald Duckworth, 1988).
8. Adapted from Murray, LCL.
9. Adapted from Fairclough and Goold, LCL.

11. PLUTARCH, *ROMAN QUESTIONS* 267A

Plutarch lived during the first and second century CE and was a philosopher and biographer. In a series of questions that range from the subjects of sacrifice to wedding rites, Plutarch puts forth the following questions about the conduct of sons and daughters at their father's funeral.

> Why do sons cover their heads when they accompany their parents to the grave, while daughters go with uncovered heads and hair let down? Is it because it is necessary for fathers to be honored as gods by their male descendants, but mourned as dead by their daughters; therefore, the custom has assigned to each gender its proper role and for both has assigned what is most appropriate?[10]

12. PLINY THE ELDER, *NATURAL HISTORY* 7.46

Pliny the Elder (23–79 CE) wrote an encyclopedia of contemporary knowledge called the *Natural History*. In a discussion of M. Agrippa and his misfortune due to his breach birth, Pliny points out the connection between breach birth and the symbolism of reverse birth in burial rites. As a symbol of ushering the deceased to the next world, the body is carried out of the house in breach position and is then turned headfirst as the body is led to the grave.

> It is part of nature's rite that humans are born headfirst; it is human custom that they are carried out of the house feetfirst.[11]

13. SOPHOCLES, *ELEKTRA* 51–53

Sophocles was an Athenian tragic playwright from the fifth century BCE. At the beginning of the *Elektra*, Orestes arrives once again at his home, plotting revenge upon his mother, Clytemnestra, who killed his father. As a part of the plot, he encourages his tutor, Plyades, to go into the house and claim that he, Orestes, has been killed while at the Pythian Games. During the telling of his plot, Orestes notes some ritual elements for visiting his father's tomb (libations and offering a lock of hair).

> Meanwhile, we will first crown my father's tomb with libations as the god ordered and the lavish tribute of a severed lock.[12]

---

10. Adapted from Babbitt, LCL.
11. Adapted from Rackham, LCL.
12. Lamoreaux, *Ritual, Women, and Philippi*, 69.

14. PLUTARCH, *LETTER TO APOLLONIUS* 113A

Plutarch lived during the first and second century CE and was a philosopher and biographer. In his *Letter to Apollonius,* he discusses the nature of grief and what people do in response to it. Plutarch refers to the practices of the Lycians and notes that mourning is labeled a woman's place in Greek culture. While misogynistic, it gives insights into how an ancient male author viewed the role of women in the process of burial rituals.

> They say that the lawgiver of the Lycians ordered his citizens, whenever they mourned, first to dress in women's clothing and then to mourn, wishing to make it clear that mourning is feminine and shameful to honorable men who lay claim to the education of the freeborn. Yes, mourning is very feminine, and weak, and lacking in honor, since women are more prone to it than men, and barbarians more than Greeks, and lesser men more than better men.[13]

FESTIVALS

15. OVID, *FESTIVALS* 3.531-38

Ovid (43 BCE–17 CE) was a Roman poet who is famous for his *Metamorphoses.* In his lesser known work *Festivals* (*Fasti*), he wrote about calendrical events in the life of the Romans. *Festivals* provides a substantial example of calendrical rites that involve entire communities. In the following passage, Ovid tells of the festival in honor of Ana Perenna in Italy. Normal, everyday pursuits are put on hold for the community as it takes part in ritual songs, dance, and revelry.

> They are roused with sun and wine, and pray for years
>> To take their cups in full and count all their drinks.
> There you will find a man drinking Nestor's years,
>> By the drinking of cups in full, a woman changed to Sibyl.
> There they sing whatever theater tunes they learned
>> And wave graceful hands in time to the lyrics.
> They drop the wine-bowl and join the dance,
>> And a kindly girl skips and tosses her hair.[14]

13. Adapted from Babbitt, LCL.
14. Adapted from Frazer, LCL.

16. LIVY, *HISTORY OF ROME* 22.1.17–18

Livy (64 BCE–17 CE) was a Roman historian. Here he tells of ominous portents that have happened around the Roman Empire at the beginning of the third century. In response, the decemvirs decide that offerings in the contexts of festivals must be given to please the gods and divert any calamity that might befall the empire.

> In such a way, being rebuked by the decemvirs, they declared that the first offering should be made to Jupiter, a golden thunderbolt weighing fifty pounds; and that Juno and Minerva should be given silver offerings; that Juno Regina on the Aventine and Juno Sospita at Lanuvium should receive a sacrifice of superior victims; and that the matriarchs, each contributing as much as she could afford, should gather together a sum of money and present it as an offering to Juno Regina on the Aventine and there celebrate a feast for the gods; and that even the freedwomen should offer money as an offering to Feronia, as much as they can.[15]

17. DIODORUS SICULUS, *LIBRARY OF HISTORY* 4.3.3

Diodorus was a first-century BCE Greek historian. For women, festivals were often a time of ritual activity outside the household. Here Diodorus Siculus recounts stories about the incorporation of Dionysus into the Greek pantheon, giving details concerning festivals involving women's ritual activity.

> Consequently, in many Greek cities, every three years Bacchic bands of women gather, and it is customary for the maidens to carry the thyrsus and to join in the frenzied revelry, crying out "Euai!" and honoring the god; also the women, forming in groups, offer sacrifices to the god and celebrate his mysteries and, in general, with hymns, praise the presence of Dionysus, mimicking, as history records, the maenads of old who were attendants to the god.[16]

RITUALS INVOLVING MEALS

18. COLUMELLA, *ON AGRICULTURE* 11.1.19

Columella (first century CE) was the writer of the largest extant Roman agricultural manual. In his advice to masters of farm hands, Columella notes how the meal at the end of the day ought to be conducted. For ancient Mediterraneans,

15. Adapted from Foster, LCL.
16. Adapted from Oldfather, LCL.

the ritual during the meal was wrapped up in honor and position among the participants, and, therefore, this passage shows a specific situation in which a master was to change his normal mode of behavior in the midst of his workers.

> There should be no less consideration shown to those who are healthy, that those in charge of supplies should provide them food and drink without their being deceived, and he should make it routine that the farmworkers should always have meals at their master's hearth and household fire; and he should eat in the same way while with them and be an example to them of frugality. He should not recline on a couch while having a meal except on solemn holidays, and he should be generous to the strongest and most frugal among them on the celebration of feast days, sometimes even admitting them to his own table and showing himself willing also to give them honor.[17]

19. Plutarch, *Table Talk* 713a

In this portion of the *Moralia*, Plutarch recounts a discussion of the place of the flute in the context of a meal and the religious rituals involved. Here libations are also mentioned. Between the main course and the second course, a set of rituals are enacted: the tables are removed, the floor is swept, water was passed around to wash the hands, then a libation of wine was poured out in honor of the gods, and then a paean was sung. Further, garlands and perfume may be passed around to the guests. Here we see mention of the libations, garland, and the paean.

> We could not send away the flute from the table if we wanted to; it is as essential as the garland to our libations. Further, it helps to instill the singing of the paean with a religious tone.[18]

20. Plato, *Symposium* 176a

Plato (428/427–348/347 BCE) was the founder of the academy in Athens and was a Greek philosopher and mathematician. The *Symposium* is his dialogue centered on the dinner party and gives modern readers a window into Athenian social life. In this portion of the dialogue, Socrates shows up later than the other dinner guests, and they wait for him to complete his meal so they can move on to the rituals that transition into drinking and conversation.

> It seems that, after this, when Socrates had taken his place and had feasted like the others, they poured libation and sang to the god and performed the other ritual

17. Adapted from Forster and Heffner, LCL.
18. Adapted from Babbitt, LCL.

actions, as custom dictates, until they started drinking. Then Pausanias started a conversation: "Well, men, what type of drinking do we prefer? Honestly, for me, I am not feeling well because of yesterday's drinking session, and I request a little relief; I believe it is the same for the rest of you, since you were at yesterday's party: so consider what type of drinking we might prefer."[19]

Vocabulary of Domestic Ritual

HEBREW

אַזְכָּרָה (*azkarah*) . . . . memorial offering
זֶבַח (*zevakh*) . . . . sacrifice
חַג (*khag*) . . . . festival
חֲתֻנָּה (*khatunah*) . . . . wedding
יָלַד (*yalad*) . . . . to give birth
פֶּסַח (*pesakh*) . . . . passover (meal)
קְבֻרָה (*qevurah*) . . . . burial

GREEK

γάμος (*gamos*) . . . . wedding, marriage
ἑωρτάζω (*heōrtazō*) . . . . to celebrate
σπονδή (*spondē*) . . . . libation
τελεσσίγαμος, -ον
    (*telessigamos, -on*) . . . . consecrating a marriage
τελεστήριον (*telestērion*) . . . . thank offering
τελεστής (*telestēs*) . . . . priest
τελεσφορέω (*telesphoreō*) . . . . to bring an offering (in the passive)
τελεσφορία (*telesphoria*) . . . . initiation into the mysteries
τελετή (*teletē*) . . . . ritual
τέλος (*telos*) . . . . services or offerings to the gods, marriage
                                    rites
θυσία (*thysia*) . . . . sacrifice
θυσιάζω (*thysiazō*) . . . . to offer sacrifice

19. Adapted from Lamb, LCL.

LATIN

celebratio........................ celebration of a festival
celebritas .... solemn procession of the dead
donum .... offering, gift
feriae........................... festivals
lectisternium..................... feast of the gods
piaculum......................... sin-offering
rite............................. according to religious use
ritualis .... ritual
ritus............................. form and manner of religious observances
sacrificium....................... sacrifice
sacrifico .... to offer sacrifice

Select Bibliography

DeMaris, Richard E. *The New Testament in Its Ritual World*. New York: Routledge, 2008.

DeMaris, Richard, Jason Lamoreaux, and Steven Muir, eds. *Early Christian Ritual Life*. London: Routledge, 2018.

Lamoreaux, Jason. *Ritual, Women, and Philippi: Reimagining the Early Philippian Community*. Eugene: Cascade, 2013.

Nielsen, Inge, and Hanne Sigismund Nielsen, eds. *Meals in a Social Context: Aspects of the Communal Meal in the Hellenistic and Roman World*. Aarhus: Aarhus University Press, 2001.

Parca, Maryline, and Angeliki Tzanetou, eds. *Finding Persephone: Women's Rituals in the Ancient Mediterranean*. Bloomington: Indiana University Press, 2007.

Uro, Risto. *Ritual and Christian Beginnings: A Socio-Cognitive Analysis*. Oxford: Oxford University Press, 2016.

Additional Texts

CHILDBIRTH

Aristotle, *Politics* 1335b12–14
Exodus 13:13–16

Euripides, *Hippolytus* 161–75; *Iphigeneia at Tauris* 381–84

Genesis 21:1–4
The Greek Anthology 6.59, 201, 202, 286
IG II² 1514.7–38; IV 121–22
LSS 115A.16–20
Luke 1:57–66; 2:7

Plato, *Theaetetus* 149b–e
Plutarch, *Roman Questions* 288a–e
SEG 9.72
Statius, *Silvae* 4.8
Theophrastus, *Characters* 16.9

MARRIAGE

Achilles Tatius, *Leucippe and Clitophon*
  2.11.2–4
Apuleius, *Apology* 76.4; *The Golden Ass*
  4.27
Aristophanes, *Thesmophoria* 900
Arnobius, *Against Nations* 2.67
Cicero, *For Cluentius* 14
Claudian, *Fescennine Verses* 4.2–3
Code of Hammurabi 128
Demosthenes, *For Phormio* (*Or.* 36)
  30–32
Dio Cassius, *Roman History* 54.16.7
Diodorus Siculus, *Library of History*
  16.91.4–16.92.1
Dionysius of Halicarnassus, *Roman
  Antiquities* 11.34
Euripides, *Alcestis* 918–19; *Daughters
  of Troy* 353–58; *Iphigeneia at Aulis*
  440–69; *Iphigeneia at Tauris* 818–19
Gaius, *Institutes* 1.136–37a
Genesis 24
The Greek Anthology 6.207, 277
Heliodorus, *Ethiopian Story* 5.30–33; 6.8
Homer, *Iliad* 18.490–96
ILS 8393
Isaeus, *Pyrrhus* 3.77–80; *Ciron* 8.18
Isaiah 61:10
John 2:1–10
Laws of Eshnunna 28–29
Livy, *History of Rome* 38.57

Lucan, *Civil War* 2.360–64
Lucian, *The Carousel* 41; *Parliament of
  the Gods* 5.4; *A Professor of Public
  Speaking* 8; *Timon* 52
Macrobius, *Saturnalia* 1.15.21
Mark 6:17–19
Matthew 22:1–14
Menander, *Samia* 124–25; 673–74
Pausanias, *Description of Greece* 3.13.9
Persius, *Satires* 2.70
Plato, *Republic* 459d
Pliny the Elder, *Natural History* 10.148;
  21.46
Plutarch, *Artaxerxes* 26; *Bravery of
  Women* 244e; *Lycurgus* 15.1–3; *Solon*
  20.4; *Table Talk* 666f–667a
Julius Pollux, *Onomasticon* 3.39–40
Ruth 4:1–12
SEG 9.72
Sappho 44
Strabo, *Geography.* 10.4.20–21
Thucydides, *History* 2.15.5
Tobit 8:19–21; 11:18
Ulpian, *Digest* 35.1.15; *Rules* 6.1–13
Xenophon, *Cyropaedia* 5.2.12

BURIAL

Acts 9:37–39

Aeschylus, *Libation-Bearers* 23–31,
    423–28

Antiphon, *Speeches* 6.34

Apuleius, *Florida* 19; *The Golden Ass* 8.14

CIL 14.2112

Demosthenes, *Against Macartatus* (*Or.*
    43) 62

Genesis 37:34–35; 50:1–14

Herodotus, *Histories* 6.58.1

Homer, *Iliad* 6.414–20; 7.64–84, 421–32;
    Odyssey 11.424–26; 24.280–301

ILS 7212

John 19:38–42

Josephus, *Against Apion* 2.205

Judith 16:23–24

Leviticus 21:1–5

Livy, *History of Rome* 5.41.2; 34.7.2–3

Lucian, *Charon* 181–82; *Funerals*
    10–13, 21–24; *Salaried Posts in Great
    Houses* 28

Lucretius 197–99

Luke 23:50–24:1

Mark 15:42–16:2

Matthew 27:57–61

Mishnah
    Mo'ed Qatan 1.6
    Sanhedrin 6.6
    Shabbat 23.5

Ovid, *Letters from the Black Sea* 1.102;
    Festivals 2.533–42; *Sorrows* 3.3.29–46;
    4.3.31–47

Plato, *Laws* 947d, 959e–960a

Pliny the Younger, *Epistles* 5.16

Plutarch, *Aristides* 21; *Roman Questions*
    272d–e; *Consolation to His Wife* 612a

2 Samuel 1:11–12

Sophocles, *Antigone* 423–40, 891–903;
    Electra 1126–41

Valerius Maximus, *Memorable Deeds and
    Sayings* 2.6.8

Vergil, *Aeneid* 6.212–35; 9.486–87

FESTIVALS

Aristophanes, *Thesmophoria* 214–40,
    571–80

Callimachus, *Hymns* 6.119–33

Deuteronomy 16:1–16; 25:5–10

Euripides, *Bacchanals* 72–82

Exodus 12:1–28; 23:14–19

IG V 11390

Isaeus, *Pyrrhus* 3.80; *Ciron* 8.19–20

Leviticus 16, 23

Lycophron 859–65

Numbers 9:1–14; 28:26–31; 29:1–6,
    12–40

Pausanias, *Description of Greece* 4.17.1;
    4.19.4–5; 6.23.3

P.Hibeh 54

Plato, *Republic* 459d–e

Plutarch, *Aristides* 21; *Camillus* 42.4–5;
    Lycurgus 14.2–3; *Greek Questions*
    299e–300a

SIG 2653

Xenophon, *Hellenica* 5.2.29

MEALS

Athenaeus, *The Dinner Sophists* 1.11–18; 2.38; 4.146–49; 11.462

1 Corinthians 8:1–13; 11:17–34

Exodus 12:1–28, 43–13:2

Herodotus, *Histories* 6.57

Homer, *Iliad* 9.199–224; *Odyssey* 3.29–64, 404–76; 7.153–66; 13.24–62; 17.170–83

Horace, *Odes* 4.11

Lucian, *The Carousel* 43; *Salaried Posts in Great Houses* 14–18

Luke 14:7–14; 22:14–23

Mark 7:1–23; 14:22–25

Matthew 26:26–30

Philo, *On the Life of Joseph* 201–6

Pindar, *Isthmian Odes* 6

Plato, *Symposium* 175a, 213e

Plutarch, *Advice to Bride and Groom* 140b; *Table Talk* 615d–616a, 616f–617e, 619b–d, 679d–e

Rule of the Community (1QS) VI, 1–8

Rule of the Congregation (1QSa) II, 17–22

Xenophon, *Symposium* 2.1

11. Ritual, Public

Amy Marie Fisher

Introduction

While another chapter has looked at domestic ritual and collective festivals, this chapter explores the ritual of public cult centers, particularly with respect to the political importance of these rituals. While the public cult center was certainly not the only, or necessarily the most important, place of ritual for most in antiquity, these sites did play an important role in ancient societies, most notably in the realm of ideology.

Public cult sites took many shapes and forms; they could be temples of various size and shape, smaller shrines, secured areas, or natural sites rendered sacred on account of some event, mythic or historical. Temples in antiquity were not houses of worship the way churches and synagogues are today. Rather, they were the earthly possessions or holdings of the god to whom the place was dedicated. Most ritual activity took place before the temple, but within its sacred precinct. The sacred precinct of the temple was demarcated by a boundary known as the *temenos* in Greek (see **chap. 8, Space**). Rituals were performed, however, at the site of a future temple, to dedicate a new temple, and even, in the case of the Israelite temple in Jerusalem, within the temple itself. These rituals frequently focused on creating and maintaining the sacred nature of the site and structure. In addition, these rituals were thought to create and maintain lines of communication between the human suppliants and the gods.

The altar, located before a temple or shrine, was the spot of most activity in a temple precinct. Altars, like the temples behind them, varied greatly in size and decoration but were mainly large rectangular structures. The altars of Greece and Rome were usually of hewn blocks, with carved relief; in contrast, the altar before the temple in Jerusalem was of uncut stones, placed together into a rectangular shape.

Until quite recently, the act of animal sacrifice was considered the heart of Greek and Roman cult and ritual; recent studies have challenged this notion.

While it is true that public cult involved much more than just sacrifice, almost every temple and shrine from the ancient world had an altar in front of it, which speaks to the importance of the act of sacrifice. Altars, however, were not used as the receptacles of only burnt offerings, but also of liquid offerings, particularly of wine. Incense too was burned upon the altars of temples. Thus, it is perhaps best to view the act of *offering* to the gods, be it animal, vegetable, incense, or libation, as the focal point of most public cult rituals in antiquity, rather than the specific act of animal sacrifice. The overemphasis of the act of specifically animal sacrifice and the pouring out of blood may come from a fixation with the trope among early Christ-followers (and to a lesser extent Judean writers). This, however, may in part stem from the great number of explicit references to sacrifice and blood in the Hebrew Bible. To suggest that Israelite cult was solely fixated by the act of sacrifice would be to reduce a complex religion of many rituals down to a single act.

While the priests of ancient Israel were tied explicitly to the temple in Jerusalem, most priests in ancient Rome were associated with specific festivals rather than specific cult sites. These cult officials gained their positions through elaborate rituals, and as priests and officiates, their main job was the performance of various rituals aimed both at the continuity of tradition and the reshaping of society and the environment into better and improved states.

This idea of reshaping society through ritual acts relates to the role of ritual in certain ancient ideologies. Such rituals were generally practiced at the state level and either for or by the rulers of the state. Ideological rituals could both give and take away power from an individual. One sees the refusal of certain rituals to the empress Livia following her death, because it was deemed inappropriate to give to a dead empress the same level of ceremony as to a dead emperor (see **chap. 9, Gender**). In contrast, an ideological deployment of power was the Roman practice of *evocatio deorum*, when a general attempted to gain a military victory by calling on a local god to leave the side of the enemy, in exchange for a new (and better) life in Rome (see **chap. 3, Patronage**).

Here we look at passages describing rituals that have to do with the topics above: temples, public cult officials, altars, and the act of sacrifice in collective and public moments. The passages below give a wide range of examples of these topics, striving for diversity, though that diversity is far from complete. The lack of explicitly Christian references stems from the fact that this chapter is devoted to an exploration of public acts of ritual in public cult sites, something the first followers of Jesus and even the early church lacked (e.g., Matt 9:13). One does see resonance of some Judean ideas regarding proper ritual in texts associated with Christ-followers, and this is reflected, for example, in the Latin Apocalypse of Paul.

Ancient Texts

TEMPLE

1. Ezra 3:10–11

The building of the Second Temple in Jerusalem following the Babylonian exile was a moment well recorded in various books and annals. Here the author of Ezra-Nehemiah describes the rituals surrounding the laying of the foundation of this new temple.

> And when the builders had founded the house of the LORD, the priests in full regalia stood together with trumpets, and the Levites, the sons of Asaph, with cymbals, to praise the LORD, according to the directions of David king of Israel; and they answered one another, with praising and thanksgivings to the LORD, [saying] "Because he is good, for his loving-kindness to Israel endures for all eternity." And all the people raised a loud shout, when they praised the LORD, on account of the founding of the house of the LORD.

2. Bacchylides, *Epinicians*, *Ode* 3.15–20

Bacchylides was a lyric poet of Greece, dating to the fifth century BCE. His *Epinicians* is a collection of fourteen odes dedicated to various people and gods. In this ode, dedicated to Hieron of Syracuse, Bacchylides immortalizes the charioteer Hieron's victory in a race and bids the man to do what is right—honor the god Apollo at his temple, which he describes in vivid detail (see **chap. 4, Honor**).

> Indeed, the sacred precincts are full to bursting with oxen-slaying festivals; the streets are full to bursting with hospitality. Gold shines and sparkles, the gold of the high and richly wrought tripods standing before the temple. In that place, Delphians manage Phoebus's great grove, beside the Castalian stream.[1]

3. Livy, *History of Rome* 3.7.6–8

Livy (59 BCE–17 CE) was a historian active during the time of the emperor Augustus. Livy's *History of Rome* was an epic work, first consisting of a mere five books, but later growing to 142 books. Here, in book 3, Livy writes of how the Romans attempted to avert an outbreak of the plague, in a time of war no

---

1. Adapted from Campbell, LCL.

less, through dramatic and panic-filled rites at the temples, when nothing else had worked.

> The destruction of Rome by the disease was the same as that of her allies by the sword. The lone surviving consul died, and among the brilliant men struck down were the augurs, M. Valerius and T. Verginius Rutilus, as well as Ser. Sulpicius, the Curio Maximus; and among the lowborn people, the ravages of the disease were extensive. Lacking all human-based aid, the senate directed the people to make vows to the gods: They were ordered, along with their wives and children, to go as supplicants and to beg for pardon from the gods. Called forth by public judgment to do what each one's own misfortune was urging him to do, they filled every temple. Prostrate matrons, sweeping the sanctuaries with their hair, everywhere were begging pardon from enraged heaven and asking for a limit on the plague.[2]

4. OVID, *METAMORPHOSES* 1.367–83

The *Metamorphoses* is a book of poetic retellings of many archaic tales from Rome by the poet Ovid. This passage is taken from the tale of Deucalion and Pyrrha, who were the only survivors of a great flood. Here they perform rites at an oracular temple in order to learn what to do, now that they are the only ones left on the earth. Their supplications and right actions elicit a response from the goddess.

> After he had spoken and they wept a bit, it was decided
> to call upon the heavenly powers and to seek aid through sacred oracles.
> Without delay, they approached to consult the Cephissian waves,
> which not yet still water, lashed about in its former channel.
> There, as soon as they had dropped, like dew, a little liquid on their clothes and
>   heads,
> they turned their footsteps to the shrine of the sacred goddess:
> Its pediments blanched out with ugly lichens,
> and the altars stood without any fires.
> And when they reached the steps of the temple,
> they fell upon the ground, terrified,
> and kissed the icy rough stone with trembling lips,
> and they said; "If just prayers soften the will of the gods,
> and if the wrath of the gods may be prevailed upon,
> speak, O Themis! From where

2. Adapted from Foster, LCL.

and by what art might this injury to humankind be repaired?
Give aid, most mild one, to this sinking affair!"
The goddess, moved by their appeals, replied;
"Depart from the temple and veil your brows; ungird
the ties of your robes, and scatter behind you, as you go,
the bones of your great mother."[3]

PUBLIC CULT OFFICIALS

5. EXODUS 40:12–15

In this passage, we read the traditional account of the establishment of the Israelite priesthood through a straightforward investiture ceremony. God is the speaker in this passage, and he is telling Moses what to do to establish the priesthood.

> Then you shall present Aaron and his sons at the tent of meeting's opening, and you shall wash them with water and place the holy garments on Aaron, and you shall anoint and consecrate him, in order that he may serve as a priest to me. You shall bring his sons as well and place tunics on them and anoint them, just as you anointed their father, that they may serve me as priests: and their anointing shall be their admission to a perpetual priesthood throughout their generations.

6. CICERO, *ON THE LAWS* 2.20–21

Cicero (107–43 BCE) was a spokesman, orator, and prolific writer at the end of the Roman Republic. In his book *On the Laws*, he offered a discussion on natural law, Roman religion, as it had been under the kings of Rome, and the need for certain reforms in the Roman constitution. Here, in his section on Roman religion, Cicero explains the differences between the various colleges of priests in Rome.

> There will be three sorts of priests of the state: one who is in charge of religious ceremonies and sacred things; another who interprets the unknown utterances of those prophesying and the bowlegged men; and those who have knowledge of the senate and of the nation, the interpreters of Jupiter the Best and Greatest, the augurs of the nation, who will discern the future from signs and auspices and will hold fast to their discipline. And these priests shall take the auguries for the

3. Adapted from Miller, LCL.

vineyards and groves, as well as for the welfare of the people; those conducting matters either of war or common things will be warned ahead of time regarding the omens, and they shall obey them; the priests will discern the anger of the divine ones, and they will yield to it; they will observe the signs of heaven by lightning, and they will regulate and keep the city free, both the territory and the places for observation. Anything an augur should declare as unjust, impious, defective, or awful will be of no effect and not done.[4]

7. Livy, *History of Rome* 5.40.7–10

In Rome, the Vestal Virgins were the most famous of the priestesses. They lived and worked on the Palatine hill in the temple to Vesta, goddess of the hearth and household. The main job of the Vestal Virgins was to ensure that the hearth of Rome in the temple of Vesta never went out. Here we read of their escape from Rome, when it came under attack by the Gauls.

> Meanwhile, the Flamen Quirinalis and the Vestal Virgins, disregarding any care for their own affairs, deliberated over which of the sacred things should be carried with them, because they lacked the strength to carry everything, and which ones would be left behind, or which spot would best keep the sacred items safe; they decided it best to place them in small casks and bury them next to the house of the Flamini Quirinalis, where it is now a religious offense to spit. For the remaining items, having divided the load between themselves, they carried them off by way of the road, which goes on the pile bridge to Ianiculum. When Lucius Albinus, a Roman common person, whose wife and children were riding in a cart, noticed them on that hill, in the midst of the rest of the mob, who, unfit for warfare, were leaving the city, the separation between divine and human things was preserved even then; judging it unscrupulous that the priestesses of the state went on foot and the sacred items of the Roman nation were carried by hand, while his own family was seen in a carriage, he ordered his own wife and children to climb down, put the virgins and sacred items into the cart, and conveyed them to Caere, where the priestesses were intending to go.[5]

8. Aristophanes, *Lysistrata* 646

The Athenian Aristophanes (ca. 446–386 BCE) wrote a number of comedic plays, which reflect and lampoon a variety of social conventions. Men were not the only active participants in ancient Greek public cult; women also took on var-

4. Adapted from Keyes, LCL.
5. Adapted from Foster, LCL.

ious roles, and in Athens girls did as well. In this excerpt from a female chorus, an anonymous woman of noble Athenian status recounts all the various public cult roles she fulfilled when a child, preteen, and just before marriage. She uses this cultic activity as proof of the veracity and sagacity of the advice she wishes to give.

> It is suitable, for I
> Have been a sharer
> In all the luxurious splendour
> Of the proud city.
> I, for my part, carried the holy vessels
> At seven, then
> I was a barley-meal-making maiden
> At the age of ten,
> And wearing saffron-dyed robes,
> Soon after this,
> I was Little Bear to
> Brauronian Artemis;
> Then wearing a necklace of figs,
> Grown tall and fair,
> I was a Basket-bearer,
> And so it follows that I should
> Give you advice that I think good,
> The very best I can.[6]

THE ALTAR

9. 1 MACCABEES 4:44–51

First Maccabees recounts the attempts of the Maccabees to free Israel from its Hellenistic overlords, who have, among other slights, profaned the temple in Jerusalem. Here the Maccabees are content to purify the temple, rather than destroy it, but decide to completely destroy and reconstruct the altar in front of it, as it is upon the altar that their sacrifices to God are burned, meaning it must be extremely pure.

> They debated what to do with the altar of burnt offering, which had been defiled.
> And they decided it best to tear it down, so that it would not stand as a lasting

6. Adapted from Henderson, LCL.

humiliation for them. So they tore down the altar and stored the stones in an appropriate place on the temple hill until a prophet might arrive and decide what to do with them. Then they took unhewn stones, according to the law, and built a new altar resembling the old one. They also repaired the sanctuary and the interior of the temple and consecrated the temple courtyards. They made new holy utensils and brought the lampstand, the altar of incense, and the table back into the temple. Then they offered incense on the altar and lit all the lampstand's lamps, and these lit up the temple. They set the bread on the table and put up the curtains. And with that, they completed all their work.

10. AESCHYLUS, *PERSIANS* 200–10

In his tragedy, the Greek playwright Aeschylus (ca. 523–456 BCE) allows his audience a glimpse into the royal palace of their chief rivals, the Persians. Despite the setting, the manner of worship is very Greek in the play. Here the Queen Mother Atossa recounts how, after a dream full of terrible portents, she ran out to offer a sacrifice upon an altar to save her son. Unfortunately, her actions are too late, as she receives a second portent in bird form once outside. Note the proximity of the different gods' altars.

> When I had risen and touched my hands to the beautiful flowing stream, I approached an altar with [incense in my hand], hoping to make a burnt offering of honey cake to the gods who avert evil, the ones to whom such offerings are due. But I saw an eagle fleeing toward the altar of Phoebus: and in sudden dread I stopped speechless, friends. Immediately after, I saw on wing a hawk rushing in flight and plucking with its talons at the eagle's head, which, in truth, did nothing at all, but cower in fear and submit.[7]

11. ISAEUS, *ON THE ESTATE OF MENECLES* 2.31–32

Altars were more than mere receptacles of offerings to the gods; they were also fixed and public sites. As such, other activities might be conducted at altars, such as the swearing of oaths. In this passage from the Athenian orator Isaeus (ca. 420–348 BCE), we hear of a court case over a property dispute that is arbitrated before the altar of Aphrodite.

> And those people [the arbitrators], having affirmed by oath to us at the altar of Aphrodite at Cephale that they would determine what would be most expedient, arbitrated that we should give up that which my opponent claimed and offer it up

7. Adapted from Sommerstein, LCL.

as a gift: for indeed, they asserted that there was no other means of release from the matter except that he should receive a share of Menecles's property. They declared that for all remaining time, we must do good to each other, both in word and in deed, and they forced both sides to swear at the altar that they would do this. And so we swore to do good to each other for the future, insofar as lay in our power, both in word and in deed.[8]

12. LUKE 1:8–11

In this passage from the Gospel of Luke, the future father of John the Baptist, Zechariah, is presented as a priest at the temple in Jerusalem. What follows is a description of his tasks within the temple. Note that at the Jerusalem temple, some cultic activity was conducted within the building, here at the site of the altar of incense.

> Once, while he [Zechariah] was fulfilling the priest's office before God and his priestly division was on duty, according to the priestly office's custom, he was selected by lot to enter the temple of the Lord and burn incense. Now, a whole throng of the people was praying at the hour of incense outside. At that moment, one of the Lord's angels appeared to him, standing on the right side of the altar of incense.

SACRIFICE

13. 2 CHRONICLES 29:27–28

Various traditions record different rituals surrounding the act of sacrifice at the temple in Jerusalem. Second Chronicles contains one of the earliest accounts, which tells of music accompanying the entire ritual of sacrifice.

> Hezekiah ordered the sacrifice of the burnt offering on the altar. As the offering began, singing to the Lord did as well, which was complemented by trumpets and the musical instruments of David, king of Israel. Everyone present bowed down in worship, while the musicians continued to play and the trumpets continued to sound. All this was kept up until the completion of the sacrifice of the burnt offering.

14. 1 SAMUEL 1:24–28

In this passage, also from the Hebrew Bible, we read of Samuel's mother Hannah and her sacrifices at the temple. Note that rather than go to the

8. Adapted from Forster, LCL.

temple following her period of impurity after childbirth to sacrifice at most a lamb and pigeon, as is required in Lev 12:6–8, Hannah waits until Samuel is weaned and her offering is a bull. While Hannah clearly understands the importance of sacrifice following a birth, she adapts the traditions to her own end in this event.

> When she [Hannah] had weaned him [Samuel], she took him with her, along with a three-year-old bull, an ephah of flour, and a wineskin. She brought him to the house of the Lord at Shiloh; and the boy was very little. Once there, they sacrificed the bull, and they brought the child to Eli. And she said, "Oh, my lord! As you live, my lord, I am the woman who stood here previously praying to the Lord in front of you. This child is the one for whom I was praying; and the Lord has granted me the appeal that I made to him. Therefore, I have loaned him to the Lord; as long as he lives, he belongs to the Lord."

15. Aristophanes, *Birds* 847–55
In this passage, Pisthetaerus, a middle-aged Athenian turned would-be king of the birds, despite having flipped the world on its head in many other aspects, still offers sacrifice in the standard Greek manner. The Chorus explains the process of the ritual.

> *Pisthetaerus*: Go, good one, where I send you, for without you that which I command would not be accomplished. I, for myself, wish to sacrifice to the new god, and I will call the priest who must conduct the procession. Slave! Slave! Take up the basket and the basin.

> *Chorus*: (singing) Agreeing with you, I wish as you wish, and I join in recommending that you offer mighty and august prayers to the gods, as well as offer a little sheep as a burnt offering on account of our gratefulness. Let us sing the chant of Apollo and let Chaeris sing along with us.[9]

16. Homer, *Odyssey* 3.165–79
Many instances of sacrifice at altars appear in the *Odyssey*. In this passage, Nestor of Gerenia explains the ill-fated journey of those attempting to return from Troy, and then he recounts a case where, having safely completed a section of the journey, they offered sacrifice to Poseidon in thanks.

---

9. Adapted from Henderson, LCL.

[B]ut I with the full company of ships that followed me fled on, for I knew that the god [Zeus] was devising evil. And the warlike son of Tydeus fled and urged on his men; and late upon our track came fair-haired Menelaus and overtook us in Lesbos, as we were debating the long voyage, whether we should sail seaward of rugged Chios, toward the isle Psyria, keeping Chios itself on our left, or land-ward of Chios, past windy Mimas. So we asked the god to show us a sign, and he showed us one and told us to cleave through the midst of the sea to Euboea, that we might the sooner escape from misery. And a shrill wind sprang up to blow, and the ships ran swiftly over the teeming waves and at night put in to Geraestus. There on the altar of Poseidon, we laid many thighs of bulls, thankful to have traversed the great sea.[10]

IDEOLOGY

17. JUBILEES 16:20–25

Here we have a retelling of the institution of the Festival of Booths by an angel, who attributes this most important of Judean festivals to Abraham, who, we are told, introduced it to the world. By moving the introduction of the Festival of Booths all the way back to the time of the patriarchs and naming the forefather of Judaism as the festival's creator, the festival becomes both a link to the past for celebrants and a sign of the religion's longevity to the world.

And there he built an altar to the Lord who had freed him and who was making him rejoice in the land of his sojourning, and he celebrated a joyful festival for seven days of this month, near the altar, which he had built at the Well of the Oath. And on this festival, he built booths for himself and for his servants, and he was the first person on earth to celebrate the feast of tabernacles. And during those seven days, each day he brought a burnt offering for the Lord to the altar for a sin offering—two oxen, two rams, seven sheep, one male goat—so that through them he might atone for himself and his offspring. And, as a thank offering, seven rams, seven kids, seven sheep, and seven male goats, along with their respective fruit offerings and drink offerings; and he burnt all the fat of them on the altar, for a sweet-smelling scent, a chosen offering to the Lord. And both in the morning and in the evening, he burnt fragrant substances, frankincense and galbanum, and stacte, and nard, and myrrh, and spice, and costum; all seven of these he offered, crushed, pure and mixed together in equal parts. And he celebrated this feast for

10. Adapted from Murray and Dimock, LCL.

seven days, rejoicing with all his heart and with all his soul, he and all those who were of his household, and there was no foreigner present there, nor a single one who was uncircumcised.[11]

18. HOMERIC HYMNS 2.265–74

The Homeric Hymn to Demeter is one of a set of thirty-three "hymns" from ancient Greece. In antiquity, the collection was attributed to Homer, though they are actually compositions of many poets and redactors, created over a period of some two hundred years. All the poems are dedicated to a certain god or goddess and highlight the deity's chief characteristics and, on occasion, recount an important event for the deity's identity. Demeter's hymn is one such hymn and contains the fullest ancient account of her daughter's abduction by Hades and Demeter's attempt to get her back. The poem is also an etiology for the temple to Demeter in Eleusis and the Eleusinian mystery cult practiced there. Here we read of Demeter demanding this temple from the royal mortals with whom she has been living, following her daughter's disappearance from the earth.

> I am that Demeter who has honor and is the best help and creator of advantage for both the undying ones and the mortals. But now, let all the people build me a magnificent temple with an altar at its base, beneath the city and its steep wall and above Callichorus's spring, upon a rising knoll. And I will teach my mysteries myself, so that from now on you may perform them respectfully and thus placate my mind.[12]

19. TACITUS, ANNALS 1.14

Tacitus (56–117 CE) was a Roman senator, governor, and historian. In this section of the *Annals*, he recounts Tiberius's refusal to allow his recently deceased mother the elevation to god that Augustus had received. Here we note that, ideologically speaking, the emperor must be clearly supreme to all others, in death as in life.

> The emperor repeatedly emphasized that there must be a limit to the honors paid to women, and that he would observe similar moderation in those bestowed on himself, but annoyed at the offensive proposal, and in fact seeing a woman's ele-

11. Orval S. Wintermute, "Jubilees," in vol. 2 of *The Old Testament Pseudepigrapha*, ed. James H. Charlesworth (Garden City, NY: Doubleday, 1985).
12. Adapted from West, LCL.

vation as a slight to himself, he would not allow even a single lictor to be assigned her, and he forbade the erection of an altar in memory of her adoption, or any other distinction.[13]

20. LIVY, *HISTORY OF ROME* 1.20.1–7

The history of the priesthoods in Rome was one with mythic roots. Here Livy sets forth one account of how the first king of Rome, Numa, created all the major Roman priesthoods as part of his larger creation of Roman culture and identity.

Then he [Numa] set his mind to creating the priesthoods, even though he conducted numerous sacred rites himself, in particular those belonging to the flamen of Jupiter. But he suspected that in a time of war, kings would be more like Romulus than Numa, that is, actively fighting in battle. Thus, to guard against the performance of the king's sacred rite being interrupted, he appointed a flamen as the perpetual priest to Jupiter, and he ordered that the priest wear a clearly marked outfit and sit in the royal curule chair. He also appointed two more flamens, one for Mars and the other one for Quirinus; he then picked virgins to serve as priestesses to Vesta.... In the same way, he chose twelve "Salii" for Mars Gradivus and assigned them a particular outfit of an embroidered tunic, with a brazen cuirass on top of it.... The next priesthood filled was the pontifex maximus. Numa appointed a senator's son, Numa Marcius, and he was put in charge of all the religious regulations, which were written out and sealed.... He then put all other sacred events, whether public or private, under the direction of the pontifex, so that the people would have an authority to consult, meaning that there would be no trouble from the adoption of foreign rites or the neglect of their own ancestral rites.[14]

Vocabulary of Public Ritual

HEBREW

בֵּית הַמִּקְדָּשׁ (*bet hammiqdash*) .... temple
הֵיכָל (*hekal*) .... temple
זֶבַח (*zevakh*) .... sacrifice
כֹּהֵן (*kohen*) .... priest

13. Adapted from Moore and Jackson, LCL.
14. Adapted from Foster, LCL.

186

מִזְבֵּחַ (*mizbeakh*) . . . . altar
עֹלָה (*olah*) . . . . burnt offering
קָרְבָּן (*qorban*) . . . . sacrifice, offering

GREEK

βωμός (*bōmos*) . . . . altar
θυσία (*thysia*) . . . . sacrifice
ἱερεύς (*hiereus*) . . . . priest
ναός (*naos*) . . . . temple
τέμενος (*temenos*) . . . . sacred precinct

LATIN

aedes (*sacra*) . . . . temple
ara . . . . altar
donum . . . . offering
flamen . . . . priest from the college of the pontifices
pontifex . . . . priest
sacerdos . . . . priest
sacrificium . . . . sacrifice

Selected Bibliography

DeMaris, Richard E. *The New Testament in Its Ritual World.* London: Routledge, 2008.
Faraone, Christopher A., and F. S. Naiden, eds. *Greek and Roman Animal Sacrifice: Ancient Victims, Modern Observers.* Cambridge: Cambridge University Press, 2012.
Hayward, C. T. R. *The Jewish Temple: A Non-Biblical Sourcebook.* London: Routledge, 1996.
Jensen, Jesper Tae, George Hinge, Peter Schultz, and Bronwen Wickkiser, eds. *Aspects of Ancient Greek Cult: Context, Ritual and Iconography.* Aarhus Studies in Mediterranean Antiquity. Aarhus: Aarhus University Press, 2010.
Kloppenborg, John S. "*Evocatio Deorum* and the Date of Mark." *JBL* 124 (2005): 419–50.
Knust, Jennifer Wright, and Zsuzsanna Várhelyi, eds. *Ancient Mediterranean Sacrifice.* Oxford: Oxford University Press, 2011.

Additional Texts

TEMPLE

Acts 2:46; 3:1–3, 8–10; 4:1; 5:20–25, 42;
  14:13; 19:27, 35; 21:26–30; 22:17; 24:6,
  12, 18
Aeschylus, *Suppliant Women* 490–99
Amos 7:13; 8:3
Appian, *Syrian Wars* 10.63
Apuleius, *The Golden Ass* 11.22–24
Aristophanes, *The Rich Man* 620–26
Baruch 1:8
Bel and the Dragon 10, 14, 22
1 Chronicles 9:33; 10:10; 28:11; 29:1, 19
2 Chronicles 2–4; 7; 26:16; 29:3, 16, 20;
  35:20
Daniel 5:2, 3, 23; 11:31
1 Esdras 1:2–15, 41, 49, 53–55; 2:7, 10, 18,
  20, 30; 4:63; 5:44, 56–58, 67; 6:18–19
Euripides, *Andromache* 1110–15; *Electra*
  167–89; *Ion* 82–111
Ezekiel 40–48
Ezra 3; 4:1–3; 5
Habakkuk 2:20
Herodotus, *Histories* 2.44; 6.105; 7.140
Homer, *Odyssey* 12.345
Isaiah 6:1–4; 15:2; 44:28; 66:6
Isaeus, *Philoctemon* 6.50
Jeremiah 7:4; 24:1; 41:5; 43:13; 50:28;
  51:11; 52:13, 17–23
John 2:13–15, 19–21; 5:14; 7:14, 28; 8:2,
  20, 59; 10:23; 11:56
Jonah 2:4, 7
Judith 4:1–3, 11–12; 5:18–19; 8:24
1 Kings 6–8
2 Kings 10:21–27; 18:16; 23:4; 24:13; 25:9,
  13–17
Letter of Jeremiah 13, 18, 20–21, 31, 55

Livy, *History of Rome* 1.10.5–7; 1.19.1–3;
  4.20.2–4; 4.25.3–5; 4.29.7; 10.19.17–
  18; 10.42.7; 27.37.7–15; 35.9.1–6
Luke 1:9, 21–22; 2:27, 37, 46; 4:9; 18:10;
  19:45–47; 20:1; 21:5, 37, 38; 23:45;
  24:53
1 Maccabees 1:21–23, 45–47; 2:8; 4:36–
  38, 41–50, 57; 6:2; 7:36–37; 10:41–43,
  83–84; 11:4; 13:52; 15:9
2 Maccabees 1:13–16, 18; 2:9, 19, 22;
  3:2; 6:2, 4; 8:2; 9:2; 11:3, 25; 12:26;
  14:31–36; 15:17
3 Maccabees 1:10, 13, 16; 3:16–17
4 Maccabees 4:8–11
Malachi 1:10; 3:1
Mark 11:11, 15–16, 27; 13:1, 3; 14:58; 15:29,
  38
Matthew 4:5; 12:5–6; 21:12, 14–15, 23;
  24:1; 26:61; 27:5, 40, 51
Micah 1:2
Nehemiah 2:8; 6:10–11
Plato, *Laws* 738, 854
Plutarch, *Consolation of Apollonius* 109a
Prayer of Azariah 31
Psalms 5:7; 11:4; 18:6; 27:4; 29:9; 48:9;
  65:4; 68:29; 79:1; 138:2
Revelation 3:12; 7:15; 11:1–2, 19; 14:15, 17;
  15:5–8; 16:1, 17; 21:22
1 Samuel 1:9; 3:3; 31:10
2 Samuel 22:7
Sirach 45:9; 49:12; 50:1–2, 7; 51:14
Strabo, *Geography* 8.12
Tobit 1:4; 14:4–5
Wisdom 3:14; 9:8
Zechariah 6:12–15; 8:9

CULT OFFICIALS

Aulus Gellius, *Attic Nights* 1.12; 10.15

1 Chronicles 15:24

2 Chronicles 7:6; 23:4; 31:4; 36:14

Cicero, *On Divination* 2.51–53; *On the
Nature of the Gods* 1.122

Deuteronomy 21:5

Dionysius of Halicarnassus, *Roman
Antiquities* 2.19.3–5; 2.67; 2.73.1–2;
4.62.5–6

Euripides, *Iphigenia in Tauris* 34–40

Exodus 19:22; 28:1–4, 41; 29:30, 44;
30:30; 40:13, 15

Ezekiel 22:26; 42:14

Ezra 2:61–63; 8:24; 9–10

Genesis 14:18

Homer, *Iliad* 6.297–310

Isaiah 61:6

Jeremiah 14:18

Joel 1:13

Judges 17:5–13

Letter of Jeremiah 18, 28

Livy, *History of Rome* 1.36.3–6; 22.10;
25.16.1–4

1 Maccabees 10:18–20

2 Maccabees 3:15

3 Maccabees 2, 6

Malachi 2:7

Numbers 3, 4, 18

Pausanias, *Description of Greece* 1.27.3

Plato, *Laws* 909e

Plutarch, *Numa* 8–13

Prayer of Azariah 62

Psalms 110:4; 132:9

1 Samuel 2:35

Sirach 45:7, 15; 50:1–21

Zephaniah 3:4

ALTAR

Acts 17:23

Apollodorus, *Library* 2.7.7

1 Chronicles 6:49; 21:18–26

2 Chronicles 15:8; 28:24; 30:14; 32:12;
33:3–5, 15–16; 34:4–5

Deuteronomy 27:5–6

Dionysius of Halicarnassus, *Roman
Antiquities* 7.72.15–16

1 Esdras 5:50

Exodus 17:15; 20:24–26; 21:14; 24:4;
27:1, 5–7; 28:43; 29:37; 30:1; 32:5;
38:1–7; 39:38; 40:10

Ezekiel 6:6; 43:18–27

Ezra 3:2–3; 7:17

Genesis 8:20; 12:7–8; 13:4, 18; 26:25;
33:20; 35:1

Herodotus, *Histories* 1.183.1–3

Hesiod, *Theogony* 535–57

Homer, *Odyssey* 3.179; 8.364

Joshua 8:30–31; 22:10–34

Judges 6:24–31

1 Kings 8:22; 16:32; 18:30–40

2 Kings 16; 23:1–20

Leviticus 1:5–12

Livy, *History of Rome* 10.23.4–9

Lucretius, *Nature of Things* 1.80–101

Luke 1:11

1 Maccabees 1:21, 47, 54, 59; 2:23–25,
45; 5:68

2 Maccabees 6:5; 10:2–3

Malachi 1:7, 10; 2:13

Nehemiah 10:34

SACRIFICE

Psalms 20:3; 27:6; 40:6; 50, 5, 8, 14,
  23; 51:16–17, 19; 54:6; 66:15; 106:28,
  37–38; 107:22; 116:17; 141:2
Revelation 2:14, 20
Romans 12:1
1 Samuel 1:3–4, 21; 2:13, 29; 6:15; 9:13;
  11:15; 15:15, 21–22; 16:3, 5; 20:6, 29
2 Samuel 6:13; 15:12

Sirach 7:31; 28:5; 30:19; 35:1, 4, 9, 15;
  38:11; 45:14, 16, 21; 46:16
Sophocles, *Antigone* 998–1011
Tobit 1:4–5
Wisdom 18:9
Xenophon, *Anabasis* 6.1.17–24
Zechariah 14:21
Zephaniah 1:7–8

IDEOLOGY

Daniel 5:2–4
Livy, *History of Rome* 5.21.1–7
Macrobius, *Saturnalia* 3.9.7–8

Zechariah 6:9–15
Plutarch, *Alexander* 3.3–5
Suetonius, *Nero* 13

12. Purity

RITVA H. WILLIAMS

Introduction

As a generic human activity, purity refers to the process of ordering, classi-
fying, and evaluating persons, places, things, times, events, and experiences
so that everyone and everything is in its proper place and time. The result of
this process is a system with a set of rules governing it. What is in its proper
place is sacred, pure, clean, acceptable, and appropriate. What is not in place is
profane, impure, unclean, inappropriate, or just simply "dirt" (i.e., matter out
of place). The result is a culturally defined conceptual map of reality in which
everything and everyone has a defined place. With this map, individuals and
groups are able to determine what is socially acceptable for particular persons
in any given situation, time, or place (see **chap. 18, Deviance**). Purity rules are
symbolic expressions of a group's identity and core values.

Anomalies are experiences that blur, confuse, or transgress the categories,
lines, and boundaries that define where everyone and everything is supposed
to fit. They often arouse a range of emotions, from curiosity to discomfort to
disgust. Anomalies evoking strong feelings of revulsion or hatred may be labeled
abominations. Social groups may deal with anomalies and abominations by
(1) adopting a single interpretation of reality that simply eliminates them from
public discourse; (2) physically removing them temporarily or permanently
through quarantine, incarceration, exile, or execution; (3) creating rules or laws
that explicitly forbid anomalous persons, things, or behavior in specific places
and times; (4) labeling them as public hazards; and (5) giving them limited time
and space in rituals that call attention to other levels of meaning.

The generic activity of purity produces symbolic systems in which specific
purity rules are replicated throughout the social order. Almost universally, the
individual human body is a central symbol of the social group. The physical

body is treated as a microcosm of the social body, which draws on body symbolism selectively in response to its own special risks and problems. Purity rules that focus on bodily surfaces and orifices often replicate a social group's anxiety about the boundaries between itself and its neighbors. Rules about clothing, jewelry, hairstyles, and body art can reinforce social location and values (see **chap. 9, Gender**). Hierarchically organized social structures find expression in comparisons of persons to various body parts. How physical bodies that have too much or too little of a desired quality are treated can reveal the group's underlying anxieties. Purity rules surrounding individual physical bodies serve to reinforce the core values of the social body. For example, the Pharisees' project of eating in a state of physical cleanness to avoid ingesting impurity and defiling the body's interior replicates anxieties about God's holy people (the social body) assimilating and accommodating dominant Greco-Roman values and practices (see **chap. 8, Space**).

Researchers have traditionally sought to distinguish between ritual or cultic purity, on the one hand, and moral purity, on the other. Careful observation, however, reveals a more complex spectrum of often overlapping purity systems within any given social group. Below I attempt to classify the various forms of purity and impurity found in ancient Mediterranean texts, based on whether they result in temporary, long-term, or permanent pollution, whether they are transferable, whether they originate from inside or outside the body, and how the impurity is resolved.

Temporary physical pollution occurs when things that properly belong inside the body leak out—for example, vital bodily fluids that are lost during menstruation, ejaculation, childbirth, disease, or death. These are natural biological processes that are frequently unavoidable and arise from carrying out normal social obligations. Yet the affected person is considered ineligible to interact with God, the gods, or the sacred realm until a specific ritual of cleansing is complete. Temporary physical pollution is often transferrable. Not only is the body of the affected person, together with any personal items that he or she has touched (e.g., clothing, bed, chair, saddle), temporarily defiled, but so is anyone who touches any of these items. In this way, temporary physical pollution may arise not only from inside one's own body, but also from physical contact with persons and things outside one's own body. While it is regarded as a definite obstacle to interaction with the sacred, it may, but need not always, limit other social activities. Physical purity rules are concerned about the maintenance of boundaries between bodies (physical and social).

Ingested pollution results in a long-lasting, perhaps even permanent defilement of the physical body. Here the pollution originates outside the body and results from ingesting things that are prohibited. Sometimes the food is forbidden because it does not measure up to some specific cultural criteria of what is fit for human consumption. Following the logic of "you are what you eat," it may be that the nature or character of what one consumes is thought to affect one's attitudes and behaviors. At other times, a particular food item may be forbidden because it is too sacred (i.e., it is devoted to or set apart for a particular deity). Social identity and social location may be demarcated by what one eats, when, where, and with whom. Purity rules related to food seek to maintain the internal order, coherence, and integrity of the body (physical and social), even as they seek to prevent inappropriate or unacceptable elements from entering it.

Internal personal pollution manifests itself in particularly heinous behavior, such as murder, idolatry, or incest. Such behaviors point to something disordered within the core of the individual body, a deep-seated stain or defilement that is long lasting, perhaps even indelible. While rarely physically transferrable, internal personal pollution leaves a residue that can pollute a whole community or an entire land. Cleansing is often difficult, even impossible, so that the internally polluted person has to be permanently removed through exile, excommunication, or execution in order to protect the wholeness and health of the social body. Internal personal purity rules are intended to protect relationships within families, between neighbors, and with God/gods.

Ancient Texts

TEMPORARY PHYSICAL POLLUTION

1. LEVITICUS 12:1–5 (LXX)
Leviticus is an Israelite text that in its current form emerged no earlier than the Babylonian exile of the sixth century BCE. Sometimes called the "Priests' Manual," Leviticus contains instructions about sacrifice, diet, how to avoid pollution, and how to deal with unavoidable pollution. In this text, childbirth, sexual intercourse, menstruation, and childbirth are sources of pollution to be dealt with by washing with water, waiting a specific length of time, or engaging in a ritual of sacrifice.

> If a woman conceives and bears a male child, then she shall be unclean seven days. She shall be unclean as in the days of her menstrual separation. . . . She will then continue in her blood uncleanness for thirty-three days. She is not to touch any

sacred thing, nor come into the sacred place until the days of her cleansing are complete. But if she bears a female child, she shall be unclean twice seven days as in her menstrual separation, and she shall continue in her blood uncleanness for sixty-six days.[1]

2. SEG 9.72

The Cyrene cathartic law refers to a fourth-century BCE inscription located in the *frigidarium* of the baths connected to the Apollo sanctuary in Cyrene (see **chap. 8, Space**). The text attributes Cyrenaean customs of purification and abstinence to the god Apollo. It includes provisions for averting disease and death, the use of wood growing in sacred precincts, and cleansing rituals associated with sex and childbirth.

> When a man pulls out from a woman, if he has slept with her in the night, let him sacrifice what he wishes; if having slept with her he pulls out by day, he goes, after washing, wherever he wishes, except to [*two lines missing*]. The woman in the marriage bed pollutes the house. On the one hand, the one within she pollutes; she does not pollute the one outside, unless he comes in. The person who is inside, he shall be polluted for three days, but he will not pollute others, not wherever this person goes.[2]

3. 11QT XLV, 7–12

The Temple Scroll (11QT) found in Cave 11 at Qumran is an Israelite text dating from the second half of the second century BCE. It presents itself as divine instructions to Moses, concerning the construction of the temple, the sacrificial rites to be conducted there, together with purity regulations related to the temple and the holy city. The latter are more stringent than their biblical parallels.

> As for a man, if he has a nocturnal emission, he may not go to the entire sanctuary until he shall complete three days: he shall wash his clothes, and he shall bathe on the first day, and on the third day he shall wash his clothes, and he shall bathe, and the sun will set; afterward he may go to the temple. If a man has intercourse with his wife, [producing] a puddle of semen, he shall not go to the entire temple city where I cause my name to dwell for three days.[3]

---

1. Adapted from Albert Pietersma and Benjamin G. Wright, eds., *New English Translation of the Septuagint,* trans. Dirk L. Büchner (Oxford: Oxford University Press, 2007).

2. Adapted from P. J. Rhodes and Robin Osborne, *Greek Historical Inscriptions, 404–323 BC* (New York: Oxford University Press, 2003), 494–505.

3. Adapted from Mayer I. Gruber, "Purity and Impurity in Halakic Sources and Qumran

4. SEG 28.421

A second-century BCE Greek inscription from the temple of Isis, Sarapis, and Anoubis in Megalopolis instructs potential worshippers that they must be cleansed in order to offer sacrifice. Among the conditions that necessitate cleansing are childbirth and menstruation (i.e., forms of temporary physical pollution), as well as ingesting meat, shedding blood, and having an abortion.

> For someone wishing to enter the temple to sacrifice: cleansed from childbirth on the ninth day, on the forty-fourth day from an abortion, on the seventh day from the natural cycle, seven days from bloodshed, on the third day after goat and sheep meat.[4]

5. TIBULLUS, *ELEGIES* 1.3.23–26

The first book of elegies by Albius Tibullus (55–19 BCE), a Roman of equestrian rank, features his love affair with a woman he calls Delia. The third poem is written during an illness that kept Tibullus from accompanying a friend on a campaign to the east. He both questions Delia's devotion to the goddess Isis and prays that it will bring him healing. In doing so, he reveals the need for, and inconvenience of, maintaining physical purity.

> What now is your Isis to me, Delia?
> What benefit was there in so often rebuffing the moment at hand?
> What good was your pious cultivating of holiness by bathing purely, and as I remember, purifying yourself by sleeping alone in your bed?[5]

6. VERGIL, *AENEID* 2.717–20

The *Aeneid*, a Latin epic poem composed by Publius Vergilis Maro between 29 and 19 BCE, recasts the Trojan hero Aeneas as the legendary ancestor of the Romans. Aeneas, a character noted for his scrupulous *pietas*, epitomizes the idealized values and virtues of the Roman people. An example of his reverence for the gods is demonstrated in his request that his father carry their household gods out of burning Troy because his own hands are bloodstained.

Law," in *Wholly Woman, Holy Blood: A Feminist Critique of Purity and Impurity*, ed. Kristin De Troyer et al. (Harrisburg, PA: Trinity Press International, 2003), 70–71.

4. Adapted from G. J. M. J. Te Riele, "Une Nouvelle Loi Sacrée en Arcadie," *BCH* 102 (1978): 325–31.

5. Adapted from Postgate and Goold, LCL.

You, Father, take in your hands our holy and native Penates.

For me, newly come from such great battle and bloodshed,

to touch them would be an unspeakable sacrilege

until in some living stream of water I shall be cleansed.[6]

7. *IG* II² 1366.2–7

From the second or third century CE, an inscription recorded on a stele in
the Attic region gives directions to the worshippers of Men, the Phrygian god
of the moon, concerning who can enter the sanctuary (see **chap. 8, Space**).
Washing is the prescribed ritual for cleansing those who have become polluted
by sex, menstruation, contact with corpses, or ingesting certain foods.

> Also, nobody polluted is to enter [the sanctuary of Men Tyranos]; let them be
> purified from garlic and pig-flesh and women. After washing their whole body on
> the same day, they can enter. And having washed her whole body for seven days
> because of that which makes her a woman [e.g., menstruation] a woman may enter
> on the same day, and for ten days after [touching] a corpse.[7]

EXAMPLES OF INGESTED POLLUTION

8. LEVITICUS 17:10–13 (LXX)

Leviticus also contains instructions about "clean" and "unclean" animals (11:1–
47). The prohibition against consuming blood emerges not from the uncleanness of blood but from its sacred purposes.

> And if anyone of the children of Israel, or any resident aliens living among them
> eats any blood, I will set my face against that person who eats blood, and will
> cut him off from the people. For the life/soul of the flesh is its blood, and I have
> given it to you to make atonement for your lives/souls on the altar. For the blood
> makes atonement for its life/soul. Therefore, I said to the children of Israel: no
> one among you shall eat blood, nor shall any resident alien living among you eat
> blood. When any of the children of Israel or the resident aliens living among them
> hunts down an animal or bird that may be eaten, they shall pour out its blood and
> cover it with earth.[8]

6. Adapted from Fairclough and Goold, LCL.

7. Adapted from *NewDocs* 6:920–21.

8. Adapted from Pietersma and Wright, *New English Translation of the Septuagint*.

9. Herodotus, *Histories* 2.41.1–3

Herodotus's *Histories* (ca. 450–402 BCE) is a primary source of information about the lands and ancient peoples of western Asia, northern Africa, and Greece. Book 2 contains descriptions of the geography, fauna, culture, politics, and religious practices of Egypt. This passage explains why Egyptians do not sacrifice cows, and avoid kissing Greeks or using their cooking utensils.

> All Egyptians sacrifice clean bulls and bull-calves; they may not sacrifice cows; these are sacred to Isis. For the images of Isis are in woman's form, horned like an ox, as the Greeks picture Io, and all Egyptians alike revere cows far above all cattle. For this reason, no Egyptian man or woman will kiss a Greek man on the mouth, or use a knife belonging to a Greek man, or a spit, or a caldron, or taste the flesh of a clean ox that has been cut up with a Greek knife.[9]

10. 1 Maccabees 1:62–63

First Maccabees is extant as a Greek text that tells the story of the Maccabean Revolt (ca. 167–160 BCE). The revolt is precipitated by Antiochus IV Epiphanes's edicts to suppress ancient Israelite traditions, including their dietary practices, and replace them with non-Israelite customs, such as sacrificing swine. In this text, refusing to ingest unclean meat becomes the defining act of Judean socioreligious identity and allegiance.

> Yet many in Israel grew strong and determined in themselves not to eat unclean things. They chose rather to die than be defiled by foods or profane the holy covenant. So they died.[10]

11. Juvenal, *Satires* 6.01–6 (Oxford Fragment)

Juvenal's *Satires*, dating from the late first and early second century CE, offer a blistering and often vulgar critique of marriage as practiced among the Roman elites. Most often read as invective against women, it casts men as agents and enablers of female vice (see **chap. 9, Gender; chap. 18, Deviance**). It provides evidence, however problematic it is, of Roman views of gender and sexuality. This controversial excerpt from the "Oxford Fragment" points to bodily fluids as a source of pollution.

---

9. Adapted from Godley, LCL.
10. Adapted from *The Orthodox Study Bible*, Thomas Nelson, 2008.

In any house where one professing obscenity lives and sports, and a trembling right hand permits anything, you will come upon every kind of filth, such as sodomites. They are permitted to pollute the food and the sacred rites of the table. Cups that should be broken to pieces as soon as the mouth that practices cunnilingus or touches female genitalia has drunk from it are simply washed.[11]

12. ROMANS 14:14–17

Romans was dictated by the apostle Paul to Tertius and delivered by Phoebe to a Christ group in Rome about the year 56/57 CE. He seeks to strengthen his audience's social identity and sense of community. He presents being "in Christ" as an overarching identity that sublimates the previous ethnic, religious, and cultural identities that manifest themselves in practices such as observing holy days and dietary restrictions.

> I know and am persuaded in the Lord Jesus that nothing is unclean in itself; but it is unclean for those who think it is unclean. If your brother [or sister] is injured because of what you eat, you are no longer walking according to love/in solidarity. Let not what you eat destroy one for whom Christ died. Let not your good be slandered. For the kingdom of God is not food and drink, but justice and peace and joy in the Holy Spirit.

13. STATIUS, *THEBAID* 8.758–66

The *Thebaid* is a Latin epic poem composed by Statius (45–96 CE), retelling the feats of the seven champions of Argos against the city of Thebes. Book 8 closes with a scene from the battlefield where the wounded Tydeus slays his enemy and devours his head. The impurity of this deed is underscored by the goddess Athena's response.

> And now, Tritonia [Minerva/Athena], her father appeased, comes bearing immortal glory to the wretch, and lo—sees him drenched with the brain's shattered waste, and his jaws defiled by living blood, his companions not strong enough to take it from him. Stood the Gorgon, hair sticking straight up before her face, overshadowing the goddess. Shrinking away she flees from where he is cast down, not yet entering heaven until the mystic light and guiltless Helios has cleansed her vision with much water.[12]

---

11. Adapted from Braund, LCL.

12. Adapted from J. H. Mozley, *Statius, with an English Translation*, 2 vols. (New York: G. P. Putnam's Sons, 1928).

EXAMPLES OF INTERNAL PERSONAL POLLUTION

14. Ezekiel 33:25-26, 28-29

Ezekiel was a Judahite priest and prophet exiled to Babylon in 597 BCE, along with the royal family and other notables from Jerusalem. The book that bears his name presents the tragedy of the Babylonian exile as divine punishment for the sins of Judah and its leaders. Here he indicts them for idolatry, bloodshed, and sexual immorality, the very sins that caused God to cast out the previous inhabitants of the holy land (see **chap. 8, Space**).

> Thus says the LORD God: You eat [meat] with blood, you raise your eyes to your idols, and you shed blood, and despite this you assume you will inherit the land. You stand by your sword, you perform abominations, to a man you defile your companion's wives, and despite this you assume you will inherit the land. . . . I will give the land over to devastation and waste; her arrogant strength will end, and the mountains of Israel will be desolate with no one passing through. And they will know that I am the LORD when I give the land over to devastation and waste because of all the abominations that they performed.[13]

15. Demosthenes, *Against Neaera* (Or. 59) 86

This is a courtroom speech of Apollodorus against Nearea, dating from the mid-fourth century BCE. Neaera, a foreign-born courtesan, is charged with illegally marrying an Athenian citizen, giving her daughter in marriage to the king-archon and thus enabling an alien and alleged prostitute to perform religious duties on behalf of the city. Apollodorus explains the rationale for a law that bars from public religious ceremonies women taken in adultery.

> The laws prohibit access to the public sacrifices to these women alone who have been found with an adulterer; but if she attends and defies the laws, anyone who wishes may inflict on her with impunity any punishment short of death. . . . For this reason, the law was made that permits inflicting on her any outrage short of death with no recourse to justice, so that neither pollution nor sacrilege comes into the temple.[14]

16. Plato, *Laws* 872e-873a

Plato's *Laws* is a fourth-century BCE work presented as a dialogue between a Cretan politician, a Spartan citizen, and an Athenian stranger, the goal of

13. Adapted from *The Jewish Study Bible* (Oxford University Press, 2004).
14. Adapted from Murray, LCL.

which is to create laws for a new Cretan colony. Book 9 is concerned with criminal offenses against the gods, the state, and other members of society. The murder of kin results in a pollution that can be removed only when the doer of the deed suffers the same fate.

> For the pollution of common blood, there is no other cleansing, nor does the pollution wish to be recognized as washed away before the trapped soul suffers murder for murder, like for like, and through propitiation the anger of all the kindred sleeps.[15]

17. CICERO, *FOR ROSCIUS AMERINUS* 66

In 80 BCE, at the age of twenty-seven, Marcus Tullius Cicero defended Sextus Roscius Amerinus, who was accused of murdering his father of the same name. Cicero's first criminal case resulted in an acquittal. In this excerpt from his defense speech, Cicero describes the seriousness of the permanent stain that parricide leaves on a person's soul.

> Do you not perceive what the poets have handed down to us: those, who for the sake of avenging their father, inflicted punishment on their mother, especially in response to the command and oracles of the immortal gods, yet the Furies hound them and never suffer them to rest, because they could not be pious without pollution? And this is the truth, O judges. The blood of one's father and mother has great power, great obligation, great sanctity, from which, since it produces a stain, there is not only no power that can wash it clean, but it permeates the soul, so that extreme frenzy and madness follow it.[16]

18. CATULLUS, *POEMS* 64.397–405

Gaius Valerius Catullus (84–54 BCE) was a Latin poet of the late republic. His work is preserved in an anthology of 116 poems. Poem 64 is the most substantial of these, a mini-epic retelling of the story of Ariadne. It ends with an epilogue in which the poet suggests that human impurity brought an end to the golden age in which gods walked the earth.

> But when the earth was saturated with abominable pollution and everyone drove justice from their greedy minds, brothers drenched their hands in brothers' blood, the child stopped grieving the parents' death, the father chose to bury his firstborn, that unconstrained he might take possession of the flower of unmarried

15. Adapted from Bury, LCL.
16. Adapted from Freese, LCL.

stepmother, the impious mother spreading herself beneath her ignorant son, the pious without reverence polluted the gods of the family: everything lawful and abominable, madly confused, turned away from us the just mind of the gods. Therefore, they will not condescend to visit such unions, nor permit themselves to be met in the bright light of day.[17]

19. EPICTETUS, *DISCOURSES* 4.11.3–8

These discourses purport to be verbatim shorthand notes taken down by a student, Arrian, during the philosophy classes offered by the Stoic teacher Epictetus (55–135 CE). The extant collection consists of ninety-five discourses arranged in four books. Book 4, chapter 11 consists of a discourse on purity. Epictetus asserts that human habits of purity are received from the gods by way of reason, hence the highest form of purity is of the soul.

> Since the gods by their nature are clean and undefiled, so far as humans approach them by reason, so far do they cling to cleanliness and to habits of cleanliness. Since it is impossible for human nature to be altogether clean . . . reason endeavors to make human nature love cleanliness. In fact, the first and foremost cleanliness is that which is in the soul; and the same is true of pollution. But you would not find the same pollution in a soul as you would in a body. As for the soul, what else would you find to cause it to be filthy but its own work? The work of soul is choice, refusal, desire, aversion, preparation, purpose, and assent. What then is it in these works that cause it to be filthy and unclean? It is nothing but its own wretched decisions. Therefore, the soul's pollution arises from wicked principles, and its cleansing in forming right principles. A clean soul is one having right principles, for only this soul is free of confusion and pollution in its work.[18]

20. JOSEPHUS, *JEWISH ANTIQUITIES* 20.165–66

Jewish Antiquities, written by Flavius Josephus (37–100 CE), recounts the history of the Judean people, from the creation of the world. Completed in the final year of Emperor Domitian's reign, he offers an apologia for the antiquity and importance of his people in the aftermath of their disastrous revolt against Rome. He interprets the destruction of Jerusalem and its temple in 70 CE as cleansing it of the murderous impiety of the rebels.

---

17. Adapted from Cornish, LCL.
18. Adapted from Thomas Wentworth Higginson, *The Works of Epictetus, His Discourses, in Four Books, the Enchiridion, and Fragments* (New York: Thomas Nelson & Sons, 1890).

[They committed these murders] not only in other parts of the city, but sometimes in the temple, for there too they dared to commit murder, regarding not even this as impiety. It is because of this, I suppose, that God, hating their impiety, turned his back on both our city and temple, judging it to be a clean dwelling no more, and brought the Romans upon us, and cleansed the city by fire, and cast us into slavery together with our wives and children, determining to teach us a lesson by misfortune.[19]

Vocabulary of Purity

HEBREW

חָלָל (*khalal*) . . . . profane, common, unholy

טָהוֹר (*tahor*) . . . . clean, pure

מִקְוֶה (*miqveh*) . . . . pool for ritual cleansing

קָדוֹשׁ (*qadosh*) . . . . holy, sacred

שֶׁקֶץ (*sheqets*) . . . . abomination, specifically tabooed animal flesh

תּוֹעֵבָה (*toevah*) . . . . abomination, detestable aberration, irregularity

GREEK

ἁγιάζω (*hagiazō*) . . . . to make sacred, holy, set apart

ἁγιαστήριον (*hagiastērion*) . . . . holy place, sanctuary

ἅγιος, -α, -ον (*hagios, -a, -on*) . . . . sacred, holy, set apart by or for someone, exclusive, of high value

ἁγνός, -ή, -όν (*hagnos, -ē, -on*) . . . . pure, chaste, holy

ἀκάθαρτος, -ον
(*akathartos, -on*) . . . . unclean

ἀλίσγημα (*alisgēma*) . . . . pollution, defilement

βδέλυγμα (*bdelygma*) . . . . abomination

καθαρός, -ά, -όν
(*katharos, -a, -on*) . . . . clean, cleansed, free of adulterating matter

19. Adapted from Feldman, LCL.

κοινός, -ή, -όν (*koinos, -ē, -on*)........common, profane, that which is shared col-
lectively or communally, ordinary and of
relatively little value

μιασμός (*miasmos*)..................stain, defilement, pollution or corruption
arising from shameful deeds or crimes

μολυσμός (*molysmos*) ....stained, defiled

LATIN

abluo...........................to cleanse, wash away

eluo ....to wash off, cleanse

maculo ....to stain, defile, pollute

nefas ....contrary to divine law, impious deed

obscenus, -a, -um ....lewd, impure, indecent

purgo...........................to make clean, purify

purus, -a, -um ....clear, pure, unstained

sacro...........................to set apart, consecrate, dedicate

scelero.........................to pollute, defile

turpo...........................to soil, defile, pollute

Select Bibliography

Douglas, Mary T. *Natural Symbols: Exploration in Cosmology*. New York: Pantheon,
1970.

———. *Purity and Danger*. London: Routledge & Kegan Paul, 1966.

Klawans, Jonathan. *Impurity and Sin in Ancient Judaism*. New York: Oxford University
Press, 2000.

Malina, Bruce J. *The New Testament World: Insights from Cultural Anthropology*. 3rd ed.
Louisville: Westminster John Knox, 2001.

Neyrey, Jerome H. "Readers Guide to Clean/Unclean, Pure/Polluted, and Holy/Pro-
fane: The Idea and System of Purity." Pages 159–82 in *The Social Sciences and
New Testament Interpretation*. Edited by Richard L. Rohrbaugh. Peabody, MA:
Hendrickson, 1996.

Parker, Robert. *Miasma: Pollution and Purification in Early Greek Religion*. Oxford:
Clarendon, 1985.

Additional Texts

TEMPORARY PHYSICAL POLLUTION

Achilles Tatius, *Leucippe and Clitophon* 4.7.7–8

Cicero, *Against Catiline* 1.29; *On the Laws* 2.19, 24

Deuteronomy 23:11–12

Diodorus Siculus, *Library of History* 16.20.5

Dionysius, *Letter to Basilides*, fragment 5, canons 2, 3, 4

Epictetus, *Discourses* 4.11

Euripides, *Helen* 1430

Herodotus, *Histories* 2.37.2–3; 2.47.1

Historia Augusta, Alexander Severus 29.2

Josephus, *Against Apion* 1.289–92; 1.305–7; *Jewish Antiquities* 3.11.260–69; 4.127; *Jewish War* 1.152–54; 2.149; 6.426

Leviticus 11:24–40; 13–14; 15:2–17, 19–24, 25–30

Livy, *History of Rome* 1.45.6–7; 6.41.8–9

Luke 5:12–16; 7:11–17; 8:40–56; 11:37–52; 17:11–19

Mark 1:40–45; 5:21–43; 7:1–23

Matthew 9:18–26; 15:1–20

Numbers 19:11–13, 14–19, 20–22

Ovid, *Festivals* 4.657

Pliny the Elder, *Natural History* 7.13

Plutarch, *Isis and Osiris* 352c–f; *Roman Questions* 289e–291b

Propertius, *Elegies* 2.33.1–6

Seneca the Elder, *Controversies* 1.2.3–7

Soranus, *Gynaecology* 1.19–29

Tibullus, *Elegies* 1.3.23–26

Valerius Maximus, *Memorable Deeds and Sayings* 3.8. ext. 3

Vergil, *Aeneid* 5.412–13

INGESTED POLLUTION

Acts 15:20, 29

Aristotle, *Politics* 1278b7–1279a8

1 Corinthians 8:1–11:1

Deuteronomy 12:23

Didache 6.2–3

Epistle of Barnabas 10.1–11

Ezekiel 33:25

Herodotus, *Histories* 2.37.1, 4–5; 2.39.4; 2.47.2–3

Hippolytus, *Refutation of All Heresies* 8.12

Hosea 9:3

Joseph and Aseneth 8:5–7

Josephus, *Jewish Antiquities* 3.259–60; 6.120–21; 10.190–94

Jubilees 22:16–18

1 Maccabees 1:41–64

2 Maccabees 5:27; 6:18–7:42

Matthew 15:1–20

Leviticus 11:1–47; 17:10–16

Petronius, *Satyricon* 37

Philo, *Special Laws* 4.17–23

Plutarch, *Roman Questions* 286e, 289e–290d

Revelation 2:14, 20

Romans 14:1–23

Tosefta

Demai 2, 11

Tertullian, *On Fasting*

Vergil, *Aeneid* 3.225–28

INTERNAL PERSONAL POLLUTION

Aeschines, *Against Timarchus* 18–19, 188; *On the Embassy* 148–49

Aeschylus, *Agamemnon* 205–25; *Eumenides* 155–75, 250–85, 313–20, 324–29, 470–80, 600–603; *Libation-Bearers* 1014–17, 1026–28; *Seven against Thebes* 677–82, 736–40; *Suppliants* 260–69

Apollodorus, *Epitome* 2.9; *The Library* 2.4.6; 2.4.12; 2.5.12

Cicero, *On Divination* 1.121; *On the Nature of the Gods* 2.71

Demosthenes, *Against Leptines* (*Or.* 20) 158; *Against Nausimachus* (*Or.* 38) 21–22; *Against Pantaenetus* (*Or.* 37) 58–59

Diodorus Siculus, *Library of History* 10.9.6; 13.29.6–7

Epictetus, *Discourses* 2.8.12–14

Euripides, *Hippolytus* 316–17; *Hercules* 1219–31; *Phoenician Maidens* 1044–54

Herodotus, *Histories* 1.35.1–4

Josephus, *Jewish Antiquities* 2.24, 55–56; 3.274–76; 4.220–22; 6.303; 7.92, 371–72; 11.297–301; 19.42; 20.163–66; *Jewish War* 1.500–501; 2.139–41; 4.150, 159, 163; 4.201–2, 215, 241–42, 323, 560–63; 5.10, 99

Leviticus 18:24–30

Plato, *Cratylus* 405a–b; *Laws* 716e, 759c, 831a, 865, 868–71, 881

Plutarch, *Aristides* 24.2; *Pericles* 39.2; *Solon* 12; *Theseus* 12.1

Sophocles, *Oedipus the King* 94–99, 235–44, 310–15, 350–53, 1012

13. Alternate States of Consciousness

Colleen Shantz

Introduction

Among the many elements of religious life and adherence that are vital to Mediterranean antiquity are experiences arising from alternate states of consciousness, or ASCs. In Greek, Roman, and Semitic cultures, such experiences were sometimes valued as an indication of contact with the divine realm. For that reason, the use of ASCs was institutionalized in particular practices and social roles. Thus, dreams, visions, trances, possession, and out-of-body experiences were cultivated in religious contexts, whether in the healing cult of Asclepius, the oracle of Delphi, or the earliest assemblies of the Jesus movement in Greco-Roman cities (see **chap. 8, Space**).

For some time, the designation *altered states of consciousness* has been used, but this assumes one normal state of consciousness against which others are contrasted, normally pejoratively. The better approach is to speak of *alternate* states of consciousness. Although consciousness is a relatively fluid spectrum, so-called normal consciousness can be distinguished by its attention to the material realities in the subject's immediate context. Consciousness of this kind evolved as the most common orientation for human beings because of its self-evident effectiveness in helping the species to respond quickly to threats and benefits. However, human beings also have the capacity to alter consciousness and, moreover, to learn a level of control over such changes. In fact, some anthropological literature uses the term *polyphasic* for societies that recognize and cultivate changes in consciousness as valued cultural practices, distinguishing those societies from monophasic cultures, which see deviations from common waking consciousness as abnormal or impaired. The neurological bases of ASCs are now being studied and applied to ancient contexts. However, beginning with interest in shamanism, anthropology remains the primary lens through which they are studied.

A landmark survey of ethnographic data conducted in the 1960s showed that the majority of the world's cultures (80 percent) practice some form of institutionalized alteration of consciousness. Thus, urbanized, north Atlantic cultures are unusual in valuing a single phase of consciousness at the expense of all other states. While certain neurological universals make ASCs possible, the hosting culture also influences their character, preparing individuals for alterations, shaping the nature of the experience, and interpreting the alterations after the fact. So, although many people have experienced occasions of dissociative states, the practice was institutionalized in the Delphic oracle and Hebrew prophets, for example. Similarly, sages in Judean and diaspora contexts (e.g., Philo) and philosophers in Hellenistic contexts (e.g., Plotinus) employed meditation as a means to gain philosophical insight. In a more democratizing form, initiation rites like those of Mithraism seem to have been designed to alter the consciousness of participants.

Nonetheless, the ancient world was not without its debates about which forms or instances of ASCs were authentic experiences of the divine. For example, Lucian provides significant detail for the prophetic performances of Alexander, alleging that he chewed on soapwort to simulate foaming at the mouth and that he rigged a serpent puppet from cloth with horsehair controls (*Alexander* 13–14). Less vehement but equally skeptical, Thucydides was not convinced by the claim that Apollo spoke through the oracle at Delphi (*War* 2.17; 5.26). Lucan, who recognized the prophetic status of Phemonoë, nonetheless accused her of sometimes faking her possession. In the case of dreams, Herodotus, who was otherwise skeptical of divine signs, saw dreams as reliable sources of knowledge, whereas in the passage we see below, Aristotle offered only qualified support.

Yet for each of these objections, one can find numerous credulous reports of the same phenomena. Thus, the historical record attests to active cultivation of changes in consciousness and interest in their significance. Sometimes these practices were institutionalized, especially in the case of Israelite prophecy and Roman oracles. Other practices were circumstantial. For example, in many ancient settings, dreams were occasionally cultivated as a source of reliable information. In the healing cult of Asclepius, petitioners would purify themselves and offer sacrifice in the hopes of receiving a dream that would tell them how to treat their ailment. Obviously, their preparation also included a kind of priming, referred to as dream incubation, of the issue for which they were seeking insight.

The ensuing examples are categorized primarily according to the most salient embodied phenomenon in the text. While there is often overlap among these phenomena (e.g., between dreams and visions, or auditions and trance), some combination of the perceptual, biological experience and the social, cultural context stands out as the dominant feature in most cases. Other physical characteristics, like pain or anxiety, are not uncommon in these descriptions, but they do not belong to a recognized cultural category and so are not distinguished in what follows. As we see below, little ancient vocabulary is specialized to alterations of consciousness. The absence of specialized language offers oblique support for the sense that alterations of consciousness were considered a normal part of the cultural fabric. For example, visions are described with the ordinary language of seeing, and the phrases like "the spirit of the Lord is upon me" suffice to describe occasions of positive possession.

In addition to texts, some archaeological remains testify to the contexts in which changes in emotion and perception were cultivated. Indeed, in some cases, like the tauroctonies (relief carvings of Mithras sacrificing a bull) and standardized temple architecture used by Mithraists, or the abaton at Epidaurus (a dormitory used to incubate dreams as part of healing), these archaeological remains are the only evidence of these practices. Caves were a common site for oracles of various kinds, and, in the cult of Asclepius, the descent (*katabasis*) required in preparation for dreams also suggests cave-like features.

Ancient Texts

DREAMS

1. ARISTOTLE, *ON PROPHECY IN SLEEP* 462B

Aristotle was the eminent fourth-century BCE Athenian philosopher and scientist, student of Plato, and teacher of Alexander the Great. In this passage, Aristotle weighs the evidence for and against the divine source of dreams. He is characteristically levelheaded in considering whether they are divinely inspired; however, his deliberations suggest something of the broad appeal that dreams had in the popular culture of his time.

> With regard to prophecy that takes place in sleep and that is said to arise from dreams, it is not easy either to reject it or have confidence in it. . . . In addition to its other unreasonableness, it is absurd to conceive that it is a god who sends such dreams and sends them not to the best and wisest, but to anyone and everyone.

However, if we eliminate causation by the god, none of the other causes seems probable: some people do foresee [in dreams].[1]

2. Genesis 40:5–8; 41:15–16, 25

Israelite religion, along with other cultures of the ancient Near East, seems to have valued dreams and their interpretation as sources of information and insight. For example, the interpretation of dreams figures significantly among the many other virtues that distinguish the young Israelite Daniel in the foreign court of Nebuchadnezzar. Even as late as Josephus, we see claims of the inspired ability to interpret the divine import of dreams (*Jewish War* 3.351–54). Nowhere does the interpretation of dreams figure so prominently in biblical narrative as in the Joseph saga. Interestingly, while the God of Israel is notably absent from the action, he is nonetheless credited as the (passive) source of Joseph's interpretations. Here no apology is offered for the validity of dreams; rather their reliability, and the superiority of those who can read them, is assumed.

> Both the cupbearer and the baker of the king of Egypt, who were being held in prison, had a dream the same night, and each dream had its own meaning. When Joseph came to them in the morning, he saw that they were disturbed. So he asked Pharaoh's officials who were with him in custody in his master's house, "Why are your faces sad today?" They answered, "We both had dreams, but there is no one to interpret them." Then Joseph said to them, "Do not interpretations belong to God? Tell them to me." . . .
>
> Pharaoh said to Joseph, "I dreamed a dream, and no one can interpret it. But I have heard it said of you that when you hear a dream you can interpret it." Joseph answered Pharaoh, "It is not of me, but God will answer Pharaoh favorably." . . .
>
> Then Joseph said to Pharaoh, "The dreams of Pharaoh are one dream. God has told to Pharaoh what he is about to do."

3. Aelius Aristides, *Sacred Tales* 50, 68

The second-century CE Greek orator, Aelius Aristides, was a devotee of the healing god Asclepius, whose help he sought for a range of ailments. Interestingly, Aristides visits an Asclepion (i.e., the healing center) in response to the prophecy he received from the oracle called Colophon. Among the techniques deployed in the cult of Asclepius, the cultivation of dreams figured prominently. After recovering his health, Aristides recounted over a hundred dreams in six speeches.

---

1. Adapted from Hett, LCL.

I had a dream . . . like this: I thought that I was giving an oratorical speech and spoke among a group of people, and during the speech with which I contended, I called upon the god in this way: "Lord Asclepius, if in fact I excel in rhetoric and excel greatly, give me health and make the envious burst." I happened to have seen these things in the dream, and when it was day, I picked up some book and read it. Then I found in it what I had said. In awe I said to Zosimus, "Look, what I dreamed that I said, I find written in the book."[2]

SPIRIT POSSESSION

4. MARK 1:23–27A

Anthropological literature sometimes distinguishes positive and negative possession, the former being welcomed and the latter overtaking individuals against their will. A strong tradition of negative possession pervades the Synoptic Gospels. "Unclean spirits" or demons inhabit people, displace their voluntary bodily control, and manifest remarkable, often harmful, behavior through them.

And immediately there was in their synagogue a man with an unclean spirit, and he cried out, saying, "What do you want with us, Jesus Nazarene? Have you come to destroy us? I know who you are—God's holy one." But Jesus disrespected him, saying, "Shut up and come out of him!" And after convulsing the man and crying out with a loud voice, the unclean spirit came out of him. And everyone was in awe.

5. LUCIAN, *LOVER OF LIES* 14–18

Although the second-century CE Greek satirist Lucian of Samosata was mocking accounts like those recorded in the Gospels, he provides evidence of the persistence of negative possession in Christian circles a century after the Gospel of Mark (see **chap. 19, Mockery and Secrecy**).

It is ridiculous of you, Ion said, to doubt everything. You know, I should really like to ask you what you have to say about all those who deliver men possessed by demons from their terrible predicament by—and there is no doubt about it—exorcising them! No need for me to dwell on this. Everybody knows about the Syrian from Palestine, the expert in these matters, and how many people he took care

2. Adapted from Behr, LCL.

of—those who collapsed before the full moon, those who rolled their eyes, those whose mouths filled with foam—and yet he made them well and sent them home in a normal frame of mind, having healed them from whatever plagued them, *for a substantial fee.* They lie there, and he stands beside them and asks, "Where do you come from? Whence did you enter this body?" The patient himself says nothing, but the demon answers, either in Greek or in a foreign language, depending on the country he comes from, and tells him how and from where he entered this person. Then he swears an oath, and if the demon does not obey, he threatens him and drives him out. As a matter of fact, I saw one coming out, all black and smoky.[3]

6. JOSEPHUS, *JEWISH ANTIQUITIES* 4.118–19

In antiquity, the term prophecy is used quite broadly to cover a variety of phenomena; however, the texts in this section are all examples that express the displacement of the personality or mind of the prophet. In embellishing the traditional story of Balaam, Josephus explains the extraordinary events as due to the intervention of God's spirit. The passage serves as an example of positive spirit possession.

In this way, Balaam spoke by inspiration, not coming from his own power, but moved by the divine spirit to say what he did. But then Balak was displeased and said that he had broken the contract he had made, through which Balak and his allies had invited Balaam to come with the promise of great presents: for rather than coming to curse their enemies, he had pronounced encomium upon them and had declared that they were the happiest of men. To this, Balaam replied, "O Balak, if you think rightly about this whole matter, can you imagine that it is in our power to be silent, or to speak anything, when the spirit of God grasps us?—for he puts in our mouths whatever words he pleases, and speeches that we ourselves are not conscious of."[4]

VISIONS

7. EZEKIEL 1:4–8A

Of all the visions attributed to Hebrew prophets, that of the sixth-century BCE Ezekiel has pride of place. The vivid sensory detail and disturbing imagery fueled the meditations of later *hekhalot* and *merkabah* mystics, among

---

3. Georg Luck, *Arcana Mundi: Magic and the Occult in the Greek and Roman Worlds* (Baltimore: Johns Hopkins University Press, 1985), 109.
4. Adapted from Thackeray, LCL.

others. Thus, whatever the relationship of this passage to an original ASC, it was subsequently used to stimulate many such experiences. In fact, early rabbis considered it such a powerful expression of visionary experience that the Talmud warns against reading it publicly or allowing children to access it.

> I looked, and behold, a stormy wind was coming from the north, a great cloud with fire and brightness flashing around it, and in the middle of the fire something like glowing amber. Within it was the manifestation of four living creatures, and this was their appearance: They had human appearance, and each one had four faces, and each had four wings. Their legs were straight, and their feet were like those of a calf, and they sparkled like polished brass. Under their wings they had human hands.

8. 2 BARUCH 6:2–7

Second Baruch is a pseudepigraphic account of the visions attributed to Baruch, who was purported to be Jeremiah's scribe. Many apocalyptic visions are pseudepigraphic and hence do not provide direct evidence of ASCs. However, regardless of whether the specific accounts are actual, their popularity in late Second Temple literature suggests a practice among those who composed the texts.

> And I was grieving over Zion and lamenting the captivity that had come upon the people. And look, suddenly a strong spirit lifted me and bore me aloft over the wall of Jerusalem. And I looked, and behold four angels standing at the four corners of the city, each of them holding a torch for fire in his hands. And another angel descending from heaven said to them: "Hold your lamps, and do not light them until I tell you. For first I am sent to speak a message to the earth and to place in it what the Lord the Most High has commanded me." And I saw him descend into the holy of holies and remove the veil, and holy ark, and the mercy seat, and the two tables, and the holy clothing of the priests, and the altar of incense, and the forty-eight precious stones with which the priests were clothed, and all the holy vessels of the tabernacle.[5]

9. MARK 9:2–8

Materials from early Christ-followers contain a few accounts of visions involving Jesus. In this passage, the details of bright light, the literal mention of metamorphosis, and the stimulation of fear are all indications of ASC.

5. R. H. Charles and William John Ferrar, *The Apocalypse of Baruch and the Assumption of Moses* (Boston: Weiser, 2006).

And after six days, Jesus took Peter and James and John and led them to a high summit, away from the others, on their own. And he was transformed in front of them; his cloak became gleaming, utterly white to a degree that no clothmaker on earth could whiten it. Then Moses and Elijah appeared to them, talking with Jesus. Responding, Peter said to Jesus, "Rabbi, how good that we are here; let us make three shelters—one for you, one for Moses, and one for Elijah." For he had not known how to respond, for they were terrified. Then a cloud appeared, overshadowing them, and a voice emerged from the cloud: "This is my Son, the beloved, listen to him." And suddenly, looking around, they no longer saw anyone but Jesus alone with them.

AUDITIONS

10. 1 Samuel 3:3b–5

In Hebrew texts, *voice* often substitutes metonymically for God's specific commandments or general purposes. This cultural feature couples with the ASC phenomenon of hearing ideas as if they were spoken. The two features come together in stories such as the commissioning of Samuel.

Samuel was reclining within the temple of the LORD, where the ark of God is. Then the LORD called, "Samuel! Samuel!" and he said, "Here I am!" and ran to Eli, and said, "Here I am, for you called me." But Eli said, "I did not call; lie down again." So he went and lay down.

11. Augustine, *Confessions* 8.12.29

Augustine of Hippo (354–430 CE) was trained as a philosopher and rhetorician. He had affiliated with Manichaeism for most of a decade, but over time, he was exposed to Christian orators and friends who were sympathetic to Christianity, and he began to feel uncertain about his choices. This section from the autobiographical *Confessions* is Augustine's account of an event that occurred after a conversation with one of these friends, when Augustine was in a state of frustration about his own indecision.

I was saying these things and weeping in the most bitter contrition of my heart, when suddenly I heard the voice of a boy or a girl—I don't know which—coming from the neighboring house, chanting again and again, "Take it, read it; take it, read it." Immediately I stopped weeping and began to wonder whether it was usual for children in some kind of game to sing such a song, but I could not remember ever having heard anything like it. So, stopping up the flood of my tears, I stood, for it seemed to me that this was a divine command to open my book of Scripture and read the first passage my eyes should fall upon.[6]

12. PLATO, *APOLOGY* 31C–D

The fifth-century BCE Greek philosopher Plato is one of two sources (the other being Xenophon) that claim of Socrates that he once heard a voice that he took to be divine. Plato presents this phenomenon as part of the general case brought against Socrates at his trial. In this passage, Socrates defends to his jurors his choice to refrain from public life.

> The reason for this is something you have heard me frequently mention in different places—namely, the fact that I experience something divine and demonic, as Meletus has written in his indictment, by way of mockery. It started in my childhood, the occurrence of a particular voice. Whenever it occurs, it always deters me from the course of action I was intending to engage in, but it never gives me positive advice. It is this that has opposed my practicing politics, and I think its doing so has been absolutely fine.[7]

ASCENT

13. 2 CORINTHIANS 12:2–4

Although stories of ascent experiences are not uncommon in antiquity, they are often presented as stylized accounts after the fact, and any originating event is shrouded under their elaboration. In a few extraordinary cases, first-person accounts of cosmic travel have survived, and Paul's description is one of those. Although it too has been shaped for rhetorical purposes, it is exceptional for its straightforward expression of confusion about the status of his body. This somatic disruption correlates well with contemporary studies of out-of-body experiences. Despite the use of third-person construction, the passage is an autobiographical account.

> I know a man in Christ, who fourteen years ago—whether in the body I do not know or whether out of the body I do not know, God knows—this man was seized

---

6. Augustine, *Confessions*, trans. Henry Chadwick (Oxford: Oxford University Press, 2008).

7. Thomas G. West, *Plato's Apology of Socrates: An Interpretation, with a New Translation* (Ithaca, NY: Cornell University Press, 1979).

up to the third heaven. And I know that this man—whether in the body or apart from the body I do not know, God knows—he was seized into paradise and heard inexpressible things that it is not possible for a human being to speak.

14. 1 ENOCH 70:1–4A

Accounts of out-of-body experiences are particularly prominent in early Judaism, when traditions about the ascent of exemplary figures developed. But, in contrast to the preceding account, the *Parables* or *Similitudes of Enoch* (1 Enoch 37–71) illustrate the complex relationship between literary accounts and real experiences of ASCs. Genesis 5:21–24 states tantalizingly that Enoch "walked with God and then was no more because God took him," and that gap in information inspired several imaginative accounts, including this one. The Similitudes recount the secrets of the heavens as they are revealed to Enoch in his own journey through the heavens, but it is impossible to judge whether a particular experience lies behind these accounts. What 1 Enoch does provide is another piece of evidence that such revelatory journeys were the object of increasing interest in this period.

> And it happened after that, while [Enoch] was living, he was lifted up from among those who live on the earth to the presence of that son of man and to the presence of the Lord of spirits. And he was lifted up on the chariots of the spirit, and his name vanished among them.
>
> And from that day, I was no longer counted among them. And he placed me between the two winds, between the north and the west, where the angels took cords to measure for me the place for the chosen and righteous.[8]

TRANCE

15. PLATO, *TIMAEUS* 71E–72A

This passage appears in a section of the dialogue in which Plato discusses philosophical anthropology and the properties of various human organs. In these lines, he describes the alternate consciousness of the mantic prophets as the displacement of their mind/intellect (*nous*). Such alterations of personality are a key characteristic of the anthropological category of trance.

---

8. George W. E. Nickelsburg and James C. VanderKam, *1 Enoch*, Hermeneia (Minneapolis: Fortress, 2012).

There is good reason for believing that divination is the god's gift to uncontrolled thinking: no one in their mind attains true and inspired divination, but only when the power of the intellect is fettered in sleep or they are distraught by some disorder or because of divine possession. It is to individuals in their ordinary thinking to recollect and interpret the utterances, in a dream or waking life, of divination or possession, and by reflection to discern for whom they are significant whether for good or evil in the future, past, or present. But when individuals have been overtaken by frenzy and continue in that state, it is not for them to decide the meaning of their own visions and utterances.[9]

16. 1 CORINTHIANS 14:13–15

Here Paul discusses the distinctive trance practice of ecstatic speech known as glossolalia or "speaking in tongues." He describes the trance state as displacing or neutralizing the activity of one's mind and the concomitant dominance over one's spirit.

> Therefore, the one speaking in a tongue should pray so that he can interpret it. For if I pray in a tongue, my spirit prays, but my mind is fruitless. So then, what should I do? I will pray in the spirit, and likewise I will pray in the mind; I will sing in the spirit, and I will sing with the mind as well.

17. ACTS 10:9–13

The author of Acts relates several narratives of dreams and visions in the period immediately following Jesus's death. The one in question is frequently described as a vision (and sometimes even a dream, although Peter is not portrayed as sleeping). Such overlap of categories is not unusual. I have placed it here because of the opening details in which Peter is described as hungry before ecstasy (*ekstasis*) came upon him. Thus, this scene rounds out a wide range of biocultural phenomena of ASCs in Acts.

> About the sixth hour, Peter went up to the roof to pray. But he became hungry and wanted to eat; however, while they were making preparations, an ecstasy fell on him, and he saw the heaven opening and a certain container descending like a huge sheet being let down upon the earth by the four corners, and in which were all the quadrupeds and walking things of the earth, and birds of heaven. And a voice came to him, "Rise up, Peter, kill and eat!"

9. Adapted from Bury, LCL.

MEANS OF ACHIEVING

18. 1 Kings 18:26–29a

Some groups in antiquity cultivated alterations of consciousness through rehearsed meditation, sensory stimulation or deprivation, or the use of alcohol or psychotropic drugs. The scene of a sacrificial contest between the prophets of Baal and Asherah, on the one hand, and the prophet of YHWH, on the other, presents several "bottom-up" means of inducing alterations in consciousness: vigorous vocalization, synchronized movement, self-inflicted pain, and fasting.

> Then they took the ox that was given to them, and they prepared it and shouted the name of Baal from the morning until the midday, saying: O Baal, answer us! But there was no voice, and there was no one answering. So they jumped upon the altar they had made. And it happened that at noon Elijah ridiculed them, saying: Shout with a louder voice, for he is a god—either he is busy, or turned away, or on a journey, or maybe he is asleep and has to be awakened. And they shouted with a loud voice and cut themselves, as was their practice, with swords and spears until blood was streaming all over them. So as midday passed, they performed prophetic actions until it was time for the evening sacrifice.

19. Thanksgiving Hymns (1QH) V, 30–33

Another effective means to focus and shift consciousness is through the stimulation of heightened and exceptional emotions. The Qumran community understood their worship to take place in the presence of angels (Damascus Document [4QDª]). When the *maskil* (instructor) of the Qumran community performed the *hodayot* poems in front of the community, he alternated dramatically between language of exaltation and descriptions of personal debasement in an emotional paradox that Carol Newsom calls "the masochistic sublime."

> How is a spirit of flesh to interpret all these things and to grasp the secret counsel of your greatness? And what is the child of a woman in the midst of all your awesome works? He is a thing composed of dust and kneaded with water. Sinful guilt is his foundation, ignominious shame, and a source of pollution, and a spirit of fault rules him. And if he acts wickedly, he will become an eternal sign and a warning for generations, an eternal horror among mortals.[10]

10. Carol Newsom, "Religious Experience in the Dead Sea Scrolls," 213.

20. PLOTINUS, *ENNEADS* 1.9

The third-century CE philosopher Plotinus is credited as the founder of Neo-platonism. He greatly valued the insights that derived from some ASCs, and he reflected on their metaphysical significance in his philosophical writings. In this passage, he discusses the means by which one might appropriately achieve freedom from one's body, distinguishing it from the means that he deems illegitimate (viz. psychoactive drugs).

> The soul will wait for the body to be fully severed from it. In those circumstances, it does not depart; it simply finds itself free. But how does the body become separated? The separation occurs when nothing of the soul remains bound up with it. The harmony of the body through which the soul was kept is broken, and it can hold its guest no longer. But when a man devises the dissolution of the body, he is the one who has used violence and ripped himself away, not the body that has let the soul slip from it. . . . To rely on drugs to release the soul seems a strange way of assisting its purposes.[11]

Vocabulary of Alternate States of Consciousness

As discussed in the introduction to this entry, the vocabulary associated with ASC includes quite ordinary words like "see" and "hear," which are of course far too numerous to be included here. In monophasic cultures, like most industrialized north Atlantic societies, special words (like hallucinate) are created to label perceptions in various states of consciousness as less reliable than quotidian perception.

HEBREW

חָלַם (*khalam*) . . . . to dream
כָּבוֹד (*kavod*) . . . . glory/radiance
נָבִיא (*nabi*) . . . . prophet
רוּחַ (*ruakh*) . . . . spirit

11. Adapted from MacKenna, LCL.

GREEK

ἀποκάλυψις (*apokalypsis*) . . . . revelation
δαιμόνιον (*daimonion*) . . . . demon
δόξα (*doxa*) . . . . glory/radiance
ἔκστασις (*ekstasis*) . . . . ecstasy, dissociation, astonishment
ἐξίστημι (*existēmi*) . . . . to stand apart, be beside oneself, be amazed
μαντεία (*manteia*) . . . . vision
νοῦς (*nous*) . . . . mind
ὄναρ (*onar*) . . . . dream
ὅραμα (*horama*) . . . . vision
πνεῦμα (*pneuma*) . . . . spirit
προφήτης (*prophētēs*) . . . . prophet
ψυχή (*psychē*) . . . . soul, mind, psyche

LATIN

anima . . . . soul
daemon . . . . demon
insomnium . . . . dream
mantis . . . . soothsayer, diviner
mens . . . . mind
visio . . . . vision

Select Bibliography

Beck, Roger. *The Religion of the Mithras Cult in the Roman Empire: Mysteries of the Unconquered Sun.* Oxford: Oxford University Press, 2006.

Craffert, Pieter. *Life of a Galilean Shaman: Jesus of Nazareth in Anthropological-Historical Perspective.* Eugene, OR: Cascade, 2008.

Newsom, Carol A. "Religious Experience in the Dead Sea Scrolls: Two Case Studies." Pages 205–22 in *Linking Text and Experience.* Vol. 2 of *Experientia.* Edited by Colleen Shantz and Rodney Alan Werline. Early Judaism and Its Literature 35. Boston: Brill, 2012.

Shantz, Colleen. *Paul in Ecstasy: The Neurobiology of the Apostle's Life and Thought.* New York: Cambridge University Press, 2009.

Taves, Ann. *Religious Experience Reconsidered: A Building-Block Approach to the Study of Religion and Other Special Things.* Princeton: Princeton University Press, 2010.

Additional Texts

DREAMS

Acts 16:9–10

Appian, *Civil Wars* 1.12.105; 2.16.115;
4.14.110; *Roman History* 8.1.1; 8.20.136;
11.9.56; 12.2.9; 12.4.27

Aristotle, *On Dreams*; *On Prophesying by
Dreams*

Cicero, *On Divination* 1.60

Daniel 2:24–47

Diodorus Siculus, *Library of History*
13.97.6; 16.33.1; 17.103.7

Diogenes Laertius, *Lives of Eminent
Philosophers* 1.11.117; 2.5.35; 3.2, 5

Dionysius of Halicarnassus, *Roman
Antiquities* 1.56.5; 1.57.4; 3.67.3; 5.54.2;
7.68.3–5; 20.12.1–2

Herodotus, *Histories* 1.34, 209; 2.139,
141; 3.30, 124; 5.56; 6:107, 118; 7.12–14,
17–19

Josephus, *Jewish Antiquities* 1.11, 19; 2.2,
5; 10.10; 17:13; *Life* 42

Livy, *History of Rome* 36

Lucian, *The Passing of Peregrinus* 26

2 Maccabees 15:11–17

Matthew 1:18b–25; 2:12–15, 19–22; 27:19

Philostratus, *Life of Apollonius* 1.5, 9–10,
23, 29; 4.34; 8.12

Plutarch, *The Obsolescence of Oracles* 412a–b; 434d–e

Tacitus, *Annals* 1.65; 2.14; 11.4; 12.13;
Histories 4.83

POSSESSION

Acts 2:1–13

Babylonian Talmud
Sanhedrin 65b

1 Corinthians 14:1–2

Euripides, *Hippolytus* 141–50; *Medea*
1167–77

Ezekiel 2:2; 3:24

Josephus, *Jewish Antiquities* 6.214,
221–23; 9.35

Judges 14:5–6, 19; 15:14–15

Mark 1:12–13//Matthew 4:1–11//Luke
4:1–13; Mark 1:23–28; 3:20–30//Mat-
thew 12:22–37//Luke 11:14–23; Mark
5:1–20//Matthew 8:28–34//Luke
8:26–39

Numbers 11:25

Pausanias, *Description of Greece* 10.12

Philo, *On the Migration of Abraham* 35;
On the Cherubim 27; *On Drunkenness*
146–49; *On the Life of Moses* 50, 51;
Who Is the Heir? 53

Plato, *Phaedrus* 244a–b; *Symposium*
202e–203a; *Timaeus* 71d–72a

Plutarch, *The Obsolescence of Oracles*
414e–f, 418c–d

Romans 8:9–11, 14–16

1 Samuel 10:5–6; 16:14–16; 18:10; 19:9,
23–24

Sirach 48:12–14

VISIONS

Acts 2:32–36; 9:3, 10–16; 10:3–6, 9–16;
 16:9–10; 18:9–10; 22:6; 23:11; 26:13;
 27:23–26
2 Corinthians 3:17–18
Ezekiel 8:1c–3
Luke 22:41–44

Passion of Perpetua and Felicity 4, 10, 11
Philo, *On the Life of Moses* 49
Revelation 4:1–19:19
Tertullian, *On the Soul* 9; *Exhortation to
 Chastity* 10.5

AUDITIONS

Acts 9:3–9, 10–16; 22:6–10; 26:14–18
Augustine, *Confessions* 8.12.29
2 Baruch 12:5–13:6
Ezekiel 12:1ff; 13:1ff; 16:1ff; 18:1ff; 20:2ff;
 20:49bff; 22:1ff; 23:1ff
Haggai 1:1, 3ff; 2:1–9, 10–12c, 20–23
Isaiah 38:4–8
1 Kings 6:11–13; 17:2–4; 18:1; 19:9b;
 21:17–19
2 Kings 20:4–7

Mark 1:11//Matthew 3:17//Luke 3:22b
Passion of Perpetua and Felicity 3–13
Philo, *On the Decalogue* 9, 11 (46)
Philostratus, *Life of Apollonius* 8.7.2
Plutarch, *On the Sign of Socrates*
 588b–589f
Revelation 1:9–11; 14:13
1 Samuel 3:3b–5; 15:10ff
2 Samuel 7:4–17
Zechariah 1:1ff; 4:8ff; 7:1

ASCENT

Babylonian Talmud
 Hagigah 14b–15a
1 Enoch 87:3; 90:31
Ezekiel 3:12, 14; 11:1, 24

Jerusalem Talmud
 Hagigah 77
Shepherd of Hermas, *Similitudes* 9.1 (78)

TRANCE

Acts 10:10–16; 11:5–10; 22:17–21
Augustine, *Confessions* 9.10
Cicero, *On Divination* 1.113–14
1 Corinthians 14:13–19
2 Corinthians 5:13
Daniel 8:17–18
Eusebius, *Ecclesiastical History* 5.7
Isaiah 21:1–10
1 Kings 19:4–9a

Lucan, *Pharsalia* 5.146–57
Lucian, *Alexander the False Prophet*
 12–14
Philo, *Who Is the Heir?* 14 (69–70)
Plato, *Ion* 534d; *Phaedrus* 244a–b
Plutarch, *Oracles at Delphi No Longer
 Given in Verse* 397; *The Obsolescence of
 Oracles* 432c

MEANS OF ACHIEVING

2 Baruch 12:5–13:2

Cicero, *On Divination* 1.114

Daniel 8:27; 10:8–9, 15–17

Exodus 33:21–23

Ezekiel 4:4–8

1 Kings 19:9–12

Lucian, *Alexander the False Prophet* 12

Pausanias, *Description of Greece* 1.34.5

Philo, *On the Contemplative Life* 40;
  On the Decalogue 2.10–12

Philostratus, *Life of Apollonius* 4.11

Porphyry, *On the Cave of the Nymphs* 6

14. Healing

AGNES CHOI

Introduction

That the Bible contains descriptions of various illnesses and accounts of healing is undisputed. A more controversial issue, however, concerns how best to interpret these texts in the ancient context. The understanding and experience of health and illness, as well as the therapies used in restoring health, are culturally determined. Thus, healing, illness, and therapies must be considered within a specific culture in order to be understood properly.

Modern interpreters have often studied the biblical texts concerning healing and illness within a biomedical framework based on Western medicine. In scientifically oriented cultures, health is understood as the absence of *disease*, that is, when biological and psychological processes malfunction. In the biomedical model, the appropriate therapy for a disease focuses on the cause of the disease (e.g., bacteria, viruses, etc.). This therapy is called a *cure*, that is, when biological or psychological processes are made to function properly again. This model contributes very little to our understanding of the ancients' understanding and experience of health and illness.

A more useful framework can be found in medical anthropology, the study of non-Western medical systems from a cross-cultural perspective. As health and illness can be understood and experienced in different ways, medical anthropologists consider the various ways in which different cultures determine how both the person and the group understand and respond to illness and health. In cultures that are not scientifically oriented, health is understood as the condition of well-being as defined by a given culture. *Illness* "refers to the psychosocial experience and meaning of perceived disease."[1] The appropriate therapy for illness

---

1. Arthur Kleinman, *Patients and Healers in the Context of Culture* (Berkeley: University of California Press, 1980), 72.

is *healing*, which differs from curing. Healing involves seeing disease as illness, which makes it meaningful, and then attempts to reduce or eliminate the distress caused by the condition. In other words, the process of healing is intended to endow illness with meaning, as well as to alleviate symptoms.

By using the framework provided by medical anthropology, one can explore health care as a system. A health-care system typically includes presuppositions about causes and diagnosis, as well as about what options are available to the ill person, and finally the modes of therapy administered. This tripartite structure (causes, options, modes) is nearly universal; the details, assumptions, and practices within each vary considerably cross-culturally.

Health-care systems consist of three overlapping sectors: the popular sector, the professional sector, and the folk sector. The popular sector consists of the beliefs and activities of the individual, the family, social networks, and community, and it is in this sector that most illnesses are defined and treated. The professional sector is comprised of the organized healing professions, and as such involves formal institutions, professional training, and social sanctioning. Finally, the folk sector is composed of a series of different medical approaches, including, but not limited to, shamanism, herbalism, special systems of exercise, and symbolic nonsacred healing. Significantly for the ancient Mediterranean, the folk sector also involves popular healers and the use of magic and exorcism.

In the ancient world, the understandings of illness and health, as well as the health-care system, were embedded in three interrelated dimensions: the personal, the social, and the cosmic. As a result, both illness and health were understood to be experienced or caused by individuals, groups, or deities.

Ancient Texts

THE VALUE OF HEALTH

1. PLATO, *GORGIAS* 451E

The philosopher Plato (ca. 429–347 BCE) wrote a dialogue called *Gorgias*, which has Socrates (469–399 BCE) refer to a Greek drinking song attributed to Simonides or Epicharmos (sixth or fifth century BCE). In it, health is ranked as the greatest blessing for humankind, since without health, no other blessings could be enjoyed (e.g., wisdom, wealth, strength, courage, power, children, beauty, pleasure).

To be healthy is best for mortal man, second is to be of beautiful appearance, third is to be wealthy without fraud, and fourth is to be young with one's friends.[2]

2. Sextus Empiricus, *Against the Ethicists* 48–49

The second-century CE physician, philosopher, and skeptic Sextus Empiricus records a debate concerning the relative value accorded to health. This debate reveals that some disagreed with Plato's position. The Peripatetic school of philosophers, for example, claimed that health ranks second to virtue or courage, and the Stoics were indifferent to it.

At any rate, some consider health to be a good, but others [consider it] not a good; and of those who suppose [it is] a good, some have declared [it] the greatest good, but others, not the greatest; and of those saying [it is] not a good, some [consider it] "a preferred indifferent," but some [consider it] an indifferent, but not "preferred." Therefore, that [health is] good, and this first, has been said by not a few of the poets and writers and in general by all who are not philosophers [i.e., ordinary people].[3]

PERSONAL DIMENSIONS OF ILLNESS AND HEALTH

3. Libanius, *Orations* 1.248–50

Libanius (314–393 CE), born in Antioch and educated in Athens (336–340 CE), was a Greek teacher of rhetoric. His students almost certainly included John Chrysostom and probably Basil and Gregory of Nazianzus. At the age of twenty, he was struck by a thunderbolt, which resulted in a life of poor health and migraines. In Mediterranean antiquity, when one became ill, one did not ask "*What* is the cause of my illness?" but "*Who* is the cause of my illness?" In this text, Libanius attributes the onset of migraine and gout to individuals who had hidden a chameleon, a sign of ritual binding, in his classroom. Libanius implies that the identity of these individuals was known to him (see **chap. 20, Evil Eye**).

Therefore, some of my friends were urging me, and each other as well, to prosecute certain individuals who were rumored to be responsible for this, but I myself was not of the same mind as them, and I was restraining them. Instead, I said

2. Adapted from Lamb, LCL.
3. Adapted from Bury, LCL.

that it is necessary to pray rather than to arrest someone for contriving in secret. However, a chameleon appeared in the classroom from what place I do not know. . . . Nevertheless, not even after so great a revelation did I accuse anyone for its appearance, but it seemed to me that fear entered into the minds of the guilty parties, and they relaxed their pressure, and I became able to move about again.[4]

4. *IG* V 1145

Just as individuals could be the cause of illness, they could also be the cause of healing. One such individual from the professional sector of the health-care system was the physician. In exchange for a specified period of service, the city physician enjoyed public recognition and probably a specified minimum income. In this first-century BCE Greek inscription (from Gytheum in Laconia), we learn that following a vote in the council, the Spartan physician Damiadas was invited to settle in the city and to serve as the city physician. Although Damiadas is honored with language typically associated with a patron, the city physician was, nevertheless, an employee (see **chap. 3, Patronage**).

> Whereas Damiadas . . . the Lacedaimonian physician, [it] having been sent to him in writing just as it has been voted, seeing that he came to us practicing medicine, that he showed himself second to no one in his trade and noblest in life, and having procured the greatest respect of our authorities and our city, that having labored and having been contracted for the execution of this work just as he was invited to by the people, and engaging in this trade among us for two years, he did what was right for those in need, lacking nothing in zeal and love of honor in order to treat all persons equally, both poor men and rich men, and slaves and freemen. And in the dwelling and also the sojourning as a resident alien, in that which he has done, he has kept himself without offense, becoming worthy of the craft that he practices, and worthy of his own fatherland and of our city, and he kept himself without reproach in all things, behaving like a free man, acting toward all as befits a wise and educated man. And during the magistracy of Biadas in the month of Laphrios, seeing the whole city in great difficulty because of the property taxes, he offered to practice medicine freely among the people for the remainder of the year, exceeding, in our opinion, the measures of justice and giving a great demonstration of nobility and goodwill and affection to our citizens. Because of all these things, the people, showing gratitude for all the things Damiadas has done, having been seized with benevolence regarding his being well disposed to

4. Adapted from A. F. Norman, *Libanius' Autobiography (Oration I)* (London: Oxford University Press, 1965), 129.

our city and doing every sort of good thing, both in his craft and in all spheres of life, have made him a public guest and benefactor of our city. And let there be to him the right to possession of a house and property and the other benevolences and all honors that belong to the other public guests and benefactors of the city. And the Ephoroi during the magistracy of Biadas, having inscribed this public guesthood upon a stone stele to be erected on the most conspicuous place of the agora, so that the city's benefactorial memorial make manifest to all Damiadas's nobility and goodwill.[5]

5. Plato, *Charmides* 155E–156E

Magicians and miracle-workers from the folk sector of the health-care system could also be sources of healing, though physicians sometimes expressed skepticism about their efficacy. In Plato's fourth-century BCE dialogue *Charmides*, we find the first explicit reference to an amulet applied with an incantation. Socrates reveals a recipe for a headache amulet, which he learned from the Thracians while serving on a military campaign in the area.

> And I said there was a certain leaf, and there was a spell in addition to the remedy, which if someone [said the] spell at the same time [that one applied the remedy] to one's body, the remedy makes [one] altogether healthy; but without the spell, there was no advantage from the leaf.[6]

6. 1 Kings 17:17–22

The biblical prophet Elijah is an example of a folk healer. In this text, Elijah acts as the mediator between God and the son of the widow of Zarephath, who is ultimately restored to health.

> And it came to pass after these things [that] the son of the woman, the mistress of the house, became ill. And his illness was so severe that there was no breath remaining in him. And she said to Elijah, "What have you against me, man of God? You have come to me to mention my iniquity, and to kill my son." And he was saying to her, "Give your son to me." And he was taking him from her bosom, and he brought him up to the upper room in which he himself was living, and he laid him upon his bed. And he was calling to the Lord and he was saying, "Lord my God, have you done evil against the widow with whom I sojourn, by killing her son?"

---

5. Adapted from H. F. J. Horstmanshoff, "The Ancient Physician: Craftsman or Scientist?" *Journal of the History of Medicine and Allied Sciences* 45 (1990): 191–92.

6. Adapted from Lamb, LCL.

And he was stretching himself on the boy three times, and he was calling to the Lord and he was saying, "Lord my God, let the life of the boy return to his body." And the Lord was hearing the voice of Elijah, and the life of the boy returned to his body and he was revived.

7. JOHN 9:1–7

Jesus is frequently depicted as a folk healer in the Gospels. In the Gospel of John, the reports of Jesus's healings are frequently associated with questions about the source of Jesus's power. In this text, we can observe the concern to identify the individual(s) responsible for the man's blindness (the man or his parents), as well as the demonstration of Jesus as a mediator of God's healing.

> As he [Jesus] was passing by, he saw a man blind from birth. And his disciples asked him, saying, "Rabbi, who sinned, this man or his parents, that he was born blind?" Jesus answered, "Neither this man sinned, nor his parents; but [he was born blind] in order that the works of God might be revealed in him. It is necessary for us to work the works of the one who sent me while it is day; night is coming when no one is able to work. As long as I am in the world, I am the light of the world." Having said these things, he spat on the ground and made mud from the saliva and smeared the mud upon the man's eyes and said to him, "Go, wash in the pool of Siloam" (which means "sent"). Then he departed and washed and came back seeing.

8. HIPPOCRATES, *ON THE DISEASES OF YOUNG WOMEN* 1.7

Hippocrates was a physician in the fifth century BCE. The Hippocratic corpus that bears his name was intended to instruct students and practitioners of medicine and is crucial literary evidence for our understanding of early Greek medicine, including their understanding of women's health. The Hippocratics believed that female flesh was more porous than male flesh. As a result, menstruation was thought to be important because it allowed a woman to release the moisture retained by her porous flesh. In addition, sexual intercourse was thought to be necessary for women's health, for intercourse prevented the womb from moving around the body and suffocating a woman (see **chap. 9, Gender**).

> If suffocation occurs suddenly, it will happen especially in women who have not had intercourse with men and more often in older women than the younger ones, for their wombs are lighter. It usually occurs because of the following: when the woman has an emptiness of the vessels, and works harder than is customary, her

womb, becoming heated from the hard work, because it is empty and light, turns on itself because of the hard work. For there is in fact an empty space in which it is able to turn, because the belly is empty, and when the womb turns, it hits the liver and they go together and strike against the abdomen. For the womb runs toward and goes upward toward the moisture, because it becomes unusually dry by the hard work. The liver is moist, and when the womb hits the liver, it produces suffocation when the breathing outlet is stopped around the belly.[7]

9. Hippocrates, *On the Diseases of Young Women* 8.466–70

If a woman failed to menstruate, the blood would collect in the region of the heart and lungs, causing her to exhibit symptoms of "hysteria," including nightmares, fever, and suicidal attempts (the term "hysteria" comes from the Greek word for "womb"). Marriage, sexual intercourse, and pregnancy constituted the appropriate course of treatment (see **chap. 9, Gender**).

Then from such a vision, many people strangled themselves, actually more women than men, for the womanly nature is more fainthearted and sorrowful. And the virgins in the season of marriage who remain unmarried, they suffer these visions more frequently, especially in the descent of their monthly period, although before they have had no such bad dreams of this sort. For later the blood collects in the womb in preparation to stream forth; but when the mouth of the exit is not opened wide, and more blood keeps on flowing into the womb because of the food and the growth of the body, which does not have an outlet, because of its abundance, it rises up to the heart and to the diaphragm. Then when these parts are filled, the heart becomes sluggish, then because of the sluggishness, numbness, then because of the numbness, madness seizes the woman. . . . Now, I urge the virgins who might suffer a condition of this kind to cohabit with men as quickly as possible; for if they become pregnant, they become healthy.[8]

SOCIAL DIMENSIONS OF ILLNESS AND HEALTH

10. Plato, *Republic* 406d–e

Plato offers in his *Republic* (380–370 BCE) a description of a state's or city's essential necessities: not only food and shelter, but also the principle of the

---

7. Adapted from Ann Ellis Hanson, "Hippocrates: Diseases of Women 1," *Signs* 1 (1975): 576.

8. Adapted from Potter, LCL.

division of labor. In the midst of Socrates's comments on this last principle, he offers a satirical description that illuminates the economic burden of illness such that when an individual became ill, the group to which he belongs might not assume the responsibility of caring for him. Socrates contrasts the experience of illness of the poor carpenter, who could not afford the economic burden of a long-term illness, and the rich man, who was free to pursue a life as a valetudinarian (i.e., one unduly anxious about one's own health).

> "A carpenter," I said, "being ill expects from the physician a remedy [that will act as] an emetic [lit. a drink that causes vomiting] on the disease or having been treated to be set free by purgative or by cautery or by knife. But if anyone might prescribe a long regimen to him, placing felt around the head and these accompaniments, he quickly says that he has no leisure to be ill, and it is not profitable to live in this way, turning one's mind to disease, and being neglectful of the work that lies before him; and after having said farewell to a physician such as this, going on to his usual way of living, having become healthy, he lives to manage his affairs; but if his body might not be sufficient to go forward, having died, he is set free of [his] circumstances."[9]

11. Hesiod, *Works and Days* 238–45

In his poem *Works and Days*, the eighth-century BCE Greek poet Hesiod encourages his brother Perses to live a life of justice and hard work. In the section focusing on justice and injustice (202–85), Hesiod emphasizes that Zeus rewards the former but punishes the latter. That illness could be experienced not only by individuals, but also by groups is illustrated as Hesiod recounts the suffering of an entire city, including death and infertility, inflicted by Zeus.

> But to those who are interested only in evil violence and cruel works, far-sounding Zeus, Cronos's son, ordains punishment. Often even a whole city suffers because of an evil man who sins and devises wicked deeds. And the son of Cronos inflicts from heaven great misery, famine together with plague, and the people perish; women do not give birth, and households become few through the cunning of Olympian Zeus.[10]

12. *The Poem of the Righteous Sufferer*, lines 95–96

The Poem of the Righteous Sufferer (*Ludlul bēl nēmeqi*) is an Akkadian poem almost certainly dating to the Cassite period (ca. 1500–1200 BCE). The poem

---

9. Adapted from Shorey, LCL.
10. Adapted from Most, LCL.

likely consisted of four tablets and was 400–500 lines in length. In the poem, a certain noble, Šubši-mešrê-Šakkan, engages in a monologue describing how he endured all manner of suffering. If the group assumed the responsibility of caring for an ill member, then healing assumed a social dimension. One locus of healing was the home, as illustrated by the homecare that Šubši-mešrê-Šakkan received during his prolonged illness.

> I take to a bed of bondage; going out is a pain; my house has become my prison.[11]

13. Pausanias, *Description of Greece* 10.32.12

Pausanias, a second-century CE Greek author of travel literature, offers in his *Description of Greece* a guidebook to the province of Achaia (modern-day Greece) that pays particular attention to, among other things, sanctuaries of healing, the most prominent of which were associated with Asclepius, the god of medicine. The social dimensions of healing may be observed in the therapies of the Asclepieia that were provided by temple personnel and the various buildings for housing and treatment of the ill (e.g., gymnasia for exercises; bathhouses). This passage contains a description of the lodgings available for the ill seeking healing from Asclepius (see **chap. 8, Space**).

> And seventy stades distant from Tithorea is a temple of Asclepius, called Archagetas. . . . Within the precincts are even dwellings for both the suppliants and the servants of the god. And in the middle is the temple and a statue made of stone, having a beard more than two feet long. A couch is placed to the right of the statue.[12]

14. Mark 2:1–4

The social dimension of illness and health can be observed in Jesus's healing of a paralyzed man. In this text, we observe the efforts of the paralytic's four friends as they carried him and dismantled the roof in order to present the paralyzed man to Jesus.

> And [Jesus] returning again to Capernaum after some days, it was reported that he was at home. And many gathered together so that there was no longer room for another, not even in front of the door; and he was speaking the word to them. And they came, carrying to him a paralyzed man, carried by four of them. And

---

11. W. G. Lambert, *Babylonian Wisdom Literature* (Oxford: Clarendon, 1959), 45.
12. Adapted from Jones, LCL.

being unable to approach him because of the crowd, they uncovered the roof above him; and after having dug through it, they let down the pallet on which the paralyzed man lay.

COSMIC DIMENSIONS OF ILLNESS AND HEALTH

15. HIPPOCRATES, *THE SACRED DISEASE* 4.21–33

Illness included a cosmic dimension, as deities could be the cause of a particular illness. Thus, the act of diagnosing an illness included identifying the deity responsible. Although Hippocratic doctors (i.e., from the professional sector) understood illness to have natural rather than divine causes, they failed to convince many of their contemporaries, whom they deride in this text for ascribing various symptoms to specific deities.

> If the patient imitates a goat, if he roars, or convulses on the right side, they say that the Mother of the Gods is responsible. If he utters a shrill and vigorous cry, they liken him to a horse and say Poseidon is responsible. And [if] there might be some excrement, which often happens under the force of the disease, the surname Enodia is assigned. If it is more frequent and thinner, like that of a bird, it is Apollo Nomius. And if he produces foam from the mouth and kicks with his foot, Ares has the responsibility. And if at night occur fears, panics, and madness, leaping up from bed and fleeing outside, they say that Hekate is assaulting or that heroes are attacking.[13]

16. DIODORUS SICULUS, *LIBRARY OF HISTORY* 1.25.2–5

In his "Library," the Greek author Diodorus Siculus (first century BCE) offers a universal history from the mythical period to 60/59 BCE. Originally consisting of forty books, only fifteen books have survived fully (books 1–5 and 11–20), with other books preserved only in fragments. Book 1 considers the myths, kings, and customs of Egypt. In Diodorus's description of Egypt's temples, we learn that deities could be the cause not only of illness, but also of healing. In this text, Isis was recognized for her skills in healing sight (see **chap. 3, Patronage**).

> And the Egyptians say that Isis discovered many health-giving drugs and had great experience in the scientific knowledge of medical arts; therefore, now that she

13. Adapted from Jones, LCL.

has obtained immortality, she takes the greatest pleasure in the healings of men, she gives assistance in their sleep to those who are worthy, plainly exhibiting both her own presence and her beneficence to men who beg. And to prove this, as they say, they bring not legends, as the Greeks do, but manifest facts; for practically the entire inhabited world bears witness to these things, in that it eagerly contributes to these honors because of her presence in the healings. For standing above the sick in their sleep, she gives remedy for their illnesses, and she works incredible healings upon those who submit to her; and many who have been given up in despair by their physicians because of the difficulty of their illness are healed by her, and many who have been altogether maimed in the eyes or some other parts of the body, whenever they turn to this goddess, are restored to their former condition.[14]

17. Exodus 15:26

The God of Israel was also acknowledged as a source of healing.

And he was saying, "If you will listen carefully to the voice of the Lord your God, and do what is right in his eyes, and you will listen to his commandments and you will keep all his laws, all the illnesses that I set among the Egyptians I will not set upon you, for I am the Lord, the one who heals you."

18. Plutarch, *Pericles* 13.7–8

The Greek philosopher and biographer Plutarch (ca. 50–120 CE) wrote a series of comparative biographies of leading Greek and Roman figures. In his life of the fifth-century BCE Athenian politician Pericles, Plutarch illustrates that religious and secular sources of healing were sometimes combined, in his account of a seriously injured workman who experienced a full recovery as the result of a medical treatment that Athena Hygieia prescribed to him in a dream.

And the Propylaea of the acropolis were brought to completion in five years, Mnesicles being their architect. A fortunate and marvelous thing happened in the course of their building, which revealed that the goddess was not standing aloof, but was taking part and helping to accomplish the work. For one of the most productive and devoted of the craftsmen lost his footing, and he fell from the heights and was wretched in a sorry plight, despaired of by the physicians. And Pericles being disheartened, the goddess appeared in a dream and prescribed a course of treatment, which, having used it, Pericles quickly and readily healed the man. And

14. Adapted from Oldfather, LCL.

because of this, he set up a bronze statue of Athena Hygieia in the acropolis near the altar, which was there before, as they say.[15]

19. Sirach 38:1–9

Religious and secular sources of healing are also combined in this biblical description of the physician. According to Israelite Deuteronomistic theology, illness was caused by God as a punishment for sin. However, in this text, God is identified as the ultimate source of medicine and healing. God also creates the physician and the pharmacist/perfumer and endows them with skills and knowledge that should be recognized.

> Honor the physician for his services, for the Lord also created him; for healing is from the Most High, and he has received a gift from the king. The skill of a physician exalts his head, and it will be marveled at in the presence of the great. The Lord created remedies from the earth, and a prudent man does not despise them. Was not water sweetened from a tree in order that its power might be known? And he gave skill to men that he might be glorified in his marvelous works. By them he healed, and he took away his suffering; the pharmacist makes a mixture from these things. And his works will never be complete; and from him, peace is upon the face of the earth. Child, when you are ill, do not look askance, but pray to the Lord, and he will heal you.

20. Cato, *On Agriculture* 160

Marcus Porcius Cato (234–149 BCE) was a general, philosopher, orator, historian, and expert in jurisprudence and agriculture. Although he is considered to be the father of Latin prose literature, only one of his works survives intact. *On Agriculture* contains practical advice for the owner of a slave-staffed villa producing wine and olive oil for sale (see **chap. 1, Economy**). In these instructions on how to treat a dislocation, we learn that what are commonly thought of as magical sources of healing were sometimes combined with secular sources (see **chap. 18, Deviance**).

> If there is any dislocation, it will be healed by this incantation. Take a reed for yourself that is green and four or five feet long, split the middle, and have two men hold it along your hip bones. Begin to chant: "Grant, grant, grant; you will seek out that two become one" until they meet. Be sure to brandish a knife up above them. When the two pieces have met and touch one to the other, take the knife

15. Adapted from Perrin, LCL.

firmly in your hand and cut on the right and on the left sides. Bind them against the dislocation or against the fracture; it will be healed. And nevertheless, be sure to chant every day, even if you have suffered only a dislocation, in the following way: "I will harm your hurts."[16]

Vocabulary of Healing

HEBREW

אֲרוּכָה (*arukah*) .... healing
חֲלִי (*kholi*) .... sickness
רָפָא (*rafa*) .... to heal

GREEK

θεραπεία (*therapeia*) .... medical or surgical treatment or cure
θεράπευμα (*therapeuma*) .... care of the body, surgical treatment
θεραπεύω (*therapeuō*) .... to treat medically
ἴατρα (*iatra*) .... doctor's fee, thank offering for cure
ἰατραλείπτης (*iatraleiptēs*) .... surgeon who practices by anointing, friction
ἰατρεία (*iatreia*) .... healing, medical treatment
ἰατρεῖον (*iatreion*) .... surgery, remedy, doctor's fee, expense of a cure
ἰατρεύω (*iatreuō*) .... to treat medically, cure
ἰατρικός (*iatrikos*) .... tax for maintenance of a doctor, one skilled in medicine
ἰατρίνη (*iatrinē*) .... midwife
ἰατροκλύστης (*iatroklystēs*) .... physician who uses douches
ἰατρολογία (*iatrologia*) .... study of medicine
ἰατρομαθηματικοί
    (*iatromathēmatikoi*) .... practitioners of medicine with astrology
ἰατρός (*iatros*)..................... one who heals, physician, surgeon
μαγεία (*mageia*) .... magic
μαγεύω (*mageuō*).................. to be a Magus, to use magic arts, bewitch
μάγος (*magos*) .... enchanter, wizard, magical
ὑγεῖα (*hygeia*)..................... health

16. Translated by Tyler T. Travillian.

φαρμακεία (*pharmakeia*) .... use of drugs, potions/spells, poisoning,
witchcraft, remedy
φάρμακον (*pharmakon*) .... drug, healing remedy, medicine

LATIN

aegritudo........................ illness
medicamen .... drug
medicor......................... to heal
medicus......................... physician
morbus .... illness
sanitas......................... health
sano............................ to heal
valetudo .... health

Select Bibliography

Avalos, Hector. *Illness and Health Care in the Ancient Near East: The Role of the Temple in Greece, Mesopotamia, and Israel.* Harvard Semitic Museum Publications 54. Atlanta: Scholars Press, 1995.

Guijarro, Santiago. "Healing Stories and Medical Anthropology: A Reading of Mark 10:46–52." *BTB* 30 (2000): 102–12.

King, Helen, ed. *Health in Antiquity.* London: Routledge, 2005.

Kleinman, Arthur. *Patients and Healers in the Context of Culture.* Berkeley: University of California Press, 1980.

Nutton, Vivian. *Ancient Medicine.* Sciences of Antiquity. 2nd ed. London: Routledge, 2012.

Pilch, John J. *Healing in the New Testament: Insights from Medical and Mediterranean Anthropology.* Minneapolis: Fortress, 2000.

Additional Texts

DEFINITIONS OF HEALTH

Ariphron, *Hymn to Hygieia*
Aristotle, *Rhetoric* 1394b13
Athenaeus, *The Dinner Sophists* 15.694e

Galen, *On the Therapeutic Method* 1.5.4
Hesiod, *Works and Days* 102–4

Hippocrates, *Ancient Medicine*; *Precepts* 6

Lucian, *A Slip of the Tongue in Greeting* 6

Philo, *On the Contemplative Life* 2; *Hypothetica* 2.11–13

Plato, *Republic* 406e; *Laws* 631b–d

Plutarch, *Moralia* 126c, 127d, 129a, 136e–f, 693e–695d

Sextus Empiricus, *Against the Ethicists* 57

PERSONAL DIMENSIONS OF ILLNESS AND HEALTH

Acts 2:22, 43; 3:1–10; 4:22, 30; 5:12–16; 6:8; 7:36; 8:7–13; 9:34–42; 10:38; 14:3, 8–10; 15:12; 19:11–12; 28:1–10

Acts of Andrew 400–402

Acts of John 19–25, 30–33

Aeschylus, *Agamemnon* 306; *Prometheus Bound* 469–75

Apuleius, *Apology* 40.1

Aristophanes, *Acharnians* 1029; *Wasps* 1432

Aristotle, *Politics* 1282a

Arnobius, *Against the Gentiles* 1.43.5

Carmina Latina Epigraphica 987

Celsus, *On Medicine*, preamble 8

2 Chronicles 16:12; 26:16–21

Cicero, *Brutus* 217; *On Duties* 1.42; *Letters to Friends* 248

CIL 8.2756

Colossians 4:14

1 Corinthians 12:9–10, 28, 30

2 Corinthians 12:12

Deuteronomy 4:34; 6:22; 26:8

Dio Chrysostom, *Refusal of the Office of Archon* (*Or.* 49) 13–14

Exodus 7:3; 8:19

Galatians 3:5

Galen, *On Examining the Best Physicians* 9.22, 33

Genesis 50:1–3

Herodotus, *Histories* 3.129–37

Hippocrates, *The Sacred Disease* 2.1–10

Homer, *Iliad* 4.213; 5.899–906; 9.514–15; 11.833–35; *Odyssey* 4.219–32; 17.383–87; 18.383–85; 19.457–59

ICret 4.168

IG I² 152; *IG* II/III² 304, 374, 483, 604, 772, 931; *IG* IX, 2, 1276; *IG* XII, 1, 1032

Infancy Gospel of Thomas 4:1; 9:1–3

Isaiah 29:18–19; 35:5–6; 38

Isidore of Pelusium, *Epistles* 5.196, 275

James 5:14–16

Jeremiah 8:22; 46:11; 51:8

Job 13:4

John 4:46–54; 5:1–18; 11:1–44

Josephus, *Jewish Antiquities* 8.44–45; *Jewish War* 2.136

1 Kings 14:1–18; 17:17–24

2 Kings 1:2–16; 4:8–37; 5; 8:7–15

Lucan, *Pharsalia* 6.507–830

Lucian, *Salaried Posts in Great Houses* 7; *The Lover of Lies* 7–9, 11

Luke 4:18–21, 23, 25–27, 40; 5:12–17; 6:6–11, 18; 7:1–17, 21; 8:40–56; 9:1–6, 37–43, 49–50; 10:1–12, 17–20; 11:20; 13:10–17, 32; 14:1–6; 17:11–19; 18:35–43

Mark 1:32–34, 40–45; 2:1–12; 3:1–6; 5:1–43; 6:6–13, 53–56; 7:24–37; 9:14–29, 38–41; 10:46–52

Martial, *Epigrams* 5.9

Matthew 2:1; 4:23; 8:1–13; 8:16; 9:1–8,

SOCIAL DIMENSIONS OF ILLNESS AND HEALTH

COSMIC DIMENSIONS OF ILLNESS AND HEALTH

Aelian, *Nature of Animals* 11.31, 33;
  Fragments 101
Aelius Aristides, *Orations* 47.70–73;
  Sacred Discourses 1.4, 7; 2.72; 4.5–7,
  48–57; 5.1–10, 29, 36
Aristophanes, *Heroes* 58, 692a
CIL 2.4314; 6.68
Damascus Document^a (4QD^a) frag. 6,
  I, 9–13
Deuteronomy 28:27
Diogenes Laertius, *Lives of Eminent
  Philosophers* 5.76
Exodus 11:1
Galen, *Corpus Medicorum Graecorum*
  3.812; 10.971–72; 11.314–15; 19.18
Genesis 12:10–20; 20:1–18; 28:1–4
Herodotus, *Histories* 1.105; 4.205
Herondas, *Mimiamboi* 4.1–95
Hesiod, *Works and Days* 100–104;
  238–45
Hippocrates, *The Sacred Disease* 6.354–
  64; *On Regimen in Acute Diseases*
  6.642, 652, 656–68
Homer, *Iliad* 1.8–474; 2.729–31; 4.405;
  11.518; 21.483–84; 24.605–7; *Odyssey*
  9.411; 11.171–73
Hosea 11:3
IG I³ 506; 824, b.4; II/III², 772; II² 074;
  334.8–10; 1496.109–10, 133–35, 150;
  483; 4960 fr.a.1–20; IV 428; IV²
  1.121–23, 17, 33, 39, 44
IG IV², 1, nos. 121–22, 125

IG XIV, no. 966
ILS 2194, 3411, 3513
Isaiah 35:3–6a; 38:16–20
Jeremiah 17:14; 30:17
Job 2:1–10
1 Kings 8:37–39; 13:1–25
2 Kings 20:1–11
LABS 236:11–12
LAS 2:174
Livy, *History of Rome* 10.47; 11
Luke 8:43–48
MAMA 4.279–85
Mark 5:25–34
Ovid, *Metamorphoses* 15.625–744;
  19.625–744
Pausanias, *Description of Greece* 1.31.6;
  2.11.6; 2.26.8; 5.26.2–5; 10.32.17
PGM VII. 756
Philostratus, *Epistles* 18; *Life of Apollo-
  nius* 1.11; 4.17
Pindar, *Pythian Odes* 3.47–54
Psalms 6:2; 30:2; 41:4; 103:3
1 Samuel 1, 4–6
SGDI 1561 B, 1564, 1566, 1582, 1587
Sophocles, *Ajax* 172–86, 756–77;
  Oedipus 1–150; *Philoctetes* 1325–29,
  1332–33, 1437
TAM VI,1 509
TDP 62:26; 76:51; 78:68; 80:8
VAT 7525
Wisdom of Solomon 16:12

PART IV

Social Commodities

15. Loyalty

Jason T. Lamoreaux

Introduction

Loyalty in the ancient world is housed in the social matrices of honor and shame and patron-client relations (see **chap. 4, Honor; chap. 5, Shame; chap. 3, Patronage; chap. 16, Friendship and Gifts**). Following this introduction, there is a selection of texts from the domains of loyalty as they are conceived in ancient Mediterranean contexts. Included are texts that, along with references to loyalty in general, indicate loyalty within the contexts of the gods, client kingship, slavery/manumission, and philosophical schools. The concept of loyalty is worked out with greatest clarity in the Roman writers of the time, particularly in the philosophical, rhetorical, and political works of Seneca and Cicero. Of course, the Greeks had a fully realized understanding of loyalty, and so did Hellenized Judeans at the turn of the millennium. At the center of patron-client relationships is a loyalty that pertains to both parties, although loyalty from a client is quite different from that shown by the patron. The loyalty that a patron shows to his client is shown through protection, which the patron holds based on his position of power. The loyalty of a patron to a client cannot be legally regulated and is often voluntary; therefore, when patrons falter, the client is left to complain or perhaps vilify their patron in writing.

Loyalty on the part of a client, however, carries with it a weightier obligation, because the client is in a position of need. While a patron is not obligated to demonstrate loyalty, a patron can demand that a client do so on demand. The client, unlike the patron, is obligated to show loyalty, making the client's loyalty real and concrete and the patron's ideal and abstract. The client needs the protection of the patron, but the client is not without something to offer that the patron would like in return. As indicated in the chapter on **Patronage** (**chap. 3**), the client gives back to the patron honor and personal high status simply by being attached to the patron, through being a client, and through praising and complimenting the patron in the community. Since loyalty is described in this manner through ancient texts, scholars understand that ancient concepts of loyalty are not centered in internal qualities (e.g., emotions), but rather in actual external actions (e.g., behavior).

Since loyalty is not an internal quality for ancient Mediterraneans, two features of loyalty stand out. First, while some examples show that loyalty is accompanied by emotional attachment, many examples illustrate loyalty being met with hostility. In other words, there are examples in ancient texts where a client or a patron will do what loyalty requires but still feel hostile toward the person to whom they are expressing that loyalty. Further, the loyalty of the person who is hostile is never brought into question in these scenarios. Actions are enough to prove proper loyalty, and the feelings are beside the point. Second, there were attempts to legislate loyalty, particularly in regards to freedpersons, which points toward actions rather than any sort of feeling.

Loyalty can also be reflected in the actions humans take toward and on behalf of the gods, as well as the gods toward and on behalf of humans. In Judean literature, there is often a call to abide by the commandments found in the Hebrew Bible. While many translations will render Greek words like *pistos* as "faithful," the fact that there are actions to be taken in cultic contexts (i.e., to follow the commandments) points toward a call to loyalty toward the deity. For Judeans, exclusive loyalty to a singular god set them apart from their Mediterranean neighbors, sometimes causing friction between people groups and challenging group identity. The Roman senate also was very careful about demonstrating proper loyalty to the gods, because they saw Rome's power as a divine right. If the sacrifices and rituals to the gods were done incorrectly, this would demonstrate a lack of loyalty on the part of the Roman senate, and the gods would abandon their protection of the state (see **chap. 11, Ritual, Public**).

Political loyalty extends beyond that of appeasing the gods. Client kingship relied on the loyalty of international allies and kings to maintain imperial rule in conquered lands. The Romans did not demand that conquered people change their political infrastructures, but rather that they vow loyalty to the Roman Empire. Client kings would show loyalty in a number of ways, including taking the names of prominent Roman citizens or names such as *philorōmaios* (friend of Rome) and the like, minting coins showing honor to Rome, building and dedicating monuments to the Roman emperor, building entire cities in honor of the emperor and his family (i.e., Caesarea Maritima), and renaming already established cities.

Loyalty that involved manumission was the only type of loyalty that was enforced by legislation. When a slave was freed by a master, the slave moved from a relationship of master-slave to one of patron-client. Setting a slave free was, in fact, seen as a benefit to the slave. Because of this, the relationship between the former master and slave did not dissolve upon manumission. The freedperson (the one manumitted) therefore showed obedience to the former master through loyalty and gratitude for the benefaction of being set free. At the same time, the master also gained a client.

Within the context of philosophical schools, the pattern of human patronage parallels that of patronage within the context of ancient religions. The philosophers, however, offer enlightenment and salvation that constitute benefactions, and the clients of the philosophers are their disciples. Philosophical movements are centered on founding figures, and disciples who followed, even in subsequent generations, would write honoring the figure who spawned their loyalty.

Ancient Texts

LOYALTY: GENERAL

1. DEMOSTHENES, *OLYNTHIAC* 3.25–26

Demosthenes was a Greek orator in Athens during the fourth century BCE. In his *Third Olynthiac*, Demosthenes utilizes what prior generations had left behind for the good of Greece as a model for the current generation as a right expression of loyalty to the country. That loyalty is demonstrated through moderation in private affairs, alongside larger gifts that contribute to the common good.

> Among the Greeks they were so honorable; you will see what manner of men they were among the things you will see in this city, in that which is both public and private. Therefore, they furnished with public funds on our behalf buildings and many beautiful things, temples and votive offerings, so that we, being born after them, might despair of surpassing them; but in private matters, they were temperate and exceedingly steadfast in the use of the constitution, so that the house of Aristides and the house of Miltiades, both of great fame then, as anyone among you can see, that they were not more extravagant than their neighbors. For not one of them took more than needed in their management of state affairs, but each thought it necessary to increase the public good. So from their loyalty for their

fellow Greeks, and their loyalty to the gods, and the equality among themselves, they naturally deserved to govern over a great prosperity.[1]

2. Cicero, *On Duties* 1.23

Cicero was a Roman philosopher and orator who lived in the first century BCE. In this section of *On Duties*, Cicero provides a brief line about the foundation of justice within a larger exposition about justice in general. At its core, justice is undergirded by *fides*, a word translated "loyalty" here.

> However, the basis of justice is loyalty, that is to say, coming together in agreement and truth.[2]

3. Seneca, *On Benefits* 3.14.2

Seneca was a Roman Stoic philosopher from the first century CE and a tutor and advisor to Nero. In this section of *On Benefits*, Seneca expounds on the idea that there ought to be checks on benefits given to others. The question becomes, what are the boundaries of giving to others said benefits, and where does one draw the line? Further, greed, accusations, and discord may become an issue, particularly in a situation where benefits or goods become a matter of merchandise for profit. In the following passage, Seneca notes that no law dictates how much one gives in benefits, and, therefore, there is no recourse to the law when taken advantage of in such a situation. Therefore, one must rely on the loyalty of the receiver.

> You are at fault if you think that the judge will support you; no law will restore you in full, you must only look to the loyalty of the receiver.[3]

4. Cicero, *For Plancius* 80

In this section of *For Plancius*, Cicero stands before a judge arguing a case and, in his statements, begins to expound on the concept of virtue. Here, thankfulness or gratefulness is at the center of what it is to be loyal. In his estimation of what is the greatest of all virtues, he creates a parallel between filial piety (loyalty to one's family) and loyalty to the state.

> Truly, judge, although I wish to be gifted with every virtue, still there is nothing that I prefer to recognize more highly than showing thanks. Namely, this one virtue is

1. Adapted from Vince, LCL.
2. Adapted from Miller, LCL.
3. Adapted from Basore, LCL.

not only the greatest but is also the mother of all remaining virtues. What is loyalty if not voluntary gratitude toward one's parents, who are good citizens, both in war and at home, deserving well of their country who recall the kindness they have received from their country? Who are pious, who cultivate reverence for the gods, but those who with proper honors and with good memory oblige themselves to the immortal gods the honor owed them? What pleasure is there in life if friendship suffers? And, furthermore, what friendship can exist between thankless people?[4]

5. Sophocles, *The Women of Trachis* 540–42

Sophocles was a Greek tragedian in fifth-century BCE Athens. In this section of *The Women of Trachis*, Deianeira, the wife of Herakles, speaks about a woman he has taken in a siege against the city of Oechalia and sent to his home to be his lover, alongside his wife. The title of "loyal" here is clearly sarcastic and used to highlight Herakles's disloyalty to his marriage.

Such is the gift that my loyal and wellborn Herakles sends home to make up for his long absence.[5]

6. Pindar, *Pythian* 1.85–92

Pindar was a Greek lyric poet from Thebes who lived between 522 and 443 BCE. In his *First Pythian Ode*, Pindar wrote a poem in honor of Hieron of the Aetna Chariot Race in 470 BCE. Hieron is the son of Deinomenes, the king of Syracuse. In this section of the ode, Pindar gives stately advice to the prince of Syracuse in order that he might maintain loyal witnesses for his actions. He notes that a ruler ought to strive for the good, to remain noble in one's temper, and to steer clear of greed.

Nevertheless, since envy is better than pity, do not abandon the good. Steer your people with the rudder of duty; forge your tongue on the anvil of truth. If only a small spark is produced, it is borne out as a great thing when it is from you. You are the overseer of many things. You have many loyal witnesses for both the good and the bad. But remain in a noble temper, if, indeed, you esteem with affection always hearing pleasant things; do not be exceedingly distressed by expenses, but, like a steersman, send yourself off. Do not be led astray, friend, by dishonest profits.[6]

4. Adapted from Watts, LCL.
5. Michael Jameson, "The Women of Trachis," in *Sophocles II*, ed. David Grene and Richard Lattimore (Chicago: University of Chicago Press, 2013), 540–42.
6. Adapted from Race, LCL.

7. Cicero, *On Oratorical Partitions* 9

In this text, Cicero asks, "What is the next step then" in the process of finding which are the proper arguments to use in oratory? Once the proper arguments are selected, one must determine what is the best way to incite the emotions. Evoking loyalty to a position is based in reputation, while the passions are directly connected to tapping into listeners' emotions.

> Loyalty is a firmly established reputation, while passion is the excitement of the intellect either to pleasure or to distress or to anxiety or to desire.[7]

LOYALTY TO THE GODS

8. Philo, *On the Life of Abraham* 268

Philo of Alexandria was a Jewish philosopher (25 BCE–50 CE). He was a prolific writer, and many of his works have survived. In *On the Life of Abraham*, Philo discusses why the idea that "Moses trusted in God" is such a powerful phrase. He lists pursuits that one might endeavor for in this life, such as honor, fame, beauty, health, and so forth. His conclusion, however, is that loyalty to God is the greatest good of all.

> Therefore, the only trustworthy and reliable good is loyalty to God, the comfort of life, the fulfillment of worthy prospects, the barrenness of evils, the productiveness of the good, the rejection of misfortune, knowledge of loyalty, the inheritance of good fortune, the improvement of the soul in all things having been ultimately tested and having been supported by the cause of all things, who is able to do all things but wills to do what is beneficial.[8]

9. Sirach 15:13–15

Ben Sira is traditionally known as the author of Sirach and a teacher in Jerusalem. He wrote sometime between 200 and 180 BCE. Because Sirach contains Judean wisdom literature, much of what we encounter in the text is aphorisms and sayings about right action. In chapter 15, Ben Sira provides wisdom on one's freedom of choice and how choosing to preserve God's commandments and practicing loyalty lead to life. To do otherwise is to choose death.

7. Adapted from Rackham, LCL.
8. Adapted from Colson, LCL.

The Lord hates every abomination; they are not beloved by those who fear him.
He made humans in the beginning and left them in the hand of their own counsel.
If you are willing, you will preserve the commandments and practice loyalty of
your own free will.

10. 4 MACCABEES 16:18–22

The identity of the author of 4 Maccabees is unknown, but it was probably
written sometime between the middle of the first century CE and the early
second century CE. Fourth Maccabees 14–16 expands on 2 Macc 7:41 about a
mother who dies a martyr after watching her seven sons executed. She is val-
orized since she watched each of her seven sons tortured and executed, while
she still remains loyal to God. In this section, she is seen telling her tortured
sons to stand fast and not give in to evil by emulating those in the past who
have been honored for their loyalty to God.

> Remember that it is through God that you have a share in the world and that you
> enjoyed life, and because of this, you ought to endure every affliction on account
> of God. On account of him also, our father Abram made haste to sacrifice his
> son Isaac, the father of our nation; and seeing his father's hand with sword in
> hand plunging toward him, he was not afraid. And Daniel, the righteous one, was
> thrown to the lions, and Hananiah, Azariah, and Mishael were thrown into the
> fiery furnace and remained loyal to God. Therefore, you, having the same loyalty
> toward God, do not be angry.

11. GALATIANS 2:15–16

Paul, a Christ follower writing during the first century CE, sent his letter to the
Galatians who resided in Asia Minor. In this section of the letter, Paul contrasts
following the law with loyalty to Christ, which for him is the basis of justification. Paul goes on in the letter to note that this justification is the reason that
Christ died, and if the law is still in operation, then Christ died for nothing.

> We are Judeans by nature and not sinners from the gentiles; since a person is not
> justified by the works of the law except through loyalty to Jesus Christ, even we are
> loyal to Christ Jesus, in order that we might be justified from our loyalty to Christ and
> not from works of the law, since all flesh will not be justified by the works of the law.

12. SOPHOCLES, *PHILOCTETES* 1433–44

Sophocles was a Greek tragedian during the fifth century BCE in Athens. Toward
the end of Sophocles's play *Philoctetes*, Heracles appears as a ghost to Philoctetes

and Neoptolemus in order to tell them to take Troy together and, in the process, kill Paris. Once done, loyalty must be shown to the gods as Zeus expects.

> I advise you in the following way, son of Achilles,
> For without him neither are you able
> to conquer Troy, nor he without you.
> Like lions, you keep watch together, this one over you
> and you over him: But I will send you, Asclepius,
> to the one who cures sickness in Troy.
> For it is proclaimed that Troy will fall a second time
> by my bow. Consider this, when you destroy the land:
> To show loyalty to the gods:
> thus, father Zeus holds this to be most important of all things;
> For such devotion will not die with mortal man;
> even if he lives or if he dies, it is not destroyed.[9]

13. Ps.-Aristotle, *Rhetoric to Alexander* 1423b

Rhetoric to Alexander was once thought to have been written by Aristotle. This section recounts a discussion about how sacrificial rites ought to be changed. The first discussion covers issues surrounding adding to the sacrificial rites, determining whether increasing the content and cost of a sacrifice will gain increased benefactions for the state. The second discussion determines the reasons for a reduction in the sacrificial rites. The initial determination centers on the financial condition of the state at the time of the sacrifices and why it might be financially necessary to reduce the sacrificial burden. In determining this, the following statement is made about loyalty to the gods and its importance.

> Then argue that it is likely not the expense of the sacrifices but rather the loyalty of those who perform the sacrifices in which the gods delight.[10]

CLIENT KINGSHIP

14. Dio Chrysostom, *Kingship 3* (Or. 3) 86–89

Dio Chrysostom was a Greek orator, philosopher, and historian from the first century CE. He wrote four discourses on the proper king or "true king," who

---

9. Adapted from Lloyd-Jones, LCL.
10. Adapted from Hett and Rackham, LCL.

was to be fiercely loyal to the gods and to watch over his subjects like Zeus watches over all people. In the context of a discussion on the importance of friendship, the loyalty of friends is determined to be the most valuable of assets to any king. Of course, these "friends" are actually clients who are politically under the king's patronage and include client kings (see **chap. 3, Patronage; chap. 16, Friendship and Gifts**).

> Moreover, the king esteems, among all things, friendship to be his fairest and most hallowed possession. For it is not more shameful to be king without resources than it is to be king without friends, and that he maintain his well-being not by fortune, or by armies, or by another power, as by the loyalty of friends.[11]

15. POLYBIUS, *HISTORIES* 3.30.1

Polybius (200–118 BCE) was a Greek historian who lived during the Hellenistic era. His *Histories* covered the period 264–146 BCE. In this section, he recounts that the Sagutines willfully became client kings to Rome. Further on in the text, the fact that they called upon the Romans rather than the Carthaginians for protection is presented as proof of their relationship to Rome. The benefaction of protection is utilized by a client king, while loyalty is given in return.

> These things being the case, it was agreed that Saguntum had given to the Romans his loyalty several years before the time of Hannibal.[12]

16. STRABO, *GEOGRAPHY* 4.5.3

Strabo (64 BCE–24 CE) was a Greek geographer, philosopher and historian. In book 4 of his *Geography*, he discusses the cultures and geography of Gaul, Britain, and the Alps. In this passage, Caesar has conquered some of the tribes in Britain, and some have become his "friends," offering their loyalty as client kings on the island.

> Now, however, any from among the chiefs who were there, by their embassies and service, have obtained the friendship of Caesar Augustus, dedicated votive offerings on the Capitoline, and caused the entire island to be as close kin with the Romans. They pay reasonable duties on both imports and exports from the land of the Celts (which include ivory bracelets and necklaces, amber, vessels made of

11. Adapted from Cohoon, LCL.
12. Adapted from Paton, LCL.

glass, and other small goods), so that it is unnecessary to post a garrison on the island, for, at the very least, it requires one division and some cavalry so that they might exact the tribute from them; and the expense for the army would be equal to the tribute received; for it would be necessary to diminish the imports if a tribute was being imposed, and, at the same time, some hazard would be encountered if force were utilized.[13]

SLAVERY/MANUMISSION

17. SENECA, *ON BENEFITS* 3.25

In this section of Seneca's *On Benefits*, he tells the story of a slave who is willing to die in his master's place. According to Seneca, this is a "rare display of loyalty."

> During the civil war, a slave concealed his master, who had been made an outlaw, put on his rings and clothing, went out to meet the soldiers, and, after declaring that he would not lower himself to beg them not to follow through with their orders, offered his neck. Such a rare thing for a slave to be willing to die for his master, what a rare display of loyalty when few are willing to die for their master! To be found king among a cruel public, loyal among a treacherous people! When such rewards were offered for treachery, you desired the reward of loyalty, though it was death.[14]

18. MATTHEW 24:45–51

Although the author of the Gospel of Matthew is unknown, it was probably written sometime between 80 and 90 CE. This passage is found in a long chapter that expands on Mark 13, also called the "little apocalypse." In this part of Matthew's chapter, there is a discourse on the loyal and the disloyal slave. The loyal slave does the duty that his master trusted him with, while the disloyal slave abuses the master's household while he is away. The loyal slave receives benefaction, while the disloyal slave receives death and torture.

> Who is the loyal and prudent servant whom his master puts in charge of his household to give them food at the correct time? Blessed is that slave whom his master, when he comes, finds accomplishing his task in this way. Amen I say to you that the master will place that servant over all his possessions. But if that evil servant

13. Adapted from Jones, LCL.
14. Adapted from Basore, LCL.

says in his heart, "my master lingers," and begins to beat his fellow servants and eat and drink with other drunkards, the master of that slave will come on a day when the slave does not expect him and at an hour that he does not know; he will cut him in two and deposit him with the hypocrites; in that place, there will be weeping and the grinding of teeth.

PHILOSOPHICAL LOYALTY

19. LUCRETIUS, *ON THE NATURE OF THINGS* 3.9–15, 30

Lucretius was a Roman poet and philosopher who lived during the first century BCE. His work that has survived is called *On the Nature of Things* and is a poem centered in the ideas of Epicureanism. In this section of a longer hymn to Epicurus, the founder of Epicureanism, Lucretius speaks of the light that Epicurus left his disciples, the access to knowledge, which later generations attempt to copy, and describes Epicurus as if he is the father of all who commit to the Epicurean philosophical tradition. This short hymn is but one small demonstration of the loyalty of a disciple to his philosophical founder.

> You, father, are the discoverer of truths, you supply us with a father's instructions, from your pages, glorious man, as bees in the flowering pasture drink all the nectar, in like manner we feed off all your golden words.[15]

20. SENECA, *EPISTLES* 90.28

Seneca was not only a philosopher and orator, but also a letter writer. In this letter, he provides an example of philosophical loyalty on par with loyalty to the gods. Here philosophical wisdom is personified, and she is the benefactor of all knowledge. Philosophy provides the progress of humanity, and Seneca provides a list of benefits to humans when one is loyal to philosophical teaching.

> Whatever things are evil, whatever things appear to be evil; she strips our minds of falsity, she shows us what things are evil and what things are seemingly evil; she strips our minds of vain illusion. She grants a substantial greatness to us, but she restrains that which is puffed up and showy yet vacuous. She does not allow us to be ignorant of the difference between that which is great and that which is puffed up; she bestows the knowledge of the totality of nature and of her own nature. She discloses what the gods are and what their nature is; what are the gods

15. Adapted from Rouse and Smith, LCL.

of the underworld, what are the lares and the genii, what are the souls among the secondary divinities who are eternal, where they abide and what they do, what power they have, and what is their will. Such are her rites of initiation, through which are not a municipal shrine, but the enormous temple of all the gods, the heavens themselves, whose true image and likeness she offers to our mind's eye. For our sight is too dull for such a great spectacle.[16]

Vocabulary of Loyalty

HEBREW

חֶסֶד (*khesed*)...................... favor, loving-kindness

GREEK

ἄπιστος, -ον (*apistos, -on*) .... disloyalty, not trustworthy, unfaithful
δίκαιος, -αια, -ον
   (*dikaios, -aia, -on*) .... justice, loyalty
ἐρίηρος, -ον (*eriēros, -on*)........... faithful, loyal
εὐνομία (*eunomia*)................. loyalty to divine law, virtuous
εὐσέβεια (*eusebeia*) .... respect, loyalty
πίστις (*pistis*)...................... loyalty, trust
πιστός, -ή, -όν (*pistos, -ē, -on*) .... loyal, faithful
πιστότης (*pistotēs*) .... loyalty, honesty
φιλόκαισαρ (*philokaisar*) .... friend of Caesar
φιλορώμαιος, -α, -ον
   (*philorōmaios, -a, -on*)............. friend of Rome
φιλοσέβαστος, -ον
   (*philosebastos, -on*)............... friend of Augustus

LATIN

fides............................. loyalty
pietas............................ loyalty, duty

16. Adapted from Gummere, LCL.

Select Bibliography

Ando, Clifford. *Imperial Ideology and Provincial Loyalty in the Roman Empire.* Berkeley: University of California Press, 2000.

Crook, Zeba. "BTB Readers Guide: Loyalty." *BTB* 34 (2004): 167–77.

Dmitriev, Sviatoslav. *The Greek Slogan of Freedom and Early Roman Politics in Greece.* Oxford: Oxford University Press, 2011.

Fears, J. Rufus. "The Cult of Virtues and Roman Imperial Ideology." *ANRW* 17.2:827–948. Part 2, *Principat*, 17.2. Edited by H. Temporini and W. Haase. New York: de Gruyter, 1981.

Lemche, Niels Peter. "Kings and Clients: On Loyalty between the Ruler and the Ruled in Ancient 'Israel.'" *Semeia* 66 (1994): 119–32.

Rich, John. "Patronage and Interstate Relations in the Roman Republic." Pages 117–35 in *Patronage in Ancient Society.* Edited by Andrew Wallace-Hadrill. London: Routledge, 1989.

Additional Texts

LOYALTY: GENERAL

Aeschylus, *Persians* 1–15

Aristophanes, *Lysistrata* 1185

Caesar, *Gallic Wars* 1.19.3; 1.41.4

Chariton, *Chaereas and Callirhoe* 8.2.13; 8.8.7, 12

2 Chronicles 24:22

Cicero, *Agrarian Law* 2.22; *On Invention* 1.47; *On Duties* 2.33; *For Roscius Amerinus* 6.15

CIL 6.1779

1 Corinthians 1:9; 3:3–9, 16–23; 6:9–11; 11:2, 27–34; 14:33–36

Demosthenes, *Olynthiac* 3.26; *Against Timotheus* 49.25–27

Euripides, *Medea* 11–15

Galatians 1:6–7, 13–14; 5:22

Genesis 19:18–19

Hebrews 13:7

Herodotus, *Histories* 3.8, 74; 9.91–92, 106

Homer, *Iliad* 16.144–47

Horace, *Epistles* 2.1

Isocrates, *Orations* 10.58

James 1:2–3

3 John 5

Luke 7:1–10

4 Maccabees 17:2–34

Matthew 8:5–13

Philippians 1:14

Pindar, *Nemean Odes* 8.40–49

Proverbs 19:22; 20:6

Romans 1:29–32

Ruth 3:10

Sallust, *Cataline War* 19

1 Samuel 20:12–17

2 Samuel 16:15–19

Sophocles, *Antigone* 290–304
Thucydides, *History* 5.108
1 Timothy 6:9–11

2 Timothy 2:22
Xenophon, *Anabasis* 1.1.5; *Hellenica*
1.3.12; 2.4.30

LOYALTY TO THE GODS

Aeschylus, *Agamemnon* 337–40
1 Clement 15
Exodus 15:13; 20:4–6
Ezra 3:11
1 Chronicles 17:13–14
Cicero, *On the Laws* 2.19, 28
Colossians 1:7
1 Corinthians 10:13
2 Corinthians 1:18
Galatians 2:16; 3:22
Genesis 6:8; 12:1–9; 15:1–21; 24:27
Hebrews 2:17; 10:23
Herodotus, *Histories* 2.141
Hosea 6:6
Isaiah 54:10; 63:7
Isocrates, *Orations* 12.124
1 John 1:9
Jonah 2:8
1 Maccabees 2:52
4 Maccabees 15:24
Nehemiah 13:22
Numbers 14:19
Philippians 3:7–11
Pindar, *Olympian Odes* 3.41

Plato, *Republic* 615a–d; *Symposium*
193a, d
Pliny the Elder, *Natural History* 28.3
Plutarch, *That Epicurus Actually Makes
a Pleasant Life Impossible* 1101c–d
Psalms 5:7; 6:4; 17:7; 26:3; 31; 33; 36;
40:10–11; 44:26; 48:9; 59:16–17; 63:3;
66:20; 86:13; 89; 94:18; 98:3; 100:5;
103:11; 106:1, 7, 45; 107; 108:4; 109:26;
115:1; 117; 118:1–4; 119:124; 127; 136;
138; 143:8, 12; 144:1–2; 147:11
Revelation 1:5; 2:10–13
Romans 1:8, 25, 28, 31; 3:3, 22
2 Samuel 7:14–15
Sophocles, *Ajax* 709–13; *Electra*
960–69, 1090–97; *Oedipus the King*
1438–39, 1442–45
Theognis, fragments 1135–50
1 Thessalonians 1:8–9; 4:1; 5:24
2 Thessalonians 3:3
Thucydides, *History* 5.30
1 Timothy 6:9–10
2 Timothy 2:13, 22

CLIENT KINGSHIP

Ammianus Marcellinus, *History* 17.12.12
Caesar, *Gallic Wars* 1.14.2; 6.4.2; 7.5.2
Cicero, *On Duties* 1.43; *On the Republic*
1.43; *Against Verres* 2.5.83
CIRB 38, 978, 1046
Deeds of the Divine Augustus 5.26–34;

6.32; 32.3
Dio Cassius, *Roman History* 48.5; 53.22,
25
Florus, *Epitome* 1.36.3
IAM 2.348–50, 356–61, 384, 402
IGRR 3.137

Livy, *History of Rome* 8.1.10; 36.3.8–10;
  37.54.17; 45.20.8
4 Maccabees 8:6
P.London 3.1178.14
Polybius, *Histories* 3.15.5

Proculus, *Digest* 19.15.7
Suetonius, *Augustus* 60; *Caligula* 44.2
SEG 9.7
SIG² 814.2
Xenophon, *Cyropaedia* 7.1.43–44

SLAVERY/MANUMISSION

Cicero, *Letters to Friends* 287.2
CIL 1.1479; 6.7595, 18048, 18072, 18109,
  18136, 18156, 18188, 31665; 9.3922;
  10.26; 11.600, 3892; 12.2956
Colossians 4:7
1 Corinthians 4:2
Homer, *Odyssey* 1.346
ILS 6348
Lex Aelia Sentia

Luke 12:42; 19:17
Matthew 25:21
Petronius, *Satyricon* 57
Philemon
Plautus, *Braggart Solder*
Sallust, *Jugurthine War* 71
Suetonius, *Claudius* 25
Terence, *Andria* 1.1

PHILOSOPHICAL LOYALTY

Augustine, *Against the Academics* 3.41
Cicero, *On Oratory* 2.37; *On the Republic*
  1.10
Diogenes Laertius, *Lives of Eminent
  Philosophers* 2.113–14

Lucretius, *On the Nature of Things*
  1.62–79; 5.1–54; 6.1–42
Porphyry, *Life of Plotinus* 4–23
Pseudo-Plato, *Greater Alcibiades* 135d

16. Friendship and Gifts

Zeba A. Crook and Gary Stansell

Introduction

The formation of friendship and the exchange of gifts can be found in every society throughout time, yet they are so difficult to define and theorize. Who really counts as a friend? What, if any, social conditions must exist for friendship to develop? What are the rules and expectations that sustain friendships? And why do friendships break down? What are the rules and expectations of gifting? Is a gift always really a gift? Can a gift ever be free? And what are the social functions of gifting? Modern anthropologists and social theorists study these questions, but the questions are not at all new; they consumed ancient writers and the public every bit as much as they interest modern scholars.

Friendships are extralegal relationships that imply some personal, emotional bond (see **chap. 2, Kinship**). That is, they might involve considerable exchange of money and other things of value, but they are not susceptible to court action and charges of cheating or fraud. Thus, friendship exchange is fundamentally different from economic exchanges, despite the common exchange of things with economic value.

In another chapter, we see that patronage and benefactions are forms of asymmetrical exchange, wherein the value of what is exchanged and the social status of the people undertaking the exchange are both asymmetrical (see **chap. 3, Patronage**). Gifting, in contrast, is a form of symmetrical exchange, wherein the value of what is exchanged is considered by the parties involved to be (roughly) equal, and the social status of the people undertaking the exchange is also (roughly) equal. This relates to friendship too, in that friends are relatively close in status and, in addition, have the ability to reciprocate gifts of relatively equal value. Thus, when one person invites another to dinner, does a political favor, or gives a generous gift, the one giving can expect invitations, favors, and gifts to be reciprocated at some point in the future. If no return gift ever comes, or the return is inadequate, two things might happen: (1) the friendship might break down; or (2) it might transform into a relationship of patronage, since the failure to reciprocate makes the exchange (and the relationship) asymmetrical. In truth, there is no such thing as a "free gift," that is, a gift that does not require some form of reciprocation, either of something equivalent or of gratitude, honor, or prestige.

Also related to the question of patronage and benefaction, people in Mediterranean antiquity did not like to draw attention to status- and value-asymmetry, so the language of friendship and gift is used extensively in relationships that were clearly asymmetrical. One of the more common words for patron or client in Greek is *philos*, in Latin *amicus*, both meaning *friend*, and these were used even for the emperor or God. It can be quite difficult for modern readers to know in these instances whether patrons or benefactors were really friends of their clients (and vice versa), or whether both parties were merely using the language of friendship to mask the asymmetrical nature of the relationship and the exchanges.

One key, then, to distinguishing friendship from patronage, and gifts from benefactions, resides in status, value symmetry, and, above all, in the kind of reciprocity. Ancient writers were also concerned with friendships of convenience or, worse, taking advantage. When one was wealthy, one needed to be concerned with telling a new friend from a flatterer, someone who was using friendship merely as a means to gain access to one's wealth and influence.

Gifts also tend to be voluntary and, as such, tend to differ from taxation. Even this, however, admits to exceptions, since in ancient contexts, it was commonly expected that the recipient of a civic office (an honor) would give gifts to the city, that is, provide some things free of charge. As a rule, however, gifting was unregulated legally (as was patronage). Social mores and cultural expectations determined the rules and the sanctions one incurred for "breaking" those rules. Of course, these mores can be quite different from one location to another.

It is also useful, from an analytical perspective, to distinguish gifting from the exchanges that take place among kin. Parents may well give generously to their children, and siblings to each other, but kinship exchanges carry quite a different set of rules and expectations. For instance, the length of time between a gift and its reciprocation will be very much longer in a kinship context than in a friendship context.

As honor and shame were both highly important social values (see **chap. 4, Honor; chap. 5, Shame**), gifting must be situated with them. A gift given in public was a challenge, in that it publicly obligated the recipient to reciprocate. If the gift was too lavish and impossible to reciprocate, it had the potential deeply to shame the recipient. Thus, gifting had a dark side in the honor culture of Mediterranean antiquity.

Ancient Texts

SOCIAL IMPORTANCE AND PURPOSE OF GIFTS

1. HESIOD, *WORKS AND DAYS* 353–61

Hesiod, a Greek poet perhaps contemporaneous with Homer (eighth to seventh century BCE), in his *Works and Days* exhorts his idling brother, Perses. Concerning the exchange of gifts, he advises liberality but warns against exchanging anything with those who fail to reciprocate. Taking without giving back is highly dishonorable.

> Befriend friends, and be present for those who are present. Give to whosoever gives, and give not to whosoever gives not. Someone gave to the generous, but no one gave to the tightwad. "Give" is a "Good Woman," but "Rob" is an "Evil Woman": She dispenses death. The man who is willing, even if he gives something great, takes pleasure at the gift, and his spirit is delighted. But the person who takes for himself shamelessly, even if it is an insignificant thing, freezes his dear heart.[1]

2. LUKE 6:38

Reciprocity of gifts means that a gift, at some later time and in some appropriate way, must evoke a (different) gift. According to anthropological theory of gifts, giving appears to be voluntary but, in fact, is obligatory: one is obligated to give, accept, and return gifts. In Luke 6:38, the obligation is stated in the imperative.

> Give and it will be given to you. A fair measure, having been pressed down and shaken together, running over, they will put into your lap. For the measure you use to give will be the measure used when you receive it back.

3. 1 KINGS 10:10

When the Queen of Sheba makes a state visit to Solomon, the event is replete with traditional elements of hospitality and the exchange of gifts. After Solomon grandly displays his wealth, Sheba offers gifts (in contrast to the conventions of hospitality in Homer). The reciprocity here is between equals, heads of state, and forges a political alliance; yet the narrative makes it clear that Solomon is superior and the Queen is inferior in wealth and prestige.

---

1. Adapted from Evelyn-White, LCL.

Then she gave the king a hundred and twenty talents of gold, and a large amount of spices and precious stones; never again were delivered such an abundance of spices as these that the Queen of Sheba gave to King Solomon.

4. IV URKUNDEN DER 18. DYNASTIE 1326:1–5

This passage comes from an inscription on a column in the Karnak Temple. During the period of Egypt's New Kingdom (1570–1090 BCE), the king was central to the collection and redistribution of royal gifts. Gifts come from foreign lands to the king himself, not to Egypt as a country or political entity. In this passage, the king is not receiving gifts from equals but from social inferiors.

> The princes of Mitanni come to him with their *inw* on their backs in order to request the peace of His Majesty and that his sweet breath of life be sent.[2]

5. HERODOTUS, *HISTORIES* 3.97.2–5

Not all gifting occurred between individuals. Sometimes it happened between groups, and it usually carried deeply political implications. The fifth-century Greek historian Herodotus illustrates that tribute was a form of gift. Tribute is a kind of tax placed on a subdued people; the following passage recounts that, while Persia is tax-free and pays no tribute, other nations must render gifts and tribute to the Persian king. The passage also distinguishes between such a legal, political obligation and gifts of homage, presumably offered freely, yet in expectation of a return.

> Now, Persia is the only country I have not referred to as "tributary," for the land of the Persians lives tribute-free. There are some who are not imposed upon to pay tribute, but they bring gifts: Ethiopia, bordering on Egypt. . . . These [countries just listed] who together bring offerings every third year . . . two dry measures of unsmelted gold, two hundred ebony rounds, five Ethiopian boys, and twenty large elephant tusks. . . . Finally, the Arabians gave a thousand talents of frankincense each and every year. These were the gifts, aside from the tribute, that these people provided for the king.[3]

6. CATULLUS, *POEMS* 73

Catullus was a Roman poet from a prominent family in the first century BCE; his influence on later poets (Ovid, Horace, and Vergil) helped them become

---

2. Translation by Edward Bleiberg, *The Official Gift in Ancient Egypt* (Norman: University of Oklahoma Press, 1996), 93.
3. Adapted from Godley, LCL.

more widely known. He wrote poems on a number of different topics, including angry lampoons against people and erotic poetry. In this poem, he reflects on the importance of reciprocity.

> Stop expecting to be acknowledged in any respect by anyone,
> or for anyone to be grateful.
> All people are ingrates, and being kind is worth nothing,
> or worse, it wearies and hurts.
> So it is with me. I have never been hurt more seriously or more painfully
> Than when someone once called me his one and only friend.[4]

7. SENECA, *ON BENEFITS* 1.1.9–13

Seneca the Younger (ca. 4 BCE–65 CE) was a Roman Stoic statesman and philosopher. In his work *De beneficiis* (*On Benefits*), he prescribes that giving among humans be modeled on divine generosity, which in Seneca's opinion is unselfish. Seneca uses the word *beneficia*, which can have broad connotations of elites providing public works, circuses, monuments, feasts, or giving assistance. Though I have translated that word here as *gifts*, the category that Seneca imagines blurs the boundary between gifts and benefactions. This passage also alludes to the necessity of reciprocity.

> Let us take them [the immortal gods] for our guides as far as the weakness of our mortal nature permits; let us bestow gifts, not put them out at interest. The man who, while bestowing a gift, thinks of what he will get in return deserves to be deceived. . . . If a man does not give gifts because he has not received any, he must have bestowed them in order to receive them in return, and he justifies ingratitude, whose disgrace lies in not returning gifts when able to do so. As it is, virtue consists in bestowing gifts for which there is uncertainty in receiving any return, but whose fruit is at once enjoyed by noble minds. . . . He who does not repay a gift sins more, but he who does not bestow one sins earlier.[5]

GIFTS AND FRIENDSHIP

8. DIOGENES LAERTIUS, *LIVES OF EMINENT PHILOSOPHERS* 8.10

Diogenes Laertius wrote in Greek and lived in the third century CE. He is best known for writing biographies of famous philosophers, more than seventy-five

---

4. Adapted from Cornish, LCL.
5. Adapted from Basore, LCL.

biographical accounts in all. In this passage, he writes about the sixth-century BCE philosopher and mathematician, Pythagoras.

> Just as Timaeus said, Pythagoras was the first to say both "The things of friends are held in common" and "Friendship is equality." And his disciples brought their possessions together into one.[6]

9. HOMER, *ILIAD* 9.119–55

In Homer's *Iliad*, Agamemnon promises to the hero Achilles a whole catalog of gifts, if he will return to battle. Agamemnon, recognizing his own past blindness, wants to make amends by promising amends-gifts that will reestablish a broken relationship, give honor to the recipient, and make him wealthy. But these are gifts that also obligate, for Achilles must submit himself to Agamemnon's lordship.

> Yet because I was blind through yielding to my miserable passion, I am willing to make amends by giving innumerable compensatory gifts. . . . Let me name the splendid gifts: seven unsmelted tripods, ten talents of gold, twenty burnished kettles, and twelve solid horses. . . . I will also give seven women for noble and skilled work. . . . And I will give seven well-populated citadels. . . . All of them are near the sea . . . and in them dwell men who are rich in sheep and wealthy in oxen. They will honor him with free gifts as they would a god.[7]

10. GENESIS 32:13–15, 18, 20

Esau confronts his brother Jacob after years of estrangement. Before the meeting, Jacob sends ahead amends-gifts to his brother for earlier wrongs (he had stolen Esau's birthright). An honor challenge, his gifts call for a riposte; perhaps they are meant to humiliate Esau. Esau asks the meaning of the gifts (he is rightly cautious) and at first refuses to accept them. But Jacob urges Esau to accept his gifts, which he finally does (33:11). The gift strategy has accomplished the reconciliation yet set up the possibilities for further reciprocities.

> From what he had with him, Jacob took a gift for Esau his brother: two hundred female goat and twenty male goats, two hundred ewes and twenty rams, thirty suckling camels and their calves, forty cows, ten bulls, twenty female donkeys and ten male donkeys. . . . "[A] gift to my lord Esau." . . . Jacob said, "I might be

---

6. Adapted from Hicks, LCL.
7. Adapted from Murray and Wyatt, LCL.

atoned in his sight with a gift that precedes me, after which I will see his face. Maybe he will pardon me."

11. HOMER, ODYSSEY 1.310–13

In the opening book of the *Odyssey*, the goddess Athena appears to Telemachus as Mentes (in the shape of the Tapien chieftain), counseling him to search for his father, Odysseus, who according to rumor may still be alive. This scene exhibits many elements of the conventional hospitality scene (guest at the threshold, welcome, feast, identification). At the end of his visit, Mentes wishes to depart before taking the traditional bath for guest-friends. Telemachus, the host, following the rules of hospitality, honors his guest by offering a parting gift.

> Go to your ship with a joyful heart, bearing a valuable and very beautiful gift, which will be your treasure from me, such as dear friends give to guest-friends.[8]

NATURE OF FRIENDSHIP

12. HOMER, ILIAD 22.262–65

The great epic poet Homer described friendship through his characters. When the Trojan Hector makes an offer of friendship to the Greek hero Achilles, Achilles rejects it because their friendship would lack the fundamental feature required between friends: concord.

> Then having looked from beneath his brow, swift of foot Achilles said to him: "Hector, do not lecture me about unforgettable covenants. Just as there are no oaths of loyalty between lions and men, nor do wolves and lambs have united hearts, but relentlessly plot against one another continually, so it is that you and I cannot be friends, nor, for my part, will there be oaths between us until one or the other of us has fallen."[9]

13. HESIOD, WORKS AND DAYS 707–13

Hesiod was a Greek poet from around the seventh century BCE. *Works and Days* is among his better-known works; it is an eight-hundred-line poem about the toil of hard work and success. In this passage, he recognizes that friend-

8. Adapted from Murray and Dimock, LCL.
9. Adapted from Murray and Wyatt, LCL.

ship was complicated: not equivalent to kinship, but like it, people should be loyal but not without conditions, and friendship is susceptible to ceasing and beginning anew. Friendship should be long-term, not fickle.

> Do not make a companion equal to a brother, but if that's what happens, do not be the first to act badly. Do not tell lies with a benevolent tongue. If he should happen to be the first to speak or even do something hateful, having remembered, punish him as much as twofold, but accept if he invites you to be friends again and agrees to make amends. Cowardly is the man who keeps making other friends.[10]

14. ARISTOTLE, *EUDEMIAN ETHICS* 1236A

Aristotle famously distinguished among three types of friendship: pleasure, utility, and character. Though some claimed that only the last of these amounted to true friendship, Aristotle disagreed. As is clear from the passage below, however, he did still think it was the most noble form of friendship. Friendship based in goodness is the truest form, because it is not measured by its usefulness or pleasure.

> As was said before, one divides friendship into three categories: one division concerns virtue, another advantage, and another what is pleasant. Of these, the one concerning advantage is among the most common kind of friendship (for those who are seeking advantage befriend one another). . . . On the other hand, the friendship concerning pleasure belongs to the immature (for these ones have sense perception; hence the friendship of the immature is changeable, for their sense of what is pleasurable changes as they mature). But friendship based in virtue is the friendship of the best kind of people.[11]

15. CICERO, *ON FRIENDSHIP* 20

Cicero (106–43 BCE) was a Roman philosopher, statesman, lawyer, and orator. This philosophical treatise on friendship was composed as a dialogue between two figures from the past who discuss the meaning and qualities of friendship. It was written in 44 BCE. Though the entire piece is useful for understanding ancient friendship, this passage ties friendship and virtue closely together.

> For instance, friendship is nothing if not consensus on all matters, whether human or divine, together with benevolence and affection. In fact, I know of nothing

10. Adapted from Evelyn-White, LCL.
11. Adapted from Rackham, LCL.

given to humans by the immortal gods, other than wisdom, that is better. Some set riches above friendship, health, power, and honor. Many prefer sensual pleasures, but this is the highest aim of animals; the others are beyond transitory and uncertain; they are based not on our own careful consideration, but on chance fate. However, some place the utmost value on virtue, which is without doubt brilliant, for this virtue itself gives birth to and maintains friendship. Without virtue, friendship is not possible.[12]

16. Plutarch, *How to Tell a Flatterer from a Friend* 51C–D

Plutarch (45–120 CE) was best known as a biographer and essayist. He wrote many essays on what he considered moral topics, collected in the *Moralia*. One of his more famous treatises, this one reflects the anguish of the wealthy and elite over knowing who their real friends are, and which of their friends are there merely to gain access to their wealth and power. Plutarch, and others, referred to that second group as flatterers. The test for telling a flatterer from a friend is frankness of speech, or *parrēsia*. A true friend will speak frankly, while a flatterer will tell you only what you want to hear, thereby seeming supportive and agreeable, but not having your best interests at heart. Yet Plutarch knows that the clever flatterer can also use frankness of speech!

> Just as those who are clever at cooking food use bitter juices and harsh seasoning in order to reduce gross sweetness, thus also the flatterer; they employ frankness of speech in a way that is neither honest nor beneficial, which looks playful but from beneath a glaring brow and entertains but without effect.[13]

SYMBOLIC FRIENDSHIP

17. Plutarch, *On Brotherly Love* 479C–D

This passage comes from one of Plutarch's moral essays, entitled *On Brotherly Love*. In it he reflects on the relationship between kinship and friendship, claiming that we learn friendship from our first relationships, which are always based in family. It is easy to see why unrelated people in groups would come to use kinship terminology (brother and sister, father and mother) for each other.

12. Adapted from Falconer, LCL.
13. Adapted from Babbitt, LCL.

For many friendships are shady and imitative, in the likeness of that first friendship that nature produced, both in children toward parents and in brothers toward brothers.[14]

18. Seneca, *Epistles* 3.2–3

The Roman figure Seneca the Younger (ca. 4 BCE–65 CE), whom we encountered above, was a statesman and philosopher. Much of his philosophy, particularly his view of the world, was expressed in a series of 124 letters, all addressed to Lucilius, a self-made man and Roman knight. In one of these letters, Seneca advises Lucilius on the difference between true and false friendship. Notice how one of the defining features of friendship for Seneca, in addition to loyalty and trust, is the ability to speak boldly and freely.

> But if you consider someone a friend whom you do not trust the same as you trust yourself, you err direly and do not know what genuine friendship is. You can consult with a genuine friend on all matters, but first and foremost among matters that you should feel free to discuss is the friend himself. . . . Speak boldly with that person to the same degree that you would speak to yourself. . . . What is it, why should I hold back even a single word when in the presence of my friend? What is it, why should I not regard myself as alone when in his presence?[15]

19. Horace, *Satires* 1.6.45–65

One of the most famous patron-client relationships from antiquity is that between the Roman writer Horace and his patron (also the literary patron of many others), Maecenas. By all accounts, Maecenas was a generous and fair patron, unlike those lampooned by Juvenal (see **chap. 3, Patronage**). Note in this passage how Horace, however, uses the language of friendship rather than patronage. Yet there is no doubt: Horace was not Maecenas's equal in terms of status or wealth.

> Now, let's get back to me: the son of a freedman, disparaged by everyone as "the son of a freedman," because now, Maecenas, I share a table with you, while of old because as tribune I led a Roman legion. This situation and that one differ, for the same person who envies me for the honor of the office should not envy me your friendship, particularly since you adopt only those who are worthy, those who

---

14. Adapted from Helmbold, LCL.
15. Adapted from Gummere, LCL.

are far from prone to self-seeking. . . . Standing before you the first time, I spoke only a few stuttering words; I was prevented by quiet shame from going on. . . . You were quiet, as is your way. I went away, and nine months later you recalled me, inviting me to number among your friends.[16]

20. *IKilikiaBM* 2.201, LINES 21–34

Friends, particularly those who were members of associative groups, used the language of kinship to refer to their relationships. It was common for people to call fellow group members brother, sister, father, and mother. This applies equally to Greek and Roman cultic and professional associations, including early Christ-following groups. The following passage comes from column B of a first-century inscription that was found in a tomb in Lamos (southwest of Tarsus). It is common to reconstruct the bottom of column A to include the phrase "It is not permitted," from which column B continues:

> To sell outside of the group, but let him take thirty staters from the association, and let him withdraw. But if ever some brother wishes to sell, let the other brothers purchase it. Now, if the brothers do not wish, then let them receive the aforementioned staters, and let them withdraw from the association.[17]

Vocabulary of Friendship and Gifts

HEBREW

בּוֹא (*bo*) . . . . to bring
בְּרָכָה (*berakah*) . . . . gift, blessing
חָלַק (*khalaq*) . . . . to distribute
לָקַח (*laqakh*) . . . . to take, receive
מִנְחָה (*minkhah*) . . . . gift
נָשָׂא (*nesa*) . . . . to carry, take
נָתַן (*natan*) . . . . to give

16. Adapted from Fairclough, LCL.
17. Richard S. Ascough, Philip A. Harland, and John S. Kloppenborg, *Associations in the Greco-Roman World: A Sourcebook* (Waco: Baylor University Press, 2012), no. 215.

GREEK

ἀναπόδοτος, -ον
  (anapodotos, -on) . . . . countergift
ἄποινα (apoina) . . . . gifts
δίδωμι (didōmi) . . . . to give
δόσις (dosis) . . . . giving
δωρεά (dōrea) . . . . offering a gift
δῶρον (dōron) . . . . gift
δωτίνη (dōtinē) . . . . obligatory gift that expects a return
εὔνοια (eunoia) . . . . goodwill
κόλαξ (kolax) . . . . flatterer
ξεινήϊον (xeinēion) . . . . guest-gift
ὁμόνοια (homonoia) . . . . concord, oneness of mind
παρρησία (parrēsia) . . . . frank speech
παρρησιάζομαι (parrēsiazomai) . . . . . . speak frankly
φιλία (philia) . . . . friendship
φίλος, -η, -ον (philos, -ē, -on) . . . . friendly

LATIN

amicitia . . . . friendship
amicus . . . . friend
beneficium . . . . favor, benefit, service, kindness
do . . . . to give
munus . . . . duty, public office; a gift for the sake of an
                                                official office
munera . . . . gift
sparsio . . . . what is scattered or dropped, like seed

Select Bibliography

Crook, Zeba A. "Fictive-Giftship and Fictive-Friendship in Greco-Roman Society."
    Pages 61–76 in The Gift in Antiquity. Edited by Michael Satlow. Chichester: Black-
    well, 2013.

Fitzgerald, John T., ed. *Greco-Roman Perspectives on Friendship*. Atlanta: Scholars Press, 1997.

Gill, Christopher, Norman Postlethwaite, and Richard Seaford, eds. *Reciprocity in Ancient Greece*. Oxford: Oxford University Press, 1998.

Mauss, Marcel. *The Gift: The Form and Reason for Exchange in Archaic Societies*. Translated by W. D. Halls. New York: Norton, 1990.

Stansell, Gary. "The Gift in Ancient Israel." *Semeia* 87 (1999): 65–90.

Straten, F. T. van. "Gifts for the Gods." Pages 65–151 in *Faith, Hope and Worship: Aspects of Religious Mentality in the Ancient World*. Edited by H. S. Versnel. Leiden: Brill, 1981.

Additional Texts

SOCIAL IMPORTANCE AND PURPOSE OF GIFTS

Aristotle, *Nicomachean Ethics* 1155b–1156a, 1158a; *Rhetoric* 1381a; *Topics* 125a

BGU 8.1874

Cicero, *Letters to Friends* 431; *On Duties* 1.47; *For Plancius* 80–81

Dio Chrysostom, *Law (Or. 75)* 6

Exodus 29:41; 40:29

Genesis 4:3–5

Homer, *Odyssey* 9.267–68

IAsMinLyk 1.69

IDidyma 502

IMagnMai 321

IMylasa 571–75

IPrusaOlymp 24

ISmyrna 720

Josephus, *Jewish Antiquities* 14.202

1 Kings 10:25

2 Kings 17:3–4

Leviticus 2:1–15

Luke 11:8; 21:1–4

1 Maccabees 8:1, 12, 17; 10:16, 19–20, 23, 26, 54; 13:36; 14:18–22

2 Maccabees 11:26–30

Malachi 1:11–13; 2:12–13

MAMA 3.580, 780, 788

Martial, *Epigrams* 5.59.3

Matthew 2:11; 5:23–24; 8:4

Numbers 28:26–31

Pliny the Younger, *Letters* 9.30.1–4

Plutarch, *On Brotherly Love* 490e

P.Oxyrhynchus 3057

Psalms 20:3; 45:12; 72:10

1 Samuel 10:27; 18:1–4

2 Samuel 6:17–19; 19:42

Seneca, *On Benefits* 1.4.2

Sirach 22:20–21

Suetonius, *Caligula* 18.2–3

Theognis, *Elegiac Poetry* 253–54

Vergil, *Aeneid* 5.282

GIFTS AND FRIENDSHIP

Acts 3:6; 10:45; 20:35

Aeschines, *Orations* 19.248

Cicero, *On Friendship* 22, 31, 33, 35, 51,
101; *Letters to Atticus* 216, 367; *Letters
to Friends* 20.19

2 Corinthians 9:15

Dionysius of Halicarnassus, *Roman
Antiquities* 8.34.1–3

Ephesians 2:8

Genesis 43:11

Hebrews 5:1; 8:3–4; 9:9; 11:4

Homer, *Iliad* 6.224–31; *Odyssey* 9.370

Mark 10:21

Matthew 5:42; 10:8; 13:12

Plautus, *Prisoners* 897

Proverbs 15:27; 18:16

Romans 5:15

Sirach 6:17

Tacitus, *Germany* 21.3

Theognis, *Fragments* 861–62

NATURE OF FRIENDSHIP

Aristotle, *Eudemian Ethics* 1237a; *Nicomachean Ethics* 1155b, 1156b, 1158a,
1166b, 1168b, 1169b, 1170b, 1171a

Cicero, *Brutus* 1.15; *On Duties* 1.20, 51,
56, 158; *About the Ends of Goods and
Evils* 2.78, 82; 5.56–66; *On Friendship*
3, 15, 19–20, 22–23, 26–27, 37, 47–48,
51, 55–56, 61–65, 69–70, 74, 80, 84,
100, 104; *Letters to Atticus* 60; 4.1.7;
4.7.1; *Letters to Friends* 3, 26, 64, 96,
253; *On the Subdivisions of Oratory* 78,
88; *For Plancius* 5

Demosthenes, *On the Crown* (*Or. 18*) 109

Diodorus Siculus, *Library of History*
10.4, 8

Diogenes Laertius, *Lives of Eminent
Philosophers* 8.10, 16, 17, 23, 33, 35

Epictetus, *Dissertations* 2.22

Homer, *Iliad* 3.276; 4.360–61; 6.14–15,
119–236; 13.487; 15.710; 16.219; 17.267,
411, 655; 19.315; *Odyssey* 3.103, 126–29,
199, 211, 313, 375; 8.21

Horace, *Art of Poetry* 450–52; *Satires*
1.3.50–55

Iamblichus, *Protrepticus* 21

Job 16:20–21

Lucian, *Toxaris* 6

Mark 8:32

Maximus of Tyre, *Orations* 14

Philemon 8

Pindar, *Nemean* 8.44

Plato, *Phaedrus* 233C

Plutarch, *On the Education of Children*
12e; *How to Tell a Flatterer from a
Friend* 49c–d, 49e–f, 51a–b, 52a,
54d–f, 55a, 55d, 56a, 61b, 65a, 70e; *On
Having Many Friends* 93c–e, 94a–b,
95b, 95c, 96a, 96f, 97a; *On Moral Virtue* 451e; *On the Control of Anger* 453a,
455d, 462a; *On Brotherly Love* 481d,
483e; *On Envy and Hate* 538e

Proverbs 16:27–28; 17:17; 18:24; 22:24–
25; 27:5–6, 17

Psalm 55:1–23

Seneca, *Benefits* 6.34; *Epistles* 95.48

Sextus, *Sentences* 293

Sirach 6:14–16; 12:8–9; 19:13–15; 22:22;
27:17

Theognis, *Elegiac Poetry* 119–28, 575–76, 641–42, 811–14, 963–70, 1219–20

Xenophon, *Hellenica* 4.1.34–35; *Memorabilia* 2.9–10

SYMBOLIC FRIENDSHIP

BGU 8.1770

CCCA 6.342

Chariton, *Chaereas and Callirhoe* 1.6.4; 1.12.6; 2.2.3; 4.6.5; 5.4.12–13; 5.8.6–7; 6.8.5; 8.4.3; 8.10

Cicero, *On Friendship* 22, 31, 51, 100; *Letters to Friends* 110, 111, 155, 298, 318

CIJ 88, 93, 166, 319, 494, 496, 508, 509, 510, 523, 537, 619, 694, 720

CIL 3.633, 870, 882, 1207, 4045, 7505, 7532, 8833, 8837, 11042; 5.784; 6.8796, 10234; 9.2687, 5450; 10.1874; 11.1355, 5748–49; 14.37, 70, 256, 2408

CIRB 104, 967, 1263, 1277, 1281, 1282, 1283, 1284, 1285, 1286, 1288

CPJ 3.473

Dio Chrysostom, *Kingship 3* (*Or.* 3) 86

Dionysius of Halicarnassus, *Roman Antiquities* 3.7.3; 3.9.7; 6.32.3; 6.40.3; 6.55.3; 6.71.2; 8.1.5–6; 8.7.1; 8.7.3; 8.9.3

Exodus 33:11

Herodotus, *Histories* 6.89

Homer, *Iliad* 3.256, 323, 373

Horace, *Epistles* 1.10.33; 1.18.37–40, 67–69, 76–85, 86–87; *Satires* 2.6.85–92

IEph 234, 235, 424, 424a, 1601e

IGLSkythia 1.99; 1.100; 2.83

IGR 3.90, 191, 883; 4.908

IGUR 77, 246

IMylasa 544

IPergamon 117, 118, 120–25

ISelge 2, 17, 20

ISmyrna 844a

James 2:1, 23–24; 3:1

John 15:13–14; 19:12

Josephus, *Jewish Antiquities* 7.276; 19.328

Lucian, *Toxaris* 7, 20, 28, 32

1 Maccabees 10:20; 13:36; 15:32

MAMA 8.455, 492, 514–17a–b; 10.437

Matthew 5:22–23

NewDocs 4:124

OGIS 470.10

1 Peter 2:17; 5:9

Pliny the Younger, *Letters* 10.4; 10.26

Plutarch, *On the Control of Anger* 453c; *On Tranquility of Mind* 467d, 471e, 472b; *On Brotherly Love* 479b, 479d, 481b

Proverbs 19:6

Psalm 25:14

Romans 12:10

SEG 43.893

SIG[3] 813a–b, 854, 898, 1111

Sirach 7:12, 18

Tacitus, *Annals* 1.10

TAM III,1 14, 16, 21, 57, 58, 83, 87, 98, 105, 122–23

1 Thessalonians 1:4; 2:1; 3:2; 4:1; 5:1, 4, 12

Thucydides, *History* 2.97

Wisdom of Solomon 7:14

Xenophon, *Anabasis* 7.3, 16; *Cyropaedia* 7.1.42; *Memorabilia* 2.2.2; 3.7.9

17. Limited Good and Envy

John H. Elliott, Zeba A. Crook, and Jerome H. Neyrey, SJ

Introduction

The notion of *limited good* concerns certain social perceptions, and it influences subsequent behaviors. This concept was first identified by anthropologist George Foster in his study of peasant communities (1965, 1972) and is now taught in business courses as "zero sum game." According to this perception of reality, all good things in the world exist in a finite amount. This applies initially to material things, like land, water, food, jobs, and money. The reality of ancient economic life would certainly have turned the perception of limited good into the experience of it, particularly among the majority of the world who were quite poor. In the ancient Mediterranean, businesses were small, and the cost of land made it available only to an elite few. Therefore, wealth was collected extremely slowly, and living safely above subsistence level was beyond the hope of many. Therefore, these things must be apportioned carefully and collected or held with humility and subtlety. A person whose wealth is very high must take measures to share it (see **chap. 3, Patronage**), lest he or she become an object of envy, since wealth that one person has is wealth another cannot have. Conspicuous consumption was to be avoided by all, but the elite few, such as the emperor, had less need to care about public opinion.

This perception that all material goods exist in a limited, finite supply comes also to take on symbolic forms. Symbolically, ancient Mediterranean people believed that health, blood, beauty, masculinity, and semen were also limited goods. That is, it was widely assumed that the unhealthy or unattractive were naturally predisposed to envy of those who were healthy and attractive. Likewise, fertility (marked by having many children), and more specifically having a baby boy (so symbolically powerful because of his future potential), also risked inviting envy from those in want of both.

The final development of the perception of limited good is metaphorical. Power, influence, status, respect, honor, fame, security, and praise were also imagined as if they were limited goods. Heaping praise on someone for one's material possessions would be seen as dangerous to that person, for the observing public (see **chap. 6, Collectivism**) is invited by this praise to become envious. Conversely, moderate expression of praise for someone's generosity is doubly meaningful because a) it shows the wealthy person is not a hoarder, but generous with his or her wealth, and b) praise too is a limited good, because praise is something all people want for themselves, not for others. Honor granted to one person by the public court of reputation (see **chap. 4, Honor**) because of praise was honor denied to another. A Roman aphorism states *laudet qui invidet*, which can be rendered either "he who envies praises" or "he who praises envies."

In this vertically structured society, the status position maintained by one person means no one else can occupy that position at the same time; only by removing that person from that position could another occupy it. Thus, the perception of limited good is what makes ancient society so agonistic, because people are in competition for the limited supply of honor, status, and the more basic needs for their survival (land, food, water, wealth). The agonistic nature of peasant society is also evident in unceasing military, political, and social conflicts, as well as in endless family quarrels—always the same, endless squabbles, passed down from one generation to the next.

A small community (such as a large family or a village) can be thought of as a closed system, in that they ally together against the outside. In a closed system in which all good things are limited, there is a natural balance: Each person has a certain amount (of food, money, fertility). Because all things are limited, any rise in the amount of good going to one person or family throws off that balance, and thus that person or family becomes a threat to the whole system. The honorable person, seeking to avoid being envied or shamed, also seeks to avoid leaving the impression that he or she is seeking more than a fair share. Greed and hoarding are risky and deeply disliked traits, and the wealthy are frequently construed as thieves.

The perception of limited good is also what leads to envy and explains the sharp distinction between envy and jealousy. Envy is the pained reaction to seeing another person succeed or gain in things that are good. Jealousy is intense concern about losing to another what one already possesses, with either positive or negative valorization. Envy, always negative, is distress at what someone else possesses and wishing it destroyed. Jealousy is defensive and concerned with protecting and preserving what one has; envy is hostile aggression and targets others (through the malicious glance of an evil eye). Jealousy wants to keep what one has; envy wishes what the other has to be destroyed so that no one can have it. For this reason, envy is never represented as a positive emotion. It was considered corrosive and to originate in evil. This explains the natural link between envy and evil eye belief and practice (see **chap. 20, Evil Eye**).

Any form of success or good fortune is prone to envy: beauty, health, youth, wealth, success in warfare and athletic contests, reputation, and good social standing. Who envies whom? The ancients say that envy is a peer action. That is, a commoner does not envy the person who was appointed governor by the emperor, since the governorship was not available to that common man (and thus cannot be construed as having been taken from him).

Ancient Texts

PERCEPTIONS OF LIMITED GOOD

1. Anonymous wise saying (recorded by Iamblichus of Chalcis)
Iamblichus of Chalcis (245–325 CE) was a Neoplatonic philosopher. He is known for having collected sayings so old and traditional that no one knows their origin. In this saying, the perception of limited good is clearly articulated.

> People do not find it pleasant to give honor to someone else, for they suppose that they themselves are being deprived of something.[1]

2. Plutarch, *On Listening to Lectures* 44b
Plutarch (46–120 CE) was a philosopher, biographer, and essayist. His *Moralia* is a collection of short essays in which he is primarily concerned with moral education, in one case on how properly to listen to a lecture. In this work, he compares two listeners: one who listens too uncritically, cheering every syllable without thought. The other he describes in the passage below, which serves also to illustrate the perception of limited good.

> An offensive and tiresome listener is the man who is not to be touched or moved by anything that is said, full of festering presumption and ingrained self-assertion, as though convinced that he could say something better than what is being said;

1. H. Diels, *Die Fragmente der Vorsokratike* (Berlin: Weidmannsche Buchhandlung, 1935), 2:400.

he neither moves his brow nor utters a single word to indicate that he is glad to listen, but by means of silence and an affected gravity and pose, he seeks to gain a reputation for poise and profundity; as though commendation were money, he feels that he is robbing himself of every bit that he bestows on another.[2]

3. HERODOTUS, *HISTORIES* 7.10

The "father of history," Herodotus was a Greek historian who lived in the fifth century BCE in Asia Minor (modern Turkey). Only one of his works has survived, known as the *Histories*, but its influence has been immeasurable. This work recounts the rise of the Persian Empire (550 BCE), the wars between Greek city-states and Persia (499–449 BCE). Section 10 of book 7 is mostly a speech counseling the Persian king against renewed hostilities against the Greeks, and above all from underestimating them. The speaker, Artabanus, worries about the universal and natural principle of limited good being broken.

> Do you see how the god with his lightning always strikes the larger animals and will not allow them to grow insolent, while those of a smaller size do not aggravate him? How likewise his bolts always fall on the highest houses and the tallest trees? So he plainly enjoys bringing down everything that exalts itself.[3]

4. JOSEPHUS, *LIFE* 122

Titus Flavius Josephus (37–100 CE) was a Judean historian. Trained in Israelite and Hellenistic traditions, he notes the rise of envy in a rival, namely, the envy of John, son of Levi, at Josephus's own rise in fortune. John perceives that another's success necessarily means his own loss. In a limited-good system, success, fame, honor and prestige come at the expense of others, who surface as the most likely candidates to envy those of rising fortune.

> John, son of Levi . . . having heard that everything was working out in my favor . . . and believing that my success meant ruin for him, was driven headlong into envy.[4]

5. FRONTO, *LETTERS* (LCL 112: 72–73)

Marcus Cornelius Fronto, a Roman grammarian and rhetorician, possibly the personal secretary of Marcus Aurelius, lived 100–170 CE. After praising his recipient, Marcus Aurelius, for the unique virtue of making all live in tran-

2. Adapted from Babbitt, LCL.
3. Adapted from Godley, LCL.
4. Adapted from Thackeray, LCL.

quility, he cites the example of Orpheus, who attracted numerous friends and followers from different nations and with different characteristics. They lived together without strife, the mild with the ferocious, the gentle with the violent, the moderate with the proud, and the timid with the unmerciful. There is, then, no perception of limited good and so no envy expressed.

> But of all your virtues, one is to be principally admired, that you bring together all your friends in concord. This is more difficult than to soften with the lute the fierceness of lions and wild beasts: And you will obtain this the more easily, if you take care to root out and eradicate mutual envy and the evil eye among your friends, that they might not, if they are generous to or benevolent with another, think that this has been deprived or taken away from themselves. Envy among men is evil and utterly destructive, a severe blight on both parties.[5]

6. PHILO OF ALEXANDRIA, *ON DRUNKENNESS* 110

A hellenized Jewish philosopher, Philo (20 BCE–50 CE) explains the error of polytheism and the worship of idols in terms of limited good. Simply put, the more honor and regard given to deified mortals and human-made materials, the less honor there can be for the true God.

> Polytheism in the souls of the unwise is godlessness; and those who make gods out of mortal things negate God's honor. For they were not satisfied with fashioning images of sun and moon, or, if they consider it, even of the whole earth and all the water; but they even also give animals and plants devoid of reason a share of those honors that belong by right only to immortal beings.[6]

7. JOHN 3:26–30

This passage is the clearest example of the perception of limited good in the New Testament. The episode begins with John's disciples complaining to him that Jesus's disciples are winning so many new disciples that they and John may be ruined; thus, they perceive the situation in terms of limited good. John, however, does not, and so he does not envy Jesus or suggest any behavior typical of those who see reality in terms of limited good.

> And the disciples of John . . . came to him and said, "Rabbi, the one who was with you across the Jordan, whom you testified about, here he is baptizing, and all are

---

5. Adapted from Haines, LCL.
6. Adapted from Colson and Whitaker, LCL.

going to him." John answered and said, "It is not possible for a person to receive anything other than that which was given to him from heaven. You yourselves testify that I did not say that I am the messiah, but that I have been sent before him. The one who has the bride is the bridegroom. And the friend of the bridegroom, who stands and hears him, rejoices greatly at the bridegroom's voice. For this reason, my joy has been fulfilled. He must increase, and I must decrease."

8. MARK 10:35–37, 41

Two disciples of Jesus, James and John, ask for a unique favor: to sit at his right and left hand. This represents positions of glory, honor, and prestige, but because these things exist in limited supply, the other disciples are naturally displeased. For James and John to rise up in status, the other disciples would sink low.

> James and John, the sons of Zebedee, approached him saying to him, "Teacher, we want you to do for us whatever we ask of you." He said to them, "What do you want me to do for you?" They said to him, "Grant us to sit at your right hand and at your left hand in your glory.". . .
>
> When the ten disciples heard this, they began to be very angry with James and John.

ENVY

9. ARISTOTLE, *RHETORIC* 1387B22–25

Aristotle (384–322 BCE), a student of Plato and a teacher of Alexander the Great, was a Greek philosopher and polymath. One chapter of his *Rhetoric* offers the most valuable and used description of envy in antiquity.

> Envy is the pain one feels at seeing the success of one's peers in attaining the good things that have been mentioned, not in order that we might gain something for ourselves, but because someone else has it.[7]

10. THUCYDIDES, *HISTORY* 6.16.2–3

Thucydides (ca. 460–411 BCE) was a Greek historian recounting the wars between Athens and Sparta. He records a speech by the famed Athenian general Alcibiades, in which he claims to be best suited among men to lead the Athenians. In recounting his many honors, victories, and civic benefactions, however, he also admits that this leaves him vulnerable.

7. Adapted from Freese, LCL.

I entered seven chariots, which was never before done by a private citizen, and I won first place, as well as second and fourth, and achieved everything in a style worthy of my victory. While by custom these things do bring honor, it is by what is done that one immediately senses power. For whatever splendor I bring to the city—by providing choruses or in any other way—while by nature it causes envy among citizens, among foreigners it appears as strength.[8]

11. HERODOTUS, *HISTORIES* 1.32

This text by Herodotus illustrates the Greek notion of the envy of the gods. Interestingly, there is no parallel for this sentiment in the biblical texts, where God might be jealous to defend what belongs to God, and even zealous, but is never depicted as envious.

When Solon gave the second-place prize to Cleobis and Biton, Croesus said to Solon in anger, "O Athenian guest, is our happiness such to you that you do not make me equivalent to common men?" So Solon said, "O Croesus, I am aware that the divine is both envious and prone to trouble us, yet you enquire about the fortunes of people."[9]

12. DIOGENES LAERTIUS, *LIVES OF EMINENT PHILOSOPHERS* 7.111

Nothing is known about Diogenes Laertius, other than he lived in the third century CE and that he wrote about the history of philosophy. He credits Chrysippus, a third-century BCE Stoic philosopher, with establishing the existence of four emotions, namely, grief, fear, desire, and pleasure. Grief, he goes on to say, has several species: pity, envy, jealousy, petty rivalry, heaviness, annoyance, sorrow, anguish, and confusion. Below are the definitions offered for envy, jealousy, and petty rivalry. These succinct and nuanced definitions are representative of the Stoic view and were often quoted. Of note are the Greek words: *phthonos* (envy), *zēlos* (jealousy), and *zēlotypia* (rivalry born from jealousy).

Envy is distress at the good things befalling others; jealousy is distress at the good things befalling others, which a person desires for oneself; rivalry is distress at the good things befalling others, which one himself already has.[10]

---

8. Adapted from Smith, LCL.
9. Adapted from Godley, LCL.
10. Adapted from Hicks, LCL.

13. Cicero, *Tuscan Disputations* 4.16–17

Marcus Tullius Cicero (106–43 BCE) was a philosopher, statesman, poet, and letter writer. Of note in this passage is that, though writing in Latin, Cicero draws virtually the identical differentiation among envy, rivalry, and jealousy: *invidia* (envy), *aemulatio* (rivalry), and *obtrectatio* (jealousy). Also of note is his use of the Greek term *zēlotypia* toward the end of the passage.

> Envy is distress that comes as a result of [seeing] someone else's prosperity, even though one's having it does no harm to the person who envies him or her. . . . Rivalry [in the negative sense] is distress, should another be in possession of the object desired and one has to go without it oneself. Jealousy is what I understand to be the meaning of *zēlotypia*, distress arising from the fact that the thing one has desired for oneself is also possessed by someone else.[11]

14. Galatians 5:19–21

Like many of the moral philosophers, Paul uses vice lists in order to distinguish honorable from dishonorable behavior, distinguished in Galatians as the works of the flesh versus the fruits of the spirit. Before listing the latter, he lists the works of the flesh. Note how envy is one of them, but also distinct from jealousy. None of them are defined, as with Cicero or Diogenes Laertius. That is the nature of the vice list.

> The works of the flesh are plainly evident: unchastity, impurity, debauchery, idolatry, sorcery, hostility, discord, jealousy, rage, strife, dissension, factionalism, envy, intoxication, excess, and things like these. I say this in advance, that whoever does these things will not inherit the kingdom of God.

15. Ovid, *Metamorphoses* 2.775–82

Ovid was a widely respected Latin poet (ca. 43 BCE–17 CE). His lengthy narrative poem offers a mythologized history of the world. In this passage, he describes in lurid detail and at length the personified figure of Envy. Envy poisons people and is, in fact, so destructive that it can destroy itself even. Envy is therefore portrayed with monstrous imagery, but in keeping with ancient conceptions of gender, envy is also personified as female (see **chap. 9, Gender**).

> She is pale in the face, her entire body atrophied, her vision is keen and direct; her teeth were the color of envy and rotted, her breast green, and her tongue suffused with venom. She laughs only at the sight of suffering. She never sleeps,

11. Adapted from King, LCL.

but is awakened by watchful vigilance. She wastes away at the sight of people's successes. She tears away at others and at herself; she is her own humiliation.[12]

16. PLUTARCH, *ON ENVY AND HATE* 538D

Plutarch links envy with the evil eye, in his treatise on envy and hate.

For [those who envy] direct an evil eye against those who are thought to be good, thinking that they possess the greatest good, namely, virtue. And even if [those who envy] receive some benefit from the fortunate, they are tormented and envy them for both the intention and the power.[13]

17. CALLIMACHUS, *HYMN TO APOLLO* 105–13

Callimachus (ca. 310–240 BCE) was a Greek poet in Alexandria. The setting for this hymn is a festival for the god Apollo, at which the god himself will appear. In the context of this hymn, Callimachus appears (in parable form) to allude to a dispute with a rival poet named Apollonius of Rhodes. Callimachus wrote short poems, and Apollonius (who wrote very long poems) criticized Callimachus for it. Callimachus believes he himself is the best of poets and, in this hymn, suggests that Apollonius envies him for it. As a result, Apollonius is portrayed as envy personified, which we find also in text no. 19 below. Importantly, Callimachus represents Apollo as his protector against the envy of his rival. Apollo prefers the pure poetry of Callimachus to the verbose and polluted poetry of Apollonius.

Envy said secretly into the ear of Apollo: "I do not admire the singer who sings short songs." Apollo spurned Envy with his foot and then pronounced: "The stream of the Assyrian river is great, but it carries a lot of earthy dirt and polluted water. The priestesses of Demeter do not bear every kind of water to Demeter, but only water that is pure and undefiled, a spring from holiness." Rejoice, O Lord. And Blame—let him go where Envy is.[14]

18. BASIL, *CONCERNING ENVY* 471

Around 364 CE, Basil of Caesarea, a Christian theologian who wrote in Greek, composed a famous homily on envy and the evil eye. In it, he accuses envious persons of distorting and slandering what is praiseworthy.

12. Adapted from Miller, LCL.
13. Adapted from De Lacy and Einarsen, LCL.
14. Adapted from Mair, LCL.

The envious are skilled at making what is praiseworthy appear despicable by means of unflattering distortions and in slandering virtue through the vice to which it is closely related.[15]

19. *IAPH* 12.719.18–23

An association of traveling athletes set up this white marble inscription in Aphrodisias, a city in Asia Minor, in order to honor one of their members, Kallikrates, who was unrivaled in kickboxing (*pankration*). His size and strength were immense, his victories many and at the highest levels, and he was admired and congratulated. When Kallikrates's career was ended by a shoulder injury, they naturally assumed it was caused by people's envy, which results in the destructive gaze of the evil eye. In this inscription, envy is even personified.

> On account of all these things, evil-eyeing Envy advanced upon his superabundant glory and, grudging our communal good, took it away when it thrust into the part of the body most useful to kickboxers, the shoulders.[16]

20. ISOCRATES, *ANTIDOSIS* 141–43

Isocrates was a Greek rhetorician, listed among the ten Attic orators (436–338 BCE). Envy is aroused by the sight of virtue and success and is checked by living with moderation.

> When the decision was made against me, I examined these things, just as each of you would have done. I scrutinized my own life and actions, spending the most time on those things concerning which it seemed to me I deserved to be praised. When he heard me, one of my close friends had the courage to tell me something more amazing than anything: He allowed that, while the things of which I spoke were consistent with a love of honor, he himself not only greatly feared these things, but that many hearers might also be grieved. "For some people," he said, "have been brutalized by envy and by want and are hostile, with the result that they wage war not against wickedness but against good deeds, and they hate not only the best people, but also the most excellent pursuits. And in addition to

15. M. M. Wagner, *St. Basil: Ascetical Works*, Fathers of the Church 9 (Washington, DC: Catholic University of America Press, 1962), 471.

16. Philip A. Harland, *Greco-Roman Associations: Texts, Translations, and Commentary II; North Coast of the Black Sea, Asia Minor* (Berlin: de Gruyter, 2014), 335–36.

their other faults, they not only team up with those who act unjustly and have sympathy for them, but also they destroy, whenever they have the power to do so, whomever they might envy.[17]

Vocabulary of Limited Good and Envy

HEBREW

קִנְאָה (*qinah*) – zeal, intense devotion, jealousy, envy

GREEK

βασκαίνω (*baskainō*) . . . . to cast the evil eye
ζῆλος (*zēlos*). jealousy, zeal, intense devotion
ζηλοτυπία (*zēlotypia*) . . . . rivalry born from jealousy
ὀφθαλμὸς πονηρός
   (*ophthalmos ponēros*). . . . . evil eye
φθόνος (*phthonos*). . . . . envy

LATIN

aemulatio. . . . . rivalry born from jealousy
fascinatio. . . . . cast of the evil eye, natural ocular conveyance
                                              of envy, malice
invidia . . . . envy
liveo . . . . to envy
obtrectatio . . . . jealousy

Select Bibliography

Elliott, John H. "God—Zealous or Jealous but Never Envious: The Theological Conse-quences of Linguistic and Social Distinctions." Pages 79–96 in *The Social Sciences*

17. Adapted from Norlin, LCL.

and Biblical Translation. Edited by Dietmar Neufeld. Atlanta: Society of Biblical Literature, 2008.

Foster, George M. "Peasant Society and the Image of Limited Good." *American Anthropologist* 67 (1965): 293–315.

Konstan, David, and N. K. Rutter, eds. *Envy, Spite and Jealousy: The Rivalrous Emotions in Ancient Greece.* Edinburgh: Edinburgh University Press, 2003.

Malina, Bruce J. "Limited Good and the Social World of Early Christianity." *BTB* 8 (1978): 162–76.

Neyrey, Jerome H., and Richard L. Rohrbaugh. "'He Must Increase, I Must Decrease' (John 3:30): A Cultural and Social Interpretation." *CBQ* 63 (2001): 464–83.

Additional Texts

PERCEPTIONS OF LIMITED GOOD

Aristotle, *Politics* 1257a2–3, 1257b12, 1258a17

Cicero, *On Duties* 3.22

Genesis 27:30–40

Jerome, *Commentary on Jeremiah* 2.5.2

Josephus, *Jewish Antiquities* 2.254–57; 4.24–34; *Jewish War* 1.457–66

Judges 7:2

Luke 4:16–24; 7:4–5; 19:26

Mark 4:25; 6:4; 7:24–30; 9:38–41; 10:17–18

Matthew 13:12, 54–57; 25:29

Plato, *Laws* 626b

Plutarch, *On Love of Wealth* 525–26; *On Whether an Old Man Should Engage in Public Affairs* 787d

Pseudo-Pelagius, *On Wealth* 2

1 Samuel 18:6–9

Seneca, *On Anger* 21.6; *Epistles* 11.4, 7; 66.7, 9–10; 71.17, 20; 79.8–9; 85.20

Sirach 26:29

ENVY

Acts 5:17; 7:9; 8:23; 13:45, 50–51; 16:20–23; 17:5–7; 18:12–14; 23:2

Antisthenes, fragment 82

Aristotle, *Politics* 1284b21; *Rhetoric* 1388a38–53

Basil, *Concerning Envy* 1–5

Cicero, *On the Orator* 2.209–10; *Tusculan Disputations* 3.19–21; 4.16–18

1 Clement 4:1–13; 5:2, 5; 6:4

1 Corinthians 3:3

2 Corinthians 12:20

Cyprian, *Jealousy and Envy* 5.66–87; 7.119–21; 10.167–69

Demosthenes, *On the Crown (Or.* 18) 107–8

Dio Chrysostom, *Popular Opinion* and *Opinion (Or.* 67–68)

Galatians 4:17–18; 5:26

PART V

Social Subterfuge and Control

18. Deviance

Giovanni Bazzana

Introduction

All cultures and societies construe their own identity by highlighting their opposition to an *other* that paradigmatically reverses all the behaviors and values presented as ideologically "normal" and normative in the mainstream. In ancient Mediterranean cultures, the construction of this oppositional other was particularly evident in ethnographic writing. Authors such as Herodotus and the many who followed his lead built a fictional representation of other peoples—often located in remote countries, at the extreme limits of the geographical compass—as deviating from the communal "rules" of what was assumed to be properly human behavior (see **chap. 6, Collectivism**). Thus, peoples inhabiting the margins of human space are routinely depicted as violating in striking and revolting ways the core laws that constitute civilization (see **chap. 8, Space**). In this perspective, such descriptions function in ways that go well beyond mere entertainment, since they also strengthen the acceptance of conventional paradigms of humanness.

In the texts presented below, this is the case for the norms regulating when it is lawful to kill another human being (in war or in some instances of capital punishment as opposed to cannibalism) or with whom one is allowed to have sexual intercourse (as opposed to cases of incest). Since these norms are believed to constitute the essence of humanness, deviant behaviors are deemed to derive from a condition that slides progressively and inexorably toward bestiality. Thus, foreigners who are labeled as cannibals or as incestuous are also considered to be at best not fully human. From this perspective, labeling and othering are ideological discourses that can be mobilized also against the internal other, particularly in cases of political competition. The case of Catilina mentioned below is a well-documented instance of political conflict in which one party charged the other with political subversion rooted in deviancy and "proved" by alleged acts of cannibalism and illicit sexual habits.

Witchcraft is a specific kind of deviancy that characterizes the other in matters of religious normativity. As such, witches are frequently depicted as sharing some of the above-mentioned "deviant" features, such as cannibalism and sexual depravity. Witches, it is claimed, possess a formidable power and an esoteric knowledge that enable them to control supernatural forces for their own unethical purposes. Such purposes included damaging other human beings (often on the basis of envy; see **chap. 20, Evil Eye**) or obtaining personal and material advantages. The main conceptual difference between institutional religion and magic/witchcraft is that the former is considered proper and legitimate, while the latter is labeled as a threat for human relationships and the body politic.

The ancient discourse on witchcraft encompasses a rich terminology in Greek, Latin, and Hebrew, while the labeling of witches becomes the object of an increasingly precise legislation under the early Roman Empire and then in late antiquity. Witchcraft accusations follow a precise socioeconomic pattern and have a transparent ideological function. Thus, potential witches are usually found among people in marginal or subaltern social locations, as in the case of women (see **chap. 9, Gender**) or foreigners, whose religious deviancy becomes suddenly evident when the social body experiences a crisis. Moreover, as for the other deviance discourses, witchcraft too can be used to label an internal sociopolitical competitor (the most representative case being that of Apuleius's charge of *mageia*, clearly instigated by his successful marriage with a rich widow in the city of Oea, despite his marginal status as a foreigner).

Israelites and Judeans were the victims of all the above-mentioned types of labeling in antiquity as much as any other foreign ethnic group encountered by Greeks and Romans. Charges of cannibalism, sexual depravity, and witchcraft are quite common in ancient anti-Jewish literature. When what would eventually become Christianity started to acquire relevance in the Greco-Roman world, it too became the object of similar attacks. The extant apologetic literature demonstrates that, starting with the second century CE, Christian intellectuals spent a significant amount of energy rejecting and counteracting such labeling, as Judean authors had done beforehand (e.g., Josephus).

Of course, since what would become Christianity grew within the sociocultural context of the Mediterranean world, Christ-following writers too adopted and adapted these widespread ideological and rhetorical models. Thus, as Judean authors had occasionally represented other foreign groups as deviant, likewise Christ-following writers could so label their opponents. For instance, Paul does this when he describes the sexual depravity of the gentiles to his addressees in Rome. Interestingly enough, already while—as noted above—many second-century Christian apologists were defending themselves from "pagan" labeling, writers such as Irenaeus and Hippolytus offer a quite developed representation of their Christian competitors as deviant in matters of moral and religious behavior. The Christian employment of the ideological discourse of deviancy and witchcraft will flourish—with dire consequences— in the anti-Jewish (and eventually, anti-Semitic) and heresiological literary production of late antiquity and beyond.

Given the paucity of evidence at our disposal for the ancient world, it is extremely difficult to ascertain whether deviancy was actually assumed by marginal groups as a positive element of self-definition. Research conducted on historical periods for which documentation is richer (as, for instance, the witchcraft trials of the early modern era or the epidemic of satanic-ritual abuses of the 1980s in the USA) has demonstrated that in a small number of instances, some people—often coming from marginal social and cultural locations—might feel psychologically and socially compelled to represent themselves as victims or even accomplices of an otherwise completely fictional "evil." It is also worth noting that, given their ideological significance, deviancy and witchcraft do exercise a powerful role in constructing authority and establishing control, particularly in the context of small sectarian movements. In this perspective, one might cautiously interpret as positive instances of self-labeling the transgressive behaviors of ancient Cynic philosophers or the positive embracement of cannibalism in the factional polemic of the Johannine community. Though this happens, it is uncommon, and thus I have not provided any additional texts for this phenomenon.

Ancient Texts

CANNIBALISM

1. ARISTOTLE, *NICOMACHEAN ETHICS* 1148B20–27

Aristotle (384–322 BCE) composed several treatises concerned with moral instruction. The one addressed to Nicomachos is the longest and the one that achieved the greatest popularity in antiquity. In this passage, the Greek philosopher illustrates through several examples the key point of his ethics, that impulses and behaviors that are virtuous when governed by "natural" moderation can become vices when practiced in excess. Excess is the natural state of the other.

It is possible to observe corresponding habits with respect to each of these monstrous natural dispositions. I speak of the bestial habits, such as that of the woman who—they say—opens the womb of pregnant women and eats the fetuses or of some savages of the Black Sea, among whom some enjoy raw meat, some human flesh, and some others offer to each other their young children on the occasion of a feast, or also what is narrated regarding Phalaris. These are bestial habits, but some are caused by illness and by madness, such as the case of the man who sacrificed and ate his mother or the other who devoured his fellow slave's liver.[1]

2. EURIPIDES, *HECUBA* 1056–75

Euripides of Athens (ca. 480–406 BCE) was possibly the best-known and most-admired writer of tragedies in antiquity. In *Hecuba*, written during the Peloponnesian War to witness to the pain and destruction brought on Athens by the conflict, Euripides looks at these themes through the eyes of Hecuba, queen of Troy, in the aftermath of the ruin of her city and the slaughter of her family. In this scene, Polymestor (who has been blinded by Hecuba in revenge for the murder of her son) proclaims that he will get back at the queen and other Trojan women by killing and devouring them. Pain and brutality push human beings beyond the limits of humanity into bestiality.

> Woe to me! Where shall I go? Where shall I stand? Where shall I find haven? Is it my reward to crawl after a track like a stalking quadruped beast? Shall I take this direction or that one or the other one, since I need to seize the murderous Trojan women who have utterly destroyed me? O wretched women of Phrygia, O cursed women, in what recesses have you flown escaping from me? O Helios, I wish you could heal the bloody eyelids of my blind eyes by sending your light!
>
> Ah! Ah! Hush, I perceive the secret coming of those women. Where should I attack them, so that I will fill myself of their flesh and bones, taking food as the wild beasts, gaining mutilation as a retribution for my insults, O wretched![2]

3. HERODOTUS, *HISTORIES* 3.25

The Greek historian Herodotus (ca. 484–425 BCE) combined his historical narrative with extensive descriptions of odd and "unnatural" customs of non-Greek peoples. In this passage, the historian relates how the Persian king Cambyses—having attempted an ill-conceived military expedition against the Ethiopians—comes to fear that his soldiers might descend into "inhuman" behaviors.

1. Adapted from Rackham, LCL.
2. Adapted from Way, LCL.

Like one in madness and not in his sound mind, however, Cambyses, as soon as he heard from the Ichthyophagoi, led his army on commanding the Greeks to remain there and taking all his infantry. . . . But before his army had completed the fifth section of the journey, suddenly all the provisions were exhausted, and after the provisions, the beasts of burden were eaten up. . . . Meanwhile, the soldiers took what they could from the earth, supporting their life by eating grass, but when they came to sand, some of them did a terrible deed. Choosing by lot one man out of ten, they ate him. When he heard about this, Cambyses became afraid of the act of eating each other and gave up his expedition against the Ethiopians. He journeyed back, and he arrived in Thebes, having lost much of his army.[3]

4. SALLUST, *THE WAR WITH CATILINE* 22.1–3

The Roman historian Sallust (86–35 BCE) described in a short text the events connected with a failed coup led by the noble Roman senator Catiline. In this passage, the author reports on a rumor of ritual cannibalism ascribed to Catiline and his coconspirators. Sallust notes that this charge would be beyond measure and probably artfully spread by the opponents of Catiline in order to discredit him.

At that time, some put out the rumor that Catiline, after having drawn to a close his speech, and binding the accomplices of his crime with an oath, meted out, in cups, human blood mixed with wine. Later, when all had tasted of it after reciting a curse, as it usually happens in sacred rituals, he revealed his plan. And people spread the rumor that he had done this, so that the conspirators might be more loyal to one another, since each one of them was going to be cognizant of such a crime.[4]

5. JOSEPHUS, *AGAINST APION* 2.95–96

Josephus (ca. 37–100 CE), a Judean priest of aristocratic lineage, was implicated in the first revolt against the Romans (66–70 CE). He defected to the emperor Vespasian and was led as a slave to Rome, where he then became a freedman of the imperial household. In Rome, Josephus went on to compose a series of writings defending the Judeans from Greco-Roman prejudices and hostility. *Against Apion* refutes the slanders of the Egyptian Apion, who—among many others—reported the following story of a Greek man found by the Seleucid king Antiochus IV in the temple of Jerusalem.

3. Adapted from Godley, LCL.
4. Adapted from Rolfe, LCL.

[The man] had heard about an unspeakable law of the Judeans, according to which he was fed and that the Judeans did this at an established time every year. They used to apprehend a Greek foreigner, fatten him for the year, and, after having led him into a certain wood, kill him. They used to sacrifice his body according to their rituals, and taste of his entrails, and take an oath on the sacrifice of a Greek, that they would have enmity toward the Greeks. Then they would throw the remains of the dead man into a certain ditch.[5]

6. Minucius Felix, *Octavius* 9.5–7

Minucius's dialogue is a defense of Christianity directed against Greek and Roman attacks, composed between the end of the second and the beginning of the third century CE. In the course of the fictional conversation between the Christian Octavius and the "pagan" Caecilius, the author reports several slanders against the Christians. The following excerpt—ascribed to Fronto, an influential senator and rhetorician under the Antonine emperors—purports to describe some Christian rituals centered on cannibalism and incestuous sexual relationships.

A baby covered in mush, so that the inattentive may be deceived, is placed before the one who is initiated to the sacred rituals: The baby is killed with invisible and hidden wounds by the initiate, who is led to inflict innocuous hits by the appearance of the mush. Even more thirstily—O horror—they lick his blood; they race each other to divide its limbs. Through this victim, they form a compact; through this consciousness of a crime, they pledge themselves to reciprocal silence. . . . On a fixed day, they assemble to a banquet, with all the children, sisters, mothers, men of every sex and of every age. Then, after a great deal of eating, when the camaraderie has grown warmer and the heat of incestuous lust has been fanned by drunkenness, a dog, which had been tied to a candelabrum, is provoked to rush and jump, by throwing some dog food beyond the length of the line to which it is tied. Thus, when the light that gives awareness is overturned and put out, in the darkness that generates shamelessness, haphazardly they form couplings of unspeakable lust.[6]

SEXUAL PERVERSION

7. Cicero, *For Caelius* 14

Marcus Tullius Cicero (106–43 BCE) was a famous Roman politician and rhetorician. Several of his trial speeches have survived and have become the basis

---

5. Adapted from Thackeray, LCL.
6. Adapted from Rendall, LCL.

of modern rhetorical training. The present speech is part of the masterpiece defense for Marcus Caelius Rufus, charged of political violence. Cicero deflects the charges away from the acts of Caelius and toward the sexual conduct of his lover Clodia, who was an older widow. In this section, Cicero evokes the voices of Clodia's noble and morally uptight ancestors to castigate her licentious behavior.

> Woman, what do you have to do with Caelius? With a young man? With a stranger to your family? Why were you either so well acquainted with him to lend him gold, or so hostile to fear poison from him? . . . Why were you affected by your brother's vices more than by the virtues of your father and your ancestors, which have been replicated both in the males and also in the females of your family up until our days? Did I break the peace with Pyrrhus so that you might strike alliances every day with the vilest sexual partners? Did I bring water to Rome, so that you might use it for your incestuous purposes? Did I build the road so that you could go there together with foreign men?[7]

8. Tacitus, *Histories* 5.5

Tacitus (ca. 56–after 117 CE) wrote extensively on the history of the Roman Empire from the death of Augustus to the reigns of the Flavians. As it is usual for ancient historical writing, Tacitus's works included digressions describing foreign people. The following passage is part of Tacitus's famous description of the Judeans, in which the Roman author employs many of the anti-Jewish stereotypes mentioned also by other ancient writers.

> These rituals [of the Sabbath], however they have been introduced, are protected by their antiquity. All their other customs, which are sinister and revolting, owe their strength to their perversity. For all the worst people, holding in contempt their ancestral religious observances, have heaped there [in Judea] tributes and money. Thus, the power of the Judeans has grown and also, because among themselves they have obstinate loyalty and compassion, is always at hand, but toward all the others, they have inimical hatred. They keep themselves separated in meals, they keep their distance in sleeping arrangement, and, despite their being a people exceedingly inclined to lust, they abstain from sexual relationship with foreigners; nevertheless, among themselves nothing is not allowed. They established the practice of circumcising genitals so that they could be recognized by their difference.[8]

7. Adapted from Gardner, LCL.
8. Adapted from Moore, LCL.

9. Romans 1:22–27

Paul (ca. 5–67 CE) of Tarsus was the author of the earliest surviving written documents stemming from the Christ movement. These writings—included in the New Testament— have the literary form of letters addressed to the groups of Christ-followers that the apostle had founded in several urban centers of the eastern Mediterranean. In this excerpt from Paul's letter to the Christ groups in Rome, the author describes in stereotypical terms the moral corruption of "pagans."

> While they were stating that they were wise, they became fools, and they bartered the glory of the incorruptible God for the likeness of the image of a corruptible human being and of birds and quadrupeds and reptiles. Therefore, God delivered them in the desires of their hearts to the defilement of dishonoring their own bodies in themselves. Those who changed the truth of God into falsehood and worshiped and adored the creature instead of the creator, who is blessed forever, amen! Therefore, God delivered them to dishonorable passions. For their females changed the natural intimacy in that against nature. Likewise, the males, abandoning the natural intimacy of the female, were on fire in their yearning for each other, so that the males produced disgrace in the males and they received in themselves the reward that is due to their error.

10. Eusebius of Caesarea, *Ecclesiastical History* 3.29.1–2

Eusebius (ca. 260–340 CE) wrote the first surviving example of a complete history of Christianity from Jesus to the time of Constantine. Following a model that was going to become standard for later authors, Eusebius understood this history as a trajectory of corruption, from perfectly orthodox beliefs to various types of deviancy ("heresies") brought about by external ideas and practices. In this passage, Eusebius reports how Clement of Alexandria (another Christian author of the end of the second century) had described the perverted actions of the heretic Nikolaos.

> At the time of these events, the sect called "of the Nicolaitans" came together for the briefest of times. The Apocalypse of John mentions it too. They boasted [as the founder of the sect] a certain Nikolaos who had been among the deacons handpicked with Stephen by the apostles to serve the poor. Clement of Alexandria, in the third book of the *Stromateis*, records precisely these things about him: "Since he had a beautiful wife and—after the ascension of the Savior—had been rebuked in front of the apostles for jealousy, he led her in the middle, and he left her to whoever wanted to marry her. For they say that such an action followed the saying 'one must abuse the flesh.' And those who are followers of his sect,

imitating the action and the saying in a simplistic and superficial way, practice sexual licentiousness without restraint."[9]

11. JOHN CHRYSOSTOM, *AGAINST THE JEWS* 1.2.7–1.3.1

John Chrysostom (ca. 349–407) was bishop of Antioch and then Constantinople, a leading figure both in the theological and political controversies that tore apart Christianity between the fourth and the fifth centuries. John has been surnamed Chrysostom ("Golden-Mouthed") for the great rhetorical sophistication of his homilies, which have survived in great number. In a series of speeches delivered when he was bishop of Antioch, John attacked the Jews of the great Syrian city because he was afraid that their religious observances (Sabbath, dietary regulations, and so on) were proving attractive for Christians as well. In this violent anti-Judean polemic, John has recourse to all the ancient clichés of deviancy, including sexual immorality.

> Their [the Jews'] purpose is to fast, but their appearance is of drunkards. Listen how the prophet ordered them to fast. "Sanctify the fast," he says. He does not say, "Make a show of your fast," but "announce a religious cult, bring together the elders." But these Jews, having brought together bands of effeminate men and a great mob of prostituted women, drag all the theater and those who act on the scene in the synagogue. For there is no difference between the theater and the synagogue. . . . Where a prostitute has established herself, that place is a brothel. Moreover, the synagogue is not only a theater and a brothel, but also a den of thieves and a dwelling place of wild beasts. For [the prophet] says, "Your house has become the den of hyenas."
>
> . . . Whenever God leaves, what hope of salvation is left? Whenever God leaves, that land becomes a foundation of demons.[10]

MAGIC AND WITCHCRAFT

12. PLINY THE ELDER, *NATURAL HISTORY* 18.8.41

The elder Pliny (ca. 23–79 CE) collected in his extremely vast "natural history" an enormous wealth of historical and anthropological information concerning all the regions of the ancient Mediterranean world. The little episode of

9. Adapted from Lake, LCL.

10. Adapted from P. W. Harkins, trans., *Discourses against Judaizing Christians*, Fathers of the Church 68 (Washington, DC: Catholic University of America Press, 1977), 9–11.

Chresimus reveals the social mechanics through which witchcraft accusations (see **chap. 17, Limited Good and Envy**) came to be attached to foreigners and other marginal people.

> Caius Furius Chresimus, a former slave who had become a freedman, used to produce, from an absolutely small piece of land, far bigger harvests than his neighbors could from the most extensive properties. Thus, he became the target of great envy, as if he was enticing away other people's crops through malevolent spells.[11]

13. Lucian, *Lover of Lies* 16

Lucian (ca. 125–180 CE), a Syrian by birth but educated in the most sophisticated Hellenistic way, is the author of several satirical pieces that make fun of cultural and religious habits of his time. In this work, Lucian reports the conversation of Greek philosophers who describe in a playful way a series of miracles and "magical" acts that they claim to have witnessed. Here Lucian portrays (with features that are very close to those used for Jesus's activity in the Gospels) an exorcism performed by a stereotypical foreigner, depicting him as greedy and a charlatan.

> I will be happy to ask what you have to say about those who free the demoniacs from their terrors by chasing away so openly the ghosts with incantations. And there is no need for me to speak about this subject, since all of you have seen that Syrian from Palestine. He is an expert in such a technique and, when he is presented with those who fall under the influence of the moon with their eyes twisted and with their mouths full of foam, assuredly he restores them to their feet and sends them away with a sound mind, having freed them from their terrors in exchange for a significant compensation. After he has stood over them lying on the ground, he asks from where they have come. The sick person is silent, but the demon answers by saying—in Greek or in a barbarian language—from where and how it entered into the person. With adjurations and, if the spirit does not obey, with threats, the exorcist drives the demon out. I myself saw one go out, black and with the appearance of smoke.[12]

14. 1 Samuel 28:7–17

The Torah contains a severe rejection of the witchcraft and necromancy practiced by outsiders. Toward the end of the narrative arc concerning Saul, the

11. Adapted from Rackham, LCL.
12. Adapted from Harmon, LCL.

first king of Israel, the king—who has been rejected by God and thus cannot receive guidance through the official oracles—has recourse to the help of a "witch," thereby violating his own prohibition of such practices. In this episode, which is darkly ironic as it gestures toward Saul's imminent defeat and death, the king meets the ghost of his archenemy, the prophet Samuel, who explicitly confirms that this is God's will.

Saul said to his servants, "Locate for me a woman who controls the spirits of the dead, and I will go to her, and I will question the spirits in her."

... And the woman said to Saul, "I see a god who is emerging from the earth." And he said to her, "What is his appearance?" And she said, "An old man is emerging, and he is enveloped in a robe." And he realized that this was Samuel, and he fell to the ground with his face down. And Samuel said to Saul, "Why have you bothered me and made me emerge?" And Saul said, "I am in great distress and the Philistines are waging war on me, and God has abandoned me and he does not respond to me either through the prophets or through dreams. And I have interrogated you, so that I may know what to do." And Samuel said, "Why do you ask me, since the Lord has abandoned you and has become your enemy? The Lord has brought about by himself as he had announced through me, and he has taken away the kingdom from you and has given it to your relative David."

15. ORIGEN, *CONTRA CELSUM* 2.49

Origen of Alexandria (ca. 184–253 CE) was the first Christian author to write extensively—and with an enormous influence on later generations—on systematic theology and biblical exegesis. A major work of Origen is the long refutation of the *True Discourse*, an anti-Christian pamphlet authored around 177 CE by the Greek philosopher Celsus. The latter's attack on Christianity has survived only through the extensive quotations of Origen, as in the fragment below, in which Celsus tries to demonstrate that Jesus had been a practitioner of harmful sorcery.

"O light and truth! He [Jesus] proclaims expressly with his own voice," as you yourselves have written, that there will be among you also others, who will perform similar miracles, who will be evil men and sorcerers. And he calls Satan one who deceptively devises such tricks. So that he himself does not even deny that these operations do not have anything divine, but are appropriate for the evil. And being forced by the power of truth, Jesus in the same stroke both revealed the crimes of others and convicted himself of the same actions. How is it not wicked to extrapolate from the same actions that the one is God and the others sorcerers? For why should we infer on the basis of these actions that the others are evil rather than Jesus was legitimate, while we can employ only his own testimony? All the more so since he himself acknowledged that these are not the hallmarks of a divine nature, but of some deceivers and of thoroughly evil individuals.[13]

16. IRENAEUS, *AGAINST HERESIES* 1.13.1, 3

Irenaeus (died ca. 202 CE) was the bishop of Lyons in Gallia but hailed originally from Smyrna, in modern western Turkey. Irenaeus's major work was composed in Greek (but is preserved only in Latin) and contains a detailed refutation of the so-called Gnostics, mostly followers of the great second-century teacher Valentinus. In this excerpt, Irenaeus describes the doctrines and practices of a certain Marcus, a Valentinian teacher. As is typical for Christian heresiologists (of whom Irenaeus is a precursor of sorts), the account is not very reliable historically but employs the usual ancient strategy of stereotyping and labeling (see **chap. 6, Collectivism**) in order to cast the heretics as foreign and criminal.

> Furthermore, another of them (Valentinians), whose name is Marcus, boasts of being the corrector of his own teacher. He is a great expert in magical delusions, through which he seduces many men and not a few women. He has led them to turn themselves to him, as to the most knowledgeable and the most perfect, and to the one who has received the greatest power from invisible and ineffable places. . . . It is possible to see that Marcus possesses a familiar demon, through which he seems to prophesy, and through which he lets prophesy as many women as he considers worthy to be partakers of his favor. For he spends most of his time around women, and particularly around those who are noble, and most elegantly dressed, and most affluent. He often tries to draw them after himself and says to them in flattering tones: "I want you to partake of my favor, because the Father of all does continually see your angel before his face. The place of your greatness is among us: We need to get together in unity. Receive first favor from me and through me. Prepare yourself as a bride who is expecting her bridegroom, so that you may be what I am, and I what you are."[14]

13. Adapted from Origen, *Contra Celsum*, trans. Henry Chadwick (Cambridge: Cambridge University Press, 1980).

14. Adapted from *The Apostolic Fathers with Justin Martyr and Irenaeus*, The Ante-Nicene Fathers 1 (Edinburgh: T&T Clark, 1867).

SELF-LABELING

17. JOSEPHUS, *JEWISH ANTIQUITIES* 13.345–46

In this passage, Josephus describes a military campaign of an Egyptian king against the Judeans. The author employs the description of a brutal and inhuman behavior to cast a disapproving light on the enemy of his people. However, the final comment illustrates how such a reputation of cruelty could be cultivated in order to achieve military success.

> After the victory, Ptolemy overran all the land and—at the fall of night—took his rest in some villages of Judea. Having found these settlements full of women and children, he ordered his soldiers to slay them, to butcher them, and—after having thrown their flesh into boiling cauldrons—to offer it as a firstfruits sacrifice. The king commanded this, so that the enemies who had fled from the battle and had come together might think that their adversaries were cannibals, and on that account may be even more stricken with terror at the sight of such actions.[15]

18. DIOGENES, *EPISTLE* 7.1

Diogenes of Sinope (who lived in the fourth century BCE) was one of the most important representatives of the philosophical school called "Cynic" (which means "dog" in Greek). He was well known for his highly irregular and transgressive behaviors, such as living in an abandoned barrel and masturbating in public. The fundamental tenet of Cynic philosophy is that true happiness can be achieved only by living "according to nature" and thus by refusing all sophistications and all social and religious constraints. Probably in the first century BCE, unknown followers of the Cynic philosophical school composed and put together a collection of letters containing moral instructions, which were attributed to the pen of Diogenes.

> Do not be distressed, O father, because I am called "dog" or because I wear a double threadbare cloak or because I carry a leather pouch around my shoulders or because I have a stick in my hand. For it is not worth to be aggrieved about such things, but much better to rejoice because your son is satisfied with few things, but he is free from other people's evaluation, to which everyone, both Greek and barbarian, is enslaved.
>
> ... For I am called "dog" of heaven and not of the earth, because I make myself similar to that one, living not according to the evaluation of other people,

15. Adapted from Marcus, LCL.

but according to nature, free under Zeus, having given him credit for the good and not to my neighbor.[16]

19. JOSEPHUS, *JEWISH WAR* 6.204–13

In his narrative of the first revolt against Rome, Josephus spends a good deal of time painting the suffering and horror brought on the Judean people by the decision to fight the Romans. The following passage is part of the description of the tragic situation of the Judeans besieged within Jerusalem.

> It was by any means impossible for her [Mary] to find something to eat, and the hunger advanced in her bowels and in her brain, and the inner turmoil was even more enflamed than the hunger. Having taken counsel with the anger and with necessity, she went beyond the natural limits. Grasping her child, who was sucking at her breast, she said, "Wretched infant, for whom will I protect you in the war, in the famine, and in the revolt? There is slavery under the Romans, if we survive their attack, but the famine is even faster than slavery, and the rebels are more dangerous than both. Come! Be nourishment for me and a curse for the rebels and a story spread through the world, which is the only thing missing to complete the misfortunes of the Judeans." And as soon as she had said these words, she killed the son. Then, after having cooked it, she ate half of it, and she kept the other half hidden.[17]

20. JOHN 6:52–56

The Gospel of John (composed between the end of the first century and the early decades of the second, presumably in Asia Minor) presents a biography of Jesus that differs markedly from those of the other canonical Gospels. In particular, John does not have a narrative of the last supper with the disciples, but a long speech, in which Jesus says that one must truly eat his flesh and drink his blood. Albert Harrill has shown that John is using and appropriating the language of cannibalism, which is typical of sects and other secret political groups in antiquity. Indeed, Jesus's speech works to chase away people (first the "Judeans" and then most of the disciples) who had seemed to become followers of the prophet from Nazareth.

> The Jews were fighting among themselves, saying, "How can this one give us his own flesh to eat?" Therefore, Jesus said to them, "Amen amen, I say to you, if you

16. Abraham J. Malherbe, *The Cynic Epistles: A Study Edition* (Missoula: Scholars Press, 1977), 98.
17. Adapted from Thackeray, LCL.

do not eat the flesh of the Son of Man and drink his blood, you do not have life in yourselves. The one who devours my flesh and drinks my blood has the life of the coming eon, and I will raise him on the last day. For my flesh is true nourishment, and my blood is true beverage. The one who devours my flesh and drinks my blood abides in me and I in him."

Vocabulary of Deviance

HEBREW

אוֹב (*ov*) . . . . ancestral spirit, ghost, necromancer
זְנוּת (*zenut*) . . . . sexual immorality
שִׁקּוּץ (*shiqquts*) . . . . foreign deity, abomination

GREEK

βάρβαρος, -ον (*barbaros, -on*) . . . . foreign, barbarian, uncivilized
γοητεία (*goēteia*) . . . . sorcery
ἐπῳδή (*epōdē*) . . . . incantation
θηριώδης, -ες (*thēriōdēs, -es*) . . . . bestial, savage
κατάδεσμος (*katadesmos*) . . . . binding spell
μαγεία (*mageia*) . . . . magic
μαλακός, -ή, -όν
    (*malakos, -ē, -on*) . . . . effeminate, soft
μανία (*mania*) . . . . madness
νεκρόμαντις (*nekromantis*) . . . . necromancer
πορνεία (*porneia*) . . . . sexual immorality

LATIN

alienus . . . . foreigner
carmen . . . . incantation
defixio . . . . binding spell
incestus . . . . unholy, polluted
libido . . . . lust
striga . . . . evil spirit, witch

veneficus . . . . poisoner, witch

vitium . . . . defect, vice

Select Bibliography

Guijarro, Santiago. "The Politics of Exorcism: Jesus's Reaction to Negative Labels in the Beelzebul Controversy." *BTB* 29 (1999): 118–29.

Isaac, Benjamin. *The Invention of Racism in Classical Antiquity*. Princeton: Princeton University Press, 2006.

Knust, Jennifer Wright. *Abandoned to Lust: Sexual Slander and Ancient Christianity*. New York: Columbia University Press, 2006.

Malina, Bruce J., and Jerome H. Neyrey. *Calling Jesus Names: The Social Value of Labels in Matthew*. Sonoma, CA: Polebridge, 1988.

Schäfer, Peter. *Judeophobia: Attitudes toward the Jews in the Ancient World*. Cambridge: Harvard University Press, 1998.

Stratton, Kimberly B. *Naming the Witch: Magic, Ideology, and Stereotype in the Ancient World*. New York: Columbia University Press, 2007.

Additional Texts

CANNIBALISM (AND OTHER DESPICABLE FOREIGN CUSTOMS)

Aeschylus, *Persians* 187, 255

Aristophanes, *Birds* 1573; *Clouds* 492

Aristotle, *Politics* 1252b, 1338b

Clement of Alexandria, *Stromateis* 3.2.10.1

Demosthenes, *Against Meidias* (*Or.* 21) 150; *1 Against Aristogeiton* (*Or.* 26) 17

Dio Cassius, *Roman History* 68.32.1; 71.4.1

Dio Chrysostom, *To the People of Rhodes* (*Or.* 31) 3; *Corinthian Discourse* (*Or.* 37) 30

Diodorus Siculus, *Library of History* 3.8.2; 5.32.3–4

Euripides, *Hecuba* 1057–72; *Iphigenia in*

Aulis 1400

Florus, *Epitome* 2.12

Heraclitus, *Homeric Allegories* 107

Herodotus, *Histories* 1.58; 3.106

Irenaeus, *Against Heresies* 1.20.2

Josephus, *Against Apion* 2.8

Juvenal, *Satires* 6.78–83

Livy, *History of Rome* 23.5.12

Plato, *Statesman* 262d

Pliny the Elder, *Natural History* 6.53

Plutarch, *Cicero* 10.2

Porphyry, *On Abstinence* 3.3

Strabo, *Geography* 4.5.4; 14.2.28

Thucydides, *History* 1.3; 2.36, 97

Xenophon, *Anabasis* 5.4.34; 5.16

SEXUAL PERVERSION

Pseudo-Aristeas, *Letter* 151–52

Exodus 34:15–16

Josephus, *Against Apion* 2.199

Justin, *First Apology* 9

Leviticus 18

Philo, *On the Contemplative Life* 50–60;
    Special Laws 37–40

Sibylline Oracles 3.594–600

Testament of Levi 14

MAGIC AND WITCHCRAFT

Achilles Tatius, *Leucippe and Clitophon*
    6.7.4-5

Aeschylus, *Agamemnon* 1418; *Eumenides*
    649; *Persians* 598–708; *Prometheus
    Bound* 174

Antiphon, *Speeches* 1.14–20

Apuleius, *The Golden Ass* 1.5–19;
    2.21–30; 3.15–25

Augustine, *City of God* 7.35

Pseudo-Clement, *Recognitions* 2.5.7–15

Demosthenes, *On the Crown* (*Or.* 18)
    276; *False Embassy* (*Or.* 19) 109;
    1 Against Aristogeiton (*Or.* 26) 25

Diodorus Siculus, *Library of History*
    1.76; 4.45–48, 50–56; 5.55, 64

Euripides, *Andromache* 155–60; *Bacchae*
    234; *Hippolytus* 1038

Heliodorus, *Ethiopian Story* 3.16

Herodotus, *Histories* 1.101–28; 2.33;
    4.105; 7.113–14, 191

Hippocrates, *On the Sacred Disease*
    1.10–46

Homer, *Odyssey* 10.133–405; 19.457

Horace, *Epodes* 5, 17

Lucan, *Pharsalia* 6.413–587

Lucian, *Alexander the False Prophet*
    9–18; *The Lover of Lies* 11–13, 33–36;
    Nigrinus 15

Ovid, *Loves* 3.7.27–84; *Metamorphoses*
    7.159–351

Petronius, *Satyricon* 63

Plato, *Laws* 671a, 903b; *Phaedo* 78a;
    Republic 364b–e, 380d, 426b; *Sympo-
    sium* 202e–203d

Pliny the Elder, *Natural History* 28.92–
    106; 30.1–20

Plutarch, *Alexander* 77

Polybius, *Histories* 4.20.5-6

Sophocles, *Ajax* 582; *Oedipus at Colonus*
    1194

Suetonius, *Caligula* 50

Xenophon, *Memorabilia* 2.6.10–13

19. Mockery and Secrecy

Dietmar Neufeld and Zeba A. Crook

Introduction

Mockery is more than poking fun; it aims to be aggressive and polemical. And in a cultural context of honor and shame, vicious and sustained, or merely extremely effective, mockery can kill. Mockery was, thus, far from harmless. To be susceptible to mockery was very important, for being shame*less* (see **chap. 5, Shame**), or impervious to shaming, was to sit outside of the social order. No good person was impervious to shame, no good person impervious to mockery. But because of this connection to shame, mockery invited violence, so potentially serious a blow was mockery to honor (see **chap. 4, Honor**).

There are hundreds of terms in Hebrew, Greek, and Latin that relate to mockery, many more than can be included in the vocabulary list below: ridicule, laugh, jeer, disdain, deride, scorn, tease, vilify, disparage, and so on. The specificity and the range of words relating to mockery are breathtaking. Mockery in antiquity had consistent subject areas, namely, those relating to core attitudes and values: sexual behavior and demeanor, religion and ethnicity, political conduct or affiliation, wealth, poverty, and conspicous consumption, dress and appearance, food and drink, social status and occupation, and people's names and nicknames. In fact, any social register that mattered was ripe for mockery. It is, of course, because these social registers mattered that mockery held such potential for injury.

Mockery relies on the visual culture of antiquity, for one cannot be shamed if one cannot be seen. In order to gain honor, one had to be seen doing honorable things, but being seen made one vulnerable to shame. Attempts to gain honor could end in failure, and from there, in mockery or shame. And herein lies the relationship between mockery and secrecy: secrecy was the antidote, the prophylactic, against mockery in the ancient Mediterranean. And if secrecy is a defensive strategy, the counteroffensive strategy was surveillance:

the attempt to penetrate past veils of secrecy, in order to weaken. Secrecy was the attempt to empower, and surveillance threatened that power. And vice versa, another's secrecy was a problem to be overcome by effective surveillance. This is the case, obviously, for nations that seek to protect themselves, but it applies no less to the construction of religion: a god's power surely can be said to reside in its mystery, in what is not known. Those with secrets, as those with mysterious power, closely guard those secrets, for obvious reasons.

It is already apparent, therefore, how secrecy carries benefits and, as such, is a potent means of social interaction in political and religious systems the world over—both ancient and modern. Ancient Egyptians, Greeks and Romans, Judeans, Christians, and Gnostics made strategic resource of secrecy to manipulate, confabulate, inculcate, obfuscate, regulate, disseminate, and demarcate. Secrecy, keeping secrets, and secretive behavior were part of the social fabric of ancient Mediterranean culture; and authors, kings, queens, priests, healers, exorcists, and others embedded in such a culture used secrecy for a variety of purposes.

For example, in Greece, secrecy granted great prestige to the holders, and in Egypt, it protected potent sacred knowledge. In Egypt, words had efficacious power in liturgy, which, in the process of recitation by priests and kings, caused them to become members of the divine court. These liturgical hymns were carefully guarded and engraved not in the public spaces of temples, but in inaccessible places like the tombs of the kings. In the Greek magical papyri, letters and hieroglyphs were dicipherable only by the initiates, and their true meaning was hidden to outsiders. The motivation was not so much the protection of knowledge from outsiders, but the promotion of social closure and group solidarity.

Anthropologists define secrecy as an official, conscious, measured, and deliberate concealment (or even lying) of information, activities, or relationship that outsiders can gain only by surveillance. Secrecy is far more than simply concealment; it is a kind of guarded information but one that is freely and willfully disseminated by persons of power to those who need to know. Yet concealment is also a form of secrecy.

Secrecy performs a number of important social functions: provides/enhances the power of its holder; demarcates insiders (privy to secrets) from outsiders (uninformed); creates mystique; provides cohesion in groups; permits communities to control social relations with outsiders; shapes meaning and understanding as well as misunderstanding, misrepresentation, and misidentification; functions as a defensive strategy of exclusion against kin, neighbors, and associations; constitutes memory and identity in the acts of uncovering lies and of revealing secrets; regulates rituals of piety by demanding that they remain inconspicuous in contradistinction to those who practice them openly for all to see; guards knowledge of the ineffable against its false appropriation. In the end, it is the "not telling" that often signals more than the telling of a secret.

Secrecy deploys itself in a variety of forms: hiding, lying, evasive speech, deception, ambiguity, furtive behavior, silence, purposeful concealment, open secrets (i.e., ones known to all, but to speak them openly violates the command to be discreet about them), surveilling, spying, and subterfuge. Mystery, secrecy, and esotericism functioned in divergent contexts differently. The word for "mystery" (*raz*) in Hebrew and Aramaic texts of the Second Temple period appeared in a variety of compositions with magical, medical, astronomical, and physiognomic associations. The category of "mystery" has much to do with authority and power and the strategies of laying claim, expressing, and asserting authority and power. The social milieu of secrecy and mystery was attached to the temple, royal court, and to the cultivation of the scribal craft—ideologically motivated to support the social position of an elite group of persons and their knowledge of authority.

Ancient Texts

MOCKERY

1. Horace, *Satires* 1.3.56–58

Horace was a first-century BCE Roman poet and letter writer whose works were highly admired in his life. He excelled in lyric poetry (odes and epodes) and even wrote a poem on the writing of poetry. But he was best known for his satires, in which he lampoons many aspects of Roman life and culture. In this passage, he reflects the cultural requirement to be visible. Of course, there is potential shame in being visible, but there can be no honor without it.

> The honest one who lives among us, the man who is exceedingly unassuming, we give the family name: slow and doltish. The one who flees from every trap and does not leave a flank unguarded to the malintentioned, though we live a life where consuming envy and accusations thrive at every turn, instead of referring to his sound mind and cautiousness, we invoke his cunning and deception.[1]

2. Lucian, *Carousal* 19

Lucian was a satirist and rhetorician who lived in the second century and wrote in Greek. He composed many satiric dialogues, as well as narrative fictions and rhetorical essays. This passage is from a work that appears to have

1. Adapted from Fairclough, LCL.

been fashioned as a parody of Plato's symposium, but this one ends in drunken violence. In this passage, a clown named Satyrion has entered the dinner and makes a fool of himself. He then turns to the guests, mocking them in turn. Some laugh him off, but then his mockery goes too far, or touches a sensitive nerve, when he turns to the Cynic figure, Alcidamas. Lucian revels in the scene of a philosopher and a clown coming to blows (see **chap. 4, Honor**).

> After that, he went after Alcidamas as he had the others, calling him a little Maltese dog. Alcidamas became violently irritated . . . and having ripped off his threadbare cloak, he called him out to fight, and if he refused, he said he would lay a beating on him with his staff.[2]

3. CICERO, *ON THE REPUBLIC* 5.6

Cicero (106–43 BCE) is one of the Roman Republic's last and greatest figures. He served as consul in 63 BCE but was also a lawyer, orator, poet, and philosopher. *On the Republic* is one of Cicero's nineteen treatises; in it, he creates a philosophical dialogue between Scipio Africanus (who died before Cicero was born) and eight other historical characters. In this passage, Cicero describes mockery, and shame, as greater deterrents of bad behavior than even laws (see **chap. 4, Honor; chap. 5, Shame**).

> The best citizens are not deterred from crime by a fear of legal punishments. They are rather deterred by an innate sense of shame to fear condemnation that is not unjustified. The effective leader augments this condition by using public opinion to foster such a sense of shame and completes it through administration and instruction. As a result, shame better than fear keeps a citizen from doing wrong.[3]

4. PROVERBS 30:17

The book of Proverbs is a list of sayings, in the tradition of wisdom sayings. In Hebrew, it is known as *Mishley Shlomo*, which would be variously rendered as the *Instructions* or *Parables of Solomon*. These collections are concerned with setting the parameters of righteous living, the meaning of life, and moral behavior. This saying shows that while the mocking eye might well be a feature of life, directing it to one's parents is unacceptable: a destroyed eye can no longer mock.

> The eye that mocks a father and rejects obedience to a mother will be pecked out by the ravens of the valley and will be consumed by the vultures.

2. Adapted from Harmon, LCL.
3. Adapted from Keyes, LCL.

5. MARK 5:38–43

The author of Mark, the first of the Synoptic Gospels, had a habit of sandwiching stories together. This story has Jesus on his way to heal the daughter of a synagogue official, when a hemorrhaging woman delays them. This passage begins at the point when they continue their journey to the sick girl. But because they were delayed, the girl has died, and the people are understandably disconsolate. Notice the response of the crowd to Jesus's suggestion that the girl is merely sleeping, as if they do not know a dead person when they see one. Note also his command to secrecy at the end.

> He comes into the home of the synagogue official and sees a commotion and many wailing and shouting. And having entered, he says to them, "Why are you making a commotion and wailing? The child did not die, but is asleep." And they mocked him. But having thrown them all out, he takes the child's father and mother and those who were with him and enters the room where the child was. And having taken the hand of the child, he says to her, "Talitha kum!" (which translated is: "Little girl, I say to you, get up!"). And immediately the little girl got up and was walking around, for she was twelve years old. And immediately they were completely beside themselves. And he expressly commanded them that no one should know about this, and he said that something should be given her to eat.

6. PLUTARCH, *CATO THE ELDER* 9.5

Plutarch lived during the first and second century CE and was a Greek biographer, historian, essay writer, and also a Roman citizen. Marcus Cato, also known as Cato the Elder and Cato the Wise, was a prominent Roman citizen and consul in the second century BCE. In his *Parallel Lives*, Plutarch offers a biography of Marcus Cato, which includes a number of sayings of Cato that were critical, at times mocking of people concerning whose conduct and lifestyle he disapproved. In the two examples provided here, one such person is an overweight knight, and the other a person who enjoys fine food and drink.

> Abusing an obese knight, he said, "Where can a body such as this be useful to the city, when the space between his throat and groin is taken up entirely by his belly?" A person who was fond of pleasure wished to get together with him, but having declined, he said that it was not possible for him to live with a person in possession of a palate more sensitive than his heart.[4]

4. Adapted from Perrin, LCL.

7. PHILOSTRATUS, *LIFE OF APOLLONIUS* 4.20

Philostratus was a third-century CE Greek sophist, living in the Roman Empire. In one of his five surviving works, he writes about Apollonius of Tyana, a second-century CE Pythagorean philosopher and teacher. In this passage, Philostratus provides an example of laughter as an embodied disorder, in this case madness. It is the coarseness of the youth's laughter and insults, aimed at the philosopher himself, that alerts Apollonius to the possibility that the boy was demon-possessed. Note also, however, that the young man's behavior had been subject to social mocking in ribald song.

> While he [Apollonius] was lecturing on the question of how to perform libations, an effeminate young man, whose custom for licentiousness had become the topic of coarse drinking songs, happened to be near by. . . . The young man both heaped abusive words on him and laughed loudly and rudely. Then Apollonius looked up and said: "It is not you who commits these outrages, but the demon who controls you without your knowing it."[5]

8. ACHILLES TATIUS, *LEUCIPPE AND CLITOPHON* 2.29

It is believed that Achilles Tatius lived and wrote in second-century CE Alexandria. He has but one surviving work: a Greek comedic novel about the adventures of Clitophon and his beautiful cousin, Leucippe. In this passage, Leucippe reflects on the real and deep damage that can be caused by words. Words can be likened to weapons; the wounds they leave are bloodless and invisible, but painful nonetheless (see **chap. 5, Shame**).

> Speech is the father of all these things [shame, grief, and anger]; like a bow that watches, takes aim, and hits its mark, sending its arrows of various kinds against the soul. One of the missiles is insult, and its wound generates anger. Another is to have one's misfortunes revealed; from this missile comes grief. Another is reproach at failure, and they call this wound shame.[6]

9. LUKE 23:36–37

The trial scenes of Jesus in the Gospels are replete with Jesus being mocked. First of all, the Gospels depict Jesus anticipating his own mocking (Matt 20:19; Mark 10:34; Luke 18:32), and so it turns out in the narratives that follow. Luke's and Matthew's Jesus is mocked when the soldiers blindfold Jesus and then

5. Adapted from Jones, LCL.
6. Adapted from Gaselee, LCL.

taunt him (Matt 26:68; Luke 22:63). The passage below comes from Luke, who offers the most explicit description of Jesus being mocked at his death. The Roman soldiers are standing at the foot of the cross, as Jesus hangs there dying.

> The soldiers who were coming up mocked him, offering him vinegar and saying, "If you are the king of the Judeans, save yourself!"

10. SUETONIUS, *CLAUDIUS* 4

Suetonius (ca. 69–122 CE) was a Roman historian. He is best known for writing about the history of the Caesars, including Claudius, the fourth emperor of Rome. Claudius suffered from some childhood disease that left him with physical irregularities. The following passage is part of a letter that Caesar Augustus wrote to Livia, the grandmother of Claudius, concerning how to reduce the ridicule that will result from being seen in public. Clearly, the plan must be to enact secrecy, or hiding Claudius away if the risk of mockery is too high. Little did they know that despite these apparent limitations, Claudius would become emperor. Curiously, this Latin passage contains two dozen Greek words.

> I have conferred with Tiberius, dear Livia, concerning what is to be done with your grandson at the games of Mars. Tiberius and I are in agreement that we must determine once and for all what plan we are to follow. For if he is physically whole, *holoklēros* [a Greek word meaning the same thing], so to speak, what doubt is there that he should be put through the same grades and steps as his brother has been put through? If, conversely, we observe him to be "disadvantaged" and "disabled in the soundness of his body and of his mind," we must not provide people, "those who are accustomed in this way to mock and sneer," the occasion to ridicule him and us.[7]

THE NATURE OF SECRETISM

11. MATTHEW 12:1–2

All three Synoptic Gospels share a story in which Jesus is in a grain field with his disciples on the Sabbath (Mark 2:23–28; Matt 12:1–8; Luke 6:1–5). Suddenly, Pharisees appear to criticize Jesus and his disciples for transgressing Sabbath custom. What were Pharisees doing in a grain field on the Sabbath? Clearly, they were conducting surveillance. Surveillance was the way one

7. Adapted from Rolf, LCL.

found out others' secrets. Matthew's version of the story makes this aspect most explicit.

> At that time, Jesus was going through the grain fields on the Sabbath. His disciples were hungry, so they began to pluck and eat ears of corn. When the Pharisees saw this, they said to him, "Look for yourself, your disciples are doing that which one is not permitted to do on the Sabbath."

12. TACITUS, *ANNALS* 1.6

Tacitus (ca. 55–120 CE) was a renowned historian of the early Roman Empire. The first coining of the term "secret of the state" (*arcana domus*, literally, "secrets of the emperor's house"), as well as how state secrets work, is found in Tacitus's *Annals*. Tacitus's narration of events relating to the accession of Augustus's successor Tiberius provides a good example of state secrecy: the removal of politically inconvenient family members, the ensuing denial of the orders that led to their removal, and finally the advice of an astute and careful confidante to avoid any public debate. The murder of Augustus's grandson Agrippa Postumus and the discretion urged by Sallustius Crispus mark the first instance of the use of the term *arcana imperii* (state secrets) or *arcana domus* (secrets of the emperor's house).

> The new reign's first deed was to cut down Agrippa Postumus. He was killed by a centurion who found it a hard task, though he was a persevering murderer and the victim taken by surprise unarmed. Tiberius mentioned nothing about the affair before the senators. . . . But when, by habit of the military, he reported that he had done as commanded, he claimed that he himself had given no orders and that the thing that had been carried out would have to be returned to the senators for a response. This came to the notice of Sallustius Crispus, who was privy to the secret, for it was he who had sent instructions to the tribunes in the first place, and he was afraid that the responsibility might be shifted to himself, in which case either telling the truth or lying would be equally risky. So he warned Livia that palace secrets . . . were best undivulged.[8]

13. ROMANS 16:25–27

The authenticity of this closing passage of Romans is uncertain; in the manuscript tradition, it appears in five different locations, and sometimes not at all in the oldest manuscripts. Yet the passage is very interesting. In this scribal

8. Adapted from Jackson, LCL.

addition, the scribe builds on the theme of secrecy to express a vision of inclusion: now the whole world gains access to a mystery hidden for so long.

> Now to the one who is able to steady you by my good news and the proclamation of Jesus Christ, according to the revelation of the mystery that was kept quiet through the ages, but is now made known through the prophetic writings by the command of the eternal God to make known the obedience of loyalty to all the nations—to the only wise God, through Jesus Christ, to whom be eternal glory! Amen.

14. 1 CORINTHIANS 15:51–52
Here Paul unambiguously plays on mystery and revelation as the end of a secret and, in so doing, helps create a new sense of identity for a group of Christ followers.

> Look! I am telling you a mystery. All will not sleep, but all will be altered, in an instant, in the twinkling of an eye, at the final trumpet blast. For he will blast the trumpet, and the dead will be raised as imperishable, and we will be altered.

15. DIO CASSIUS, *ROMAN HISTORY* 53.19.2–3
Dio Cassius (ca. 150–235 CE) was born in Bithynia, the northern part of Asia Minor. Dio's historical works are key for our knowledge of the last years of the Roman Republic and the first four Roman emperors. Here is another passage that reveals the importance of surveillance to countering the threat that sometimes inheres to secrecy.

> For in an earlier time [e.g., during the republic], as we know, all things were brought before both the council and the people, even if they came to pass far away. Therefore, everyone learned about these things, and many wrote them down, and by extension the truth about them. . . . But ever since, more things began to happen secretly and covertly. And if some things somehow came out into the open, they were impossible to disprove, because they were untrustworthy.[9]

16. CICERO, *AGAINST CATILINE* 1.1
The Catilines were a Roman aristocratic family in the first century BCE. Cicero fought against the treason and attempted coup of the Catilines, by giving speeches in the senate, by thwarting their designs, and by attemping to turn

9. Adapted from Foster, LCL.

people against and away from them. Cicero makes a big deal of piercing the secrecy of the Catilinarian conspirators and using his spies. Cicero is at pains to point out that what is plotted in secrecy under the cover of darkness and privately in houses will be seen—in an ocular culture ever vigilant of those who hatch secret plots. Cicero deploys the discourse of secrecy to reveal the extent to which the plotters, despite their best attempt to hide their plots, were open to watchful public inspection. Such a discourse was designed to shape public opinion and to convince the plotters to abandon their plans.

> For what remains, Catiline, what can you expect now? Your shameful meetings can no longer be covered by the dark of night, nor can the walls of private houses conceal your conspiratorial voice. Everything is seen and displayed. . . . You are surrounded; all your plans are laid bare in the light of day; let me remind you of them.[10]

17. MINUCIUS FELIX, *OCTAVIUS* 9.2–7

Minucius Felix was a third-century Christian apologist who wrote in Latin. His only surviving work was a dialogue entitled *Octavius*, which was a critique of polytheism. In this passage, Minucius Felix recounts a slander about Christians, which he then rejects. The slander in this passage is based on the assumption and the accusation of secrecy. It is almost certain that Christians met in private, since it was illegal to be Christian, but this also fueled suspicion. So while secrecy might be intended to protect, it could also generate distrust, slander, and persecution. Note also how the author claims that the new Christian is sworn to secrecy.

> They know one another by secret gestures and insignia, and they have mutual love almost before they know one another. . . . I know not whether these reports of debauchery are untrue; certainly suspicion is applicable to secret rites done under the cover of night. . . . An infant is covered with flour, in order to fool the unsuspecting, and is placed before the initiate to the rite. The initiate, who has been summoned to inflict blows on the baby, thinks they are harmless because the flour hides the dark and secret wounds. Thus is the baby killed. Then, I shudder at the horror, they lick up the blood with great thirst, and they divide its limbs eagerly. They establish an alliance through this sacrificial victim, for jointly aware of their wickedness, they promise mutual silence. . . . They gather for a predetermined feast day with all their children, sisters, and mothers, all people regardless

10. Adapted from MacDonald, LCL.

of sex and age. In that place, drunk and engorged, they burn with incestuous desire. A dog tied to the lamp is provoked to jump and bound by throwing scraps beyond the length of its chain. Thus, the light is overturned and put out, and they are plunged into the shameless dark, where they fornicate with random partners in abominable lust.[11]

18. *PGM* IV. 2505–20

Secrecy is one of the foundational principles in the Greek Magical Papyri (*PGM*), though applied in a variety of ways for divergent purposes. The *PGM* contain comments to keep spells and procedures, divine names, divine *logoi*, and the initation rites of the magician all secret; once initiated, the new member alone has knowledge of the secret names, symbols, and forms of the deity. This spell of attraction is powerful and so is not to be performed rashly, and it contains a protective charm in the event that the goddess makes those who invoke it airborne and hurls them from aloft to the ground.

> So consequently, I have also thought it necessary to take the precaution of a protective charm so that you may perform the rite without hesitation. Keep it secret. Take a hieratic papyrus roll and wear it around your right arm, with which you make the offering. And these are the things written on it: "MOULATHI CHERNOUTH AMARÔ MOULLIANDRON, guard me from every evil daimon, whether an evil male or female." Keep it secret, son.[12]

19. DANIEL 2:19–22

Secrets produce power, for when one has secret knowledge, one controls the flow of information. God is depicted both as the one who knows all the secret wisdom and who dispenses it when appropriate. Power is inscribed as much by withholding as it is by sharing the wisdom.

> Then that night, the secret was revealed in a vision to Daniel, and he blessed the God of heaven. Daniel answered and said: "Let the name of God be blessed from age to age, for wisdom and power belong to him. He directs time and season, removes and appoints kings; to the wise he gives wisdom, and knowledge to those who know what it is to understand. He reveals things that are impenetrable and secret; he knows what is in the darkness, and light is with him.

11. Adapted from Rendall, LCL.
12. Betz, *Greek Magical Papyri*, 1:84.

20. 1QMYSTERIES (1Q27) I

This fragmentary Dead Sea scroll, in the genre of wisdom literature, extols the secret knowledge, or mysteries, that God controls and that humans can access only as God wills, by divine revelation. It helps, of course, to be a member of the righteous community. This particular text was possibly written in the first century BCE.

> mysteries of sin [. . .] but they neither knew the secret of the way things are, nor did they understand the things of old; they did not know what would come upon them, so they did not rescue themselves, since they did not have the secret of the way things are. This will be the sign that this will come to pass: when the sources of evil are locked up and wickedness is ostracized from the presence of righteousness, as darkness in the presence of light; as smoke vanishes and ceases to be, in the same way will wickedness vanish for good and righteousness be manifest like the sun. The world will be made firm, and all the adherents of the mysteries of sin shall be no more. True knowledge will fill the world, and there will never be any more folly. This is all about to happen, it is a true oracle, and in this way, it will be known to you that it cannot be averted.[13]

Vocabulary of Mockery and Secrecy

HEBREW

סֵתֶר (*seter*) . . . . covering, hiding place, secrecy
צָחַק (*tsakhaq*) . . . . to laugh at, mock
רָז (*raz*) . . . . secrecy

GREEK

ἀποκαλύπτω (*apokalyptō*) . . . . to reveal
καλύπτω (*kalyptō*) . . . . to hide
κατασκοπέω (*kataskopeō*) . . . . to spy
κατάσκοπος (*kataskopos*) . . . . spy
κρυφαῖος, -α, -ον
   (*kryphaios, -a, -on*) . . . . hidden, secret

13. Martínez, *Dead Sea Scrolls Translated*, 399.

317

λανθάνω (*lanthanō*) . . . . to hide, escape notice
μυστήριον (*mystērion*). . . . . mystery, secret teaching
πλανάω (*planaō*) . . . . to deceive
σκώπτω (*skōptō*) . . . . to mock, jeer
χλευάζω (*chleuazō*) . . . . to mock, scoff at

LATIN

derideo . . . . to mock
ludibrium . . . . mockery

Select Bibliography

Corbeill, Anthony. *Controlling Laughter: Political Humor in the Late Roman Republic.* Princeton: Princeton University Press, 1996.

Halliwell, Stephen. *Greek Laughter: A Study of Cultural Psychology from Homer to Early Christianity.* Cambridge: Cambridge University Press, 2008.

Neufeld, Dietmar. *Mockery and Secretism in the Social World of Mark.* New York: Bloomsbury and T&T Clark, 2014.

Neyrey, Jerome H. "The Sociology of Secrecy and the Fourth Gospel." Pages 79–109 in *"What Is John?"* Vol. 2 of *Literary and Social Readings of the Fourth Gospel.* Edited by Fernando F. Segovia. Atlanta: Society of Biblical Literature, 1998.

Simmel, Georg. "The Secret and the Secret Society." Pages 305–76 in *The Sociology of Georg Simmel.* Translated and edited by Kurt H. Wolff. Glencoe: The Free Press, 1950.

Tefft, Stanton K., ed. *Secrecy: A Cross-Cultural Perspective.* New York: Human Sciences, 1980.

Additional Texts

MOCKERY

Achilles Tatius, *Leucippe and Clitophon* 6.10

Acts 17:32

Archilochus, fragment 196a 33–34

Aristophanes, *Frogs* 376, 549–78, 857–58, 1089–98, 1200–47; *Knights* 319–92, 697, 1400–1402; *Peace* 476; *Lexiphanes* 5; *Lysistrata* 457–60; *Thesmepho-*

20. Evil Eye

John H. Elliott

Introduction

Evil-eye belief and practice (EEBP) is a widespread folk concept that some persons are enabled by nature to injure others, cause illness and death, and destroy any person, animal, or thing merely by a look. Also known as *fascination* (Greek: *baskania*; Latin: *fascinatio*), this belief holds that the eye is an active organ that emits destructive emanations charged by negative dispositions (especially envy, malevolence, miserliness, and withheld generosity). These emanations arise in the heart or soul and are projected outward against both animate and inanimate objects. The Roman writer Plutarch compares these emanations to the destructive rays of the sun and to "poisoned arrows" shot from a bow, while gospel writers compare them to the light beams projected from a lamp. This evil eye can be repelled and warded off by a great variety of protective words, gestures, actions, and amulets.

Extensively attested in the ancient circum-Mediterranean regions (Mesopotamia, Egypt, Greece, Rome, Israel) and ancient Near Eastern religions (Mesopotamian religion, Judaism, Christianity, and Islam) and continuing in these regions into the present day, EEBP (which includes not only belief in the evil eye, but also the numerous practices intended to avoid or repel it) can be found in all the six major regions of the world and in 67 of 186 societies across the globe, 36 percent of the total world sample. In antiquity, poets, tragedians, philosophers, historians, naturalists, artists, sages, and theologians all referred to the phenomenon. Direct reference to EEBP occurs in literary works, sacred texts, personal letters, papyri, inscriptions, philosophical and historical treatises, incantations and prayers, sermons, and theological commentaries, from the third millennium BCE through late antiquity (sixth century CE).

This evidence is supplemented by thousands of anti-evil-eye amulets uncovered in archaeological excavations and by anti-evil-eye designs, formulas, and inscriptions on door plaques, stone engravings, mosaic thresholds, public buildings, and personal jewelry, along with statuary and art (frescos, funerary art, etc.), all displaying anti-evil-eye imagery. The Bible contains some sixteen text segments explicitly referring to EEBP, though this is not apparent in most modern biblical translations. Many additional references occur in the parabiblical literature, the rabbinic writings, and the Christian church fathers. This evidence too is accompanied by a vast array of amulets and iconographic materials.

The plausibility and power, or logic, of EEBP rests on a complex of related ideas. First, the eye, deemed preeminent among the bodily organs for receiving information and conveying dispositions and feelings, is considered an *active*, not a passive, organ—a projector, not a receptor, of light and energy. The rays or particles of energy it projects are comparable to the sun and its rays or to a household lamp, which projects beams of light. That the eye functions by active emission (called the *extramission theory* of vision) was how most ancient people thought the eye operated. It was not until the 1700s that the extramission theory was supplanted in scientific circles in the West by the *intromission theory* of vision, namely, that the eye is a passive organ receiving external stimulation.

Second, the eye conveys and directs toward others the force of *emotions* that arise internally in the heart or soul. Among the negative emotions and dispositions, envy is paramount, as well as, among the biblical communities, stinginess, lack of generosity, and begrudging of aid to those in need.

The third feature of the logic of EEBP is that the evil eye, with its intense ocular gaze or hostile stare, can be an instrument of aggression. The eye directs this energy, negative in the case of an evil eye, against persons, creatures, and objects, and it can cause injury, illness, loss, decay, disintegration, and even death. While the evil eye can operate intentionally, however, it can also function inadvertently, that is, persons might not even realize that they themselves were feeling envy and thus casting the evil eye. This fact makes the evil eye that much more dangerous, for persons might unconsciously feel envy and direct the evil eye at people they have no desire to harm (e.g., family).

Fourth, it was assumed that certain people naturally possessed the evil eye and thus ought to be avoided: strangers, alien peoples, the physically deformed, blind persons and those with unusual ocular features (strabismus, double pupils, single eye, wandering eye, knit eyebrows), and social deviants. Likewise, it was assumed that some people were natural targets and especially vulnerable: the newly born, birthing mothers, children, and those who were handsome, beautiful, victorious, and successful (see **chap. 17, Limited Good**

and Envy). All persons and living creatures were both potential "fascinators" (those emitting the evil eye) as well as potential targets or victims. Fascinators can even attack themselves with the evil eye.

And finally, attack from an evil eye could be averted or thwarted through a variety of methods and means, including words, physical gestures, actions, and amulets. Avoidance strategies included restricting expressions of admiration or praise (which could veil or convey envy) or accompanying them with formulaic statements of "no evil eye intended."

EEBP belonged to a constellation of beliefs serving to explain manifestations of personal and social distress and—through protective words, gestures, and amulets—to provide a sense of safety in an otherwise unpredictable and threatening universe. Socially, the belief helped to affirm key traits of group identity and demarcate natives from evil-eyed strangers and aliens (see **chap. 6, Collectivism**). Evil-eye accusations were an effective informal mechanism for identifying and regulating social deviants and behavior inimical to the common good (see **chap. 18, Deviance**). The belief has reinforced, with extraordinary sanction, attitudes and actions fostering group cohesion and communal well-being. It has promoted the values of generosity and the sharing of possessions, while discouraging envy and miserliness. It has encouraged values and patterns of social action and personal deportment underwritten by God or the gods.

Ancient Texts

CAUSING HARM WITH AN OCULAR GLANCE

1. PLUTARCH, *TABLE TALK* 680F–681A

Plutarch (46–120 CE) was an accomplished philosopher, biographer, historian, and essayist writing in Greek. The most extensive discussion of the evil eye in antiquity is found in Plutarch's *Symposium* or *Table Talk*. Here he sums up prevailing thought on how the eye functions.

> For odor, voice, and breathing are all various emanations from living bodies that produce sensation in other bodies whenever the sense organs are stimulated by their impact. . . . In all probability, the most active stream of such emanations is that which passes out through the eyes. For vision, being very swift and borne by a substance that gives off a flame-like brilliance, radiates a wondrous power.[1]

1. Adapted from Minar, Sandbach, and Helmbold, LCL.

2. Plutarch, *Table Talk* 681d–e

Plutarch relates the extramission function of the eye to its destructive ability.

> But as regards not only the physiological but also the negative psychical effects of ocular glances, which includes the casting of an evil eye, how, Patroculus asks, can a glance of the eye spread harm to the persons who are looked at? I answered, "Are you unaware that the body is sympathetically affected when the mind is subjected to external influences? For amorous thoughts arouse the sexual organs . . . pain, greed, and jealousy cause one's body to change color and one's health to waste away. . . . Envy, ensconced by nature in the mind more than any other passion, also fills the body with evil. . . . When, therefore, individuals under envy's sway direct their glance at others, their eyes, which are close to the mind and draw from it envy's evil, then attack these other persons as if with poisoned arrows."[2]

3. Matthew 6:22–23

According to the Gospels, Jesus also presumed an active eye and an extramission theory of vision, and like Plutarch, he relates that to the evil eye. *Haplous* ("integral"), as in the Testament of Issachar (below, no. 6), conveys the sense of "generous" as an expression of moral integrity. "Evil eye" here connotes the antithesis to a disposition of generosity, as in several other biblical evil-eye passages:

> The eye is the lamp of the body. If, then, your eye is integral/generous, your whole body will be full of light. If, however, your eye is evil, your whole body will be full of darkness. If, then, the light in you is darkness, how great the darkness!

CONVEYING HOSTILE DISPOSITIONS AND EMOTIONS

4. Deuteronomy 15:9–10

This is one of several biblical texts where looking at someone with an evil eye communicates miserliness, stinginess, and a begrudging of aid to those in need. Giving generously is the best way to avoid the evil eye.

> Be careful lest there be an evil thought in your heart and you say: "The seventh year, the year of remission of debts, is near," and you look with an evil eye upon your needy neighbor, you give nothing, and your neighbor cry to the Lord against

2. Adapted from Minar, Sandbach, and Helmbold, LCL.

you, and you be guilty of sinning. Give liberally and do not grieve in your heart when you do so, for because of this, the Lord your God will bless you in all your work and in all that you undertake.

5. Tobit 4:7–8, 16

Tobit's parting advice to his son Tobias twice refers to the evil eye. The full expression "evil eye" is not present, but the notion of an active eye conveying envy and begrudging points unmistakably to an evil eye, as does its proximity to Deut 15:7–11 (cf. Matt 6:22–23//Luke 11:34).

> Give alms from your possessions to all who live uprightly, and do not begrudge with an evil eye the alms when you give them; do not turn your face away from any poor man, and the face of God will not be turned away from you. If you have many possessions, give alms from them in proportion to what you have; if you have few possessions, do not worry about giving according to the little you have. . . . Give of your bread to the hungry, and of your clothing to the naked. Give all your surplus as alms, and do not begrudge with an evil eye the alms when you give them.

6. Testament of Issachar 3:3, 4, 8

The Testament of Issachar (second century BCE to first century CE) presents Issachar, son of Jacob the patriarch and a brother of Joseph (whose brothers cast an envious evil eye upon him at Gen 37:11), reviewing his life and claiming to have been free of envy, the evil eye, and ungenerosity toward others.

> I was not envious and evil eyed toward my neighbor. . . . I lived my life with integrity of eyes. . . . With integrity/generosity of heart I supplied to the poor and oppressed everything from the good things of the earth.[3]

7. Basil, *Concerning Envy* 372.32–376.7

The Christian theologian Basil of Caesarea (ca. 330–379 CE), in his famous homily on envy and the evil eye, echoes Aristotle's definition of envy, equates envying and wielding an evil eye, and enumerates several of their pernicious aspects.

> No feeling more pernicious than envy is implanted in human souls. . . . As rust wears away iron, so envy corrodes the soul it inhabits. More than this, it consumes the soul

---

3. H. C. Kee, "Testaments of the Twelve Patriarchs," in vol. 1 of *The Old Testament Pseudepigrapha*, ed. James H. Charlesworth (Garden City, NY: Doubleday, 1983).

that gives it birth, like vipers that are said to be born by eating their way through the womb that conceived them. Now, envy is pain caused by our neighbors' prosperity. Hence, an evil-eyed person is never without cause for grief and despondency. If his neighbor's land is fertile, if his neighbor's house abounds with all the goods of this life, if he, its master, enjoys continual gladness of heart—all these things aggravate the sickness and add to the pain of the evil-eyed person. . . . What could be more fatal than this illness? It ruins our life, perverts our nature, arouses hatred of the good bestowed on us by God, and places us in a hostile relation toward him.[4]

8. Jerome, *Commentary on Galatians*, comments on 3:1a

The church father Jerome (ca. 342–420 CE), in his Latin commentary on Paul's reference to the evil eye in Gal 3:1 (see no. 13), recalls conventional wisdom on the subject, including the association of evil eye and envy. He even cites the Roman poet Vergil (first century BCE) at the end.

By these examples, we have shown either that the envious person is tormented by the happiness of another, or that he in whom there are some good things, as a victim, suffers harm by one who casts an evil eye, that is, by one who envies. It is said that the evil-eying person is particularly harmful to infants and the young of age and to those who do not yet leave behind a firm footprint. Accordingly, one of the gentiles stated, "I do not know what evil eye is evil-eying my tender lambs" [citing Vergil, *Eclogues* 3.103].[5]

POSSESSORS AND WIELDERS OF THE EVIL EYE

9. *KTU*[2] 1.96 [= RS 22.225 = CAT 1.96 = UDB 1.96]

This is an Ugaritic incantation from the site of Ras Shamra on the Syrian coast (ca. 1400–1200 BCE). It mentions various types of people who wield the evil eye.

The eye, it roamed and darted. . . . It was the eye of an evil man that saw him, the eye of an evil woman; it was the eye of a merchant that saw him, the eye of a potter, the eye of a gatekeeper.[6]

4. M. M. Wagner, *St. Basil: Ascetical Works*, Fathers of the Church 9 (Washington, DC: Catholic University of America Press, 1962), 463, 465.

5. John H. Elliott, *Beware the Evil Eye: The Evil Eye in the Bible and the Ancient World* (Eugene, OR: Wipf & Stock, 2016), 3:228.

6. J. N. Ford, "'Ninety-Nine by the Evil Eye and One from Natural Causes.' KTU 1.96 in Its Near Eastern Context," *Ugarit-Forschungen* 30 (1998): 201–78, esp. 202.

10. PLINY THE ELDER, *NATURAL HISTORY* 7.2.16–18

Pliny the Elder (23–79 CE) transmits in his *Natural History* reports concerning various foreign tribes possessing the evil eye, the damage they cause by their act of praising, their telltale ocular features, and even Roman women with two pupils—all evil-eye features conferred by nature.

Isogonus and Nymphdorus report that there are families in the same part of Africa beyond the Nasamones with the power of the evil eye, whose praising causes meadows to dry up, trees to wither, and infants to perish. Isogonus adds that there are people of the same kind among the Triballi and the Illyrians, who also injure by the evil eye and kill those at whom they stare for a longer time, especially with furious eyes, and that their evil eye is most felt by adults; and that what is more remarkable is that they have two pupils in each eye. Apollonides also reports women of this kind in Scythia, who are called the Bitiae, and Phylarchus mentions also the Thibii tribe and many others of the same nature in Pontus, whose distinguishing marks he records as being a double pupil in one eye and the likeness of a horse in the other. . . . Also among ourselves, Cicero states that the glance of all women who have double pupils is injurious everywhere. In fact, when nature implanted in man the wild beast's habit of devouring human flesh, she also thought fit to implant poisons in the whole of the body, and with some persons the eyes as well, so that there should be no evil anywhere that was not present in man.[7]

11. SIRACH 14:3–10 (LXX)

The Greek translation of the book of Jesus ben Sirach presents the most extensive comment on the evil eye in the Bible and highlights several significant features of evil-eyed persons.

Wealth is not fitting for a person of little account, and of what use is property to an evil-eyed person? Whoever accumulates by depriving himself accumulates for others, and others will live in luxury on his goods. If a man is evil to himself, to whom will he be good? He will not enjoy his own riches. No one is more evil than he who evil-eyes himself. And this is the retribution for his wickedness: Even if he does something good, he does it unintentionally and betrays his wickedness in the end. Evil is one who looks with an evil eye, turning away his face and disregarding people. The evil eye of a greedy person is unsatisfied with a single portion; and an evil eye withers life. A person with an evil eye is begrudging concerning bread, and it is lacking from his table.

7. Adapted from Rackham, LCL.

VICTIMS OF THE EVIL EYE

12. PLUTARCH, *TABLE TALK* 680D

Plutarch related that all persons, animals, and possessions are deemed vulnerable to evil-eye attack, but particularly infants, the good-looking, and the successful.

> We know, for instance, of persons who seriously hurt children by looking at them, influencing and impairing their susceptible, vulnerable constitutions.[8]

13. GALATIANS 3:1

In his letter to the Galatians, Paul implies that a competing group of Christ-followers loyal to Torah legal traditions, led by James, would have been envious of the freedom Paul had given them in not being so bound.

> O uncomprehending Galatians, who has injured you with an envious evil eye, you before whose very eyes Jesus Christ was publicly portrayed as crucified?

DAMAGE CAUSED BY THE EVIL EYE

14. BM 122691

This Akkadian tablet in the British Museum is an anti-evil-eye incantation (1830–1530 BCE). It describes the threat of the evil eye to infants and mothers in childbirth and the damage it causes when breaking into a home.

> It [the evil eye, *īnum*] has broken in, it is looking everywhere!
> It is an enmeshing net, a closing bird snare.
> It went by the babies' doorways and caused havoc among the babies,
> It went by the door of mothers in childbirth and strangled their babies.
> Then it went into the jar room and smashed the seal,
> It demolished the secluded stove,
> It turned the locked house into a shambles.
> It even struck the chapel; the god of the house has gone out of it.
> Slap it in the face! Make it turn around!

8. Adapted from Clement and Hoffleit, LCL.

Fills its eyes with salt! Fill its mouth with ashes!
May the god of the house return!⁹

15. DEUTERONOMY 28:54–57

Deuteronomy 28:47–57 elaborates on the divine curses to befall Israel because of its nonobservance of the commandments and its failure to serve the Lord with joyfulness and gladness of heart (28:47). Judah, according to Moses's forecast, will be attacked and besieged by a merciless enemy (the Neo-Babylonian invasion of 587 BCE in the reign of King Zedekiah), stripped of its cattle and food, and its population reduced to want and starvation (28:48–52). The besieged will finally resort to eating their own children (28:53). In this situation of extreme deprivation, desperation, cannibalism, and the evil eye, family members will be subject to the depraved evil eye of their very own relatives—the most extreme illustration of evil-eye behavior in all Scripture.

> The man, who is tender among you and delicately bred, will look with an evil eye against his fellow Israelite [lit. "brother"], against his beloved wife, and against the last of his children who remain to him, begrudging them [for food] the flesh of his children that he is eating because he has nothing else left to him in the siege and in the distress with which your enemy shall distress you in all your towns. The woman who is tender among you and delicately bred . . . will look with an evil eye against her beloved husband, against her son, and against her daughter, begrudging them [for food] the afterbirth that oozes from her genitals and the baby that she bears; for she shall eat them herself secretly for lack of anything else [to eat] in the siege and in the distress with which your enemy shall distress you in your towns.

16. PLUTARCH, *TABLE TALK* 682B

Persons can also evil-eye and injure themselves, illustrating how the evil eye was thought to operate automatically, unintentionally, as well as with malice aforethought. Plutarch introduces handsome Eutelidas by the river and then reports the effects of accidental evil-eying of the self.

> Handsome Eutelidas evil-eyed himself, that baneful man, beholding himself in the river's water. . . . Eutelidas, it is said, handsome in his own estimation, was struck by what he saw reflected in the water, fell ill, and lost his beauty with his health.¹⁰

9. B. R. Foster, *Before the Muses: An Anthology of Akkadian Literature*, 3rd ed. (Bethesda: CDL, 2005), 176.
10. Adapted from Clement and Hoffleit, LCL.

PROTECTION FROM THE EVIL EYE

17. ANONYMOUS EGYPTIAN FORMULA
In Egypt, in addition to the myriad of Eye-of-Horus amulets that were used to protect against the evil eye, protection also was afforded from the Saitic period (663–525 BCE) onward by the use of formulas based in personal names, mostly of women.

> Nut slays the evil eye
> Neith slays the evil eye
> Chons slays the evil eye
> Sekhmet slays the evil eye[11]

18. PLINY THE ELDER, *NATURAL HISTORY* 28.7.39
Pliny the Elder reveals another protective strategy against the evil eye, namely, spitting.

> When a stranger enters the house, or when a person looks at an infant while asleep, it is usual for the nurse to spit three times even though infants are under the divine protection of the god Fascinus.[12]

19. PERSIUS, *SATIRES* 2.31–34
Like the elder Pliny, the Roman poet and satirist Persius (34–62 CE) refers to spit as a protection against the evil eye, but also refers to an important gesture.

> Behold, how the grandmother or older aunt
> removes the boy from the crib and his forehead and moist lips
> first purifies with the notorious middle finger and atoning spittle
> knowledgeable thereby about warding off burning eyes.[13]

20. B. BERAKHOT 55B
For protection when encountering an unknown place, the rabbis advised reciting Gen 49:22 (a reference to Joseph, who survived the envious evil eye of his brothers [Gen 37:11]) and making a manual gesture.

11. Wilhelm Spiegelberg, "Der böse Blick in altägyptischen Glauben," *Zeitschrift für Ägyptische Sprache und Altertumskunde* 59 (1924): 149–54.
12. Adapted from Bostock, LCL.
13. Adapted from Braund, LCL.

If, when entering a city, a man fears the evil eye of some inhabitant, let him take the thumb of his right hand in his left hand, and the thumb of his left hand in his right hand, and say: "I, so-and-so, am of the seed of Joseph, over which the evil eye has no power, as it is written: 'Joseph spared by God from the envy of his brothers is a fruitful bough, even a fruitful bough by a well'" [Gen 49:22]. If he is afraid of his own evil eye, he should look at the side of his left nostril.

Vocabulary of the Evil Eye

HEBREW

עַיִן הָרָע (*ayin hara*) .... evil eye
רַע עַיִן (*ra ayin*) .... evil-eyed

GREEK

βασκαίνω (*baskainō*). .... to cast the evil eye
βασκανία (*baskania*) .... evil eye
βάσκανος, -ον (*baskanos, -on*). .... evil-eyed
ὀφθαλμὸς πονηρός
   (*ophthalmos ponēros*). .... evil eye
φθόνος (*phthonos*). .... envy

LATIN

fascinatio .... cast of the evil eye
oculus malus/malignus/nequam
   /obliquus .... evil eye

Select Bibliography

Dundes, Alan, ed. *The Evil Eye: A Folklore Casebook.* Rev. ed. Madison: University of Wisconsin Press, 1992.
Elliott, John H. *Beware the Evil Eye: The Evil Eye in the Bible and the Ancient World.* 4 vols. Eugene, OR: Wipf & Stock, 2015–2017.

———. "The Fear of the Leer: The Evil Eye from the Bible to Li'l Abner." *Forum* 4 (1987): 42–71.

Kern-Ulmer, Rivka Brigitte. *The Evil Eye in the Bible and in Rabbinic Literature*. Hoboken, NJ: Ktav, 1994.

Maloney, Clarence, ed. *The Evil Eye*. New York: Columbia University Press, 1976.

Additional Texts

CAUSING HARM WITH AN OCULAR GLANCE

Aeschylus, *Agamemnon* 946–47

Aristotle, *On Dreams* 459b27–32

Heliodorus, *Ethiopian Story* 3.7–9

Luke 11:34–36

Plutarch, *Table Talk* 625e–626e, 680f, 682f, 683a

Proverbs 23:6

Pseudo-Aristotle, *Problemata Inedita* 3.52

CONVEYING HOSTILE DISPOSITIONS AND EMOTIONS

Deuteronomy 15:7–11; 28:54–57

4 Maccabees 1:25–26; 2:15–16

Matthew 20:15

Mark 7:22

Mishnah

   Avot 5.13

Proverbs 28:22

1 Samuel 2:29, 32; 18:9

Sirach 14:10; 37:10–11

Testament of Issachar 3.3; 4.5

POSSESSORS AND WIELDERS OF THE EVIL EYE

Acts of Thomas 5.44

Apollonius of Rhodes, *Argonauts* 4.1635–90

Aulus Gellius, *Attic Nights* 9.4.7–8

Babylonian Talmud

   Qiddushin 82a

Chariton, *Chaereas and Challirhoe* 1.1.6; 3.2.17; 6.2.11

Demosthenes, *Against Meidias* (*Or.* 21) 209; *1 Against Aristogeiton* (*Or.* 25) 80, 83

Galatians 3:1; 4:17

Homer, *Iliad* 11.36–37

Ignatius, *Romans* 7.2

Martyrdom of Polycarp 17.1

Mishnah

   Avot 2:9; 5:19

Ovid, *Metamorphoses* 7.366–67

Philo, *Against Flaccus* 29

Philostratus, *Life of Apollonius* 7.42

Pliny the Elder, *Natural History* 7.2.16–17

Plutarch, *Table Talk* 682a–b

1 Samuel 18:8–9

4QSapiential Text (4Q424) frag. 1, II,
2–4, 7

Strabo, *Geography* 14.2.7
Theocritus, *Idylls* 6.39

VICTIMS OF THE EVIL EYE

Acts of John 20
Babylonian Talmud
  Bava Batra 118a, 141a
  Bava Metzi'a 107b
  Pesahim 50b
Catullus, *Poems* 5.9–12; 7.11–12
Euripides, *Ion* 1421
Heliodorus, *Ethiopian Story* 3.7–4.5

P.Abinnaeus 30.23–24; 35.28–29; 37.4
P.Oxyrhynchus 292, 300, 2276, 3312–13
P.Rylands 4.604
Plutarch, *Table Talk* 680d, 682a–f; *That Epicurus Actually Makes a Pleasant Life Impossible* 1090c
Sirach 14:6
Vergil, *Eclogues* 3.103

DAMAGE CAUSED BY THE EVIL EYE

Acts of Thomas 9.100
Heliodorus, *Ethiopian Story* 4.5
Horace, *Epistles* 1.14.37
Matthew 6:23/Luke 11:34
Mishnah
  Avot 2:11

Plato, *Phaedo* 95b
Plutarch, *Table Talk* 680d–e
Proverbs 23:6; 28:22
Sirach 18:18; 31:12–13
Theocritus, *Idylls* 5.13
Wisdom of Solomon 4:12

PROTECTION FROM THE EVIL EYE

Aelian, *Various History* 1.15
Athenaeus, *The Dinner Sophists* 9.50
Babylonian Talmud
  Bava Batra 118a
  Bava Metzi'a 84a
  Berakhot 20a
Charisius, *Art of Grammar* 2.15
Diogenes Laertius, *Lives of Eminent Philosophers* 6.34
Euripides, *Ion* 1421
Grattius, *Cynegetica* 399–407
John Chrysostom, *Homily on 1 Corinthians* 12:13
Julius Pollux, *Onomasticon* 7.108
Macrobius, *Saturnalia* 1.6.9

Ovid, *Festivals* 5.433–34
P.Oxyrhynchus 292, 300, 930, 3313
Petronius, *Satyricon* 131
Phrynichus of Bithynia, *Sophistic Preparations* 53.6
Plautus, *The Comedy of Asses* 2.4.84
Pliny the Elder, *Natural History* 19.19.50; 28.5.22; 28.7.35–36; 37.10.54
Plutarch, *Table Talk* 681f–682a
Pseudo-Aristotle, *Problemata Inedita* 3.52; *Problemata Physica* 20.34
Tertullian, *The Veiling of Virgins* 15.1–3
Testament of Solomon 18:39
Theocritus, *Idylls* 6.39; 7.126–27; 20.11
Varro, *On the Latin Language* 7.107

Bibliography

Albera, Dionigi, and Anton Blok. "Introduction: The Mediterranean as a Field of Ethnological Study; A Retrospective." Pages 15–37 in *L'anthropologie de la Méditerranée: Anthropology of the Mediterranean*. Edited by Dionigi Albera, Anton Blok, and Christian Bromberger. Paris: Maisonneuve & Larose, 2001.

Ando, Clifford. *Imperial Ideology and Provincial Loyalty in the Roman Empire*. Berkeley: University of California Press, 2000.

Arbel, Vita Daphna, Paul C. Burns, J. R. C. Cousland, Richard Menkis, and Dietmar Neufeld, eds. *Not Sparing the Child: Human Sacrifice in the Ancient World and Beyond*. London: Bloomsbury, 2014.

Avalos, Hector. *Illness and Health Care in the Ancient Near East: The Role of the Temple in Greece, Mesopotamia, and Israel*. Harvard Semitic Museum Publications 54. Atlanta: Scholars Press, 1995.

Balch, David, and Jason Lamoreaux, eds. *Finding a Woman's Place: Essays in Honor of Carolyn Osiek*. Eugene, OR: Wipf & Stock, 2011.

Barton, Carlin A. *Roman Honor: The Fire in the Bones*. Berkeley: University of California Press, 2001.

Batten, Alicia J. "Philemon." Pages 201–62 in *Philippians, Colossians, Philemon*. Wisdom Commentary Series. Collegeville, MN: Liturgical, 2017.

Batten, Alicia J., and John S. Kloppenborg, eds. *James, 1 and 2 Peter and Early Jesus Traditions*. London: T&T Clark, 2014.

Bazzana, Giovanni B. *Kingdom of Bureaucracy: The Political Theology of Village Scribes in the Sayings Gospel Q*. Leuven: Peeters, 2015.

Beck, Roger. *The Religion of the Mithras Cult in the Roman Empire: Mysteries of the Unconquered Sun*. Oxford: Oxford University Press, 2006.

Borowski, Oded. *Agricultural Life in Iron Age Israel*. Winona Lake, IN: Eisenbrauns, 1987.

Carney, T. F. *The Shape of the Past: Models and Antiquity*. Lawrence, KS: Coronado, 1975.

Choi, Agnes. "Between Literacy and Illiteracy." Pages 71–79 in *Scribal Practices and Social Structures among Jesus Adherents: Essays in Honour of John S. Kloppenborg*. Edited by Richard S. Ascough, Philip A. Harland, Robert A. Derrenbacker Jr., and William E. Arnal. Leuven: Peeters, 2016.

———. "Never the Two Shall Meet? Urban-Rural Interaction in Lower Galilee." Pages 297–310 in *Galilee in the Late Second Temple and Mishnaic Periods*, Volume 1: *Life, Culture, and Society*. Edited by David A. Fiensy and James Riley Strange. Philadelphia: Fortress, 2014.

Clarke, Katherine. *Between Geography and History: Hellenistic Constructions of the Roman World*. Oxford Classical Monographs. Oxford: Clarendon, 1999.

Corbeill, Anthony. *Controlling Laughter: Political Humor in the Late Roman Republic*. Princeton: Princeton University Press, 1996.

Craffert, Pieter. *Life of a Galilean Shaman: Jesus of Nazareth in Anthropological-Historical Perspective*. Eugene, OR: Cascade, 2008.

Crook, Zeba. "BTB Readers Guide: Loyalty." *BTB* 34 (2004): 167–77.

———. "Collective Memory Distortion and the Quest for the Historical Jesus." *JSHJ* 11 (2013): 53–76.

———. "Fictive-Giftship and Fictive-Friendship in Greco-Roman Society." Pages 61–76 in *The Gift in Antiquity*. Edited by Michael Satlow. Chichester: Blackwell, 2013.

———. "Honor, Shame, and Social Status Revisited." *JBL* 128 (2009): 591–611.

———. *Reconceptualising Conversion: Patronage, Loyalty, and Conversion in the Religions of the Ancient Mediterranean*. Berlin: de Gruyter, 2004.

Daniels, John W. *Gossiping Jesus: The Oral Processing of Jesus in John's Gospel*. Eugene, OR: Pickwick, 2013.

Danker, Frederick W. *Benefactor: Epigraphic Study of a Graeco-Roman and New Testament Semantic Field*. St. Louis: Clayton, 1982.

DeMaris, Richard E. *The New Testament in Its Ritual World*. London: Routledge, 2008.

DeMaris, Richard E., Jason T. Lamoreaux, and Steven C. Muir, eds. *Early Christian Ritual Life*. London: Routledge, 2017.

Dmitriev, Sviatoslav. *The Greek Slogan of Freedom and Early Roman Politics in Greece*. Oxford: Oxford University Press, 2011.

Douglas, Mary T. *Natural Symbols: Exploration in Cosmology*. New York: Pantheon, 1970.

———. *Purity and Danger*. London: Routledge & Kegan Paul, 1966.

Du Boulay, Juliet. *Portrait of the Greek Mountain Village*. Oxford Monographs on Social Anthropology. Oxford: Clarendon, 1974.

Duling, Dennis C. *A Marginal Scribe*. Eugene, OR: Wipf & Stock, 2012.

———. "Memory, Collective Memory, Orality and the Gospels." *HvTSt* 67 (2011): 103–13.

———. *The New Testament: History, Literature, and Social Context.* 4th ed. Belmont, CA: Thomson/Wadsworth, 2003.

Dundes, Alan, ed. *The Evil Eye: A Folklore Casebook.* Revised ed. Madison: University of Wisconsin Press, 1992.

Edwards, Douglas R. "Dress and Ornamentation." *AB* 2 (1992): 232–38.

Elliott, John H. *Beware the Evil Eye: The Evil Eye in the Bible and the Ancient World.* 4 vols. Eugene, OR: Wipf & Stock, 2015–2017.

———. "The Fear of the Leer: The Evil Eye from the Bible to Li'l Abner." *Forum* 4 (1987): 42–71.

———. *1 Peter: A New Translation with Introduction and Commentary.* Garden City, NY: Doubleday, 2001.

———. "God—Zealous or Jealous but Never Envious: The Theological Consequences of Linguistic and Social Distinctions." Pages 79–96 in *The Social Sciences and Biblical Translation.* Edited by Dietmar Neufeld. Atlanta: Society of Biblical Literature, 2008.

———. *What Is Social-Scientific Criticism?* Minneapolis: Fortress, 1993.

Esler, Philip Francis. "Models in New Testament Interpretation: A Reply to David Horrell." *JSNT* 78 (2000): 107–13.

Faraone, Christopher A., and F. S. Naiden, eds. *Greek and Roman Animal Sacrifice: Ancient Victims, Modern Observers.* Cambridge: Cambridge University Press, 2012.

Fears, J. Rufus. "The Cult of Virtues and Roman Imperial Ideology." *ANRW* 17.2:827–948. Part 2, *Principat*, 17.2. Edited by H. Temporini and W. Haase. New York: de Gruyter, 1981.

Finley, Moses I. *The Ancient Economy.* 2nd ed. London: Hogarth, 1985.

Fisher, N. R. E. *Hybris: A Study in the Values of Honour and Shame in Ancient Greece.* Warminster: Aris & Phillips, 1992.

Fitzgerald, John T., ed. *Greco-Roman Perspectives on Friendship.* Atlanta: Scholars Press, 1997.

Flannery, Frances, Colleen Shantz, and Rodney A. Werline, eds. *Inquiry into Religious Experience in Early Judaism and Early Christianity.* Vol. 1 of *Experientia.* Atlanta: Society of Biblical Literature, 2008.

Foster, George M. "Peasant Society and the Image of Limited Good." *American Anthropologist* 67 (1965): 293–315.

Gill, Christopher, Norman Postlethwaite, and Richard Seaford, eds. *Reciprocity in Ancient Greece.* Oxford: Oxford University Press, 1998.

Gellner, E., and J. Waterbury, eds. *Patrons and Clients in Mediterranean Society.* London: Gerald Duckworth, 1977.

Gilmore, David G., ed. *Honor and Shame and the Unity of the Mediterranean.* Washington, DC: American Anthropological Association, 1987.

Gleason, Maud W. *Making Men: Sophists and Self-Presentation in Ancient Rome.* Princeton: Princeton University Press, 1995.

———. "The Semiotics of Gender: Physiognomy and Self-Fashioning in the Second Century C. E." Pages 389–415 in *Before Sexuality: The Construction of Erotic Experience in the Ancient Greek World.* Edited by David M. Halperin, John J. Winkler, and Froma Zeitlin. Princeton: Princeton University Press, 1990.

Gluckman, Max. "Gossip and Scandal." *Current Anthropology* 4 (1963): 307–16.

Guijarro, Santiago. "Healing Stories and Medical Anthropology: A Reading of Mark 10:46–52." *BTB* 30 (2000): 102–12.

———. "The Politics of Exorcism: Jesus's Reaction to Negative Labels in the Beelzebul Controversy." *BTB* 29 (1999): 118–29.

Halliwell, Stephen. *Greek Laughter: A Study of Cultural Psychology from Homer to Early Christianity.* Cambridge: Cambridge University Press, 2008.

Hamel, Gildas. *Poverty and Charity in Roman Palestine, First Three Centuries C.E.* Berkeley: University of California, 1990.

Hanson, K. C. "All in the Family: Kinship in Agrarian Roman Palestine." Pages 27–46 in *The Social World of the New Testament: Insights and Models.* Edited by Jerome H. Neyrey and Eric C. Stewart. Peabody, MA: Hendrickson, 2008.

Harland, Philip A. "Familial Dimensions of Group Identity (II): 'Mothers' and 'Fathers' in Associations and Synagogues of the Greek World." *Journal for the Study of Judaism in the Persian, Hellenistic and Roman Period* 38 (2007): 57–79.

Hayward, C. T. R. *The Jewish Temple: A Non-Biblical Sourcebook.* London: Routledge, 1996.

Herzfeld, Michael. "Honour and Shame: Some Problems in the Comparative Analysis of Moral Systems." *Man* NS 15 (1980): 339–51.

Hofstede, Geert, Gert Jan Hofstede, and Michael Minkov. *Cultures and Organizations: Software of the Mind.* 3rd ed. New York: McGraw-Hill, 2010.

Horrell, David. "Models and Methods in Social-Scientific Interpretation: A Response to Philip Esler." *JSNT* 78 (2000): 83–105.

Horsley, Richard A. *Sociology and the Jesus Movement.* New York: Crossroad, 1989.

Isaac, Benjamin. *The Invention of Racism in Classical Antiquity.* Princeton: Princeton University Press, 2006.

Jensen, Jesper Tae, George Hinge, Peter Schultz, and Bronwen Wickkiser, eds. *Aspects of Ancient Greek Cult: Context, Ritual and Iconography.* Aarhus Studies in Mediterranean Antiquity. Aarhus: Aarhus University Press, 2010.

Kartzow, Marianne. *Gossip and Gender: The Othering of Speech in the Pastoral Epistles.* Berlin: de Gruyter, 2009.

Kern-Ulmer, Rivka Brigitte. *The Evil Eye in the Bible and in Rabbinic Literature*. Hoboken, NJ: Ktav, 1994.

King, Helen, ed. *Health in Antiquity*. London: Routledge, 2005.

Klawans, Jonathan. *Impurity and Sin in Ancient Judaism*. Oxford University Press, 2000.

Kleinman, Arthur. *Patients and Healers in the Context of Culture*. Berkeley: University of California Press, 1980.

Kloppenborg, John S. "Evocatio Deorum and the Date of Mark." *JBL* 124 (2005): 419–50.

Knust, Jennifer W. *Abandoned to Lust: Sexual Slander and Ancient Christianity*. New York: Columbia University Press, 2006.

Knust, Jennifer W., and Zsuzsanna Várhelyi, eds. *Ancient Mediterranean Sacrifice*. Oxford: Oxford University Press, 2011.

Konstan, David, and N. K. Rutter, eds. *Envy, Spite and Jealousy: The Rivalrous Emotions in Ancient Greece*. Edinburgh: Edinburgh University Press, 2003.

Kramer, Emil A. "Book One of Velleius' *History*: Scope, Levels of Treatment, and Non-Roman Elements." *Historia* 54 (2005): 144–61.

Kressel, Gideon M. "Shame and Gender." *Anthropological Quarterly* 65 (1992): 34–46.

Lamoreaux, Jason. *Ritual, Women, and Philippi: Reimagining the Early Philippian Community*. Eugene, OR: Cascade, 2013.

Lawrence, Louise Joy. *An Ethnography of the Gospel of Matthew: A Critical Assessment of the Use of the Honour and Shame Model in New Testament Studies*. Tübingen: Mohr Siebeck, 2003.

Lemche, Niels Peter. "Kings and Clients: On Loyalty between the Ruler and the Ruled in Ancient 'Israel.'" *Semeia* 66 (1994): 119–32.

Malina, Bruce J. "Collectivism in Mediterranean Culture." Pages 17–28 in *Understanding the Social World of the New Testament*. Edited by Dietmar Neufeld and Richard E. DeMaris. London: Routledge, 2009.

———. "Is There a Circum-Mediterranean Person? Looking for Stereotypes." *BTB* 22 (1991): 66–87.

———. "Limited Good and the Social World of Early Christianity." *BTB* 8 (1978): 162–76.

———. *The New Testament World: Insights from Cultural Anthropology*. 3rd ed. Louisville: Westminster John Knox, 2001.

Malina, Bruce J., and Jerome H. Neyrey. *Calling Jesus Names: The Social Value of Labels in Matthew*. Sonoma, CA: Polebridge, 1988.

Malina, Bruce J., and Richard L. Rohrbaugh. *Social Science Commentary on the Synoptic Gospels*. Philadelphia: Fortress, 2003.

Maloney, Clarence, ed. *The Evil Eye*. New York: Columbia University Press, 1976.

Martin, Dale B. *Sex and the Single Savior: Gender and Sexuality in Biblical Interpretation*. Louisville: Westminster John Knox, 2006.

Mauss, Marcel. *The Gift: The Form and Reason for Exchange in Archaic Societies*. Translated by W. D. Halls. New York: Norton, 1990.

Moxnes, Halvor, ed. *Constructing Early Christian Families: Family as Social Reality and Metaphor*. London: Routledge, 1997.

Moxnes, Halvor. "Conventional Values in the Hellenistic World: Masculinity." Pages 263–84 in *Conventional Values of the Ancient Greeks*. Edited by Per Bilde, Troels Engberg-Pedersen, Lise Hannestad, and Jan Zahle. Aarhus: Aarhus University Press, 1997.

Neufeld, Dietmar. "Dressing Down Criminals, Deviants and Other Undesirables." *HvTSt* 70 (2014): 1–8.

———. *Mockery and Secretism in the Social World of Mark*. New York: Bloomsbury and T&T Clark, 2014.

Newsom, Carol A. "Religious Experience in the Dead Sea Scrolls: Two Case Studies." Pages 205–22 in *Linking Text and Experience*. Vol. 2 of *Experientia*. Edited by Colleen Shantz and Rodney Alan Werline. Boston: Brill, 2012.

Neyrey, Jerome H. *Give God the Glory*. Grand Rapids: Eerdmans, 2007.

———. *The Gospel of John in Cultural and Rhetorical Perspective*. Grand Rapids: Eerdmans, 2009.

———. *Honor and Shame in the Gospel of Matthew*. Louisville: Westminster John Knox, 1998.

———. "'I Am the Door' (John 10:7, 9): Jesus the Broker in the Fourth Gospel." *CBQ* 69 (2007): 271–91.

———. "Readers Guide to Clean/Unclean, Pure/Polluted, and Holy/Profane: The Idea and System of Purity." Pages 159–82 in *The Social Sciences and New Testament Interpretation*. Edited by Richard L. Rohrbaugh. Peabody, MA: Hendrickson, 1996.

———. "Social Science Modeling and the New Testament." *BTB* 16 (1986): 107–10.

———. "The Sociology of Secrecy and the Fourth Gospel." Pages 79–109 in *"What Is John?"* Vol. 2 of *Literary and Social Readings of the Fourth Gospel*. Edited by Fernando F. Segovia. Atlanta: Society of Biblical Literature, 1998.

Neyrey, Jerome H., and Bruce J. Malina. *Portraits of Paul: An Archaeology of Ancient Personality*. Louisville: Westminster John Knox, 1996.

Neyrey, Jerome H., and Richard L. Rohrbaugh. "'He Must Increase, I Must Decrease' (John 3:30): A Cultural and Social Interpretation." *CBQ* 63 (2001): 464–83.

Neyrey, Jerome H., and Eric C. Stewart. *The Social World of the New Testament*. Peabody, MA: Hendrickson, 2008.

Nicolet, Claude. *Space, Geography, and Politics in the Early Roman Empire*. Translated by Hélène Leclerc. Ann Arbor: University of Michigan Press, 1991.

Nielsen, Inge, and Hanne Sigismund Nielsen, eds. *Meals in a Social Context: Aspects of the Communal Meal in the Hellenistic and Roman World.* Aarhus: Aarhus University Press, 2001.

Nutton, Vivian. *Ancient Medicine.* Sciences of Antiquity. 2nd ed. London: Routledge, 2012.

Oakman, Douglas E. *Jesus and the Economic Questions of His Day.* Lewiston: Edwin Mellen, 1986.

———. *Jesus and the Peasants.* Eugene, OR: Cascade, 2008.

———. *Jesus, Debt, and the Lord's Prayer.* Eugene, OR: Cascade, 2014.

———. *The Political Aims of Jesus.* Philadelphia: Fortress, 2012.

Oden, Robert A., Jr. "Jacob as Father, Husband, and Nephew: Kinship Studies and the Patriarchal Narratives." *JBL* 102 (1983): 189–205.

Olson, Kelly. *Dress and the Roman Woman: Self-Presentation and Society.* London: Routledge, 2008.

Osiek, Carolyn, and Jennifer Pouya. "Constructions of Gender in the Roman Imperial World." Pages 44–56 in *Understanding the Social World of the New Testament.* Edited by Dietmar Neufeld and Richard E. DeMaris. London: Routledge, 2010.

Parca, Maryline, and Angeliki Tzanetou, eds. *Finding Persephone: Women's Rituals in the Ancient Mediterranean.* Bloomington: Indiana University Press, 2007.

Parker, Robert. *Miasma: Pollution and Purification in Early Greek Religion.* Oxford: Clarendon, 1985.

Parkin, Robert. *Kinship: An Introduction to the Basic Concepts.* Oxford: Blackwell, 1997.

Peristiany, J. G., and Julian Pitt-Rivers, eds. *Honor and Grace in Anthropology.* Cambridge: Cambridge University Press, 1992.

Pilch, John J. *Healing in the New Testament: Insights from Medical and Mediterranean Anthropology.* Minneapolis: Fortress, 2000.

Pitt-Rivers, Julian. "Honour and Social Status." Pages 19–77 in *Honour and Shame: The Values of Mediterranean Society.* Edited by J. G. Peristiany. The Nature of Human Society Series. Chicago: University of Chicago Press, 1966.

Rich, John. "Patronage and Interstate Relations in the Roman Republic." Pages 117–35 in *Patronage in Ancient Society.* Edited by Andrew Wallace-Hadrill. London: Routledge, 1989.

Richardson, Peter, and Amy Marie Fisher. *Herod: King of the Jews and Friend of the Romans.* London: Routledge, 2017.

Rodd, Cyril S. "On Applying a Sociological Theory to Biblical Studies." *JSOT* 19 (1981): 95–106.

Rohrbaugh, Richard L. "Gossip in the New Testament." Pages 239–59 in *Social Scientific Models for Interpreting the Bible: Essays by the Context Group in Honor of Bruce J. Malina.* Edited by John J. Pilch. Leiden: Brill, 2001.

———. "Legitimating Sonship—A Test of Honour: A Social-Scientific Study of Luke 4:1–30." Pages 183–97 in *Modelling Early Christianity: Social-Scientific Studies of the New Testament in Its Context*. Edited by P. F. Esler. London: Routledge, 1995.

———. "Methodological Considerations in the Debate Over the Social Class of Early Christians." *JAAR* 52 (1984): 519–46.

———. "Models and Muddles: Discussions of the Social Facets Seminar." *Forum* 3 (1987): 23–33.

———. *The New Testament in Cross-Cultural Perspective*. Eugene, OR: Cascade, 2007.

———. "Peasant Reading of the Parable of the Talents/Pounds: A Text of Terror?" Pages 109–23 in *The New Testament in Cross-Cultural Perspective*. Eugene, OR: Cascade, 2007.

Romm, James S. *The Edges of the Earth in Ancient Thought: Geography, Exploration, and Fiction*. Princeton: Princeton University Press, 1992.

Saller, Richard P. *Personal Patronage under the Early Empire*. New York: Cambridge University Press, 1982.

Schäfer, Peter. *Judeophobia: Attitudes toward the Jews in the Ancient World*. Cambridge: Harvard University Press, 1998.

Scheidel, Walter, Ian Morris, and Richard Saller, eds. *The Cambridge Economic History of the Greco-Roman World*. Cambridge: Cambridge University Press, 2007.

Shantz, Colleen. *Paul in Ecstasy: The Neurobiology of the Apostle's Life and Thought*. New York: Cambridge University Press, 2009.

Shantz, Colleen, and Rodney Werline, eds. *Linking Texts and Experience*. Vol. 2 of *Experientia*. Atlanta: Society of Biblical Literature, 2012.

Shepardson, Christine. *Controlling Contested Places: Late Antique Antioch and the Spatial Politics of Religious Controversy*. Berkeley: University of California Press, 2014.

Simmel, Georg. "The Secret and the Secret Society." Pages 305–76 in *The Sociology of Georg Simmel*. Translated and edited by Kurt H. Wolff. Glencoe: The Free Press, 1950.

Spiegelberg, Wilhelm. "Der böse Blick in altägyptischen Glauben." *Zeitschrift für Ägyptische Sprache und Altertumskunde* 59 (1924): 149–54.

Stansell, Gary. "David and His Friends: Social-Scientific Perspectives on the David-Jonathan Friendship." *BTB* 41 (2011): 115–31.

———. "The Gift in Ancient Israel." *Semeia* 87 (1999): 65–90.

———. "Gifts, Tributes, and Offerings." Pages 349–64 in *The Social Setting of Jesus and the Gospels*. Edited by Wolfgang Stegemann, Bruce J. Malina, and Gerd Theissen. Philadelphia: Fortress, 2002.

———. "Honor and Shame in the David Narratives." *Semeia* 68 (1994): 55–79.

Stewart, Eric C. *Gathered around Jesus: An Alternative Spatial Practice in the Gospel of Mark*. Matrix 6. Eugene, OR: Cascade, 2009.

————. *Peter: First-Generation Member of the Jesus Movement*. Paul's Social Network. Wilmington, DE: Glazier, 2012.

Straten, F. T. van. "Gifts for the Gods." Pages 65–151 in *Faith, Hope and Worship: Aspects of Religious Mentality in the Ancient World*. Edited by H. S. Versnel. Leiden: Brill, 1981.

Stratton, Kimberly B. *Naming the Witch: Magic, Ideology, and Stereotype in the Ancient World*. New York: Columbia University Press, 2007.

Taves, Ann. *Religious Experience Reconsidered: A Building-Block Approach to the Study of Religion and Other Special Things*. Princeton: Princeton University Press, 2010.

Tefft, Stanton K., ed. *Secrecy: A Cross-Cultural Perspective*. New York: Human Sciences, 1980.

Triandis, Harry C., and Eunkook M. Suh. "Cultural Influences on Personality." *Annual Review of Psychology* 53 (2002): 133–60.

Upson-Saia, Kristi, Carly Daniel-Hughes, and Alicia J. Batten, eds. *Dressing Judeans and Christians in Antiquity*. London: Routledge, 2014.

Uro, Risto. *Ritual and Christian Beginnings: A Socio-Cognitive Analysis*. Oxford: Oxford University Press, 2016.

Van Eck, Ernest. "Invitations and Excuses That Are Not Invitations and Excuses: Gossip in Luke 14:18–20." *HvTSt* 68 (2012).

Wallace-Hadrill, Andrew, ed. *Patronage in Ancient Society*. London: Routledge, 1989.

Wikan, Unni. "Shame and Honour: A Contestable Pair." *Man* NS 19 (1984): 635–52.

Williams, Ritva H. "Constructing Identity in the Epistle of Jude." Pages 511–26 in *T&T Clark Handbook to Social Identity in the New Testament*. Edited by J. Brian Tucker and Coleman A. Baker. London: T&T Clark, 2014.

————. "The Interests of the Shrewd Steward and His Interpreters." Pages 353–68 in *To Set at Liberty: Essays on Early Christianity and Its Social World in Honor of John H. Elliott*. Edited by Stephen K. Black. Sheffield: Sheffield Phoenix, 2014.

Zerubavel, Eviatar. *Ancestors and Relatives: Genealogy, Identity, and Community*. Oxford: Oxford University Press, 2012.

Contributors

Alicia J. Batten is professor of religious studies and theological studies at Conrad Grebel University College at the University of Waterloo. Publications include two coedited volumes: *Dressing Judeans and Christians in Antiquity* (Ashgate, 2014); *James, 1 and 2 Peter, and Early Jesus Traditions* (Bloomsbury, 2014); a commentary on Philemon in *Philippians, Colossians, Philemon* (Wisdom Commentary Series, 2017) as well as books and articles on the Letter of James. She is currently co-editing *Dress in Mediterranean Antiquity* (Bloomsbury, forthcoming).

Giovanni B. Bazzana is professor of New Testament at Harvard University, the Divinity School. His most recent publication is *Kingdom of Bureaucracy: The Political Theology of Village Scribes in the Sayings Gospel Q*, and he is currently finishing a book devoted to the phenomenon of spirit possession in the traditions concerning Jesus and in the Pauline groups.

Agnes Choi is associate professor of religion at Pacific Lutheran University. She is associate editor of *Handbook of Women Biblical Interpreters: A Historical and Biographical Guide*. Her recent publications include "Never the Two Shall Meet? Urban-Rural Interaction in Lower Galilee," in *Galilee in the Late Second Temple and Mishnaic Periods, Volume 1: Life, Culture, and Society*, and "Between Literacy and Illiteracy," in *Scribal Practices and Social Structures among Jesus Adherents: Essays in Honour of John S. Kloppenborg.*

Zeba A. Crook is professor of religion at Carleton University in Ottawa. He is the author of *Parallel Gospels: A Synopsis of Early Christian Writing, Reconceptualising Conversion*, "Honor, Shame, and Social Status Revisited," and "Collective Memory Distortion and the Quest for the Historical Jesus."

John W. Daniels Jr. is teaching and learning librarian of the Proctor Library at Flagler College, and adjunct instructor in religion for the Department of Humanities. He also serves as professor of Old Testament for the Ministry Formation Program of the Diocese of St. Augustine, Florida, and is author of *Gossiping Jesus* and "Engendering Gossip in Galatians 2:11–24."

Dennis C. Duling is professor emeritus and holder of the Koessler Distinguished Faculty Award at Canisius College. He is the author of *The New Testament: History, Literature, and Social Context*, *A Marginal Scribe*, and several recent articles relating social networking, ethnicity, smell, scribalism, and collective memory in the New Testament, such as "Memory, Collective Memory, Orality and the Gospels."

John H. Elliott is professor emeritus at the University of San Francisco (retired in 2001) and a co-founder of The Context Group. Key publications include *1 Peter: A New Translation with Introduction and Commentary*, *The Evil Eye in the Bible and the Ancient World* (4 vols.), *The Elect and the Holy*, and further social-scientific studies of the Bible and its contexts.

Amy Marie Fisher works at the University of Alberta as an adjunct instructor in Religious Studies. In the summer, she is the registrar at a Roman-era archaeological site in the northern Galilee. She is a coauthor of *Herod: King of the Jews and Friend of the Romans*.

Mischa Hooker is lecturer in classics at Augustana College in Rock Island, IL. He is the author of *Origen of Alexandria: Exegetical Works on Ezekiel* (Ancient Texts in Translation).

Emil A. Kramer is a professor of classics at Augustana College in Rock Island, IL. He is the author of "Book One of Velleius' *History*: Scope, Levels of Treatment, and Non-Roman Elements."

Jason T. Lamoreaux is an adjunct of religious studies at Texas Christian University. Recent publications include *Ritual, Women, and Philippi: Reimagining the Early Christian Community*. He is a coeditor of *Finding a Woman's Place: Essays in Honor of Carolyn Osiek* and *Early Christian Ritual Life*.

Dietmar Neufeld (1949–2015) was professor of religious studies at the University of British Columbia. He is the author of *Mockery and Secretism in the*